To John,

With many happy memories of working together.
Every blessing for your new Devon adventures

Best Wishes

Dan.

WITH GOD ON OUR SIDE

A Comparative Study
of Religious Broadcasting in the
USA and the UK 1921-1995:
The Impact of Personality.

IAN ROBERTSON

Foreword by Dr.Richard Wallis

Published by New Generation Publishing in 2022

Copyright © Ian Robertson 2022

First Edition

The author asserts the moral right under the Copyright, Designs and Patents Act 1988 to be identified as the author of this work.

All Rights reserved. No part of this publication may be reproduced, stored in a retrieval system or transmitted, in any form or by any means without the prior consent of the author, nor be otherwise circulated in any form of binding or cover other than that which it is published and without a similar condition being imposed on the subsequent purchaser.

ISBN: 978-1-80369-441-2

www.newgeneration-publishing.com
New Generation Publishing

"Some said John print it, others said no. Some said it might do good, others said no"

John Bunyan (1849)

Acknowledgements

I would like to express my sincere gratitude for all those who have helped me in the course of researching and writing this book. I would particularly like to thank Professor Hugh Chignell and Dr. Richard Wallis at Bournemouth University's Media School for their patience, motivation, immense knowledge and on-going advice which was invaluable for this study.

Thanks must also go to the teams at the BBC Written Archives, The British Library, Lambeth Palace, Church of England Records Office, National Religious Broadcasters in the United States, EPLS Design and the Library staff at Bournemouth University, in particular Ian Marsland and Phil Stocks who assisted considerably with finding and securing relevant resources.

I am also indebted to all my interviewees, many of who have had considerable experience in the field of religious broadcasting and were so willing to share both their expertise and heart on the subject. Neither must I forget the inspiration of Dr. Tony Stoller, who like me was a media professional who trod this road before me and remained a source of help and information throughout.

Finally I am extremely grateful to my close family and friends who have been a constant source of encouragement, especially to my son Justin and his partner Kelsey, my daughter Penny and son-in-law John and to my late Mother and Father to whom I always promised, if life should ever deliver me this opportunity, I would seize the day.

* * * * * * *

Foreword

I vividly recall visiting the National Religious Broadcasting (NRB) Convention in the early 1990s. This exposure to the world of American religious broadcasting left a deep impression. The contrast between the US and the British experience of religious media could not have been starker. On the one hand was the unapologetically evangelistic, self-confident, deeply conservative, commercially-orientated world represented by Pat Robertson's *700 Club* and the Bakker's *PTL Club*. On the other hand was the rather staid, public-service oriented, cash-strapped religious broadcasting world represented by the BBC's *Songs of Praise*, dominated by a sense of its own diminishment.

The rising sense of lost ground that permeated religious broadcasting in the UK from the 1960s onwards, was more than just a perception. The BBC, which had been the UK's only licensed broadcaster until 1955, had been fashioned in the image of its first Director-General, John Reith. Reith was a man of strong Christian persuasion and committed to the idea that his organisation should actively promote the faith, both implicitly and explicitly. The inevitable changes that followed his departure, left religious programme makers and many within the UK's churches, with a feeling of disentitlement which only increased over time.

Despite the many notable differences between the parallel stories of religious broadcasting on either side of the Atlantic, what is common to both is the significance of their role in the development of the history of broadcasting and society more broadly. Indeed, it is impossible to properly understand the latter, without the former. In the UK context, John Reith's role at the BBC is a case in point. In the USA, in a very different way, Pat Robertson's role is similarly significant. The fact that so little has been published that reflects this reality may seem surprising. Particularly so in the light of a 21st Century acknowledgement that the forward march of secularization has faltered. Globalization, migration and the complex connection between nation and culture, have led to a renewed recognition of religion as a major social, political, and cultural force.

FOREWORD

Ian Robertson takes us on a fascinating journey from the earliest days of 'wireless' broadcasting, through to the upheavals of the 1990s on both sides of the Atlantic. It is the story of the challenges to communicate the Christian faith through the new technologies of mass communication as it was being developed throughout the 20th Century. It is also the story of particular individual pioneers, who for various reasons and in different ways, led from the front in the mission for souls via the airwaves. It is these personalities – the 'hall of fame' of the story of religious broadcasting – that is the distinctive focus of this book. Ian Robertson examines a number of the central characters of this story, many of whom became household names, some even turning their 'ministries' into multi-million-dollar enterprises. Entrepreneurism, audacity, competition, zeal and scandal all feature in the telling. Some of these individuals have, rightly, been the subject of much critical public scrutiny. (Despite processes of secularization, the media is ever quick to recognise a Pharisee.) Many characters in this story, however, seem to have been sincere: faithful to their own religious and spiritual traditions, seemingly attempting to enact the Great Commission with the tools of a modern age.

Another feature of this book is the telling of the USA and UK stories in parallel, thereby highlighting some of their similarities, as well as the very real differences that were so striking to me at the NRB all those years ago. The fact that religious broadcasting in the UK has frequently defined itself in contradistinction to that of the USA is another fascinating aspect of this story. But it is the scarcity of historical scholarship on religious broadcasting generally that makes this book especially welcome, providing an insight into an important 20th Century broadcasting phenomenon and filling a long-standing gap.

Dr. Richard Wallis
Faculty of Media & Communication
Bournemouth University, UK

Contents

Acknowledgements i

Foreword ii

Introduction 1

   1. Definitions 1
   2. Facing the Challenge 1
   3. Structure of the Book 3
   4. Digging the History 7
   Notes 10

CHAPTER 1
MAPPING THE TERRITORY
Standing on the Shoulders of Giants 13

   1. The Crucible of Mass Communications 14
   2. The Saga of Broadcasting 18
   3. The Anatomy of Religion 29
   4. The Impact of Personality/Celebrity 39
   5. Religious Broadcasting 47
   Notes 63

CHAPTER 2
GOD IS MARCHING ON
The Birth and Development of Religious Broadcasting 1921-1955 **75**

   1. The United States Blazes a Trail 75
      a) The Foundations are laid: 1921-1934 75
      b) A Time of Strategic Development: 1934-1955 80
      c) To the Ends of the Earth: Mission in the Ether 85

CONTENTS

2. The United Kingdom Learns to Inform,
   Educate, Entertain and Inspire! ... 87

   a) The Reithian Years ... 87
   b) Beyond Reith ... 95
   c) Sound and Vision ... 100

3. Summary ... 108

Notes ... 111

CHAPTER 3
NEW HORIZONS
The Expansion of Religious Television and Radio 1955-1995 ... **119**

1. The American Experience ... 119
2. The Mould is Broken in the UK ... 131
3. A Radio Revolution ... 143
4. The Battles with Regulators, Broadcasters and Government ... 147

   a) The Approach of the Central Religious Advisory Committee (CRAC) ... 147
   b) Cable, Satellite and the Channel 4 Factor ... 150
   c) The Battle for Freedoms ... 155

5. Summary ... 160

Notes ... 164

CHAPTER 4
THE HALL OF FAME
The Champions Of Religious Broadcasting ... **175**

1. A Spectrum of Significance ... 175
2. The Key Personalities ... 180

a) John C.W. Reith (1889-1971)	180
b) Rev.Dick Sheppard (1880-1937)	184
c) Rev.W.H. Elliott (1884-1957)	188
d) Aimee Semple Mcpherson (1890-1944)	192
e) Father Charles Coughlin (1891-1979)	198
f) Mother Mary Angelica (1923-2016)	201
g) Dr.Billy Graham (1918-2018)	204
h) Oral Roberts (1918-2009)	208
i) Pat Robertson (1930 –)	212
j) Jerry Falwell (1933-2007)	216
3. Summary	224
Notes	228

CHAPTER 5
OPPORTUNITY KNOCKS
The Relationship between the Churches and Broadcasting **243**

1. An American Dynamic	244
a) The Traditionalists	244
b) The Evangelicals	252
2. The British Reserve	256
a) A New Ministry Door Opens	257
b) A Whole New World	265
3. The Church on Television	273
a) An American Trilogy	274
b) Religion on Screen: Made in Britain.	275
4. Summary	278
Notes	281

CHAPTER 6
AUDIENCE IS KING
An Assessment of the Significance of Audiences to Religious Broadcasting **291**

   1. The Challenge of Research   291

   2. An American Review   293

       a) Size Matters   293

       b) The Characteristics of Religious Broadcasting Audiences   295

       c) Why Do People Watch Particular Religious Television Programmes?   300

   3. A Very British Approach   302

       a) Early Days   302

       b) The Scope of BBC Research   303

       c) What Does The Audience Research Reveal?   305

   4. A Commercial Perspective   311

       a) The Audience and Religious Television   312

       b) *Godwatching*   314

       c) *Highway and Songs of Praise*   315

       d) *Seeing is Believing*   316

   5. Summary   318

   Notes   321

CHAPTER 7
ON THE CASE
A Comparative Study of a USA and UK Religious Programme **329**

   1. Introduction   329

    2. The Cases   330

        a) *PTL (Praise the Lord) Club*   330

        b) *Stars on Sunday*   345

    3. Summary   354

    Notes   358

CHAPTER 8
CONCLUSION
Following the Evidence   **365**

    1. The Panorama Portrayed   365

    2. The Implications of the History   368

    3. The Proposition of the Book   370

    Notes   373

A BRIEF MEDIA CHRONOLOGY   **376**

BIBLIOGRAPHY   **385**

APPENDICES

    1. KEY U.K. MEDIA INSTITUTIONS   450

    2. KEY U.S. MEDIA INSTITUTIONS   455

    3. U.K. BROADCASTING REPORTS/COMMITTEES   461

    4. HIGHLIGHTS OF U.K. & U.S. BROADCASTING LEGISLATION   467

    5. A RADIO POEM   472

    6. VATICAN DOCUMENTS RE: MEDIA   473

    7. ARCHIVES CONSULTED   474

    8. INTERVIEWEES   478

    9. ILLUSTRATIONS   480

INDEX   **482**

Introduction

1. Definitions

Religious broadcasting is a specialized kind of broadcasting, as are sports, classical music, drama, news and current affairs and so on.[1] For the purposes of this book 'religious broadcasting' is defined as predominantly (though not entirely) Christian based radio and television programmes where religious ideas, experience and practice are highlighted. This all-inclusive generic ascription was adopted from the inception of broadcasting in the USA and the UK by the broadcasters themselves and followed here in line with all the literature featured.

In some countries, like the UK, religious broadcasting developed within the context of a public service structure,[2] whilst in others like America we see a more commercial context driven more by personalities and religious organisations.[3] The format for religious broadcasting tended, in the beginning, to be the transmission of worship or preaching, but eventually developed into documentaries, radio and television dramas, chat shows, films and debates.[4]

The book will attempt therefore to advance within this general context and understanding.

2. Facing the Challenge

In terms of religious broadcasting many writers, sociologists, historians, theologians and cultural analysts have described this phenomenon and tried to explain its origins and influence (Dinwiddie 1968; Wolfe 1984; Postman 1985; Nuendorf 1987; Hoover 1988; Bruce 1990; Schultze 1991; McDonnell 2009; Wallis 2020). They point to the dynamic of religious change, the popularist's innovations in worship, the large number of denominations or the growing technological advances of the 20th Century. But with few exceptions, almost none of them have dealt with one of the most important factors in the equation, the use of mass media by charismatic entrepreneurial personalities to bring the Christian message to millions of people across the western world and beyond.[5]

The other challenge within this, is creating a balance of understanding, because of the potentially contentious nature of religious broadcasting.[6] For in trying to present an authentic history of religious broadcasting there are some real paradoxes in that radio and television far from synchronizing smoothly or pointing in one direction, contributes to disjunctions, works at cross-purposes, operates out of phase with each other and rarely produces a simplistic conclusion.[7] Certainly the rhetoric of the pioneers of religious broadcasting justified the use of these new communication technologies, but tracking their effectiveness and impact in terms of building the religious community or providing more social cohesion, is a complex task.[8]

There is also the milestone of drawing together the important elements of religious broadcasting as they evolved in the USA and the UK. As will be seen, the history of religious culture in America established a very large evangelical, fundamentalist and Pentecostal subculture,[9] compared with Protestant European countries, including the UK, where church attendance was small by comparison and 'conservatives' theologically form only a small part of the Christian community.[10] In addition the book gives recognition to the different models of broadcasting – the UK, being rather closed in access and centralised in control, in comparison to the American system, which was open in access and diffuse in control.[11] The study will therefore attempt to understand the nature of the type of religious broadcasting that developed in these two disparate crucibles for radio and television.

In his Preface to *Pilgrim's Progress* (1849) John Bunyan expressed his hesitancy about writing his book, "Some said John print it, others said no. Some said it might do good, others said no".[12] Taking on board the challenge of this book is in a similar vein, as no one has attempted before such a synthesis of 20th Century religious broadcasting,[13] involving its two key contributors of the USA and UK and also sought to understand the major role personality played in creating and developing this significant genre of mass communication. I therefore commit it to print in the hope of contributing and widening knowledge on this under – researched topic.

3. Structure of the Book

The book covers a variety of themes, practices, organisations and personalities. Although some of the chapters can stand on their own, others benefit from being seen in the broader context of broadcasting and society in the USA and UK in the 20th Century.

Chapter 1, maps out the important back-drop to religious broadcasting in terms of mass communications, broadcasting, religion and personality and illustrates and examines the scholarly literature pertinent to these fields, in order to demonstrate that religious broadcasting did not emerge in a vacuum but within a historical, political and social context. In addition, despite the lack of literature on religious broadcasting, in comparison to other media studies,[14] the chapter analyses the key texts that contribute to understanding the development of religious broadcasting and those who pioneered it in both the USA and the UK.

Chapter 2, moves to examine the period 1921-1955 which incorporates what many have called the "Golden Age of Wireless".[15] The chapter demonstrates that religious broadcasting was an integral part of the broadcasting landscape in the USA and the UK from its inception. It chronicles in America the effects of the Radio Act of 1927, the development of networks like CBS and NBC and the controversies over 'sustaining time' given and taken from religious broadcasters. It also highlights the theological differences in broadcasting between the Federal Council of Churches of Christ and evangelical groups like the National Religious Broadcasters, as well giving recognition to missionary endeavours using radio across the world, by organisations such as HCJB, FEBC and Trans World Radio. Finally also featuring some of early pioneers of religious broadcasting in America such as Aimee Semple McPherson, Paul Radar, Walter A. Maier and Father Charles Coughlin.

The chapter also looks at the parallel time in the UK with the development of religious broadcasting within the BBC, championed by John Reith. There is coverage of the important 'Sunday Committee', later renamed the Central Religious Advisory Committee (CRAC), key programmes like the *Daily Service* and *Sunday Half Hour*, the controversial 'Sunday Policy', the establishment of the BBC Religious Broadcasting Department featuring its various Directors like Iremonger and Welch and their attempts to widen the appeal of religious broadcasting with productions like Dorothy Sayers's *The Man Born to Be King* (1941) on radio and T.S.Eliot's *Murder in the Cathedral* (1935) on television, as well its important broadcasts during the Second World War and the coverage of national events like Coronations and Remembrance Days. Finally much is also made of the crucial role of Lord Reith and of his key religious broadcasters Dick Sheppard and W.H.Elliott who were destined to become key figures in the religious life of the nation and beyond.

Chapter 3, moves to the era 1955-1995 and the development of television and its potential for religious broadcasting. The chapter demonstrates how the heyday for the mainline churches Roman Catholic and Protestant, allied with the National Council of Churches in the 1950s, lose their on-air prominence in the 1960s and 70s[16] to independent broadcasters nicknamed 'televangelists', who became part of the movement that was dubbed the 'electric church'.[17] This becomes the focus of the chapter, as this media phenomenon is led by charismatic entrepreneurial personalities like Dr.Billy Graham, Oral Roberts, Pat Robertson, Jim and Tammy Bakker, Jimmy Swaggart, Mother Angelica and Jerry Falwell. Robertson and Falwell becoming particularly politicized and leading to what became known as the 'religious right' and the Moral Majority movement. The chapter illustrates how the American electronic church gained immense power almost entirely through its twin pulpits of radio and television, with millions of listeners and viewers and a financial turn-over running into billions of dollars per year.

INTRODUCTION

This segment also explores the period in Britain with the breaking of the BBC monopoly and the introduction of Commercial Television, made possible by the 1954 Television Act and subsequently the setting up of regulatory bodies like the ITA and the IBA. The years 1956-1976 also see considerable growth in religious broadcasting, especially in television terms, with the *Jesus of Nazareth* (1956) drama, Sunday morning church services from all over the country and in the 60s, 70s and 80s new religious programmes like *Songs of Praise*, *Stars on Sunday* and *Highway*. The chapter further considers the role of Government with the 1962 Pilkington Committee, the 1977 Annan Report and their recommendations in relation to religious broadcasting; the 1972 Sound Broadcasting Act and the introduction of Commercial Radio and the additional opportunities for religious broadcasting at local levels; Channel 4 being introduced in 1982 and its controversial religious programmes like *Jesus the Evidence* (1984) and finally the era of battles for religious groups to gain recognition and platforms on the new cable and satellite channels, as well as a place in the media landscape made possible by the 1990 Broadcasting Act, leading to the first licenced Christian Radio station in 1995, in the form of Premier Christian Radio.

Chapter 4, importantly crystalizes the contention of the book that charismatic enterprising personalities were the driving forces in the development of religious broadcasting. The chapter takes a view of history in line with Carlyle and his portrayal of great men (1841) and additionally the Weberian perspective of the importance of 'charisma' (1915). It also notes the extension and modernising of these themes expressed by Boorstin (2006), Inglis (2010), Marshall (1997) and Rojek (2001) in talking of celebrity or stardom. The different strands of this discussion create a framework to understand the power and significance of the 'titans' of religious broadcasting, both in the USA and the UK.

The chapter emphasizes that many religious broadcasters took to the microphone and the small screen, but certain individuals in the 20th Century gained more recognition than others and whereas the book makes reference to many, the focus here is on those who became household names amongst the Christian community and beyond and therefore biographies of John Reith (1889-1971), Dick Sheppard (1880-1937), W.H.Elliott (1884-1957), Aimee Semple McPherson (1890-1944), Father Charles Coughlin (1891-1979), Mother Mary Angelica (1923-2016), Dr.Billy Graham (1918-2018), Oral Roberts (1918-2009), Pat Robertson (1930-) and Jerry Falwell (1933-2007) are featured to demonstrate the significance of these personalities in the contexts in which they lived.

Chapter 5, addresses the issue about the relationship between the Churches and the various broadcasting institutions in the USA and the UK. In terms of religious broadcasting it also focusses on the fact that not only were there charismatic personalities on radio and television, but within the churches and their organisations there were similar leaders who made a significant impact which made such broadcasting possible. For example, Charles S. MacFarland of the Federal Council of Churches of Christ (FCCC), Everett Parker of the Joint Religious Radio Committee (JRRC), Henry Knox Sherrill of the National Council of Churches (NCC) and Ben Armstrong of the National Religious Broadcasters (NRB). Here in Britain Reith appointed Cyril Forster Garbett as Chair of the 'Sunday Committee' (1923) later to be named the Central Religious Advisory Committee (CRAC). The chapter examines how that committee and the work of the British Council of Churches were to have important roles in the shaping of religious broadcasting in both the BBC and eventually in Commercial Broadcasting. The chapter also illustrates the very real tensions between denominations and conservatives and liberals in their theological and practical approach to religious broadcasting and the model they adopted in relation to UK radio and television. Finally there is a brief review of how the Church was portrayed on television, often through drama and humour, in both the USA and the UK in the latter half of the 20th Century.

Chapter 6, demonstrates that audiences for broadcasting are a key issue for programmers, marketeers and investors. The chapter outlines the issues of who and how many people were listening and viewing religious broadcasting. In America it examines the results of the survey companies like Nielson and Arbitron and the very controversial aspects of this interpreted by writers like Hadden and Swann

(1981), Horsfield (1984), Buddenbaum (1979) and Johnstone (1971). In the UK it features the work of R.J.E.Silvey (1956) and the Listener Research (later Audience Research} Department of the BBC and its various reports regarding the audiences for religious broadcasting. The chapter features the parallel research activity within the onset of commercial radio and television and the reports of the IBA and ITC and especially the work of Gunter and Viney (1994). The chapter is not just mere data-mining, but sheds light on why and how religious broadcasters sought to maximise on audiences by understanding their demographics, size and potential.

Chapter 7, takes on board a very focussed perspective to religious broadcasting and adopts a Case Study approach to two popular religious programmes, *PTL* from America and *Stars on Sunday* from the UK. It examines the ecology in which the programmes flourished, the biographical details of the presenters Jim and Tammy Bakker (*PTL*) and Jess Yates (*Stars on Sunday*) and the style and theology of these two very different programmes. Finally the chapter highlights why these two programmes were a microcosm of the religious broadcasting genre in their two nations and supports the case that it was charismatic personalities like these that were the driving force behind the impact of religious broadcasting in the USA and the UK.

4. Digging the History

The book sits within a number of academic fields, but due to the nature of the subject it stands firmly as a piece of media history, which in the past has sometimes been described as the "neglected grandparent of media studies",[18] with historians ignoring its role,[19] though in more recent years there has been a growing appreciation of this field of media history. Curran however believes that media history in fact connects to the 'mainframe' of general history and therefore it illuminates the role of media in society,[20] himself desiring to "advance a tradition of media history that seeks ambitiously to situate historical investigation of the media in a wider societal context".[21] Turow also emphasized the importance of the inter-relationship of a number of different media forming what might be called a "medium system" within the larger society.[22] The task of the media historian is then to search and 'burrow' in a creative way to reconstruct hypotheses and ideas based on what sometimes can be very limited data.[23] This is the book's approach in relation to religious broadcasting.

As already described, as this is by nature a segment of media history, it was important to provide a landscape and context in which religious broadcasting was created and developed. Some of the research with regard to this comes from secondary sources cited comprehensively in the Bibliography. But the research is not limited to this, as there was much primary source material obtained from the BBC Written Archives Centre which was vital in understanding the nature and content of religious broadcasting in Britain, supplemented also by access to the BBC's weekly *Listener* and *Radio Times* magazines, as well as *Ariel*, the BBC's own internal publication for staff communication. In parallel to this, the primary sources of the UK's developing commercial broadcasting sector was available through Bournemouth University, who host the IBA Archive, which also contains much material in regard to religious broadcasting and sheds light on how the religious broadcasting story evolved under this new environment.

In addition to these significant primary sources in the UK, the archives of Westminster Library, St. Martin-in-the-Fields, Lambeth Palace, the British Film Institute, the UK Parliament, the Churches Advisory Council for Local Broadcasting (CACLB) and the Church of England Records Centre, all proved important in understanding the impact of religious broadcasting in the UK and especially within the various Christian denominations.

In terms of America, documents held by the National Religious Broadcasters organisation, the Federal Council of Churches of Christ and the Protestant Radio & Television Centre were made available, which in a similar way to the UK helped trace the dynamic of religious broadcasting within the religious and media frameworks of America. In addition time was spent viewing/reviewing footage of a number of television broadcast series like the *700 Club* and *PTL*.

In both the situations of America and the UK, original newspaper resources also provided a historic and critical reflection on many areas covered in the book, either through hard copies, digital formats or microfilm. Many hours were spent each week in the British Library to be able to access all these important primary sources.

The concluding Case Studies were also an important vehicle in providing a real life and in-depth holistic assessment from a range of perspectives, looking at the comparative examples of religious programming in the UK and America which majored on personalities as the key feature of their output. The ITV programme *Stars on Sunday* in the UK and Jim Bakker's *Praise the Lord* (PTL) Club in the USA, were examined in terms of the personalities involved, the style of the programmes and the responses from the public.

Finally, a number of qualitative semi-structured face to face interviews were held with some strategic people who played a particular role in the religious broadcasting story of the 20th Century. Rather than adopting a general survey with these people, in the form of a questionnaire or common questions, the value of these targeted interviews was to extract as much personal experience and expertise from these interviewees in terms of whatever their interaction was in relation to religious broadcasting.

The amalgamation of these various methods represent a considered study of this significant facet of media history and help construct a clearer picture and understanding of the nature of religious broadcasting in the 20th Century.

NOTES

1. Emmanuel, D., *Challenges of Christian Communication and Broadcasting: Monologue or Dialogue?* (Basingstoke: Macmillan, 1999), p.154.

2. Bailey, M., He Who Has Ears to Hear: Christian Pedagogy and Religious Broadcasting during the Inter-War Period. *Westminster Papers in Communication and Culture*, 4 (1) 2007: 5-6.

3. Dickenson, S. H., Characterising the Message of the Electric Church. *Florida Communication Journal*, 11 (1) 1983: 21.

4. Gunter, B. and Viney, R., *Seeing is Believing: Religion and Television in the 1990s* (London: John Libbey, 1994), p.29-33.

5. Fore, W. F., The Unknown History of Televangelism. *Journal of the World Association of Christian Communication*, 54 (1) 2007: 45.

6. Howley, K., Prey TV: Televangelism and Interpellation. *Journal of Film and Video*, 53 (2/3) 2001: 24-29; Fortner, R. S., *Radio, Morality and Culture*. (Illinois: Southern Illinois University Press, 2005), p.42-43.

7. Swindler, A., Culture in Action: Symbols and Strategies. *American Sociological Review*, 51 (2) 1989: 277.

8. Schultze, Q.J., The Wireless Gospel. *Christianity Today*. 18th January (1988), p.23.

9. Elvy, P., *Buying Time: The Foundations of the Electronic Church*. (Great Wakering: McCrimmons, 1986), p.15-16; Kay, W. K., Pentecostalism and Religious Broadcasting. *Journal of Beliefs and Values*, 30 (3) 2009: 247.

10. Davie, G., *Religion in Britain: A Persistent Paradox*. 2nd edition (London: Blackwell, 2015), p.11.

11. Paley, W. S., Broadcasting Both Sides of the Atlantic. *The Listener*. 24th June (1931), p.1052-1053.

12. Bunyan, J., *The Pilgrim's Progress from This World to That Which is to Come* (London: William Pickering, 1849),p.vi.

13. Voskuil, D. N., The Power of the Air: Evangelicals and the Rise of Religious Broadcasting. *In*: Schultze, Q. J., *American Evangelicals and the Mass Media* (Grand Rapids: Academic Books, 1990), p.70.

14. Gaddy, G. D., The Power of the Religious Media: Religious Broadcast Use and the Role of Religious Organisations in Public Affairs. *Review of Religious Research*, 25 (4) 1984: 289.

15. Briggs, A., *The History of Broadcasting in the United Kingdom.* Vol. 11: *The Golden Age of Wireless* (Oxford: Oxford University Press, 1965).

16. Rosenthal, M., This Nation under God: The Broadcasting and Film Commission of the National Council of Churches and the New Medium of Television. *The Communication Review*, 4 (3) 2001: 347-348.

17. Armstrong, B., *The Electric Church* (Nashville: Thomas Nelson, 1979).

18. Curran, J., *Media and Power* (London: Routledge, 2002), p.3.

19. Marszolek, I. and Robel, Y., The Communicative Construction of Collectivities: An Interdisciplinary Approach to Media History. *Historical Social Research*, 41 (1) 2016: 329

20. Curran, J., Narratives of Media History Revisited. *In*: Bailey, M., *Narrating Media History.* (London: Routledge, 2009), p.1.

21. Ibid., p.20.

22. Turow, J., *Media Systems in Society* (London. Longmans, 1992), p.5.

23. Balbi, G., 2011. Doing Media History. *Westminster Papers in Communication and Culture*, 8 (2) 2011: 154.

CHAPTER 1

MAPPING THE TERRITORY
Standing on the Shoulders of Giants

Even a cursory glance at various aspects of media research will reveal multiple books, papers and articles on numerous media topics. They fill libraries and scores of pages on the internet. By contrast, that will not be the experience when trying to find information on religious broadcasting. As Voskuil observed, "there are no comprehensive studies of religious broadcasting",[1] a point also made by Ronald Falconer in the Baird Lectures of 1977,

> there is not much literature on the subject, probably because those who have been and are involved actively in the media are constantly under the peculiar pressures they generate and writing objectively is an unfulfilled promise.[2]

Despite its popularity amongst enthusiasts, both here and in the US, religious broadcasting remains only a sizable niche and an often forgotten player, in the vein of the comment by Garner in *On Defining the Field*, when talking about radio studies also being, "too long suffering from critical neglect".[3]

It is also important to state also that religious broadcasting is only part of the broadcasting landscape and broadcasting only part of the development of mass communications. As Hill points out, "religious radio and television did not operate in a vacuum".[4] Therefore in mapping the territory the study attempts to demonstrate the significance of the communications, broadcasting and the religious framework, as well as the impact of personality, which gave the possibility to the evolution and development of religious broadcasting in the USA and the UK.

The book touches on a wide range of subject areas, but the intention here is to set the scene in terms of the academic literature, as such, that relates to the contexts and development of religious broadcasting and the case that personality was a significant driving force behind its impact.

In terms of literature/source material, this consists of a vast array of scholarly and semi-learned journals and relevant books. Traditional techniques of library research were employed in assembling this preview. Journals of abstracts, bibliographies and literature known were used as starting points. The works cited in the Bibliography and references in each chapter indicate the key contributors in the various fields of study. The citations are used to show respect to previous scholars and as with the words of Sir Isaac Newton, "if I have seen farther, it is by standing on the shoulders of giants".[5]

Throughout, the book undertakes an extensive examination and analysis of all the relevant texts that relate to religious broadcasting, but here it will principally focus on a number of key publications that have contributed in part to different elements of the religious broadcasting story, though failed to deliver on the totality of this unique broadcasting phenomenon.

1. The Crucible of Mass Communications

As Lowery and De Fleur indicate in *Milestones in Mass Communication Research*, the word "mass" does not just refer to large numbers,[6] though by definition it does mean reaching large segments of populations, but rather we see the contemporary forms of mass communication emerging as a part of the development of a mass society,[7] mass rather denoting a sameness or homogeneity rather than the size of the audience.[8] Given this any proper understanding of society needs to incorporate the dynamics of mass communication.[9]

The concept of a 'mass society', created by the products of the mass media, has dominated critical thinking for well over half a century.[10] Hence there was a growing awareness amongst contemporary historians of the importance of mass communications in understanding media developments and therefore making a cogent informed statement about this field requires coming to terms with the diversity of theoretical perspectives.[11]

As a scholarly discipline the field of mass communication has generally considered itself to be a social science. Paul Lazarsfeld, for example, one of the most prominent sociologists made his Bureau of Applied Social Research (1944) into a major venue for the study of mass communications with the emphasis on specific content and its effects, rather than a more holistic approach. But the literature of sociologists, psychologists and mass communication scholars has tended to share a particular way of dividing up the turf of mass communications into studiable components or domains: (1) the institutions, structures and professional cohorts responsible for producing media; (2) the content, 'message systems' or 'texts' they produce; and (3) the effects of those messages on various audiences.[12] Similarly, Berelson (1959) commenting on communication research felt there were four major "approaches" or lines of inquiry in communication research, plus a number of minor ones. These major approaches are so clearly identified with and characterized by their leading proponents that they can be given names: the political approach of Lasswell (1948); the sample survey approach of Lazarsfeld (1940); the small group approach of Lewin (1948) and the experimental approach of Hovland (1949) and others.[13]

In truth, the study of mass communications has become an important backdrop to many different disciplines and areas of research, including broadcasting, as Schramm's book *Mass Communications* (1975) demonstrated, when he brought together the expertise of scholars in anthropology, psychology, political science, as well professionals in mass communications. Schramm saw mass communications as "essentially a working group organised around some device for circulating the same message, at about the same time, to large numbers of people".[14] A process for him which is not "merely academic",[15] but which had significant consequences and opportunities. Tayer makes an important point about these consequences and opportunities in stating,

> The basic dynamic in the phenomenon of mass communication, the pivotal mechanism out of which all else evolves is not technology, awesome as it became. Nor is it the 'message' or the implicit culture in the 'content' of the media. Nor is it the 'effects' which the media are purported to have. The basic mechanism inheres in the social and personal uses to which people put the media and its fare.[16]

Mass media is certainly the basic tool that bears the main functional load of mass communications.[17] Some historians of the mass media have employed the term the "communications revolution" to refer to the emergence in this era of the modern newspaper press, cinema, radio and television, though the term "mass media" itself was not widely used until the 1960s.[18] But since the 1930's there has been a marked shift in the study of mass communications compared with preceding decades, with attention being paid to the dual aim of interrelating the different elements of the communication process and linking mass communication activities to the wider social structures.[19] McQuail, considered to be one of the most influential writers in the field of mass communications, points out the longevity of this activity, "the occurrence of human communications over time and distance is much older than are the mass media now in use".[20]

So although the 20th Century can be described as the 'first age of the mass media' its roots are much earlier and the flowering much later. Briggs and Burke in their classic, *A Social History of the Media,* make the same important point,

> it was only in the 1920s – according to the *Oxford English Dictionary* – that people began to speak of 'the media' and in a generation later, in the 1960s, of a 'communications revolution', but a concern with the means of communication is very much older than that.[21]

The book argues that for those working or studying in the communications sphere they need to take history seriously and for historians, of whatever speciality, they need to take account of communication – including communication theory and communications technology.

CHAPTER 1 MAPPING THE TERRITORY

These reflections, so far indicate that mass communication is a wide ranging concept of activities dating back centuries. But Curran also feels that mass communication should not be considered part of mass media, in the way we have described, rather when we speak of mass media he is thinking specifically of modern electronic and print based media[22] and for the purpose of this book, the focus is certainly on the broadcast media of radio and television.

The analysis of this media is complicated, firstly by the implications of different perspectives and secondly by the increase in the 20th Century of rapid social change, technological innovation and the decline in some traditional forms of control and authority. As Geertz says, with the studies of communication the constant challenge is to untangle,

> a multiplicity of complex conceptual structures, many of them superimposed upon or knotted into one another, which are at once strange or irregular and inexplicit and which the student must contrive somehow first to grasp and then to render.[23]

So whether ideologically one sees the media as an indispensable component of a cohesive society (Durkheim 1895), a developing industry which adapts to changing circumstances in order to survive (Spencer 1898), a direct tool of the capitalist state (Marx 1846), an arena of conflict for sectional interests (Weber 1947) or propagators of a culture industry that has been standardised, commercialised and rigidified (Adorno 1944), the fact of the matter remains that broadcast media is a central part of American and British culture and represents the outcome of a long and continuous process that includes a vast number of technological innovations, scientific advances and new economic and social forms.

Lorimer summarises the impact and reach of this mass media when stating,

> the mass media are fully integrated with and indispensable to modern society. The media gather, analyse and disseminate current information. Individual citizens, social organisations

and businesses rely on the mass media to tell them what is going on in their community, the nation and the world at large.[24]

So what we are seeing is the history of media really slipping into being a history of society. This in itself reflects the centrality of the media in this era.[25] Marshall McLuhan, dubbed "the media guru", further enhanced the idea in his classic book *The Gutenberg Galaxy* and talked about the developing electronic media having a far reaching impact in making instant communications possible, where "the new electronic independence re-creates the world in the image of a global village".[26] This concept and reality was to have a profound effect, as much on the development of religious broadcasting as any other genre of broadcasting, in bringing the Christian message into homes across the USA and UK and ultimately across the globe.

Finally, Klapper's influential work on *The Effects of Mass Communication* (1966) highlights the power media has as a contributory agent in society,[27] helping creating opinions amongst people[28] and most significantly, "being themselves widely regarded with awe, apparently conferring status on the persons and concepts for which they are vehicles".[29]

This latter point is strategically important as we examine how through media platforms religious broadcasters gained status and notoriety both in America and in Britain.

2. The Saga of Broadcasting

As Ellens suggests, "Broadcasting is a child of the nineteenth century. The twentieth is its adolescence".[30] The thinking behind this being that the technological infrastructure that made broadcasting possible was evolved in the 19th Century and then applied in a specific way during the 20th Century.

The idea of instantaneous communication over long distances had fired the imagination of people for centuries. But it was not until 1844 that Samuel F.B. Morse was able to send a message along a copper wire between Washington D.C. and Baltimore and open the era of telecommunications. By the end of the century, radio waves had been discovered by Heinrich Hertz and adapted to a wireless telegraphy by Guglielmo Marconi. Transmission of the human voice was accomplished via the wireless telegraph and by 1906 when a few additional devices were added the age of broadcasting had become possible.[31]

When all these things were in place at the beginning of the 20th Century, the creation of radio turned into what some have called "the miracle of the twentieth century"[32] and the "greatest democratising agent since the invention of printing".[33] It also meant that the British and American governments were faced with the challenge of how to control the new broadcasting technology and maximise on its value.

H.J. Round of the Marconi Company and personal assistant to Marconi, suggested that, "serious broadcasting did not arrive in Britain until the situation in America forced the hands of those in authority here to allow it".[34] This underlines that the birth and development of radio must also be understood against a series of political and economic decisions which characterised the cultural system at the time. Governments deciding that broadcasting could not just be left to scientists; it was of too great an importance in relation to the changing social patterns of society. Hence the significance in Britain of the Sykes Committee (1923) and the Crawford Committee (1926) (See Appendix 3), ensuring that the BBC secured a "pampered monopoly"[35] for public service broadcasting and the Royal Charter stamp of approval, as it became a Corporation (1927), largely independent of government and funded by a single licence fee.

But the BBC stood for more than just a technological achievement and a new innovation, as its chief engineer, Peter Eckersley wrote in *The Power Behind the Microphone*,

> Broadcasting has the unique power to bring every living person into contact with lively minds and dramatic and portentous events. It can stimulate mass interest as much by suggestion as by direct statement. It has the power to amuse, distract and educate. It brings the listener the exciting pleasure of hearing

well-performed music of every kind and gives the ex-patriate the bitter sweets of nostalgia. It is at once a facile amusement, a university, a talking newspaper, a concert hall and a theatre. These are the handsome mosaic pieces of broadcasting.[36]

There is no doubt Eckersley was one of the greatest creative talents behind the early BBC, but every commentator on its history talks much of the vision, talent and drive of its first Director General, John Reith – a position which he held for 11 years (See Chapter 4).

McIntyre's classic biography of Reith, *The Expense of Glory* (1993) highlights the complexities of Reith in terms of his various personal relationships, as well as the volatile career-endeavours both within and beyond the BBC years. He meticulously chronicles the great achievements of this titan of the 20th Century. Another reflects Reith as,

> A tower of strength, a man of six foot seven, with a formidable jaw and heavy black eyebrows. He was a Scot bred in the unbending tradition of the Scottish church, a man with a fine record in the First World War and a determined leader of other men.[37]

That leadership was to have such a major impact on the BBC and broadcasting in the UK, not the least in relation to religious broadcasting. Reith himself in *Broadcast Over Britain* (1924) also reviews the broadcasting landscape and his own opinion of it, highlighting the growing application of radio and its wide-ranging influence beyond personal entertainment. As he reflected broadcasting was "a voyage on unchartered seas".[38] But it was from his memoirs *Into the Wind* (1949), published after the Second World War, that we gain most understanding of Reith. But as McIntyre points out, "the book runs into well over 500 pages, but he races through the first twenty four years of his life in the first eight of them" (1993, p.18). Importantly Eckersley concludes, "the form, content and influence of the broadcasting service is the product of this one dominant man".[39] However despite the major role played by Reith, other factors were coming into place with television technology on the scene developed by Baird, with all the potential that would bring. As Smith describes, the BBC had been granted its Charter at a time when its services barely filled a single radio channel. By 1950 the BBC has three radio programmes and a television channel.[40]

But while the Ullswater Committee in 1935 (See Appendix 3) recommended the expansion of the BBC in terms of its radio programmes, it was the Selsdon and the Hankey Television Committees in 1935 and 1944 respectively (See Appendix 3) that paved the way for a television service to make its impact in the hands of the BBC, until the end of its monopoly in 1955.

As we see the emergence of early radio and television in the UK, a parallel activity was happening in the United States. "In the Roaring Twenties radio would play a big part in communication of that frenzied lifestyle".[41] The first tabloid newspaper the *New York Daily News* was launched (1919) followed by a stream of magazines – *Readers Digest* (1922), *Time* (1923) and the *New Yorker* (1925). A surge of activity covered every area of life and within this environment of national change, radio broadcasting evolved. Matheson comments,

> the whole American people, radio manufacturers, newspapers, advertisers and listeners showed a characteristic quickness in welcoming this new arrival.[42]

So full blown broadcasting made its debut, with most Americans associating the birth of broadcasting with the station KDKA in Pittsburgh in 1920. But by 1922 there were almost 600 licenced stations and an estimated 400,000 radio sets in use. By 1930 the number of sets had jumped to 13 million and by 1936 to 30 million.[43] Though unlike the model of public service broadcasting we saw created in the UK, radio in the United States was a system of free competitive enterprise within a framework of governmental regulation.[44] The comparative history of broadcasting between Britain and America can be seen as a history of difference.[45] British Broadcasting regarded itself as a service, whereas American commercial broadcasting thought of itself as a business.[46] A similar point being made by the historian Asa Briggs,

Eventually the British and American systems were to be so completely different – one based on a concept of 'public service', the other fully integrated into the business system – that in all controversies about the place of radio in society they were to be taken as the two chief contrasting types.[47]

Despite the temptations or attractions of the American broadcasting model, the British came to see it as an "unrestrained broadcasting system"[48] and in addition the BBC rejected the profit motive as the basis of its institutional existence.[49] As Lacey describes in detail in *Freedom and Communication 1914-2001* the American system by contrast was philosophically and practically consumer minded,

> what was needed was a communication system that gives the individual consumer the greatest resources to satisfy his needs for information and enrichment and that strengthens his capacity to achieve personal development and autonomy of judgement.[50]

The same theme is picked up by Mosco's *Broadcasting in the United States* with the critique that American broadcasting was, "overtly rooted in commercialism, dominated by a few large corporations, something of a cultural wasteland and insensitive to minority tastes".[51]

The story of broadcasting in America therefore is one of popular and commercial enthusiasm, with a free rein to its expression, controlled for the most part by great commercial corporations and paid for by every sort of commercial interest which advertises through it.

More specifically, the development in the early history of the electronic mass media in the USA, were the 'chains' of stations or 'networks'. Within a few years it was a dominant element of broadcasting, what Barnouw termed "the golden web".[52] So in 1926 the National Broadcasting Corporation (NBC) came into being with the Columbia Broadcasting System (CBS) arriving a few years later (1929) along with the American Broadcasting Company (ABC) in 1943 (See Appendix 2). As the President of CBS stated,

CHAPTER 1 MAPPING THE TERRITORY

> America is traditionally hostile to monopoly and especially government monopoly – so we decided on government regulation rather than government control and on orderly competition rather than monopoly.[53]

So along with the situation in the UK, American media needed regulation and regulation was regarded as a federal matter not to be left in the hands of state or local governments. So their 1927 Radio Act established the Federal Radio Commission (FRC) which could issue licences, allocate frequencies and generally regulate the developing industry, with the Federal Communications Commission (FCC) taking over the role in 1934 (See Appendix 2).

Chase's *Sound and Fury: An Informal History of Broadcasting* describes how broadcasters were awakening to the fact that radio was no longer a novelty sold only on the basis of the ability to send a voice through the air. The public wanted a good voice that had something worth while to say. The trend was moving on from technology, to the importance of content.[54] Though while radio broadcasting was still in its infancy, work was underway to find a viable television system. As America's *Radio News* reported in 1926.

> Mr Baird (John Logie) has definitely and indisputably given a demonstration of real television. It is the first time in history that this has been done in any part of the world.[55]

Television was a child of radio in many respects. But as with the UK and the US, the growth of television was interrupted by the Second World War and it was not until the late 40s that its impact began to be felt.

But as Pusateri goes on to expand,

> surpassing radio for the first time, television had clearly reached by 1954 with over 400 TV stations on the air, with two thirds of American homes owning at least one television set and with NBC beginning regular telecasts programs in colour

and advertising revenues taken by the television industry, a place of maturity.[56]

In Britain also television was becoming a significant media development, as William Haley a former Director General of the BBC reflected,

> Television has become an integral part of broadcasting. The essence of broadcasting is that it is a means of communication, capable of conveying intelligence in every home simultaneously.[57]

From the time of its inception the attraction of television for British audiences never dimmed. Up until the 1950s the pattern for radio was not dissimilar. In 1927 there were over 2 million radio licences, a figure that quadrupled over the next twenty years. In 1947 there were only about 15,000 combined radio and television licences, but by the 1960s it had grown to more than 10 million licences, in addition to 4 million radio only licences. The trend and hunger for broadcasting was only on an upward direction,[58] indeed the child had grown to dwarf its parent.

The comparison of the UK and US is noted in many fields from politics to film and everything in between, but in terms of broadcasting it seems at times that each nation developed radio and television in splendid national isolation. Camporesi has made an important contribution in this field with *Mass Culture and National Traditions: The BBC and American Broadcasting 1922-1954* (2000), which is in effect a case study illustrating the British attitudes towards America in terms of broadcasting policies and programming. Hilmes also states in the classic *Network Nations: A Transnational History of American Broadcasting*,

> both for Britain and for the United States, this transnational relationship was deeply productive, providing a constant circuit of influence and adaptation that while often resisted or even reviled, nonetheless worked powerfully to enliven and expand the cultural horizons of both nations [59] ...

so it requires a real effort of will on the part of the media historian to overlook the constant and constitutive presence of Great Britain in the United States experience, and vice versa, when it comes to broadcasting.[60]

Tunstall picks up a similar theme in his summation of the media in Britain equally commenting about this relationship talking of "Anglo-American" media output. Britain being a sort of junior partner, though in some respects on a per-population, or economic product basis, Britain contributing a major amount.[61] However, as Camporesi points out when talking about input rather than output, we are talking about a relatively small amount of American material before 1955 that was featured in UK broadcasting and even when it was, it tended to be transformed into a peculiarly British flavour.[62]

As the saying goes, "when America sneezes, Britain get a cold". So by the mid 1950s, despite the hopes of the *Beveridge Committee* in 1951 (See Appendix 3) to preserve the monopoly of the BBC and resist commercialisation, the monopoly game was over, and the *Television Act of 1954* (See Appendix 4) paved the way for the establishment of Independent Television (ITV) in 1955.

But this was not unanimously welcomed. Sir William Emrys Williams, the Secretary General of the Arts Council at the time, spoke for many in an article in *The Times*,

> Its not the merits of competition or the advantages of variety, but rather the values behind the two systems of television. One is based on public service, the other on selling goods.[63]

However, the dye was cast and commercial television underway. But it was a boat that brought the demise of the total BBC monopoly. Street in his comprehensive book *Crossing the Ether: British Public Service Radio and Commercial Competition 1922-1945* (2006) and his *Historical Dictionary of British Radio,* writes of Radio Caroline as,

> the first of the UK pirate radio stations of the 1960s and extremely important in the development of post-war British

Radio. Radio Caroline shaped the music radio revolution that led to the creation of BBC Radio 1 by the BBC and ultimately, the launch of commercial radio in Britain in 1973".[64]

Relating to this latter point it is worth pointing out a difference in terms relating to this new innovation. Stoller is his comprehensive recounting of this story in *Sounds of Your Life: The History of Independent Radio in the UK* makes the point that,

> Independent radio was introduced into the UK in the early seventies. It was intended to be local, public service radio, funded by advertising but meeting a social as well as a market purpose. It was deliberately and avowedly not commercial radio.[65]

Adding to the commentary on this era, the much respected historian Asa Briggs wrote his major series entitled *The History of Broadcasting in the United Kingdom*. The fifth of his series – *Competition 1955-1974* and the longest, focusing on the massive changes that started in this period and were to be ongoing. *The Pilkington Committee* in 1962 (See Appendix 3) led the way for the establishment of a second BBC Channel – BBC 2 and BBC Local Radio, the *1972 Broadcasting Act* (See Appendix 4) set up the Independent Broadcasting Authority (IBA) responsible for commercial television and commercial radio, the *1977 Annan Committee* (See Appendix 3), the *1980 Broadcasting Act* and the development of Channel 4 (See Appendix 4).

Amidst this 'melting pot' of activity Madge believes big changes were already underway,

> when Channel 4 opened, British Broadcasting had developed into a highly structured "duopoly" in which one part mirrored the other, competing not for revenue but for audiences, using high quality programmes as bait.[66]

Interestingly, while the UK was moving closer in part to the US model of broadcasting in the 1970s, the USA with the recommendation of the Carnegie Commission (1967) passed the Public Broadcasting Act of

1967 (See Appendix 4) which established the Corporation for Public Broadcasting. Engelman says,

> this represented the apparent triumph of the movement to establish a non-commercial broadcasting system in the United States dating back to the earliest days of radio. The legislative victory followed nearly a half a century of promising initiatives dashed by political defeats.[67]

But as Hendy in *Radio in a Global Age* points out, it was public service radio but not as we know it,

> what makes the American model of public service radio different, though, is that it is a much less costly service which dispenses with the most popular forms of programmes on the basis that they are provided in any case by commercial operators. Instead, it concentrates solely on broadcasting the sort of cultural and information programmes which might otherwise be unavailable.[68]

So by the 1970s we see a UK and US broadcasting industry with some similar trends, though recognition needs to be made that comparatively speaking only recently have European governments permitted private ownership of broadcasting facilities, the American government always permitted it.[69]

But while the BBC in the following years was being challenged by the competition in both the television and radio arenas, Seaton in her controversial book *Pinkoes and Traitors: The BBC and the Nation 1974 – 1987* asserts that,

> the Peacock Report, published in July 1986 , did what the Corporation had been unable to do for itself : refresh the legitimacy of the BBC... The Peacock Report marked a decisive moment in the Corporation's survival and success for the next twenty years.[70]

Commentators at the time recognised that Britain was entering something of a period of uncertainty caused by the Broadcasting Acts of 1984 and 1990 which meant a greater de-regulation and the expansion of cable and satellite potential and the concern that the new media of that time would destroy the established order. McDonnell, for example, in his Reader *Public Service Broadcasting,* which featured various luminaries of the broadcasting world writes,

> The public service tradition in Britain has proved remarkably adaptable and resilient. But never before however has it had to face such a concerted effort by Government to alter the basic framework of broadcasting regulation.[71]

So what we have in the 1980s and 90s is the initiative of the Thatcher Government to open up the airwaves and create more competition, leading to what has been called "Broadcasting's Big Bang" in the form of the *1990 Broadcasting Act* (See Appendix 4) with its "lighter touch" regulation and widening opportunities for broadcasters including for religious groups.

Coppens and Downey concluded that by the 1990s,

> the British broadcasting system is one that can be characterised as competitive, with three commercial terrestrial television channels with a variety of public service obligations, battling it out for advertising revenue, a number of cable and satellite channels and a public broadcaster that has evolved into a tough player on the international media stage.[72]

The reality is that the United States did not share the same cultural traditions as Britain, particularly in the field of communication. America had allowed railroads, telegraph, telephony and broadcasting communications to develop with little or no government development,[73] whereas Britain's historic regulatory framework provided a different and some feel a more creditable basis for the cultural leadership of the nation.[74] However the comparative broadcasting landscapes of the US and UK both provided in their own unique way a cradle for the birth and development of religious broadcasting which was to make a significant impact in the 20th Century.

3. The Anatomy of Religion

Another part of the puzzle, as we move to the consideration of religious broadcasting, is the part played in the USA and UK by religion itself. It is worth establishing here again we are predominantly, but not entirely, talking about Christianity.

It is also worth pointing out that religion is not only seen as controversial in this era, but as hugely complex in its definitions and comprehension. Durkheim at the beginning of the 20th Century defined religion as,

> a unified system of beliefs and practices relative to sacred things, that is to say things set apart and surrounded by prohibitions, beliefs and practices that unite adherents in a single moral community called a church.[75]

Many variations on this have been offered, which is probably why O'Day for example describes religious history as a "compendium of many games" [76] or Bowker's view of religion as "a journey of exploration and discovery".[77] Though all reflect on its importance, some going so far as to describe it as "a central force in intellectual and political history".[78] The reality is that,

> Any large population will display different degrees of religious practice, awareness and sensibility and Church membership only represents one part of the continuum of religiosity on which these degrees must be measured.[79]

Across all variables it is widely accepted that Christianity has had a major role in shaping British culture over centuries. Although Britain has changed, the legacy of the past cannot and should not, be ignored. The role of religion in American society is equally important, although the religious landscape of America is not as simple or as uniform as it might originally appear. But it is hard to think of a single aspect of American culture, past or present, in which religion has not played a major part.[80] Brekus and Gilpin's major work, *American Christianities: A History of Dominance and Diversity* (2011) describes how many Christian traditions arrived in the cultural luggage of immigrants from Europe or Asia, from Ethiopia or from the Caribbean. Other groups including the Assemblies of God and the Latter-day Saints (Mormons) arose as new Christian movements in the United States. Still others emerged in the aftermath of controversies over doctrines, ethnic differences or regional tensions, such as those that fractured Methodists, Baptists and Presbyterians in the years preceding the American Civil War. In addition the immigration flow was to incorporate the influence of the other major world religions such as Buddhism, Hinduism and Islam.[81]

One of the greatest challenges to determining the religious diversity of America by numbers is finding widely agreed-upon statistics. The Gallup Survey in 1990 stated that 92% of Americans describe themselves as having some form of religious affiliation, but the fullest and most recent study is the American Religious Identification Survey (ARIS) 2008, based on a survey of more than 50,000 Americans. This survey shows that the majority of Americans (over 80%) identify themselves as religious and the vast majority of them (95%) identify with some form of Christianity and an average of 40% attend a worship service each week.[82] About one third of Christians are Catholics and about two thirds (about half the US population) identify with some form of Protestantism. The total of Americans that identify with other religious traditions (Judaism, Islam, Buddhism and Hinduism) adds up to less than 4% of the population.[83]

Many scholars would agree with Beal that numbers of the mainline Protestant denominations have played leading roles in many aspects of American life, including politics, business, science, education and most relevant for this study – broadcasting.[84] So as we see broadcasting developing in the early 1920s, the emerging Pentecostal Church (part of Protestantism) with its emphasis on the gift of speaking in tongues and the Baptism of the Holy Spirit, began to have an influence on the wider Christian community in the US,[85] with many of its members or sympathisers taking to the airwaves, like Aimee Semple McPherson (See Chapter 4). Her pioneering in this area influenced others and most of the denominations from Catholics to Southern Baptists, saw the potential of this new way to proclaim the Christian faith and build the Church.

However what also emerged within the Protestant network was a differing theological approach, which impacted the broadcasting output. So there were 'conservatives' who adhered to orthodox evangelical Christianity, believing the Bible as their sole authority, but on their fringe were groups of 'fundamentalists' (a title first coined in 1920 by Curtis Laws Editor of the Baptist paper the *Watchman Examiner*) who interpreted the Bible in a literalistic way and were sceptical of those that didn't. On the other hand there were the more 'liberal' minded mainline churches who did not subscribe to an infallible view of Scripture and were more questioning and open-minded about the Christian faith and theology.[86] Despite the different approaches both groups found a niche on the airwaves.

When television first began in the post-war years, the mainline churches were experiencing the peak of their membership and influence in society. Consequently, when the networks and stations sought a representative religious voice they turned to the mainline churches. The mainline co-operative and moderate approach to religious programming also suited the legislative and public relations needs of the newly emerging medium of television. The evangelicals and fundamentalists, who were not seen as major force within the mainstream of American cultural and religious life, existed mainly on the fringes of the influence within the television industry at that time.[87]

The Year Book of American and Canadian Churches documents trends within Christianity and designates itself as a "snapshot of religious activity", characterized denominations as being in constant flux. So in the early 1950s things began to change with Protestant denominations declining: the Episcopal Church, the Evangelical Lutheran Church in America, the Presbyterian Church USA, the United Church of Christ and the United Methodist Church. On the other hand, considerable increases were seen in the Roman Catholic Church, the South Baptist Convention, the Church of Jesus Christ of Latter Day Saints and the Assemblies of God. The Pentecostal Church becoming the fifth largest denomination in the United States.[88]

In parallel to these major changes it was the development of what was to be know as the 'electronic church' and the explosion of 'televangelists' in the 1950s who were largely evangelical, fundamentalist or Pentecostal (or all three), that was to play the most significant role in religious broadcasting in the United States and redesigned the map of American religious life.[89] So people like Dr.Billy Graham, Pat Robertson, Jim Bakker, Oral Roberts, Jimmy Swaggart, Jerry Falwell and many others (See Chapter 4) were destined to become household names. But whereas the 'religious revival' of the 1950s can be mostly seen as depicted by these vivid personalities, its substratum it has to be said was much broader than suggested by just personality cults. Religion in general was considered 'popular' in people's minds, reflecting the belief that any religion was a 'good thing'.

Herberg points out that a sense of religious belonging has long been important to Americans.[90] Hence again there was an increased church attendance, increased church giving, increased church building and an increased public esteem.[91] It prompted one commentator to reflect that,

> a close look at the evangelical communications network should convince even the sceptic that it was the most important cultural force in America at that time.[92]

In many ways the situation in the UK was more complex and controversial, with multiple strands that make up the landscape of religion.[93] Lindsay in *Mind the Gap: Religion and the Crucible of Marginality in the United States and Great Britain,* makes the point that,

> comparisons between the United States and Great Britain reveal many similarities in broad based religious concerns and values. Nonetheless, surveys over the last 40 years document

a widening gap between the two countries in individual-led religious commitment.[94]

In contrast to America, but in common with many European countries, the UK had a national church in the form of the Anglican Church where there is a relationship of State and Church, which historically provided the cornerstone of both civic and ecclesiastical life.[95] Further to this there was a growing ecumenism, drawing together Catholicism, Anglicanism and the Non-Conformist churches in the UK, ensuring a strength of co-operation which was to benefit the drive in religious broadcasting.

At the beginning of the 20th Century most people saw Britain as clearly a Christian country, the predominant culture being one largely imbued with Christian belief. It appeared to be leading the world economically, morally and religiously, exporting Christianity throughout the Empire. English Christian religion was then dominated by the Church of England which made up 60-70% of the faith community, with a further 30% also Christian, 10% of which was Roman Catholic; the remaining numbers were non-conformists like Methodists, Congregationalists, Baptists and a few Unitarians, Presbyterians, Quakers and Salvation Army. In addition there was a growing Jewish community and sects like Jehovah's Witnesses and Mormons. [96]

But at the point when broadcasting was launching in Britain, people may have had the view that religion was flourishing after the First World War. But the reality was that there was a creeping secularization which Bruce and Glendinning, in *When Was Secularization?* trace to the decline of church-going in the mid-19th Century. For them, after that period, there was an incremental process, with acceleration in the late 1950s and 1960s.[97]

Others like Brown see rather the social and cultural changes of the 1960s as the real trigger of a sudden and substantial decline of Christian culture and institutions in Britain.[98] McKibbin generally agrees that, "by the standards of many European countries or the United States, England was a 'de-Christianised' country".[99] But in those inter-war years when the BBC was still developing, the majority view reflected by Field in his article *Gradualism or Revolutionary Secularization? A Case Study of Religious Belonging in Inter-War Britain 1918-1939*, having examined data from across the country, he concluded that secularisation in Britain had to be seen as a progressive and protracted process and not a catalyst of the 1960s.[100] Edwards matches this by making the point that "secularisation seems to occur when supernatural religion becomes private, optional and problematical".[101]

Considering the post-war years, Davie's first volume – *Religion in Britain Since 1945* (subtitled – *Believing without Belonging*) also explains the concept that religion became privatized rather that institutionalized,

> the majority of British people – in common with many other Europeans – persisted in believing (if only in an ordinary God), but saw no point to participate with even minimal regularity in their religious institutions. [102]

In her revised edition *Religion in Britain: A Persistent Paradox*, she develops many of her original themes, but one of her statements really captures the flavour of religion in the period after the Second World War to the 1990s, namely that,

> Britain remains a Christian country in terms of its culture and history. Nothing will alter that. Significant sections of the population are, however, becoming not only more secular but noticeably more critical of religion.[103]

There is general agreement that there was a clear drift from the churches after the Second World War, but the reasons are many and complex mostly as a result of social changes outside the control of the churches.[104] The decline in institutional religion had become an established feature of all the churches to a greater or lesser extent, although it was not the same for all.[105]

Coming back to the comparison with the US – none of these survey trends have been mirrored in the United States, the USA being known for its religious 'exceptionalism' which runs counter to the declining impact of Christianity in the majority of western countries.[106] Early snapshot surveys in the USA and in Great Britain between 1948 and 1952 reveal church membership in the USA around 57% church membership, whilst in the UK is was 21.6%. Lindsay also asserts in that in religious service attendance, the percentage of monthly attendance in Britain dropped by 19% over the last 20 years, whilst the figure of attendance remained at approximately at 60% over the same time in the United States.[107] His study finally suggests that, "America expresses its identity through religion in ways that are weighty and powerful and in ways that people in Britain do not".[108] Secularists have a habit in Europe of turning religion into a problem where it encroaches on public life, whereas in America, religion is not only vibrant but welcomed as the source of essentially positive values.[109] Schneider also concludes,

> Religion whatever else it might be, is one of America's biggest businesses and remains a pervasive institution. It gets mixed up with education, media, politics and business and there is nothing free from its grasp and grasping.[110]

An important contribution to this discussion can also be found in Berger, Davie and Fokas's book *Religious America and Secular Europe: A Theme and Variations* (2016), where the authors maintain that it is not the vibrant evangelical religiosity of America that is exceptional, rather it is the radical and growing secularity of European societies, including Britain.[111] Despite what seems here a negative comparison it is important to remember, as Pierard and Lewis point out there were links of evangelicalism between Britain and America with many common features, especially in the realms of hymnody, theology and denominational development, all emphasizing the importance of the Bible, personal conviction and Christian social action.[112] However, after the Second World War we see Western evangelicals forming into a highly complex grouping, having a growing global presence but not a coherent organisation like a denomination.[113] The differences are most highlighted again in the comparison of America and the UK with contrasting social and political attitudes, worship styles and their theological views, with the rapid growth and influence of an almost militant Pentecostalism and Fundamentalism in America becoming the seed-bed for many of the religious broadcasters.[114] Whereas in the UK, as Marsden reflects, in *Fundamentalism as an American Phenomenon: A Comparison with English Evangelicalism* (1977), the characteristics were more about piety and spirituality and evangelicalism here did not have the same level of impact on the churches and the culture.[115]

A further development of this is seen by Callum Brown chronicling how the battle for Christian Britain was taken to the airwaves, as the BBC resisted the tide of secularisation and the growing Humanist influence of the 20th Century. In fact Brown believes with the help of the powerful Central Religious Advisory Committee (CRAC) and the like minded managers at the BBC, the place of religion within the BBC system kept significant humanists like David Tribe (the President of the National Secular Society) and his colleagues from getting airtime,[116] believing the desirability of religious and ethical broadcasting was in the interests of the nation and social order.[117] The result being that the Christianity, CRAC and the BBC's Religious Broadcasting Department were in effect and extension of the British religious establishment,[118] as Brown asserts by 1945 the Religious Broadcasting Department, carefully engineered by CRAC, inserted Christianity into the core of Britain's radio culture".[119]

Brown believes that fearing the creeping secularisation in Britain, the churches who were the most influential external body in the management of the BBC, conspired since the formation of the Corporation in 1927 to exclude Humanists and Atheists like Julian Huxley, Bertrand Russell and A.J. Ayer from prominent airtime on radio[120] and also reduced controversy about religious matters that might undermine the Christian faith. [121]

Despite the exclusion of Humanists from religious and ethical broadcasting, it did not prevent their rising role in the 1950s in other areas of public culture.[122] However, further attempts to secure representation of Humanist thought on the BBC by figures like E. M. Forster stalled in the face of influential Directors of Religious Broadcasting like Francis House who believed that religion was part of the post-war recovery[123] and Roy McKay who insisted on the priority of Christian belief on the BBC (1958). The battle fought for Christianity's central role had been won in the 1940s and 1950s, but from the 1960s there was a new role for non-Christian religions; religion and clergy became the object of unprecedented humour; Humanists took to the air tackling controversial topics and atheists like Jacob Bronowski with his series *The Ascent of Man* made the case that religions had been guilty of holding back the advance of human knowledge [124].

All this led to the extent to which the vocabulary and the narrative of debate about modern society fell into the hands of those without religious affiliation[125] with broadcasting reflecting what had become the liberalisation of Britain, with media contributing to the ongoing secularisation process and taking over key parts of the position, authority and functions of religious institutions in society, leaving Christianity just part of a multi-cultural and multi-faith, but largely secular society.

Brown's conclusions are largely correct, its monopoly had gone, but he seriously underestimates the influence of what was dubbed "the return of religion"[126] that was to continue to the end of the 20th and into the 21st Century, not withstanding the creeping secularisation and the declining affiliation to the Christian Church in the UK as noted by Heyck [127] and Gilbert [128] (precise definitions and factual accuracy are virtually impossible to achieve in this area because of differences between membership and attendance as stated by Svennevig,[129]) certainly since the late 60s the Christian Church, including in the UK, saw a resurgence in activity across most denominations in terms of the 'Charismatic Movement', which adopted the beliefs and practices 'similar' to traditional Pentecostalism from America. It can be argued this new style Pentecostalism was not a religion of reason or pre-eminently of faith or decision, but of experience.[130] The movement too was clearly no respecter of ecumenical or political divisions, or divisions of education, class or churchmanship either,[131] but in an arena of declining church attendance in the UK, it provided what many saw as the green shoots to a new revival in religious belief and spirituality.

Writing in the 1980s Gilbert asserts in his classic, *The Making of Post Christian Britain*,

> The conventional wisdom about the role of religion in the modern world is that religious convictions and religious influences are less pervasive and less important than has been in the past and that decline is likely to continue.[132]

Which as Abercrombe and Warde point out that leaves religion in Britain as something of a paradox,

> on the one hand formal religion appears to be in decline. On the other hand there is a considerable amount of religious activity… while people are not publically as religious as they were, they continue to have religious beliefs.[133]

Although over the course of the 20th Century religion became less important to western social scientists and to the media as a way of understanding and interpreting the world, with academic discussion of religion becoming the domain of sociologists, anthropologists and theologians trying to make sense of institutions and ways of life that had increasing less resonance in Western Europe and amongst American liberals, but the attack on the Twin Towers on 9/11 changed all that, when it moved religion from the inside pages to the front pages with academics rushing into print to re-discover religion as the missing dimension in politics and international relations.[134]

Hoover's important writings on religion and media match this when he observed,

> earlier paradigms in media studies were deeply rooted in the view that religion was a residual and fading feature of the social landscape worthy of study only in the most cursory way.[135]

But circumstances changed, as also noted in *Media Portrayal of Religion and the Secular Sacred* by Knott, Poole and Taira, arguing that the media is now a key source of popular information 'about' religion and that the trend has moved,

In the early 1980's when Britain was held to be in the grip of secularization, the media reflected and contributed to the retreat of religion from the public domain ... now religion because of events and controversies, has never been far from the top of the media agenda.[136]

This thumbnail analysis provides a useful sketch of the foundations and issues connected with religion and the church, which were to influence the way in which religious broadcasting was able to launch, develop and make an impact in both America and Britain.

4. The Impact of Personality/Celebrity

The case of this study is that the major impact of religious broadcasting was made possible not simply by churches, broadcasting institutions or governments, but by significant 'charismatic' personalities in their own particular eras, both in the USA and in the UK.

This theory adopts a particular slant on the historical process, whilst accepting there are a range of perceptions in analysing any movement or media development. As Fisher points out,

> everyone who has read much history is made sensible of the extreme complications of human affairs and of the difficulty of framing any large propositions to which exception may not be taken.[137]

The task of the historian is to shed light on the what, why and how of the past, based on the available evidence. But this basic tenet is viewed from different perspectives which could be called "theories of history".[138] One view sees history as *Cyclical* where history just repeats itself and there is no progress. Understanding history is about understanding patterns of activity. By contrast the *Linear Theory* sees that history is about progress and heading in an ultimate direction with a strong concept of cause and effect. Another approach dubbed the *Everyman Theory* suggests that the world is shaped by the efforts of ordinary people, not small groups or individuals. To others

Geography is the destiny where history is about location and access to resources and for *Marxists* it is about the struggle between different social classes: powerful groups controlling the wealth and resources and the powerless groups who struggle to survive. Finally there is the *'Heroic in History'* (or the *Great Man Theory*) associated with Thomas Carlyle (1795-1881) who believed that individual people and/or small groups through the power of their character or intellect determine the course of history,

> in all epochs of the world's history we shall find the Great Man to have been the indispensable saviour of his epoch – the lightening without which the fuel would never have burnt.[139]

Prior to the mid 20th Century the Great Man Theory held sway in the minds of those seeking to define the most elusive quality of leadership, because there was agreement that leaders differed from their followers and that fate or providence was a major determinant of the course of history, the contention being that *leaders are born not made* was widely accepted.[140]

With the rise of the behavioural sciences the Great Man Theory fell out of fashion and leadership was not seen as a trait, but learned behaviour and had little to do with innate personal qualities. Bennis and Nanus are typical of the scholars who consider the proposition that *leaders are born not made* to be a myth.[141] But regardless of whether leaders are born or made, it is unequivocally clear that leaders are not like other people [142] and it would be a profound disservice to leaders to suggest that they are just ordinary people who happened to be in the right place and the right time. Zaleznik further contends that the ability of leaders is directly linked to one's personality. Leaders and managers are not the same. Managers tend to favour maintenance of the status quo, whereas leaders seek to transform what is, into what should be.[143] The rise in popularity of what many now term *transformational leadership* (originally coined by James V. Downton in 1973 and developed by James MacGregor Burns in 1978) seems to support Zaleznik's proposition. Transformational leaders are those who achieve success by being magnetic, charming and visionary. Charisma being an essential ingredient.[144]

The origins of great leaders might be too complex to fathom with just one single simplistic theory alone, like the Great Man Theory and any dialogue about history has to take on board the timely emergence of situational forces, but equally the power of charismatic leadership is a legitimate and meaningful avenue which still needs due recognition and as Spector concludes that the Great Man Theory despite its lack of scientific rigour, remains fully relevant in many areas of society today, including in business and management.[145]

It is elements of this last perspective that has most resonance with the impact of religious broadcasting. Carlyle's assertion that "the history of the world is but the biography of great men",[146] fits in part with the portrayal in the book, that it was the power of the personalities of particular 'charismatic' Christian leaders that were responsible for the way in which religious broadcasting was to develop both in the USA and the UK, albeit operating within the social, political and economic circumstances of their own era.

Carlyle's approach to biography and its relationship to history was also taken up by the American Ralph Waldo Emerson for whom biography offered a way of understanding the past in terms of a more holistic approach. He says, "the world is upheld by the veracity of good men, they make the earth wholesome".[147] The German sociologist and historian Wilhelm Dilthey (1833-1911) had a similar view in that his theories centre upon how and why world-views and life-ideals get shaped in the psychic life of the individuals and more particularly in the great man.[148] Thus people are the creative agents in a given historical and social milieu and provide a new stage of historical and social development.[149]

The use of biography to better understand history has not always been fashionable as Gentili and Cerri illustrate in their *History and Biography in Ancient Thought* (1988). Roland Barthes, the French philosopher almost calling the biographical approach heresy[150] and MacMillan's *History's People* (2015) further illustrates the academic tension that exists in literature,

> Historians complain the biographers do not properly understand or short change the context of history, while biographers feel that historians miss out on the individuals who help to make history.[151]

But biography has long been seen as part of history enlivening the past as, "more human, more vivid, more intimate, more accessible, more connected to ourselves".[152] But despite the tensions, as Caine points out in her significant observations in *Biography and History* (2010), biography has now moved to occupy a more central ground, "able to show the great importance of practical locations and circumstances and multiple layers of historical change and experience".[153]

The importance of personality and biography in history and especially media history has recently been reflected in a significant way by media commentator David Hendy, who felt that is has been seriously marginalized,[154] but telling a person's life story is "the nexus through which larger structures might be revealed and understood.[155] A point re-enforced by the BBC's official historian Jean Seaton in suggesting that the accounts of individuals are useful supplements to archival research because they "animate the files, explain the real story and give you a flavour of the people and their concerns".[156] The application of this has been adopted in the *Religious Broadcasting Hall of Fame* in Chapter 4.

Adjibolosoo puts this most succinctly,

> the more I reflect on the issue of the determinates of the course of human history and development, the more each day I become convinced that, in most cases, it is people who makes things happen or not happen in society.[157]

When this gets translated into the context of religious leadership it has a profound effect. As van Kaam describes, "the religious personality knows himself as a unique creation with an irreplaceable divine vocation".[158] The pioneers of religious broadcasting had a strong belief that they were called by God to their ministries and were able to bring their endowed 'charisma' and inspiration to bear on building the structures and networks needed to make a real impact.

The term 'charisma' originates with an ancient Greek word meaning 'gift'. As used by the early Christian Church, the derivative *charismata* described "gifts from God that allowed receivers to carry out extraordinary feats such as healing or prophesy.[159] It should be noted that this notion of charisma being a gift from God, implies it is an innate character trait rather than one that can be developed.

Early references to charismatic leadership inevitably lead back to Max Weber (1864-1920), the renowned German sociologist who had a view derived directly from the Christian theological idea of grace and extended it to the endowment of the individual with exceptional powers. Weber says,

> the term 'charisma' will be applied to a certain quality of an individual personality by virtue of which he is set apart from ordinary men and treated as endowed with supernatural, superhuman, or at least specifically exceptional powers or qualities. These are such as are not accessible to the ordinary person, but are regarded as of divine origin or as exemplary and on the basis of them the individual concerned is treated as a leader.[160]

Since Weber, the concept of charisma has long been used in the social sciences more widely to describe extraordinary leaders and leadership. An important contribution to that was made by House in his *A 1976 Theory of Charismatic Leadership*, where he identifies the personal characteristics of such leaders as having high levels of self-confidence, dominance and a strong conviction in the moral righteousness of his/her beliefs.[161] In a similar vein the much acclaimed Conger and Kanungo's *Charismatic Leadership in Organisations* (1998) also gives recognition to the fact that charismatic leadership is found in a variety of contexts such as political, organisational as well as religious,[162] where their impact is shown as transformational, as described by Bass in *Leadership and Performance Beyond Expectations* (1985) as inspirational, as in the military sphere for example.[163]

So as the study relates to the context specifically of modern media, the reality, as Aberbach expounds, in *Charisma in Politics Religion and the Media* is that,

> television, radio and film have enormously expanded the meaning of charisma. No sooner as a new medium is invented than it is used as a vehicle for charisma.[164]

As will be illustrated, these new platforms became an important vehicle for faith communities in reaching their immediate constituencies more effectively, but also beyond their normal horizons to new audiences, both at home and abroad, led by personalities who exercised immense influence. Though Weber's ideas on charisma still offer a potentially fruitful perspective, so long as they are not adopted slavishly,[165] House Spangler and Woycke (1991) offer a similar helpful definition on this charismatic phenomenon as being,

> the ability of a leader to exercise and diffuse an intense influence over the beliefs, values and behaviour and performance of others through his or her behaviour, beliefs and personal example.[166]

So focussing on not just the general media, but specifically religious broadcasting, this style of charisma is perfectly demonstrated through the men and women who took to the airwaves and channels in the USA and the UK. Their powerful broadcasts created what Stutje describes as a "charismatic bond"[167] between them as a leader and their subordinates.

There is also a need to understand that charismatic leadership is also affected and influenced by the characteristics of those who are led,

> There was a time when leadership was studied almost exclusively in terms of personal traits. It was believed that certain traits tended to accompany successfully initiated leadership; thus there was hope that potential leaders could be identified by the number of leadership traits they possessed...Now, the

tendency is to consider leadership as a product of environmental factors, especially of group norms and follower expectations.[168]

It is true that leaders depend somewhat upon the perceptions of people for their charismatic authority, but nonetheless they also must be exceptional to gain such recognition.[169] As many commentators observe, "Charismatic leadership is a very special sub-type of leadership with unusual qualities not found in leadership in general".[170] House and Howell (1992) concluded that there is support for the general perspective that personality traits differentiate charismatic leaders from non-charismatic leaders. Relevant traits include personal assertiveness, creativity and innovation, risk-seeking propensity, self confidence, social sensitivity and sensitivity to follower's needs.[171] Howell, further offers too another helpful perspective in his *Two Faces of Charisma: Socialized and Personalized Leadership in Organisations* (1988) where he talks of two types of charismatic leadership: socialized and personalized. Socialised leaders tend to have goals which originate with the followers: their wants their needs and their developments. By encouraging their followers to meet these goals socialised leaders foster an environment of autonomy, which survives beyond the leader's tenure with an organisation. On the contrary, personalised leaders exhibit personally dominant and authoritarian behaviour which leads to a close relationship between leaders and followers. Since personalised leaders evoke feelings of obedience and loyalty, an environment of dependence and conformity develops. The net result of personalised leaders is that their influence rarely continues after their departure.[172]

This commentary really also preludes what is a more modern discussion of the role of celebrity, something that is now so embedded into our cultural landscape.[173] But as the social historian Barbara Goldsmith comments in the *New York Times*, "celebrity and personality have become interchangeable in our language".[174] Every epoch has had its form of "celebrity" with different periods of history and different parts of the globe possessing ways of being well known and publically renowned, shaped by the structure of public life as it is created by particular social, political and economic conditions that prevail.[175] Various scholars have expressed their own reflections on this. Boorstin talked of the transition of terminology and understanding of "men of truly heroic stature"[176] being replaced by "celebrities" – those image obsessed publicity seekers, well known for their well-knownness.[177] Rojek, in his much cited book on celebrity produced a sociological analysis of the rites and semantics of fame, drawing on classical sources like Weber, Durkheim and Bourdieu and talking of the emergence of celebrity being the result of three major interrelated historical processes; first the democratization of society, second the decline or organised religion and thirdly the commodification of everyday life,[178] illustrating this with an array of both celebrated and notorious figures. In a similar vein Fred Inglis's *A Short History of Celebrity* (2010) also serves as a powerful corrective to the belief that celebrity was the invention of the 20th Century PR industry, although it made a serious contribution to its mutation, but rather it was a product of 200 years of social change. Finally the notable media theorist Dyer, in his acclaimed book on "Stars" (1982), took the discussion almost to another level. He argued the star image is manufactured and artificial and that individual stars have their own selling point to grab and hold our attention, therefore "stars are involved in making themselves into commodities, they are both the labour and that which the labour produces".[179] So stars have capital value and their ability to attract audiences has ability to attract money. It is worth noting there has been quite a lot of scholarship talking about the differences between stars and celebrities, including Dyer, but in reality they share more in common than that which divides them and therefore many scholars use the terms interchangeably.[180]

Undoubtedly, the personalities/celebrities of religious broadcasting had a real understanding of the 'community of interest' (their audiences) they served and how to garner their following and their tangible support in terms of listenership, viewing and financial backing, where that was required. But as Hutch in his important contribution *Religious Leadership Personality History and Sacred Authority* (1991) illustrates, these men and women did not stand as mere "tradition managers", they were innovators of significant movements driven by their "charismatic" personalities and what they believed was divine inspiration,[181] becoming popular nationally and internationally and high on a spectrum of significance in the society of their day.

Barnes's article *Charisma and Religious Leadership: An Historical Analysis* (1978) has a way of blending these different strands together, stating that these charismatic leaders and pioneers had an intimate connection with a transcendent or immanent divine source,[182] and their presence arose during an appropriate socio-historical circumstance [183] and while they can emerge from within a particular religious organisation/denomination, sometimes their initiatives and ministries result in a whole new religious tradition with them at its centre.[184] Jesus being the archetype of all charismatic individuals.[185]

In terms of the context of religious broadcasting, the book throughout (and specifically in Chapter 4) will attempt to demonstrate, that there were "charismatic personalities", "celebrities" and "stars" that were in fact the principal actors in a social movement of monumental importance in the 20th Century in America[186] and of real significance in the broadcasting panorama of the UK as well.

5. Religious Broadcasting

As already noted, the subsequent chapters of the study will attempt to chronicle in detail the birth and development of religious broadcasting and how its impact was largely driven by entrepreneurial charismatic personalities both in the USA and the UK. But in terms of literature, as some scholars have pointed out, "religious broadcasting as a whole has been a relatively neglected area of study within social science".[187] However, that is not to say there have not been some important contributions in this area and therefore this is an appropriate place to highlight some of those studies, as well as the leading lights in this field and also identify the particular input they have made to our knowledge and understanding of religious broadcasting.

In terms of America, there a number of bodies of relevant material, all of which tend to focus on different elements of the religious broadcasting story.

Firstly there are those which have undertaken a more panoramic reflection of religious broadcasting in the 20th Century (Dubourdieu 1933; Hutchinson 1941; Knock 1982; Fishwick and Brown 1987; Fore 1987; Ferre 1990; Suman 1997). *Prime Time Religion* (Melton, Lucas and Stone 1997) for example is a compendium with an encyclopaedic treatment of the topic and helps to track the continuing cultural and political effects that faith based belief systems had on the American social fabric. It covers every aspect of religious broadcasting from its inception in 1921 to the end of the 20th Century, with over 430 entries chosen for their historical importance, national or international impact and longevity in the field of religious broadcasting. The book also covers all the religious groups that have turned to radio and television to promote their messages. A similar volume *Religious Radio & Television in the United States 1921-1991* (Erickson 1992) is characterised by a collection of 400 profiles of persons, programmes and organisations in the first 70 years of religious broadcasting from the *Lutheran Hour* and *Hour of Decision* to Jim Bakker and the Christian Broadcasting Network (CBN) and many other ministries. A different approach is adopted by *Air of Salvation* (Ward 1994). Ward starts from the earliest beginnings of radio and television and breaks down the story of Christian broadcasting into date-related segments. Apart from looking at fascinating stories, like how the first religious broadcast was concocted by Westinghouse to sell radios and how the first radio ministry began with a publicity stunt from the Mayor of Chicago. Ward highlights the extraordinary people involved in religious broadcasting and tries to answer questions like why NBC, CBS and ABC tried to ban gospel broadcasts and why did it take the FCC to get television started? The book is a solid historical record from the context of the evangelical community, but perhaps underplays the broadcasting work of the Federal Council of Churches of Christ and its affiliates. The final contribution in this section is *Airwaves to the Soul: The Influence and Growth of Religious Broadcasting in America* (Hill 1987). This is a serious scholarly text which spans 60 years of radio history and 22 years of television history. Like others it chronicles some of key pioneers of Christian broadcasting, but its unique contribution is that it examines some of the empirical data on religious broadcasting featuring helpful surveys, analysis of programmes, audience research and how the developing satellite technology was turning religious radio and television into a business of industrial proportions. This volume is well matched too by Hill's second publication (co-authored with Lenwood Davis) *Religious Broadcasting 1920-1983: A Selected Annotated Bibliography* (1984). This helps to identify published material about the ever expanding field of religious radio and television, providing also a variety of coverage from personality profiles to autobiographies of leading religious broadcasters.

The next segment illustrates literature which tries to place the development of religious broadcasting clearly within the cultural context of America and especially within the religious landscape of America (Haldane 1978; Hoover 1982; Tyson 1990; Wanner 2016). *Redeeming the Dial* (Hangen 2004) as an example focusses on the growth of radio from the 1920s to the 1950s but probes its audience and the covert/overt conflicts with commercial and theological forces. Hangen portrays a picture not of religious declension but of revival religion and secular entertainment yoked in dynamic and cultural tension. While Hangen's narrative follows a historical arc, she valuably explores the relevance of mass communication and audience reception theories to her work. Its main shortcoming is that the commentary was not extended into the 1960s, when radio still had a significant role, but when the age of television became increasingly more important. Fortner takes a similar perspective in *Radio, Morality & Culture 1919-1945* (2005) in ignoring the economic or biographical or legislative history of broadcasting's first decade, rather he focusses on a comprehensive profile of the development of radio as a bi-product of its birthplace and modern market capitalism, something he reflects through an examination of the USA, Canada and Britain. In Britain the BBC reflecting largely the values of the established church leadership, the USA embracing public interest rather than a public service model and religious broadcasting in Canada being a hybrid of both. The enriching volume does much to help the understanding of the cultural context of religious broadcasting, but probably attempts too much with its geographical spread. By contrast Bob Lochte's more journalistic approach in *Christian Radio: The Growth of a Mainstream Broadcasting Force* (2006) looks at a narrower history of US fundamentalism and evangelical broadcasting, though both taken together illuminate well the background of the achievements and disappointments of church involvement in radio.

The third body of literature in respect of the United States surrounds the evolution of what was to be termed the "electric church" and the growth of the televangelist phenomenon (Benson 1973; Flake 1982; Oberdorfer 1982; Elvy 1986; Frankl 1987; Rosen 1988; Jackson 1991; Peck 1993). As indicated, although there have been many authors commenting on this important component of American religion, there are some particular contributors that are significant, including Ben Armstrong the man who coined the expression the "electric church" and wrote the book *The Electric Church* (1979) – a historical survey of religious radio and television from single programmes to entire stations and networks. Armstrong was the Executive Director of the National Association of Religious Broadcasters and the study focusses on the successes of many evangelical and fundamentalist broadcasters and their ministries, but is largely uncritical and has an unrelenting optimism on the presence and future of broadcast religion. However its appendices are helpful in outlining the Code of Ethics for the National Religious Broadcasters and Principles and Guidelines for Fund Raising, which was destined to become a big issue in this genre of broadcasting. A more scholarly and much quoted work is *Mass Media Religion: The Social Sources of the Electronic Church* (Hoover 1988). It is neither contemptuous of the phenomenon, nor signed up to the anti-evangelical scare language so often encountered by non-apologists of the electric church. Hoover in a sensitive multi-method and interdisciplinary way examines the quantitative findings on who is watching religious television related to the 1983 Gallup Poll and the qualitative data from interviews about audience motivation which had been much lacking. Through a focus on Pat Robertson's Christian Broadcasting Network (CBN) he illustrates how televangelism is a multi-media phenomenon, highlighting the institution of the para-church as the newest and probably the most significant contribution of the work. These interdenominational and ecumenical religious societies of voluntary Christian action probably represented the greatest competition to the established denominations in America. Hoover argues convincingly that the electronic church is not so much a threat to the established churches, more a symbol of what is wrong with them. The fact that the electronic church provides comfort for adherents and focuses religious activity outside of the denominational structures seems to portend a diminished role for the established churches in the future. Another very significant commentary is *American Evangelicals and the Mass Media* (Schultze 1990). Here Schultze as editor co-ordinates a diverse, knowledgeable group of evangelical scholars and journalists to examine the history, as well as the philosophical and theological underpinnings of the complex love-hate relationship between the mass media and evangelical Christians. Their essays discuss book and magazine publishing, popular music, and broadcasting. A common theme is that evangelicals, dazzled by media possibilities, often confuse means with ends, failing to utilize the media effectively in their mission to evangelize the whole world. This is matched well with his own *Televangelism and American Culture: The Business of Popular Religion* (1991). Here he shows how the message of most televangelism has more in common with American culture than it does with the Bible, the preachers becoming media gurus with vast power and popularity and wealth. Schultze's survey unearths three main dynamics. Firstly that most televangelists emphasize the dramatic and downplay the ordinary, often talking about healing, miracles and speaking in tongues. Secondly that televangelism is personality-driven. Personalities are manufactured leading to books, conferences and seminars and other promotional events. Thirdly the element of televangelism being entertainment orientated, copying much of the secular media. Schultze also goes on to explode the myth that televangelists are reaching the masses, showing that they often exaggerate everything from their audience figures to the number of their converts. The book however is more than a critique of religious broadcasting; it is a perceptive analysis of how television affects the gospel and its messengers. A final contribution is *Pray TV: Televangelism in America* (Bruce 1990). The author writes as a British sociologist, with a slightly different slant. *Pray TV* covers most of the same territory as several other books about religious broadcasting. They all locate religious broadcasting in American religious history, profile the leading televangelists, discuss the beliefs of the broadcasters, describe the organization of their broadcast empires, offers viewers profiles, disclose audiences sizes and connects the broadcasters' ventures into conservative politics.

Whilst acknowledging the effect of TV evangelism in revitalizing and strengthening the American conservative subculture, Bruce sees televangelism responding to and ultimately furthering secularizing tendencies. In contrast to those who have viewed televangelism as an important element in a burgeoning social movement, Bruce sees its influence as limited and modest and is highly critical of a world he does not respect.

A further portion of literature relates to the issues of audiences for religious broadcasting. (Dennis 1962; Robinson 1965; Solt 1971; Buddenbaum 1979; Martin 1981; Clark and Virts 1985; Abelman 1987). This is not just about data, but about demographics and characteristics that became important to broadcasters in matching their presentations and linking with their core audiences. Johnstone in his tenure as Director of Research for the Lutheran Council, using a national survey constructed a profile of the typical radio programme listener reported in *Who Listens to Religious Radio Broadcasts* (1972), discovering that nearly half of the United States adult population listen to a religious radio programme at least occasionally. His research looked at factors like denominational affiliation, age, sex, educational level, geographic region, degree of religious commitment and interest and frequency of attendance at religious services. It was natural also that he used the programme *The Lutheran Hour* as a test-bed within the research, which was a serious attempt at getting some empirical data about religious broadcasting. Another attempt in this arena was *The Television-Radio Audience and Religion* (Parker, Barry and Smythe 1955) a highly objective research study using New Haven Connecticut as a laboratory to determine, in terms of religious broadcasting, what classes of people watch or hear and what programmes and with what effect. There is a description of the social and cultural history of the city and a breakdown of the population according to religious affiliation. Considerable attention is paid to the various religious programmes and the study is buttressed by in-depth interviews with selected individuals. The book reveals the effects on family life, the relative insignificant role of the religious programmes and the failure of religious broadcasters to make their programmes sufficiently broad in appeal. Obviously a city study is only a microcosm, but it does serve as an interesting model. Looking at a bigger picture *Prime*

Time Preachers: The Rising Power of Televangelism (Hadden and Swann 1981), despite its rather thumbnail approach in reviewing the development of religious broadcasting, serves as a key contribution by its authors in looking at hard audience data, especially focussing on the 1980 Arbitron survey on the audience sizes of the TV Preachers, along with some demographic descriptions showing the audiences to be largely southern, female and old. The significant conclusion however is that the data seems to show that audiences for religious broadcasters are much less than the preachers often claim. However, in spite of the use of the Arbitron data, they still only present rather vague information about viewers, their perception of programmes and their participation patterns in local churches. What Hadden and Swann did though significantly, apart from looking at the methods, theology and influence of religious broadcasters on the American religious scene, was to raise the challenge that more research in this arena was clearly needed to understand this phenomenon. *Religious Television: The American Experience* (Horsfield 1984) goes a long way to take up that mantle especially in the realms of television. In this thorough study of religious television in America, Horsfield asserts that the Gospel has been diluted and distorted by being subservient to the medium, in essence compromising basic religious principles in order to co-exist within the competitive environment of commercial television. He goes on with a comprehensive overview of empirical and available research in order to answer the following questions (a) Has there been a growth in air time devoted to religious broadcasting and how has the mix changed between sustaining and syndicated programming? (b) How large is the current audience for such programming and has this audience grown over time? Is religious television evangelical in the sense of attracting new converts? (c) What are the demographic and religious profiles of the viewers of religious programming? (d) What impact does religious programming have on people's attitudes toward religion and their attendance and contributions to the local church? (e) How important is religious television's influence in the political arena, especially in presidential elections? Horsfield concludes that it is not enough for television to provide a hospitable context for the message of evangelical fundamentalists; television has also had a major impact on the way the message of religious broadcasters has been formulated. The book has its limitations because the research is not vast, but it still remains a significant and standard text on this topic. A final study is the contribution by Hoover, a prolific writer on religious broadcasting, *The Religious Television Audience: A Matter of Significance or Size?* (1987). Hoover seeks to examine the misleading claims about the numbers of people who view religious television; much he claims is down to the unreliability of audience research techniques. Equally social, cultural, institutional and theological factors also combine to misunderstand viewing behaviour. The author concludes religious television viewing was socially desirable for most Americans, but was an infrequent behaviour which was engaged in for short periods of time and the aggregate for religious television was quite small by conventional standards.

It would be wrong to conclude that all religious broadcasting is identical, even religious broadcasting in America. Ellens in *Models of Religious Broadcasting* (1974) makes an important contribution to this in describing what can be called different "models" of broadcasting. He outlines a "pulpit" model with a sermon as the focal point, an "instructional" model which makes extensive use of documentaries, lectures and dramas, the "leaven" model with religious slots inserted into regular commercial programming and finally what he calls the "mighty acts of God" model which is the one that many evangelists adopted on television, characterised by dramatic staging, careful timings and altar calls. It is this last category that introduces the last canon of literature which focusses on important religious broadcasting personalities in terms of biographies, autobiographies, articles or commentaries. So just some of the key people featured would be Dr.Billy Graham (Temple 1954; Pollock 1985; Graham 1997; Wyland 2013; Finstuen 2017; Wacker and Wills 2017; Martin 2018); Aimee Semple McPherson (Austin 1980; Blumhofer 1993; McPherson 1996; D'Antonio 1998; Sutton 2007; Maddux 2012; Barfoot 2014); Pat Robertson (Robertson 1972; Donavan 1988; Green 1993; Boston 1996; Marley 2007; Harrell Jr 2010); Father Charles Coughlin (Ward 1933; Magil 1939; Marcus 1973; Brinkley 1983; Sayer 1983; Athans 1987; Warren 1996; Carpenter 1998; Jeanstone 2012); Oral Roberts (Roberts 1972; McIntire 1980; Harrell 1985; Schultze 1987; Arnett 2009); Mother Angelica (Erickson 1992; Arroyo 2005; Vitello 2016); Jerry Falwell

(D'Souza 1984; Falwell 1997; Harding 2000; Winters 2001; Gilgoff 2007; Fineman 2007; Applebone 2007; Falwell 2008; Williams 2010) and finally Jim Bakker (Bourngault 1985; Shepard 1989; Bakker 1996; Messner 1996; Albert 1998; Weinberg 2012; Wigger 2017).

As noted, literature on religious broadcasting is quite restricted compared with other media categories. If that is true in the American setting it is even truer in the UK. That being accepted there are some significant general sources which are worth highlighting. The most significant of these is *The Churches and the British Broadcasting Corporation 1922-1956* (Wolfe 1984). This pivotal book provides an authoritative study of religion and public broadcasting during one of its most important periods. The thirty-five years covered in the volume run from the beginning of broadcasting to the early days of commercial broadcasting. It features the first discussions of the possibilities and limits of religious broadcasting, the eventual response of the Church of England and the ongoing disputes as to what representation other churches should have in broadcasting. It details too the attempts to provide religious educational programmes, the problems over broadcasting worship, especially communion and the controversies over religious dramas like Dorothy L. Sayers' *The Man Born to Be King* (1941). In addition Wolfe draws attention to key personalities who made significant contributions to religious broadcasting including John Reith, the BBC's first Director General; early on-air preachers like Dick Sheppard and W.H. Elliott and Directors of Religious Broadcasting like James Welch. The book is a serious attempt to chronicle the history of religious broadcasting using a forbidding mass of evidence available inside and outside the BBC Archives in the same vein as Asa Briggs undertook (who wrote the Foreword to this book) with the more generic UK broadcasting history. A second volume to this publication was indicated but it never transpired. Two other general historical approaches prove useful; Cooper's *Religious Broadcasting in Britain 1922-1939* (1962) for example is also an excellent treatment of the religious broadcasting story in pre-war Britain. She demonstrates how in this period religious broadcasting is operating under the monopoly of the BBC, though many of its traits being picked up in other generations. Cooper is at pains early on to emphasize the importance of Lord Reith in this era and how his views are reflected in the way religious broadcasting developed in terms of the engagement with churches, with committees and with content. She demonstrates how in those early years religious broadcasting engaged substantially with national events, like Coronations and how the different programmes emerged and attempted in every way to reflect mainstream/orthodox Christianity. Cooper also highlights the times of controversy in the way that different church groups responded to the religious output, whether broadcasting would affect church attendance and how the Sunday broadcasting policy was dealt with. Despite the growing respect for what was called "BBC religion", she does point out its limitations for expressing all church worship especially the Communion Service through radio. The key point Cooper illuminates in the study is that at a time of waning Church attendance pre-war, religious broadcasting provided a faith dimension to people's lives that had been lost by many. The second work is similar, but the emphasis is less historical and more empirical, *The Production of Religious Broadcasting: The Case of the BBC* (Noonan 2009) examines the way in which media professionals negotiate the occupational challenges related to television and radio production. It has used the subject of religion and its treatment within the BBC as a microcosm to unpack some of the dilemmas of contemporary broadcasting. In recent years religious programming evolved in both form and content, leading to what some observers claimed was a 'renaissance' in religious broadcasting. However, any claims of a renaissance have to be balanced against the complex institutional and commercial constraints that challenged its long-term viability. Noonan documents attempts by producers to overcome the ghettoization of religious broadcasting of the past, with the opening of religious issues to a wider listener/viewer audience. It uses a wide-reaching engagement of resources both historical and observational to unravel what could be seen as the rather private world of religious broadcasting at the BBC.

The second category of UK literature has a lower historical and a clearer philosophical as well sociological approach and moves more into the direction of television and the developments of a commercial environment. *God in a Box* (Morris 1984) reflects a television documentary presented by Colin Morris, who was formerly a Methodist missionary in Africa and became the Head of Religious Broadcasting at the BBC. He uses the arena of television as the frame in which we view the dimensions of our society and how this media became so influential and all-pervasive. The book falls into three parts, the first is a guided tour of the curious world of television and the culture it creates, the second deals with the challenges presented by religious television and finally Morris gives his own thoughts about Christian mission in a television age. He writes almost as a "mole" being an insider of both television development and the Church and sometimes one gets the impression he is not comfortable with either, as his companion volume *Wrestling with an Angel* (1990) indicates. However his scepticism is dwarfed by comparison with the journalist and humourist Malcolm Muggeridge, who was the most uncompromising evangelical opponent of doing anything righteous on television. His *Christ and the Media* (1977) suggested that the nature of television violates the intensely personal and spiritual nature of genuine revelation and therefore a flawed platform for the presentation of faith. However a more optimistic picture is portrayed by Peter Elvy, who was specialist in religious broadcasting commissioned by the Jerusalem Trust to conduct a major study into European Religious Broadcasting in what would be a deregulated future. The book *The Future of Christian Broadcasting in Europe* (1990) is based on more than one hundred interviews and was presented to a special conference in 1991 after the 1990 Broadcasting Act was passed. Elvy reflects an understanding of communication theory and its developments and highlights how technology was changing, frontiers were coming down and regulations were being liberalised. All of which would affect the Church engaging in media. His follow-up publication *Opportunities and Limitations in Religious Broadcasting* (1991) continues this general discussion with contributions from 25 distinguished practitioners covering a range of subjects such as the opening up of Eastern Europe, evangelical broadcasting, the potential of satellite, cable and video, as well as the status of public service broadcasting. Although written in the early 1990s it resonates some very important issues still relevant today. The final item in this genre takes a very different approach to the previous ones quoted, *Hidden Agendas: The Politics of Religious Broadcasting in Britain 1987-1991* (Quicke and Quicke 1992) not only deals with the religious, social and regulatory prelude to the 1990 Broadcasting Bill in Britain, it argues there was a hidden agenda on the part of regulators like the IBA (later to become the ITC) to see religious broadcasting more strictly controlled after 1990 than in the past. This motivated by a desire to protect the UK from the sort of abuses of the American televangelists. The author's micro-examination of this period looks at the churches, regulators and government involvement in religious broadcasting and especially the struggle by evangelical Christians to gain official access to air-time on radio and television, allowing all shades of Christian opinion to get a fair hearing without the excesses of the American model. The book excels in featuring the complexities faced by religious broadcasters in relation to bureaucratic institutions and their attempt to reflect faith as being an integral part of all societies and therefore meriting a significant platform. This is also complimented well by an incisive paper by Leigh (1992) which looks at the regulation of religious broadcasting especially related to the 1990 Broadcasting Act and concludes that religious broadcasting still appears closely tied to a public service broadcasting model, in a regulatory and economic climate in which most other broadcasting areas have moved on.

A further small but important sector of literature relates to audience research applied to religious broadcasting. In terms of the BBC, R.J.E. Silvey built up the Listener Research Department (later Audience Research) and laid the foundations for gathering and analysing data. A publication, *Religion of the Air: Audiences for Religious Broadcasting* (1956) was produced from his St. Paul's Lecture on the subject, indicating that more church goers listen to religious broadcasters than non-church goers. Silvey's approach was surveying religious broadcasting as part of the overall programming output of the BBC. But in terms of commercial radio and television there seemed to be a higher level of investigation regarding the audiences for religious broadcasting. *Seeing is Believing: Religion and Television in the 1990s* (Gunter and Viney 1994), was really a follow-up to the previous *Godwatching* Report (1988) produced by the IBA. *Seeing is Believing* was a Television Research Publication from the ITC and examined the opinions of majority and minority religious groups in the UK about religious television. The first part comprised a qualitative research in which a series of focus group discussions were run with

Christians, atheists, agnostics and religious broadcasting professionals. The second part was a national survey with a representative sample of minority groups and groups of satellite and cable viewers. The research revealed the endorsement of viewers of television's role in covering a wide range of religious beliefs and promoting understanding, whilst rejecting the misuse of television to raise money for churches or to proselytize for new members. Such research was an important contribution to understanding the status of religious broadcasting and an indication for policy.

The final body of literature relates to the individual personalities from the UK who made significant contributions to religious broadcasting, the first of these being Lord Reith (Allingham 1938; Boyle 1972; Leishman 2008). Specifically, *The Expense of Glory: A Life of John Reith* (McIntyre 1993) is probably now accepted as the definitive biography on Lord Reith and the early days of the BBC. McIntyre highlights the complexities of Reith in terms of his various personal relationships, including with his younger male friend Charlie, but also with his volatile career endeavours, both within and beyond the BBC years. The author illustrates the tidal wave of words that Reith and his contemporaries poured out, but uniquely he has an excellent grasp of Reith's strong Calvinistic Christian convictions that influenced his decision making and his actions. Although as an employee of the BBC McIntyre might be too close to it to write a history with any sense of detachment, making it rather quirky and unbalanced in places, it does remain a must-read classic of one of the greatest public figures of the 20th Century. In tandem with books about Reith, it is important to acknowledge the books penned by Reith himself. *Into the Wind* (1949) is essentially a composite of Reith's own diaries. A diary that he accumulated of four million words since he began it in 1910. In essence it is Reith's memoirs and therefore an authentic record of Reith's personal relationships, his career, with a natural focus on his BBC years and the numerous political interactions in which he was involved. From the book, one senses the pains as well as his enthusiasms of this complex man, often hard on himself, troubled and confused, reaching for the sky but sometimes plummeting the depths. A workaholic but sometimes paralysed into inactivity. It shows a man of vision who probably died feeling he had never been given a big enough job to do. History, especially media history, clearly disagrees. Unlike *Into the Wind*, Reith's first book, *Broadcast Over Britain* (1924) was his personal review of the broadcasting landscape. He starts by highlighting the growing application of radio and its wide ranging influence beyond personal entertainment. In terms of the BBC, he emphasizes the need for good governance of the institution, but supports broadcasters having creative imagination on air. Whatever the criticisms, Reith believed the BBC monopoly was vindicated both from a technical point of view and for quality value. As he saw radio not to be a passing craze, it needed a stricter control than American broadcasting which had started earlier. Reith then begins chapter by chapter to talk about the unifying influence of music, the importance of variety, the way that broadcasting can improve the standard of English, engaging children through dedicated programming and popularising issues of religion without any association to a particular creed or denomination. His conclusion is that broadcasting should not be seen as an end in itself but rather carries multiple benefits for society in general, as well as to the individual in their home.

Allied to Reith are two London churchman he brought into broadcasting, who became UK household names, H.R.L.Sheppard, more commonly known as Dick Sheppard, (Northcott 1937; Friends 1938; Roberts 1942) the Vicar of St. Martin-in-the-Fields and W.H. Elliott, Vicar of St Michael's Chester Square (Elliott 1951; Beeson 2006). The biography *Dick Sheppard* (Scott 1977) points out that when radio came, no voice was better known. His broadcasting attracted multitudes, as did his church which became one of the most famous centres for social work in London, with people queuing to come inside and sit on the chancel steps to hear him preach. Scott manages to convey well the life and ministry of this complex man – a man of passion and frustration who often suffered bouts of debilitating illness. His ardent pacifism and his establishment of the Peace Pledge Union brought him more antagonists than allies, but in the heart of the nation he remained a burning shining light. Equally Elliott was a key player in religious broadcasting and was dubbed the "radio chaplain". His autobiography *Undiscovered Ends* (1951) is as one would imagine, his story-telling of his many scenes of life, from childhood and education through to his Christian ministry at St. Paul's and St. Michael's. The latter experience he describes unusually as just hell, because of the internal struggles he had inherited and experienced. However the chapter he calls "London Calling" focusses more on the opportunities that arose from the call he received in 1931 from Lord Reith, which was to eventually establish him as a hugely important religious broadcaster with a regular midweek programme. Despite normal attendances at St Michael's of 2000 people and a significant listenership to Elliott's broadcasts, very little has been written about him, but recently *The Canons* (Beeson 2006) which features various past personalities of St. Paul's Cathedral, includes a significant chapter on Elliott which deals with his career, but especially with a crucial description of his successful days with the BBC.

Apart from these two charismatic and influential broadcasters it is important not to forget the context in which they and the church operated in relation to the BBC regarding religious broadcasting. This brings into focus the work of the Central Religious Advisory Committee (CRAC) and those that led it. Important in this regard was *Cyril Forster Garbett* (Smyth 1959). The biography admirably conceived and sensitively written enables the reader to survey a whole period of church and national history through the lens of the life's work of one of the most compelling churchmen of his era. Garbett endeavoured in every way he knew to strengthen the position of the Church of England in the nation's life; we read of his concern for social welfare, his influence in the formative years of religious broadcasting, his efforts to help the press to give a fair account of what churchmen were thinking and doing. Although not a broadcaster himself, undoubtedly his role in chairing CRAC from 1923 to 1945, set a pathway for the church's relationship with broadcasting and became a momentous contribution, by someone Smyth describes as its champion and guide.

Finally it is important to register literature related to the UK's most popular religious programmes. *Highway* (1985) by Harry Secombe is the story of the highly successful programme he presented on television for many years. He travelled up and down the British Isles visiting towns and cities. The book contains the highlights of those visits and he weaves together many of his memories of those places and tells his readers about what makes each place special, whether it be its historic past or their famous sons and daughters, or the many "ordinary" people making extraordinary contributions to their communities. *Songs of Praise* the mainstay of the BBC's religious broadcasting output (BBC 1984; Barr 2001) has serious longevity. *Celebrating Songs of Praise: 50 Years* (Barnes 2011) is an admirable attempt to reflect this significant BBC production. Barnes points out the programme evolved over the years and whilst the people, body and packaging had changed, the heart of the programme remained rooted in a musical celebration of the Christian faith. Congregational singing is shown as the bedrock of the show and the book traces the programme through the decades with the different and well-known presenters and many international artists, politicians, entertainers, sports personalities and well known churchmen that were featured. The book was intended as a tribute to the past and present staff who had featured in this popular BBC series. Lastly we come to the Yorkshire Television production for ITV, *Stars on Sunday* presented by Jess Yates. Given the huge viewer ratings for this programme it is surprising so little was written about this programme except in newsprint. The main reflection comes from one of its producers Peter Max-Wilson (1976). His book was really dedicated to the many artists who took part in the programme and the millions of viewers who helped maintain *Stars on Sunday*, in its era, as Britain's most popular religious programme. Max-Wilson gives a colourful account of the seasons of the programme and the interactions with the people who featured on screen, who collectively were really the "Who's Who" of singers, actors, film stars, politicians and churchmen of the day, with a special feature by Dr. Donald Coggan the Archbishop of Canterbury. The author really produced a travelogue through *Stars on Sunday*, but what it failed to do was to address many of the controversial issues that surrounded the programme, that was left to Fleet Street and the Independent Broadcasting Authority (IBA).

As a footnote it is important to state that there is a significant amount of material related to religious broadcasting in articles in journals, magazines, newspapers and within a wide range of archive resource centres, which have been included and referred to in the main body of the text.

CHAPTER 1 MAPPING THE TERRITORY

NOTES

1. in Schultze, Q. J., *American Evangelicals and the Mass Media* (Grand Rapids: Academic Books, 1990), p.70.

2. Falconer, R., *Message, Media & Mission: The Baird Lectures* (Edinburgh: St Andrews Press, 1977), p.2.

3. Garner, K., On Defining the Field. *The Radio Journal: International Studies in Broadcast and Audio Media*, 1 (1), 2003:7.

4. Hill, D. G. H. and Davis, L., Religious *Broadcasting: A Selected Annotated Bibliography*. (New York: Garland Publishers, 1984), p.xii

5. Newton, I., *Letter to Robert Hooke* (1676), www.physicsforums.com.

6. Lowery, S. and De Fleur, M.L., *Milestones in Mass Communication Research* (New York: Longman, 1983), p.4.

7. Ibid., p.11.

8. Parker, E. C., Barry, D. W. and Smythe, D.W., *The Television/Radio Audience and Religion* (New York: Harper Brothers Publishers, 1955), p.159.

9. Smith, J., Understanding the Media: A Sociology of Mass Communications (New York: Hampton Press, 1995), p.xii.

10. Ward, K., *Mass Communications in the Modern World* (London: Macmillan, 1989), p.9.

11. Ibid., p. 23-24.

12. Hoover, S. M., Media. *In*: Ebaugh H.R., *Handbook of Religion and Social Institutions* (London: Springer, 2006), p.305.

13. Berelson, B., The Present State of Communication Research. *Public Opinion Quarterly*, 22 (2) 1959: 178.

14. Schramm, W., *Mass Communications*. 2nd edition (Illinois: University of Illinois, 1975), 115.

15. Ibid., p.465.

16. Tayer, L., Mass Media and Mass Communication: Notes Towards a Theory. *In*: Budd, R. W. and Rubens, B. D., *Beyond Media: New Approaches to Mass Communication* (New Brunswick: Transaction Books, 1988), p.63.

17. Tavokin, E. P., Mass Communication in the Modern World. *Herald of the Russian Academy of Sciences*, 81 (6) 2011: 613.

18. Seymour-Ure, C., *The British Press and Broadcasting since 1945* (Oxford: Blackwell, 1996), p.6.

19. McQuail, D., *Media Performance*. (London: Sage, 1992), p.30.

20. McQuail, D., *McQuail's Mass Communication Theory*. 6th edition (London: Sage Publications Ltd, 2010), p.24.

21. Briggs, A. and Burke, P., *A Social History of the Media: From Gutenberg to the Internet*. 3rd edition (Cambridge: Polity Press, 2009), p.1.

22. Curran, J., Communications, Power and Social Order. *In*: Gurevitch, M., *Culture, Society and Media* (London: Methuen, 1982), p.202-203.

23. Geertz, C., The *Interpretation of Culture* (New York: Basic Books, 1973), p.10.

24. Lorimer, R., *Mass Communications: A Comparative Introduction* (Manchester: Manchester University, 1994), p.39.

25. Seymour-Ure (1996), p.271

26. McLuhan, M., *The Gutenberg Galaxy: The Making of Typographic Man* (Toronto: University of Toronto Press, 1962), p.36.

27. Klapper, J. T., *The Effects of Mass Communication* (New York: The Free Press, 1966), p.8.

28. Ibid., p.60.

29. Ibid., p.129.

30. Ellens, J. H., *Models of Religious Broadcasting* (Grand Rapids: W. B. Eerdmans, 1974), p.13.

31. Lowery and De Fleur (1983), p.15.

CHAPTER 1 MAPPING THE TERRITORY

32. Drinker, F. E. and Lewis, J. J., Radio: *Miracle of the 20th Century* (Philadelphia: National Publishing Company, 1922), p.3-4.

33. Cantril, A.H. and Allport G. W., *The Psychology of Radio* (New York: Peter Smith, 1941), p.19.

34. in Pugh, P., *Headline Britons* (London: Icon Books,2017), p.141.

35. Beachcroft, T. O., *British Broadcasting* (London: Longman Green & Co. 1948), p.24.

36. Eckersley, P. P., *The Power behind the Microphone* (London: Jonathan Cape, 1941), p.243. See also Appendix 5

37. Beachcroft,T.O. (1948), p.15.

38. Reith, J. C. W., *Broadcast over Britain* (London: Hodder and Stoughton, 1924), p.23.

39. Eckersley, P.P. (1941), p.55.

40. Smith, A., *British Broadcasting*. (Newton Abbott: David & Charles Ltd. 1974), p.63.

41. Sterling, C. H. and Kittross, J. M., *Stay Tuned: A Concise history of American Broadcasting*. 3rd edition (New Jersey: Edward Arnold,2002), p.55.

42. Matheson, H., *Broadcasting* London: Thorton Butterworth Ltd. 1933), p.28.

43. Lowery and De Fleur (1983), p.16.

44. Siepmann, C. A., *Radio, Television and Society* (New York: Oxford University Press, 1950), p.3.

45. Coyer, K., *Its Not Just Radio: Models of Community Broadcasting in Britain and the United States*. (PhD). Goldsmith's College, London (2009), p.143.

46. Paulu, B., *Television and Radio in the United Kingdom* (London: MacMillan, 1981), p.395

47. Briggs, A., *The History of Broadcasting in the United Kingdom. Vol. 1: The Birth of Broadcasting* (London: Oxford University Press, 1961), p.59.

48. Scannell, P. and Cardiff, D., *A Social History of Broadcasting Vol.1. 1922-1939* (Oxford: Basil Blackwell, 1991), p.5.

49. Ibid., p.17.

50. Lacey, D. M., *Freedom and Communication 1914-2001* (Urbana: University of Illinois, 1961), p.78-79.

51. Mosco, V., *Broadcasting in the United States* (New Jersey: Ablex Publications, 1978), p.10.

52. Barnouw, E., *The Golden Web: A History of Broadcasting in the United States*. Vol.2: *1933-1953* (New York: Oxford University Press, 1968), p.3.

53. Paley, W. S., Broadcasting Both Sides of the Atlantic. *The Listener*. 24th June, (1931), p.1052.

54. Chase Jr. F., *Sound and Fury: An Informal History of Broadcasting* (New York: Harper Brothers, 1942), p.19.

55. Kamms, A. and Baird,M., *John Logie Baird – A Life* (Edinburgh: National Museum of Scotland Publishing,2002), p.4.

56. Pusateri, C.J. *A History of American Business* (Illinois. Harlan Davidson, 1988), p.284.

57. Haley,W., The Church and Television. *Coventry Evening Telegraph*. 6th November, (1952), p.9.

58. Carter, M. D., *An Introduction to Mass Communications: Problems in Press and Broadcasting* (London: McMillan, 1971), p.76.

59. Hilmes, M., *Network Nations: A Transnational History of British and American Broadcasting* (New York: Routledge, 2012), p.3.

60. Ibid., p.10.

61. Tunstall, J., *The Media in Britain*. (London: Constable, 1983), p.5.

62. Camporesi, V., *Mass Culture and National Traditions: The BBC and American Broadcasting 1922-1954.* (Fucecchio: European Press Academic Publishing, 2000), p.636-637.

63. Williams, W.E., Seven Decisive Years for Sound and Vision. *The Times*. 28th August (1957), p.1

64. Street, S., *Historical Dictionary of British Radio* (Plymouth: Rowman & Littlefield, 2015), p.271.

65. Stoller, T., *Sounds of Your Life: The History of Independent Radio in the UK*. (New Barnet: John Libbey Publishing Ltd. 2010), p.1.

66. Madge, T.S. and Pusateri, C. J., Great Britain and USA. *In*: Rosen, P.T., *International Handbook of Broadcasting Systems* (New York: Greenwood Press, 1988), p.108.

67. Engleman, R., *Public Radio and Television in America* (London: Sage, 1996), p.1.

68. Hendy, D., *Radio in a Global Age* (Cambridge: Polity Press, 2000), p.18.

69. Smith, J., Understanding the Media: A Sociology of Mass Communications (New York: Hampton Press, 1995), p.245.

70. Seaton, J., *'Pinkoes and Traitors': the BBC and the Nation, 1974-1987*. Revised edition (London: Profile, 2015), p.327.

71. McDonnell, J., *Public Service Broadcasting*. (London: Routledge, 1991), p.9.

72. Coppens,T., Downey, J. and Pusateri, C.J., Great Britain and USA. *In*: Haenens, L. and Saeys, F., Western *Broadcasting at the Dawn of the 21st Century* (Berlin: Meuton de Gruyter, 2001), p.334.

73. Fortner, R. S. (2005), p.68.

74. Paulu, B. (1981) p.396.

75. Durkheim, E., *The Elementary Forms of Religious Life* (Trans. Cosman, C., 2001). (Oxford: Oxford University Press, 1912), p.46.

76. O'Day, R., What is Religious History? *History Today*, 35, (1985) 48.

77. Bowker, J., *Religious Beliefs and Practices in Britain Today* (London: BBC, 1983) p.10.

78. Wolfe, J., *God and Great Britain: Religion and National Life in Britain and Ireland 1843-1945* (London: Routledge, 1994), p.13.

79. Currie, R., Gilbert, A. and Horsley, L., Churches *and Churchgoers: Patterns of Church Growth in the British Isles since 1700* (Oxford: Clarendon Press, 1977), p.6.

80. Beal, T., *Religion in America: A Very Short Introduction* (Oxford: Oxford University Press, 2008), p.5.

81. Albanese, C. L., *In:* Brekus, C. A. and Gilpin, W. C., *American Christianities: A History of Dominance and Diversity* (Chapel Hill: University of North Carolina Press,2011), p.25.

82 Hadaway, C. K., and Marler, P. L., How Many Americans Attend Worship Each Week: An Alternative Approach to Measurement. *Journal for the Scientific Study of Religion*, 44 (3) 2005: 307.

83. Beal, T. (2008), p.35.

84. Ibid., p.5.

85. Kay, W. K., Pentecostalism and Religious Broadcasting. *Journal of Beliefs and Values*, 30 (3) 2009: 247.

86. Bruce, S., *Pray TV: Televangelism in America* (London: Routledge, 1990), p.20.

87. Horsfield, P. G., *Religious Television: the American Experience* (New York: Longmans, 1984), p.15.

88. Bedell, K. B., *Yearbook of American and Canadian Churches*. (Nashville: Abingdon Press, 1994), p.40.

89. Jorstad, E., *Popular Religion in America: The Evangelical Voice* (Westport: Greenwood Press, 1993), p.36.

90. Herberg, W., *Protestant, Catholic and Jew* (New Jersey: Doubleday, 1955), p.32

91. Ibid., p.20.

92. Rifkin in Fishwick, M. and Brown, R. B., *The God Pumpers: Religion in the Electronic Age* (Ohio: Bowling Green Press, 1987), p.174.

93. Woodhead, L. and Catto, R., *Religion and Change in Modern Britain* (London: Routledge, 2012), p.34.

94. Lindsay, D. M., Mind the Gap: Religion and the Crucible of Marginality in the United States and Great Britain. *The Sociological Quarterly*, 49 (4) 2008: 653.

95. Berger, P., Davie, G. and Fokas, E., *Religious America, Secular Europe? : A Theme and Variations* (Oxford: Routledge, 2008), p.25.

96. Brown, C. G., *Religion and Society in 20th Century Britain*. (Harlow: Pearson Education, 2006), p.15-18.

97. Bruce, S. and Glendinning,T., When was Secularization? *British Journal of Sociology*, 61 (1) 2010: 107-110.

98. Brown, C. G., *The Death of Christian Britain* (London: Routledge, 2001), p.176.

99. McKibbin, R., *Classes and Cultures* (Oxford: Oxford University Press, 1989), p.276.

100. Field, C., Gradualism or Revolutionary Secularization: A Case Study of Religious Belonging in Inter-War Britain 1918-1939. *Church History and Religious Culture*, 93 (1) 2013: 92-93.

101. Edwards, N., Secularisation and Modernisation. *Journal of Popular Culture*, 8 (2) 1974: 37.

102. Davie, G., *Religion in Britain since 1945: Believing without Belonging* (Oxford: Blackwell, 1994), p.2.

103. Davie, G., *Religion in Britain: A Persistent Paradox*. 2nd edition (London: Blackwell, 2015), p.37.

104. Perman, D., *Change and the Churches: An Anatomy of Religion in Britain* (London: Bodley Head, 1977), p.23.

105. Ibid., p.33.

106. Hunt, S., Transformations in British Religious Broadcasting. *In*: Bailey, M. and Redden, G., *Mediating Faiths and Religion and Socio-Cultural Change in Twenty-First Century* (Burlington: Ashgate, 2011), p.35.

107. Lindsay, D. M. (2008), p. 654.

108. Ibid., p.676.

109. Casanova, J., *Public Religions in the Modern World* (Chicago: Chicago University, 1994), p.29.

110. Schneider, H. W., *Religion in 20th Century America* (Cambridge: Harvard University Press, 1952), p.57-58.

111. Berger, P., Davie, G. and Fokas, E., *Religious America, Secular Europe? : A Theme and Variations*. (Oxford: Routledge, 2016), p.44.

112. Pierard, R.V. and Lewis, D.M., *Global Evangelicalism: Theology, History and Culture in Regional Perspective* (London: IVP, 2014), p.110.

113. Krabbendam, H., Review of a Short History of Global Evangelicalism. *Church History and Religious Culture*, 94 (1) 2014: 165.

114. Pierard, R.V. and Lewis, D.M. (2014), p.124.

115. Marsden, G., Fundamentalism as an American Phenomenon: A Comparison with English Evangelicalism. *Church History* 46 (2) 1977:223-224.

116. Brown, C.G., *The Battle for Christian Britain*. (Cambridge: Cambridge University Press,2019), p.116.

117. Ibid., p.118.

118. Ibid., p.120.

119. Ibid., p.123.

120. Ibid., p.130.

121. Central Religious Advisory Committee, 1946-1947. *Freedom of Religious Discussion*. WAC.File Ref: R6/21/5

122. Brown, C.G., (2019), p.136.

123. Central Religious Advisory Committee, 1946-1947.

124. Bronowski, J., *The Ascent of Man* (London: BBC Books, 1973), p.143-168.

125. Brown, C.G., (2019),p.273.

126. Gabor, G. and De Vriese, H., *Rethinking Secularisation and the Prophecy of a Secular Age*. (Newcastle Upon Tyne: Cambridge Scholars Publishing, 2009), p.ix.

127. Heyck, T. W., The Decline of Christianity in the Twentieth Century Britain. *A Quarterly Journal Concerned with British Studies*, 28 (3) 1996: 440.

128. Gilbert, A. D., *The Making of a Post-Christian Britain*. (London: Longman, 1980), p.2.

129. Svennevig, M., Haldane. I., Spreis, S. and Gunter, B., *Godwatching: Viewers, Religion and Television*. (London: John Libbey, 1988), p.19.

130. Perman, D. (1977), p.72.

131. Ibid., p.215.

132. Gilbert, A.D. (1980), p.xii.

133. Abercrombie, N. and Warde, A., *Contemporary British Society*. 3rd edition. (Cambridge: Polity, 2000), p.321-322.

134. Marsden, L. and Savigny, H., 2009. *Media Religion and Conflict*. (Farnham: Ashgate, 2009), p.7-8.

135. Hoover, S. M., Religion Media and Identity: Theory and Method in Audience Research on Religion and Media. *In*: Mitchell J. and Marriage, S., *Mediating Religion: Conversations in Media Religion and Culture* (London: T & T Clark, 2003), p.11.

136. Knott, K., Poole, E. and Taira, T., *Media Portrayals of Religion and the Secular Sacred: Representation and Chance* (Farnham: Ashgate Publishing, 2013), p.7.

137. Fisher, H. A. L., A Sociological View of History. *The Sociological Review*, 1 (1) 1908: 2.

138. Standford, M., *An Introduction to the Philosophy of History* (Oxford: Blackwell, 1998).

139. Carlyle, T., On *Heroes, Hero Worship and the Heroic in History* (New York: Appleton & Co. 1841), p.83.

140. Cawthon, D.L., Leadership: The Great Man Theory Revisited. *Business Horizons*, 39 (2) 1996:1-4.

141. Bennis, W. and Nanus C. *Leaders. Handbook of Leadership: Theory and Practice*. (New York: The Free Press, 1997), p.207

142. Kirkpatrick, S.A. and Locke, E.A., Leadership Do Traits Matter? *The Executive*, 5 (2) 1991: 48-60.

143. Zaleznik, A., Managers and Leaders: Are They Different? *Harvard Business Review*, 70 (2) 1992:126-135

144. Cawthon, D.L. (1996), p.3.

145. Spector, B.A. Carlyle, Freud and the Great Man Theory More Fully Considered. *Leadership*, 12 (2) 2016: 250-260.

146. Ibid., p.16.

147. Emerson, R. W., *Uses of Great Men in Essays & Lectures 1841* (New York: Literary Classics of the United States, 1983), p.615.

148. Kornberg, J., *History & Personality: The Theories of Wilhelm Dilthey*. (PhD). Harvard University (1964), p.12.

149. Ibid., p.75.

150. Calvert, L. J., *Roland Barthes 1915-1980* (Paris: Flammarion, 1990), p.235-245.

151. MacMillan, M., *History's People: Personalities and the Past*. (London: Profile Books, 2015), p.xi.

152. Caine, B., *Biography and History* (Basingstoke: Palgrave Macmillan, 2010), p.1.

153. Ibid., p.2.

154. Hendy, D., Biography and the Emotions as the Missing 'Narrative' in Media History. *Media History*, 18 (3-4), 2012: 361.

155. Ibid., p.375.

156. Seaton, J., Writing the History of Broadcasting. In: ed.D.Cannadine., *History and the Media* (London: Palgrave Macmillan, 2004), p.155.

157. Adjibolosoo, S. B. S., *The Human Factor in Shaping the Course of History and Development*. (Lanham BD: University of America, 2000), p.9-10.

158. Kaam, V., *Religion and Personality* (New York: Mage Books, 1968), p.59.

159. Conger, J. A., Kanungo, R.N., Menon, S.T. and Mathur, P., Measuring Charisma: Dimensionality and validity of the Conger-Kanungo scale of charismatic leadership. *Canadian Journal of Administrative Sciences*, 14 (3) 1997: 291.

160. Weber, M. K. E., *The Theory of Social & Economic Organisations*. Trans. Parsons, T., 1947 (New York: Free Press, 1915), p.358-360.

161. House, R. J., A 1976 Theory of Charismatic Leadership. In: Hunt, J. G. and Larson, L. L., *Leadership: The Cutting Edge*. (Carbondale: Southern Illinois University Press, 1977), p.193.

162. Conger, J. A. and Kanungo, R. N., *Charismatic Leadership in Organisations* (London: Sage, 1998), p.4-5.

163. in Yukl, G. A. and Van Fleet, D.D., Cross-Situational Multi Method Research on Military Leadership Effectiveness. *Organisational Behavior and Human Performance*, 30, 1982:87-108.

164. Aberbach, D., *Charisma in Politics Religion and the Media: Private Trauma Public Ideals* (Basingstoke: Macmillan, 1996), p.75.

165. Dickson, G., Charisma: Medieval and Modern. *Religions*, 3 (3) 2012: 780.

166. House, R. J., Spangler, W. D., and Woycke. J., Personality and Charisma in the US Presidency: A Psychological Theory of Leader Effectiveness. *Administrative Science Quarterly*, 36 (36) 1991: 364.

167. Stutje, J. W., *Charismatic Leadership and Social Movements: The Revolutionary Power of Ordinary Men and Women* (New York: Berghahn Books, 2012), p.3.

168. Downton, J., *Rebel Leadership: Commitment and Charisma in the Revolutionary Process* (New York: Free Press, 1973), p.84.

169. Willner, A., and Willner, D., The Rise and Role of Charismatic Leaders. *Annals of the American Academy of Political and Social Science*, 358, 1967: 77-88.

170. Willner, A. R., *The Spellbinders: Charismatic Political Leadership* (New Haven: Yale University Press, 1984), p.5.

171. House, R. J. and Howell, J.M., Personality and Charismatic Leadership. *Leadership Quarterly*, 3 (2) 1992: 81-108.

172. Howell, J. M., Two Faces of Charisma: Socialized and Personalized Leadership in Organisations. *In*: J. A, Conger and R. N. Kanungo., *Charismatic Leadership: The Elusive Factor in Organisational Effectiveness* (San Franscisco: Jossey-Bass, 1988), p. 213-216.

173. Williamson, M., *Celebrity: Capitalism and the Making of Fame*. (Cambridge: Polity, 2016), p.74.

174. Goldsmith, B., The Meaning of Celebrity. *New York Times*. 4th December (1983), p.75.

175. Williamson, M. (2016), p.75.

176. Boorstin, D., From Hero to Celebrity: The Human Pseudo-Event. *In:* Marshall, P. D., *The Celebrity Culture Reader*. (London: Routledge, 1961).

177. Ibid., p.58.

178. Rojek, C., *Celebrity*. (London: Reaktion Books, 2001), p.13.

179. Dyer, R., *Stars*. (London: British Film Institute, 1982), p.5.

180. Williamson, M. (2016), p.12.

181. Hutch, R. A., *Religious Leadership: Personality History and Sacred Authority* (New York: Peter Lang, 1991), p.167.

182. Barnes, D. F., Charisma and Religious Leadership: An Historical Analysis. *Journal for the Scientific Study of Religion*, 17 (1) 1978: 3.

183. Ibid., p.4.

184. Ibid., p.6.

185. Stark, W., *The Sociology of Religion* (New York: Fordham University Press, 1970), p.9.

186. Hadden, J. K., Religious Broadcasting and the Mobilization of the New Christian Right. *Journal for the Scientific Study of Religion*, 26 (1) 1987: 1.

187. Gaddy, G. D., The Power of the Religious Media: Religious Broadcast Use and the Role of Religious Organisations in Public Affairs. *Review of Religious Research*, 25 (4) 1984: 289.

CHAPTER 2

GOD IS MARCHING ON
*The Birth and Development
of Religious Broadcasting 1921-1955*

In this chapter the aim is to demonstrate how radio became an instrument of religion, the nature of that religious broadcasting, the groups responsible for these broadcasts and above all to illustrate the thesis that religious broadcasting was more driven by personalities and their vision, than the Church itself.

1. The United States Blazes a Trail

a) The Foundations are laid: 1921-1934

Technically speaking, over-the-air religion began with the first message tapped out on Samuel Morse's telegraph in 1844: 'What God Hath Wrought'.[1] It might be one of the few times in the next century and a half that the name of God would be invoked on the airwaves, without causing controversy.

From the earliest days of radio broadcasting the zeal of religious America was there to use this medium of communication to propagate their faith. Historians have sometimes overlooked religion's presence in radio's infancy. However the interrelationship between religion and radio was profoundly significant for both.[2] After years of experimentation, radio was launched in America with the first licensed commercial station, KDKA in Pittsburgh Pennsylvania, taking to the airwaves in late 1920. From the very first, religion was an important part of the material which was pumped into the ether.[3] So as part of an attempt to test out a diversity of broadcasting including political speeches, music and sport, KDKA also scheduled what was recognised to be the first religious programme on January 2nd 1921, only a couple of months after the station had begun its regular schedule. So a very nervous Rev. Lewis B. Whittemore, the assistant minister of Calvary Episcopal Church led the 'first radio church service' on station KDKA. A first for religious broadcasting and another first for KDKA in its attempt to build an audience in this new pioneering medium.

The premiere religious broadcast was very successful and the Rev. Edwin Van Etten who conducted most of the later services from Calvary, declared that the historic first broadcast symbolised the "universality of radio religion". [4] Actually a position that was not universally accepted amongst the ministers of the day, some thinking it was on a level with the 'sinful' frivolities of motion pictures and the stage and any contact with radio equipment or personnel was at odds with morality. However many others saw the potential of radio as a way to reach, enlighten and possibly convert an audience far larger than any church, tabernacle or revival tent could ever accommodate.[5]

In the years following, the momentum grew with a whole range of broadcasting pioneers. People like Paul Rader in Chicago[6] and Aimee Semple McPherson, "the live wire of Los Angeles",[7] eventually setting up their own stations, broadcasting church services, morning prayer programmes and inspirational talks. Early adopters also included the Moody Bible Institute in Chicago and its WMBI station, which featured Bible-centred programming, in the form of its *Moody Presents* – a weekly half hour of music and Bible teaching. As observers pointed out,

> the founder of the Moody Bible Institute, Dwight L. Moody, spoke to as many as fifty thousand people at once and preached to hundreds of thousands in his lifetime. Even in his fondest dreams he did not hope to have a potential audience of almost forty million people.[8]

Others like Rev.R.R.Brown of the Omaha Gospel Tabernacle, Nebraska, broadcast on existing commercial stations like WOAW.

Brown came to see his *Radio Chapel Service* audience as a new form of church. He even invited listeners to join the *World Radio Congregation* with official membership cards. Within a decade the *Radio Chapel Service* had a weekly audience of half a million and Brown gained the reputation as the "Billy Sunday of the Air", pastor of America's first radio church. In the same vein the Greater New York Federation of Churches established programmes on New York's WEAF working with central organisations representing Protestant, Catholic and Jewish groups.[9] One of the key programmes was the *National Radio Pulpit* which continued when eventually WEAF became part of the National Broadcasting Company (see Appendix 2).

Within just a few short years more than five million homes in the USA had radios and there was a rush to establish stations. By 1923, 12 religious organisations held radio licences and by 1925, 63 of the 600 stations operating were church owned.[10] Others, as described, offered free programming on non-religious outlets. Broadcasting in the United States essentially was privately owned and commercially supported.

As Ward states,

> by 1927 more than sixty religious groups, from individual churches to evangelistic organisations, had obtained licences to operate radio stations. But radio was choking on its own growth.[11]

In reality radio's success had outgrown the few government regulations in place to control it, like the 1912 Radio Act, which was never intended to cover broadcasting.[12] 'Inadequate' and 'chaotic' were words used to characterize broadcasting regulation in the 1920s under the Radio Act of 1912.[13] As one Federal Radio Commissioner later commented chaos was to ensue, "many stations jumped without restraint to new wave-lengths which suited them ... some older stations also jumped their power".[14] In 1922, two Washington stations even broadcast three successive Sunday services from two churches at the same time on the same wavelength.[15]

So under the guidance of Congress, a National Radio Conference asked the Secretary of Commerce, Herbert Hoover, to regulate radio station broadcast times, signal strengths and frequency assignments to avoid the confusion that had occurred. By the following year Congress took action and in 1927 a Radio Act was passed and the Federal Radio Commission was formally set up (See Appendix 2). The Act established the principle that the radio spectrum belongs to the public and that a broadcaster is merely licensed to use a particular frequency for a specified period of time, but acquires no ownership rights of that frequency.[16] All the new regulations and standards were to work against religious stations, and broadcasters who did not fulfil the Commission's criteria were denied the renewal of their licenses. By 1933 the number of stations owned by religious groups was cut by more than half – to less than thirty.[17]

Although regulatory and broadcasting policies did not encourage Christian broadcasters to continue station operations, probably the dire economic conditions of the Great Depression did the most damage. The many churches who had funded religious broadcasting could no longer afford full-time radio ministries and most of the evangelists had already decided that producing individual programmes funded by donations from listeners made more financial sense. By placing these on powerful radio stations and networks with established audiences, they could reach more people at less cost. So, as stated, by 1933 less than half of the original 63 licences remained on the air.[18] In the new era of commercialism and government regulation, churches and independent religious groups could not compete on the same level as previously. The combination of government regulation and industry self-regulation forced evangelicals to deal realistically with the commercial market place. They fought for broadcasting time, took risks and learned how to produce programmes that would attract audiences and elicit contributions.[19]

But despite the restrictions, displaced broadcasters took to buying time on other stations, on a largely city by city basis, as little national network time was available. People like Walter A.Maier from the Lutheran Church began petitioning national networks,[20] like the Columbia Broadcasting System (See Appendix 2) because he wanted a nationwide programme – *The Lutheran Hour*, a programme that was heard around the world by an estimated 20 million listeners, with Maier being credited as having preached to more people than anyone else in history up to that point in time.[21]

But a result of various controversies, including a response to the politicized and aggressive radio preaching of Father Charles Coughlin (See Chapter 4), the two major networks of CBS and NBC denied 'paid time' to religious groups, so they could not monopolize the airwaves. But because religion was thought to provide a public benefit by its mere presence on the airwaves, what the networks offered was 'sustaining time' – free airtime (predictably sometimes the least profitable time slots) donated by the networks on the basis that the broadcasts should be non-sectarian and scrutinised – guided by a series of self-regulatory guidelines concerning network religious broadcasts and producing programmes like *The Church on Air* on CBS.[22]

In the same vein, in this controversial period, the Federal Council of Churches of Christ which tended to represent the more liberal mainstream churches, rather than the conservative evangelical groups, created a set of guidelines to establish some standards into this sector of the industry, which were for example adopted by NBC virtually without change:-

1. The National Broadcasting Company will serve only the central great religious faiths, as for example the Roman Catholics, the Protestants and the Hebrews, as distinguished from individual churches or small group movements where the national membership is comparatively small.

2. The religious message broadcast should be non-sectarian and non-denominational in appeal.

3. The religious broadcast message should be of the widest appeal – presenting the broad aim of religion, which is not only in building up the personal and social life of the individual, but also aids in popularising religion and the Church.

4. The religious message broadcast should interpret religion as the highest and best so that as an education factor it will bring the individual listener to realise his responsibility to the organisational Church.

5. The national religious message should only be broadcast by the recognised outstanding leaders of the several faiths.[23]

But as *The Lutheran Hour* was about to launch on CBS, a new voice came on the scene in the form of Charles E. Fuller, a pastor of Calvary Church, Los Angeles. By 1930 the church was ready to broadcast over California's KGER, a slot that continued for three years with an estimated audience of 15,000 listeners. But because of various disputes within the church, Fuller resigned and declared his intention to launch an independent broadcast ministry.[24] So in March 1933 his programme *The Pilgrims Hour* took to the airwaves on KGER. By 1934 his programmes were expanding with broadcasts from KNX Hollywood, a station that could be heard in eleven western states, plus Alaska and western Canada. A new station and a new programme *The Old Fashioned Revival Hour* was destined to become one the largest network religious programmes of its time.[25]

b) A Time of Strategic Development: 1934-1955

In several ways 1934 was a crucial year for on-the-air religion. The Federal Radio Commission morphed into the Federal Communications Commission (FCC) and became the key media regulator. In the same year the Greater New York Federation of Churches gave up involvement in network radio allowing the Federal Council of Churches of Christ (FCCC) through its Department of National Religious Radio to assume responsibility for religious content on NBC and CBS. By this time the FCCC had 25 denominations within its jurisdiction. But from 1934 onwards a large number of religious groups sought to gain their share of the 'sustaining time' allocations proposed by the major networks. It soon became apparent there was not enough airtime for everyone who wanted it. To address this problem in a rational and fair manner, an agreement was reached among the networks and such national ecumenical bodies as the Federal Council of

Churches, the Southern Baptist Convention, the Jewish Seminary of America and the National Council of Catholic Men agreed to sort out the competing demands of their constituents and decide which programmes should be allocated to the available sustaining time.[26] But an unforeseen consequence of this in 1934 was the formation of the Mutual Broadcasting System (MBS), the first new network to offer real competition since the early days of NBC and CBS and unlike its rivals was willing to sell time for paid religious programmes. By 1943 over 25% of the network's airtime was being purchased by religious broadcasters. But then a blow came to every radio preacher in America when the Mutual Broadcasting System, following the policy of other networks, announced restrictions on paid-for religious programmes and it made it virtually impossible for radio preachers to survive on air because they could no longer buy time as before.[27] A new and challenging era had begun.

The MBS announcement sparked a nationwide protest from the evangelical community and around 150 broadcasters arrived on April 7th, 1944, for a two day radio session of the National Association of Evangelicals Conference. It was decided to "form a national association of gospel broadcasters, to be affiliated with the National Association of Evangelicals" – a lobby group with an agreed Statement of Faith and Code of Ethics [28] and with a new name – the National Religious Broadcasters (See Appendix 2). It would be,

> a corporation of doctrinally evangelical individuals (and organisations) concerned for the spread of the gospel of our Lord and Saviour Jesus Christ banded together for the sake of the strength which comes from numbers united in a common cause. Thus united the religious broadcasters feel they can contribute to the improvement of religious broadcasts, better serve the interest of Christian people and more effectively minister to the spiritual welfare of the nation.[29]

A Code of Ethics was incorporated into its constitution and written in two parts: a section for producers of radio programmes and another for station owners and operators. The Code covered issues of sponsorship, character, production, co-operation, advertising, financial accountability, regulatory compliance and responsibility to uphold the gospel, the family, and the nation. So at a convention on September 21st at Chicago's Moody Memorial Church, the National Religious Broadcasters was born with its first President, William Ward Ayer. In its early years, NRB was most valuable at raising the standards of Christian radio broadcasting and eventually became the political voice for conservatives and their millions of radio listeners.[30]

Dubourdieu in his meticulous research in 1932 polled 588 radio stations to investigate the nature and impact of religious broadcasting. From the 325 that responded it showed that 8.37% of radio time was given to religion, 23% of that was on paid-time programmes and 77% (approximately three out of every four religious stations) on time donated by the station.[31] In 1939, NBC alone could report a grand total of 6,000 religious programmes, which had brought in a response of over 7 million letters from every state in the nation[32] and by the end of the Second World War in 1945, radio broadcasting was seriously beginning to get back on track in making an impact. By the end of 1945 the FCC had licensed more than a thousand stations and an estimated 60 million of American households owned a radio – up 20% from before the War.[33] In addition a new national network came on the scene, the American Broadcasting Company (See Appendix 2). The FCC ensured FM radio operations to accommodate fifteen hundred new commercial stations and with space on the dial for non-commercial stations, including religious ones. The impact of the total American religious output must have been considerable over the years. Its effect on the moral and spiritual life of the nation can never be fully assessed, but a marked return to worship emerged in many States after the War with crowded churches.[34]

This new era posed great potential for religious broadcasters and the newly formed National Religious Broadcasters moved to campaign to ensure gospel preachers obtained a share of sustaining time from the networks at both national and local levels. In terms of purchasing air time they took a slow steady approach in making its case to the executives and station owners of the industry and in 1949 the newest radio network ABC reversed its policy and accepted paid religious broadcasts. ABC signed up Charles Fuller's *Old Fashioned Revival*

Hour which was to achieve a weekly audience of around twenty million listeners.[35] Over the coming years other networks followed and religious broadcasters were gaining ground once more. NBC followed suit and Donald Grey Barnhouse's *The Bible Study Hour* launched a verse-by-verse exposition of the Epistle to the Romans. Barnhouse devoted almost a decade of broadcasts to the study of the Epistle to the Romans, taping 455 half-hour broadcasts in this series.[36]

Whilst the evangelicals were expanding their influence, the mainstream and more liberal wing of the churches was equally active. They mounted their own syndication campaign through the newly formed Joint Religious Radio Committee of the Congregational Christian, Presbyterian USA and the United Church of Canada – led by Rev. Everett C. Parker, a noted broadcaster and religious radio historian/chronicler. In 1945 the Protestant Film Commission was set up to oversee the motion picture projects of the Federal Council of Churches of Christ. Three years later the Protestant Film Commission and the Joint Religious Radio Committee merged to become the Protestant Radio Commission. These new organisations and mergers were preludes to the liberal broadcaster's plans for the upcoming television revolution and also their attempts to maintain a mainstream appeal of religious broadcasting in contrast to the revivalist movements of evangelicals, fundamentalists and Pentecostals.[37]

But with the death of the much respected Walter Maier in 1950, the new President of NRB Theodore Elsner, knew that replacing him was a vital issue for religious broadcasting and it was to be a random meeting in the beach resort of Ocean City, New Jersey, that was to provide the clue. There, he was to meet the evangelist, William Frank "Billy" Graham (See Chapter 4), fresh from his very successful Los Angeles Crusade, which had basically made him a national celebrity, thanks to the support of the newspaper mogul William Randolf Hearst.[38] Elsner's introductions and substantial funding from supporters, led Billy Graham to form the Billy Graham Evangelistic Association and take to the airwaves on the ABC network on Sunday 5th November 1950 with a programme called *The Hour of Decision* (a title suggested by his wife Ruth). In a matter of weeks, *The Hour of Decision* surpassed the previous all time high for a religious programme, amassing an audience of more than twenty million listeners. A further later media development took Graham' Crusades to film and telecasts, with a series of *The Hour of Decision* between 1950 and 1954.[39]

Even though network religious telecasts were limited, the early 1950s proved to be an era of television pioneering. So others also ventured into the newly developing medium of television, like the weekly *Catholic Hour* that debuted on CBS with Bishop Fulton J. Sheen in 1952.[39] Sheen's broadcasts and personal appearances made a big impact, even in the UK where thousands turned out to see "America's television Bishop".[40]

But others were more cautious and wanted to see if this new medium would gain traction, at the same time also considering their huge and time-consuming radio ministries. Therefore for the most part the status quo of the radio days remained in tact. The Federal Council of Churches of Christ became the National Council of Churches (NCC) in 1950 and the NCC's newly formed Broadcast and Film Commission represented the mainstream of churches and received most of the network airtime on a sustaining basis, whilst the conservative's NRB functioned with paid time both locally and in syndication.[41]

However, despite the fact that television production was enormously expensive compared to radio, in the early 1950s both liberals and conservatives recognized that audiences wanted both sound and sight, so the NCC developed projects like *Lamp unto My Feet* and *Look up and Live* on CBS and *Eternal Light* and *Frontiers of Faith* on NBC.[42] Oral Roberts' (See Chapter 4) syndicated weekly programme, made enormous strides in the field of television filming techniques,[43] while Rex Humbard who operated his own television station in Akron, Ohio, built the self-styled Cathedral of Tomorrow, specifically designed to accommodate cameras and television technicians.[44] It was another landmark period as the rapid emergence of television breathed new life into religious broadcasting and to the on-going debates.

c) To the Ends of the Earth: Mission in the Ether

Whilst it is easy to shine the spotlight on developments inside America, it needs to be recognised also in this period that the churches in America, across all denominations, were very active in sending out missionaries across the world in an attempt to share the Christian faith with those who had never heard the 'gospel' message before. Those who had seen the potential of radio already realised this new medium could be part of that outreach. As Cook recounts (1982) people like Reuben E. Larson and Clarence W. Jones in the 1930s, using state of the art international short-wave technology were chasing licences in Ecuador, until eventually the government granted the licence for the first radio station in the entire country and the first international radio station in the world, which came to be known HCJB (Heralding Christ Jesus's Blessings). By 1935 the HCJB signal was boosted to cover neighbouring countries and a new transmitter in 1940 boosted 'The Voice of the Andes' to a power of 10,000 watts. Today HCJB and its affiliated AM and FM stations can reach more than 90% of the world's population.[45]

Building 'highways in the skyways' internationally was also taken up by the Roman Catholic Church in setting up Vatican Radio with the help of the famous inventor of wireless radio Guglielmo Marconi, himself supervising the construction of a 10,000 watt transmitter with the potential to reach the faithful across the globe. Thus began a long history of propagating the Catholic faith by the airwaves.[46]

In the Far East too groups came together to form the Far East Broadcasting Company (FEBC) in 1948, realising that the medium of broadcasting was not limited by geography or political boundaries and was one of the few 'missionaries' capable of taking the gospel to the ends of the earth.[47] FEBC organised broadcasts from Manila in the Philippines, the 'hub' of East Asia, with unlimited power to reach a fifteen hundred mile radius to include Indonesia, Indochina, Malaysia, Thailand, Burma and China – a population of 1.3 billion people. Despite the vast infra-structure to all this, FEBC's field operations director Jim Bowman tried to put it in perspective by stating,

FEBC is committed to seeing listeners reached by the gospel. One hundred and twenty languages and dialects, three hundred program hours a day and thirty-two stations are meaningless statistics unless people find Christ through this vehicle.[48]

Meanwhile opportunities were to stir in Europe too, through the vision of Paul Freed, a Youth for Christ Director from North Carolina, who had heard much about the persecuted Christians in Spain under the dictatorship of Francisco Franco. Realising that broadcasting in the context of Spain would be difficult, clues came that maybe broadcasting to Spain from Tangier in Morocco might be the solution. Freed came to realise that radio would be his new ministry and in 1952 established Trans World Radio knowing that Tangiers was to be the first address. So on February 22nd 1954 the "Voice of Tangier" was on the air. To Freed, "it was a miracle of God that Trans World Radio was able to get into Europe".[49] A later base too in Monte Carlo, with a curtain of antennas, meant that Trans World Radio also had access to the Middle East, the British Isles, Scandinavia, Russia, Spain and Eastern Europe, making it probably one of the largest Christian broadcasting organisations in the world.[50] Missionary radio as with 'Gospel' radio was beginning to play a significant role in the life of the Christian Church, in and from America. Shurick in his book *The First Quarter of American Broadcasting* comments,

> with approximately 5% of all broadcasting devoted to religious and devotional programmes, radio has opened the doors of expression to the world's leaders of the church. In no other way can so vast an audience be assembled for the truths and blessings of theology. Today in a few hours, missionary work of a hundred years can be accomplished from a central pulpit in the presence of the microphone.[51]

2. The United Kingdom Learns to Inform, Educate, Entertain and Inspire!

a) The Reithian Years

Although the United States was the earliest pioneer in terms of broadcasting, the development of broadcasting in the 1920s and it's increasingly significant role in the national life, ranks as one of the most important changes of that era in Britain, as much as it was in America.

In common too with America, in Britain religious broadcasting is almost as old as radio itself. The British Broadcasting Company making its first religious broadcast on Christmas Eve 1922, 6 weeks after regular daily operations had begun.[52] But whereas in America there was no single protagonist for religious broadcasting, in Britain the first General Manager of the BBC, John Reith (See Chapter 4) who grew up in an atmosphere of rigid piety as the son of the manse, was anxious to have the Christian religion feature within the programming output of the new broadcasting company. The initiative in establishing religious broadcasting came from Reith himself, not from the Church; the latter simply accepted the opportunity offered.[53] Indeed many people judge that the BBC's notable record in the religious field was entirely due to the faith of this one man and an explanation of the BBC policy, in a cardinal issue such as religion, was down to the character and convictions of John Reith.[54] But unlike his father, Reith's congregation "would consist not just of the good people of the West End of Glasgow, but the whole population of the United Kingdom, and all its empire".[55] For by 1927, when the British Broadcasting Corporation was formed there were two and quarter million licence holders and by 1939 the vast majority of the population had access to a wireless receiver. The coming of broadcasting was truly revolutionary, for it brought into existence a totally new world of human endeavour and experience. For the Church as for society, its advent had enormous consequences which focussed in the specific issue of religious broadcasting. The whole issue of Christianity on air clearly forms a significant aspect of the religious and social life of pre-war 20th Century Britain.[56]

It has to be said too that religious broadcasting was vitally important both for radio, for churches and for the listening public, but as stated, the initiative in establishing religious broadcasting came from Reith himself, not from the churches, the latter simply adopting the opportunities offered. Reith was never a committed church man, but he was committed to the protection and promulgation of dynamic Christianity in national and personal life and Sunday was one institution he believed belonged to the maintenance of a Christian presence.[57] To the Reithian trilogy of *inform, educate and entertain* – *'inspire'* could so easily be added, as reflected by Reith's aspirations for religious broadcasting.

Indeed the whole experience of broadcasting religion was very significant for the BBC, which fulfilling its public service concept in this sphere, as every other, effectively demonstrated the workability of organising religious programmes without significant difficulties or rivalry with the churches. This was down to Reith's non-denominational approach and the setting up of an advisory committee – the 'Sunday Committee' in 1923. This consisted of Canon C.S Woodward, a priest of the Church of England, Rev. Dr R.C. Gillier, a Presbyterian minister and Mr. Herbert Ward, a member of the Roman Catholic Church. The Committee was chaired by Cyril Garbett the Bishop of Southwark and was to meet four times in 1923 and during this time more people were added to include non-conformist representation.[58] A typical action in a democratic society, this was the first step taken to give guidance to religious broadcasting.[59] By 1926 the name was changed and the committee had become the Central Religious Advisory Committee (CRAC) and was to play a significant role in shaping the religious broadcasting of the BBC and eventually that of commercial radio and television in later years.[60] The prime purpose of CRAC was to secure the active co-operation of the mainstream denominational church leaders especially in terms of authoritative advice and the presentation of church opinions and reactions at each stage of the development of religious broadcasting.[61] So early ecclesiastical caution was transformed into enthusiastic approval and suspicion and hostility virtually vanished and a long-standing alliance was established between the BBC and the mainstream churches for the religious use of the medium.

The Churches found in this new mass medium of radio, an ally and sympathetic spirit, totally absent in cinema and much less evident in the popular press. As Dinwiddie reflects, "There is a certain mysterious affinity between worship and wireless. To put it in simple terms, people wanted to tune-in to God's wavelength".[62]

The Churches benefited enormously from the public service structure and the spirit of the BBC, whose free provisions of facilities alone made possible the development of religion over the air, which so vastly increased the range and reach of the Christian message. *Radio Magazine* commented that the BBC was providing, "the largest pulpit in the world".[63]

The nature of this development was outlined in the *Radio Times* (promoted as the 'official organ of the BBC') on February 6th 1925, with a very significant article called *Religion that is Broadcast*. Speaking on behalf of the BBC it declared...

> Our aim was to communicate a thorough-going manly religion. It does not present the Almighty with the guise of what has been described as a lawyer's God policing His Universe, but as a companionable and sympathetic spirit.

In terms of the broadcast Services it went on to state...

> We are not concerned with doctrine. Familiar hymns or metrical psalms are sung. Usually there is an anthem and a fifteen minute address. Our correspondence leaves no room for doubt that the distinctive character of Sunday programmes is widely appreciated and welcomed. The exclusion of doctrinal controversy has silenced theological criticism. There are still some who thought we keep people away from church. But whatever evidence there is, points to the opposite conclusion. There is also good reason to believe that our services stimulate religious thought... Broadcasting has brought the message of religion to many thousands of men and women who might have never felt its enriching and purifying influence.[64]

The overriding principle through it all was that religious broadcasting on the BBC was to represent the 'mainstream of Christian tradition',

> The BBC confining itself to broadcast Christian religion and therefore excluding Unitarianism, Judaism, Mohammedanism and many other respectable religious creeds of the world.[65]

In reality, the BBC granted occasional talks to such groups for special occasions and equally smaller faith groups like the Society of Friends and the Salvation Army did merit and undertook occasional broadcasts.[66] But petitions from Christian Scientists, Spiritualists and Humanists were largely ignored at this time. The approach being, generally, to mirror the Christian activity of the nation.

So we see after religious broadcasting's inception at the Christmas Eve Service in 1922 given by Rev. John Mayo, Rector of Whitechapel London, religious broadcasting mushroomed with *Evensong* from Westminster Abbey and the establishment of the *Daily Service* at 10.15 each week-day morning (1926), *Epilogues, Choral Evensongs, Lift up Your Hearts* (1939) *Sunday Half-Hour* (1940), *Think on These Things* (1940), *Christian Outlook* (1948) and the *People's Service* (1948). Although the BBC discouraged the cult of 'personality' there is no doubt that radio helped to establish and enhance the nationwide reputation of certain churchmen especially the Rev.H.R.L. Sheppard of St. Martin-in-the-Fields and the Rev.W.H. Elliott of St.Michael's Chester Square (See Chapter 4), both drawing a huge listenership to their broadcasts and large crowds to their respective churches. For Sheppard this medium was unique, as he stated in his article in the *Radio Times*, "In broadcasting, Christianity has perhaps the greatest instrument for conversion that has been given to it since Jesus Christ proclaimed it".[67]

For Sheppard and others like him, a preacher is not just acting as reporter telling of his own experiences, but rather an agent of someone higher.[68] Never was that more so with the opportunity of broadcasting. In addition, the microphone was the 'annihilation of distance',[69] making the listening public for religious broadcasts vast, with more people reached week by week than attended church. The ministry of consolation, religious teaching and moral challenge presented by Sheppard and Elliott and others in the 1930s was constantly heard by millions, many of whom had little or no contact with organised religion. However, the widely popular radio ministries of men like Sheppard and Elliott was only one important strand in the total pattern of religious programmes, equally significant though less spectacular was the Sunday by Sunday broadcast worship of a great number of churches and chapels all over the country.[70] The effect of the total output upon the listening public cannot be estimated with any precision, but it can hardly have been negligible.[71] The BBC held up before listeners what Reith believed to be the basic essentials of the Christian faith and reminded them of their national heritage.

The presence of religion within the total programming of the BBC was highly significant for the nation as a whole and not just for the listening public. Some commentators believe that without religion at that time, the BBC would have been almost entirely an entertainment and informational medium and that BBC religion was a marked demonstration of its social purpose and sense of moral responsibility. However the BBC's 'Sunday Policy' proved to be controversial. In fact there was more controversy about this aspect of BBC policy during the 1930s than about anything else.[72] The basis of that policy was – dedication of certain Sunday hours to religious broadcasts, abstention from broadcasting religious or other items during normal church hours and the preservation so far as broadcasting can operate to preserve it, of the character of the 'British Sunday'.[73] There is no doubt that the policy and its existence had Reith's imprint all over it, himself declaring, "so long as I am Director-General there will be no change in the character of Sunday programmes".[74] But Eckersley, the Director of Programmes and eventually Director of Entertainment, in his commentary on the BBC in those early years observed, "the Sunday policy was in danger of defeating its own religious ends and driving the public to listening to commercial stations".[75]

The public's reaction to the Sabbatarian style of 'Reith's Sunday' (See Chapter 4) showed that any attempt to influence unduly programme content as whole, by narrowly interpreted religious consideration, was fraught with danger and ultimately the BBC in this matter could only manoeuvre effectively within the limits of public opinion. This growing disquiet led to what was termed the 'Brighter Sunday' campaign – an attempt to make the day more listener-friendly and appealing to a wider audience.[76]

Also to avoid the criticism of being too London-centric, during the 1920s the BBC had started to establish close relations with a number of churches and cathedrals. Canterbury Cathedral, York Minster, Manchester Cathedral, St George's Chapel Windsor and Liverpool Cathedral were all wired for periodical religious broadcasts. The danger of these outside broadcasts was how to maintain standards. To that end the BBC issued a brochure, *Hints to Sunday Speakers* (1928) which outlined the advice that..

> the address which should in all cases be read, is limited to 10 minutes and must avoid sectarian propaganda or provocative argument. It is intended primarily to be of a practical nature, as such a kind as may prove helpful to all listeners. You are asked to remember your vast audience is not a crowd or a congregation, but a variety of individuals to whom you are speaking in the intimacy of their homes. This is the audience to be kept in mind. The tone of voice found to have most appeal is that of the intimate and sympathetic talk rather than that of the public address.. In effect, you must not take either the interest or the knowledge of your listeners for granted. It is therefore wise to introduce the address in a human way, to treat it conversationally, and to avoid as far as possible technical terms not understood by the general listener. It should be remembered that listeners are able to stop listening at will, and thousands of them will switch off their sets if the opening is unattractive.[77]

So near or far religious broadcasting's intention was to supplement the work of the churches by making Christians more educated in their faith, keeping them in touch with important current events in all the churches and thereby helping to widen the average Christian's awareness and vision of the total Church in action. Indeed the Church of England's Convocation Report of 1931 stated...

> We wish to express our grateful appreciation of the debt which is owed to the British Broadcasting Corporation for its determination that religion shall be given its due and proper place in its programme as a whole. We rejoice that the policy which the Corporation has adopted has been endorsed by the volume of correspondence which the Corporation receives from all sorts and conditions of men.[78]

Although there was a general acceptance of the policy and practice of the BBC, not everything was sweetness and light. Despite the fact that Roman Catholics were successfully accommodated within the BBC's policy of non-controversial broadcasting, some wings of their Church felt it was unrepresented and treated more rigorously.[79] Others on a totally different plain were concerned that broadcast religion would diminish congregations especially in rural areas, the *Times* reflecting this fear,

> people are less ready to tramp long distances in order to attend Evensong at their parish church, when pressing a knob enables them to hear a service in their own cottage and farmhouse.[80]

Still others judged that the availability on-air of church services might produce a more 'passive' Christianity with listeners less engaged in the Christian community as a result and even Davidson the Archbishop of Canterbury stepped in to rebut those who felt religious broadcasting trivialised Christianity. Writing in the *Radio Times* he said,

> I am well aware that amongst religious people there are a good many who take exception to what they regard as the 'irreverent' broadcasting of religious services. I think such critics are mistaken.[81]

Despite criticisms, religious broadcasting continued to flourish with also unintended and unforeseen results, as it undoubtedly furthered the ecumenical movement, increased mutual tolerance and understanding and demonstrated that in response to this truly missionary opportunity of radio, clergy of widely differing persuasions were able to realise a unity of endeavour and testimony, far in advance of any deliberately organised ecumenical movement.[82] In parallel to this was an encouraging response from the public in this area, the BBC Handbook reporting later, "the most obvious result of 10 years of religious broadcasting, as reflected in listener correspondence, has been increased tolerance".[83]

With this sort of tangible response on many levels, religious broadcasting was under pressure to develop from early days and move ad hoc arrangements to a more permanent systematic organisation. So in 1924 religious programmes became the specific responsibility of J.C.Stobart in his capacity as Education Director, with the brief to ensure standards amongst the clergy in broadcast sermons from both church and studio.[84] It was perhaps no coincidence that the first Head of Religious Broadcasting at the BBC was also the Director of Education. Both of these aspects of the basis of religious broadcasting policy are clearly stated in the BBC's Handbook in 1928...

> In a national service to which nothing pertains to the life of men as foreign, it was natural that from the beginning religion should find its place in British Broadcasting. It could not be otherwise. Even if the programmes aimed only at providing education and recreation, religion could not be denied a place; but when those who were responsible for Broadcasting set before themselves the object of raising the national standards of values and of a constructive idealism, it was obvious that the religious service should be one of the regular programme features.[85]

As with other developments, the BBC reviewed the overall impact of its first decade of broadcasting and planned accordingly,

> the growth of religious broadcasting has been like that of a mustard seed. From small beginnings it has come almost overnight to exercise a profound and challenging influence in our life.[86]

So by the early 1930s, the bulk of Christian opinion in Britain had accepted the idea and practice of religion on the air and so in 1933 a specific Religious Broadcasting Department was created, with a Religious Director in the form of Rev. F.A. Iremonger, which was a significant shift forward. He was described by one of his colleagues as, "fearless, outspoken and an utterly kind person, who stood no nonsense and proceeded to put his ideas ruthlessly into action".[87]

Under his direction there was an extension of religious talks in the form of *The Way to God, Christian Living, Explaining the Christian Way* and *God and the World through Christian Eyes* (1933) which had originated under Stobart's reign. All geared to address the criticism that BBC Religion was an 'emasculated Christianity' and needed more apologetics. There was also a new experiment with features like the popular Sunday evening series *Melodies of Christendom* (1937), Dorothy Sayers's controversial, but much acclaimed, *The Man Born to Be King* (1941) and T.S Eliot's *Murder in the Cathedral* (1935). Equally there was a greater variety in children's religious broadcasts with a revised *Sunday Children's Hour* (first broadcast in 1923), special children's services broadcast each month and E.R. Appleton's *Joan and Betty's Bible Story* programmes (1930). The Committee of Convocation in 1931 also paid special tribute to these programmes, which it believed reached families untouched by Sunday Schools.[88]

b) Beyond Reith

Although Reith retired from the BBC in 1938, his legacy remained. His Director of Religious Broadcasting, Iremonger, moved on too to become the Dean of Lichfield and was succeeded by Dr.J.W.Welch in 1939, following very much Iremonger's brief with an overall consideration that Christianity must challenge both church and nation alike, especially the latter, through testimony to the relevance and value of Christian tradition.[89] Writing in the *St. Martin's Review* Welch stated,

> The purpose of religious broadcasting is the purpose of the Christian Church. As the Church is the extension of the Incarnation, so religious broadcasting is an extension of the church. Its methods are different, its medium new, its audience is vast, but if its fails to be the Church extending its work, it fails altogether.[90]

In line with the broader evolving internal structure of the BBC, the values and working practices of the Religious Broadcasting Department were slowly emerging and finding their place within the Corporation. Central to this was ensuring a professional standing for the output relative to other departments. Together management, staff and external contributors developed a style of programming that was non-denominational, incorporating an increasingly popular theology, delivered by an array of well known names into a style of programmes that could be termed 'BBC Religion'.'[91]

Since Reith's days, religion in broadcasting had been seen as the unique means of bringing an authoritative expression of Christian opinion to the widest public, including the committed Christian community who either would not read or had no guidance as to what they should read in order to mature and improve their Christian understanding. Iremonger had developed the Sunday talks in order to educate the Christian community. On taking up his post Welch wanted a much broader policy: the churches must not only bring the teaching of the church to bear on critical social and national questions, it must reaffirm the centrality of the Christian faith for the survival of Christian civilization. Religious broadcasting must also recognise the gulf between faith and unfaith and make every effort to reach those who were quite outside the active life of the congregation, but who were asking serious questions of believers, whether intellectuals or ordinary church people.[92] As Dinwiddie points out in *Religion by Radio* (1968) religious broadcasting developed a missionary zeal, "to challenge the careless, reclaim the lapsed and strengthen the faithful".[93]

Welch and his Director General, William Haley continually sought to encourage the Churches through broadcasting to expose Christ's creed on the electric 'areopagus',[94] in what was a challenging time when there was internal and external pressures regarding religious broadcasting and especially for a more 'secular' Sunday. This was the theme picked up by Haley in his address to the British Council of Churches stating, religious broadcasting has grown and developed; other forms of broadcasting have grown and developed as well. The BBC no longer has strictly Sabbatarian Sunday programmes. The Corporation has added religious controversy to the other forms of broadcasts. It has stated that in its duty towards the search for truth it must broadcast statements of Unbelief as well as of differing Beliefs.[95]

So it became increasingly necessary for the Corporation to wean the British away from foreign stations and their popular appeal for the Sunday audiences. Even in his day Reith had no choice but to accept that the puritan Sunday could not survive the changes in social conditions and the increasing need for Sunday leisure to be reflected in broadcasting policy. In line with this Welch wanted to shift the weight of religious broadcasting from its Sunday context to the weekday: from a liturgical and homiletical to what is called a 'practical weekday Christianity'.[96]

In its own way religious radio was creating its own ghetto,[97] but many developments took place in the years before the Second World War. The Empire Service of the BBC began officially in 1932 under Reith's reign and opened up vast possibilities of establishing and maintaining contact with Christians all over the world and making the Gospel available to those of every race and religion who were able to listen. Another major contribution was made by two series of addresses, previously mentioned, *God and the World through Christian Eyes* and *The Way to God.* They dealt with fundamental beliefs and presented the faith in a comprehensive manner and were part of the policy of the Religious Broadcasting Department in its attempt in the 1930s to provide a more intellectual and reasoned approach to the Christian faith.[98]

But whilst juggling such issues, further tensions were added for the BBC and the Religious Broadcasting Department, in terms of war breaking out in 1939. Welch was aware that amongst his ranks of Christian broadcasters were those who were keen pacifists, but there was the notion that their personal convictions should not in any way undermine the Government position as Sir Allan Powell, Chairman of the BBC Board of Governors stated,

> it would not be proper and indeed would seem insincere to invite to the microphone anyone who is known publically to be opposed to the nation's war effort.[99]

The position of the Church on the impending war and a world in crisis had been previewed as early at 1935 when the then Archbishop of York, William Temple, gave an address on the BBC entitled, *The Christian and the World Situation*, in which he declared in writing and on air,

> although war is always contrary to the will of God, it is sometimes necessary for Christians to support the use of force for the upholding of international law.[100]

The *Radio Times* commenting that, "For ourselves this is one of the most impressive uses ever made of radio as an influence of public opinion".[101]

Like Reith before him with Sheppard and Elliott, Welch had his favoured broadcasters in the form of Temple and George Macleod, the latter from the Iona community in Scotland. Both were strong personalities and powerful and compelling preachers, with substantial followings. Temple's own Penguin book, *Christianity and Social Order* (1942) selling 139,000 copies. [102] Welch wanted both Temple and MacLeod at the microphone and not merely to offer the public the required balanced view consistent with BBC policy, but in regard to the war, Welch knew that both men would proclaim support for the war effort and speak in the national interest from theological convictions which were not so much above political discourse but rather moving in similar directions on a parallel track.[103]

Others however, because of their outspoken pacifist views had to be taken off the airwaves. This created some difficulty for the Religious Broadcasting Department, as they struggled to replace some popular presenters who had the inclination and skills on air.[104] Because of the

CHAPTER 2 GOD IS MARCHING ON

unease about controversial religious broadcasting at this time, what was worked out was a *Concordat* involving Welch as the Director of Religious Broadcasting, Nicolls as the Programme Controller and Sir Richard Maconachie as Director of Talks. The agreement accepted that even in the sensitive time of war, politics and economics could not be excluded from religious talks, something that CRAC supported in its meeting in 1941.[105]

So it is not surprising that religion now figured prominently in all general discussions about broadcasting policy in the war years. Basil Nicolls at the time insisting that,

> Consideration has to be given to the part that religion can play in the crisis ... and extra services of an intercessional kind may sometimes be appropriate.[106]

But the *Concordat* did not settle everything either for the BBC Governors or some BBC officials and discussions were on-going about religious programming. Programmes developed like *The Anvil* (1942), a sort of religious *Brains Trust*, where a panel of 4, representing the main strands of British Christianity took questions from listeners and provided honest Christian answers. The programme was highly successful and following the first broadcast almost a thousand letters were received in one week. The programme fulfilled Welch's vision for Christianity to stand on its own feet and not shy away from intellectual debate, no matter how uncomfortable that might become, especially in a time of war.

But religious issues, like political issues were also international in character and the question of how to treat the enemy was at least as basic to Christian behaviour as it was to political warfare.[107] During the early stages it was the policy not to allow religion to be used as a weapon of war against Germany, but as the war went on it proved extremely difficult to draw fine distinctions between religion as propaganda and religion as a spiritual force in its own right.[108]

But there is no doubt that religious broadcasting served as 'a very present help in the time of trouble' from the National Days of Prayer in 1940 and the campaign of the Big Ben Movement calling for silence/prayer nightly before the 9 o'clock news as Big Ben chimed, to the increased programming reflecting that the purpose of war being to defend Christian values and civilisations.[109]

It was estimated by 1943 that 50% of the whole UK adult audience listened to one or more of the broadcast Services and other religious items, the *Sunday Half Hour* and the *Forces Service* being some of the most popular.[110]

c) Sound and Vision

As Temple pointed out in the early 1940's, "the end of the war is bound to usher in a vast social transformation and the Church must be ready".[111] This was to be seen in society in general, in the Church, but within the BBC as well. So what we see after the war years was the gradual process in which a religious framework shifts from being the basis of a general broadcasting policy of the BBC to becoming the basis of the broadcasting policy of the Religious Broadcasting Department alone.[112] In that too whereas wartime was marked with a single of voice of Christianity to the nation and a level of freedom, in peacetime religious broadcasting began to have to justify more its very existence in the broadcast output and sought to do so.

Indeed, religious broadcasting showed it not only benefited people individually, it helped to preserve the corporate feeling of Britain as a Christian country, in a period of decline of the traditional religious observance and erosion of faith. Had it not been for the presence of religious broadcasting the trend towards secularism would certainly have been faster. But the role of religion within the BBC's work of broadcasting helped focus the attention of the nation upon great occasions in its history, including the moments of crisis like the war and it gave the expression to the national mood and the feeling that such great events created; events such as George V's Silver Jubilee, the Coronation of George V1, the Abdication and Remembrance Day broadcasts from the Cenotaph in London which had been a part of programming since 1928.[113]

Therefore, these factors and others described, constituted a new and enormously important element in the socio-economic scene. Large numbers of people completely or almost completely unassociated with organised Christianity by church membership or attendance at public worship, were regularly listening to the Christian message and worship and events of national importance and were being influenced for good in many ways. Religious broadcasting established a unique bridge across the widespread gulf between the church and the outsider.[114]

However, the introduction of the Home, Light and Third Programmes by the BBC proved problematic for the Religious Broadcasting Department. There was an increase in the popularity of the Light Programme, which would only broadcast religion during the week-end and five minute services during the week. At the same time there was a decrease of the Home Programme (the main outlet for religion). It seemed that the audience had spoken irrespective of the importance of cultural enlightenment.[115]

But one of the most insistent post-war requests was that the Service of Holy Communion should be broadcast. This raised many problems, ecclesiastical, technical and social. It would be an entirely new departure from the recognised practice of some twenty-five years of broadcasting in Britain. Some thought that this most cherished Sacrament might be cheapened or discredited by unbelievers overhearing in the wrong surroundings or unsuitable conditions. But the Service was offered as an experiment and drew an amazing and moving appreciation from the audience. Out of the crucible of tragedy and war had come a new and successful method of bringing the very heart of the Gospel of Christ, seeking to share its benefits in days of peace.[116]

Although considerations from the Church community were important, with Welch at the helm of the Religious Broadcasting Department, his view was that broadcast religion was not a component to serve a Christian minority of the population alone, it was to proclaim the Good News to all. Welch differentiated between three different categories of listener, the 'committed' Christians, the 'half-churched' who ears were half closed and the 'forces' whose ears were shut.[117] Welch was focussed in his attempts to make religious broadcasting have the widest possible appeal.

Although all religious broadcasting was in some sense evangelistic, the BBC never regarded its function to bring non-Christian listeners from a position of enquiry to a profession of religious faith, believing the latter could only occur within the context of the local church and that the task of religious broadcasting was to supplement the work of the churches to that end. An attempt by Scottish clergymen to make religious broadcasting focus more on being a tool for conversion largely failed at this time and a more inclusive vision prevailed. Francis House, succeeding Welch in 1947, assessed the thinking at the time,

> religious broadcasting in Britain is characterized by a combination of evangelistic intention, interdenominational co-operation and concern on the part of the broadcasting organisation itself to maintain standards in religious broadcasting at least as high as those experienced from other departments.[118]

This was a crucial time for the BBC and religious broadcasting, with the appointment of the Beveridge Committee (1949) tasked to look into the future of broadcasting. Central to this activity was the involvement of Francis House as the new Head of Religious Broadcasting, but also the Central Religious Advisory Committee who had played a crucial role in religious broadcasting since the days of Reith who had established it.

House prepared a report for the meeting of CRAC in October 1948 in which he set out four important aspects of Religious Broadcasting going forward.

1. to maintain "standards of truth, justice and honesty in private and public life".

2. to explain what the Christian faith is, to remove misunderstanding of it, and to demonstrate its relevance today.

3. to lead "non-church-goers" to see that any really Christian commitment involves active membership of a "actual church congregation" while at the same time giving "church-goers" a wider vision of what church membership involves.

4. to provide opportunities for that challenge to personal faith in Jesus Christ as Saviour and Lord which is the heart of "conversion". [119]

The Beveridge Committee received a variety of papers from religious groups and felt the best solution to blending the BBC's 'impartial search for truth' and its existence as a national institution 'set up by the state in a Christian country' was to allow the BBC's Talks Department to handle controversial religious material and the Religious Broadcasting Department to concentrate on more pastoral and exegetical programmes.[120] The Report restated the policy of the BBC in terms of religion as "a positive attitude towards Christian values, to safeguard them and foster acceptance of them".[121] The application of this policy over the years culminated in a most impressive number and variety of items, not only on Sundays, but spread over every day of the week – services, talks, discussions, dramatic presentations of religious themes for schools, children at home, youth and indeed for all who cared to listen. The staff of the Religion Department both in London and the regions had grown to meet the increasing demands of listeners led by Francis House and his second-in-command Agnellus Andrew from the Roman Catholic Church.[122]

Between 1945 and 1950 there was one major change initiated by the BBC and that was to drop the pre-war 'Sunday Programme policy'. The Director General, Haley talked of "Sunday entertainment" rather than following "the strict Sabbatarian rules". There were slightly fewer religious programmes than there had been during the war and in 1948 two hours and fifty minutes were being devoted to religious broadcasting on Sunday, but on weekdays the total fell from five hours twenty minutes to four hours forty minutes.[123]

A more detailed analysis of audience reactions, based on six thousand interviews relating to two typical Sundays in March and May 1948, showed that 37% of the adult population heard at least one main religious broadcast on any given Sunday. With the total audience being around 13 million listeners to BBC religious programmes on Sundays compared well with a churchgoing population estimated at between 2 million and 4 million, 7-15%.[124] See also further Listener Research Reports in Chapter 6.

Haley continued to be a strong protagonist for the place of religious broadcasting on the BBC, despite criticisms by rationalists and others who wanted quality access to the 'microphone'. In his 1948 policy address on *Moral Values in Broadcasting*, Haley stated,

> We are citizens of a Christian country, and the BBC – an institution set up by the State – bases its policies upon a positive attitude towards Christian values ... It seeks to safeguard those values and to foster acceptance of them. The whole preponderant weight of its programmes is directed towards this end.[125]

Haley went on to explain that the BBC was not set up to be an evangelistic arm of the churches, but that the Religious Broadcasting Department itself should be regarded in that way. Haley was able to carry his approach with the BBC Governors, especially when the British Council of Churches Report in 1950 praised the Head of Religious Broadcasting for his tolerant approach.[126] This was a most significant Report as it was the first external body to make a serious study of broadcasting and the culture of the time and it was the first serious attempt by the churches to evaluate religious broadcasting since the Report of the Canterbury Convocation in the 1930s. Its positive approach was deeply encouraging making the obvious point that "what the BBC does is provide churches with an immense congregation".[127]

However, at the time of the Report, it should be noted there was a sharp difference both between the position of Britain and the United States and between Britain and some other countries in the Commonwealth, where minor sects and some fundamentalist groups paid their way to the airwaves in a pattern that was not condoned by the Religious Broadcasting Department or the BBC in general.[128]

The other issue facing Francis House as Head of Religious Broadcasting on taking office was the development of television, something that Reith strongly disagreed with, as his speech in the House of Lords revealed,

> A principle absolutely fundamental and cherished is scheduled to be scuttled.. Somebody..introduced Christianity and the uses of electricity. And somebody introduced smallpox, bubonic plague and the Black Death. Somebody is minded now to introduce sponsored broadcasting into this country.[129]

In 1947 there were very few television sets (approximately 35,000) and reception at that time was limited to the London area. But discussions were already underway previously with Maurice Gorham, the former editor of the *Radio Times* and at that time Controller of the Light Programme, who was part of the internal review of the potential of television. With regard to religion he had noted in a memo to Welch, "I do not think religious programmes can play a large part in television, but I do want to see a certain amount".[130]

Welch's successor, House, eventually produced a lengthy Report in 1950, entitled *"Religious Programmes on Television"* expressing his view, "There are signs that the Churches are beginning to become aware of the growing importance of the influence of television".[131] Apart from a few seasonal exceptions religious broadcasting on television was fairly infrequent, but House was anxious that religion on television should not be left behind. With that in mind, House sought to engage an assistant in the form of Colin Beale from the British Churches Film Council. There was little doubt that television would increase and House planned to have an 'expert' in the system.[132] Beale indeed became a valuable asset and produced a Report, *The Scope and Character of Religious TV,* for the CRAC meeting in January 1952, in which he asserted,

> Television is now more than a local curiosity, before long it will be a nationwide medium of communication. We have been assured that the door for religious programmes on television

is wide open; it cannot be overemphasized that the door must be entered.[133]

By 1955, 'God-in-a-Box' (a later title adopted by Colin Morris for his renowned book on Christian Strategy in the Television Age), was a predictable development. Beale had reported to CRAC that in 1952 there had been 12 OB Services which had continued each year. In addition there were 15 Epilogues and in Children's Television there were 9 religious plays. He proposed Epilogues to grow to 52 weekly ones by 1954 and during 1955 more regular Sunday evening transmissions.[134]

Barnes, who had become the first Director of Television in 1950, had argued that there had to be ways of conveying the Christian message through television broadcasting other than religious services. But slow was the march from experimentation to establishment. Although the BBC stated "the fundamental religious policy of the BBC is the same for television as for sound broadcasting", there was little enterprise in early programming and all the emphasis was placed on the word 'experimental'.[135]

Despite this, Francis House remained optimistic and in his address to the Annual Religious Broadcasting Department Conference held in 1955 he declared,

> As one looks to the next five years it is clear that a greater proportion of the effort of the Department will be required for television programmes. I cannot prophesy the shape of things to come in the general structure of the Corporation, but so long as the BBC continues to produce both television and radio programmes, I believe that it is of considerable importance that religious broadcasting on radio and television should be the responsibility of a single department, in order to make sure that the proclamation of the Gospel and the presentation of the life and teaching of the churches on radio and television, should be animated by the same spirit, for the same purpose and in accordance with the same standards.[136]

CHAPTER 2 GOD IS MARCHING ON

Although Beale had taken up the new post of Religious Broadcasting Organiser for Television in 1954, the hoped for developments and acceleration of programme making was disappointingly slow because of budgets and personnel, though there were some highlights like the Communion Service as part of the Coronation in 1953, the Easter Communion from Chichester Cathedral in 1955, a range of documentary programmes in 1954 on Islam, Judaism and Hinduism, the Salvation Army programme called *Missing from Home* and a range of exclusive Epilogues with people like Mrs Fisher wife of the Archbishop of Canterbury and Dr.Billy Graham who had also featured in a special discussion with Malcolm Muggeridge on *Panorama* in May 1954.

On the verge of the launch of commercial television, surveys like *Religious Broadcasts and the Public* (1955) were being conducted to analyse the nature and success of Religious Broadcasting (See Chapter 6). But the period ended not with the issues of surveys but with controversy about the broadcasts of leading humanists like Margaret Knight of Aberdeen University. The broadcasts were to cause a furore in the press,[137] consternation in the Vatican and dismay by even the likes of Winston Churchill. To many it was a flawed decision by the BBC to allow such an explosive attack on Christianity at a time of impending media competition. But by the time House stepped down in 1955, the mantle was to be taken up by the Rev. Roy McKay who not only was comfortable for Christians and Christianity to face the humanist and atheistic criticisms and propaganda, but who went on to announce a considerable extension of religious television including a new cycle of plays by Joy Harrington about the life of Christ (filmed in Palestine), five minute religious items in the July children's programmes, a Sunday night epilogue and twenty four new discussion programmes a year, some of them with the title *Christian Forum*.[138]

But as the demise of the BBC monopoly arrived, it was clear that most church opinion, both Catholic and Protestant, was hostile to the Government's initial intimations about its plans for commercial broadcasting. It was also clear that television in Britain was about to change with increasing talk of sponsorship, independent production companies and special licences and the raising of the cost of it all through advertising. All of which, it was deemed, would cause challenges for the status of religious broadcasting.[13]

3. Summary

The story of broadcasting in America is the story of an experiment which became an art and an art which became a significant history. Right from its outset religious radio programmes formed an integral part in the development of network broadcasting with radio stations connected with religious broadcasting in three ways – by selling air-time to groups who would broadcast religion; by donating air-time and by broadcasting religious programmes of their own. Certainly the new platform of radio communication raised religious understanding to a new level and catapulted the driving personalities of religious broadcasting to a national and sometimes international prominence.

Although the intention of the FCC was that all religious radio should be representative of all faith groups, the eventual reality was that religious denominational groups grew into their own niche, either on existing stations or on their own independent ones and the role of government control in religious broadcasting turned out to be minimal, merely ensuring that the developing commercialisation process did not eliminate religious broadcasting from either network or local stations.

Although the potential radio was slow to be grasped in some quarters of religious leadership, by the 1930s its impact was better understood, as so ably expressed by Dr Franklin Dunham in his address to the National Council of Catholic Men.

> Holy Scriptures admonish us to hear the Word of God and keep it ... radio possesses the power to carry the Word of God to wildernesses wherein the weary blistered feet of His missionaries have never trod. It possesses likewise the power to carry His word to the lame, the halt, the blind and the man sick of palsy. No barriers of time nor space can halt its winged

words – the quality in it 'is not strained, it literally falleth like the gentle rain from Heaven to this earth'.[140]

In summary religious broadcasting in America was shown as a powerful influence, especially in American religious life, with the founding generations of radio preachers in the 1920s and 1930s. Radio helped ensure that the voice of religion continued to shape American culture during some of the most tumultuous decades of its history.[141] That influence only grew stronger and more pervasive with the rise of Christian television and radio networks and also became something of a resistance movement countering the growing secularization of the age.[142] Moreover, short-wave transmitters and later satellite technology fulfilled the aspirations especially of evangelical Christians who saw broadcasting media as almost God's chosen instrument for spreading the gospel to every continent, people and nation on earth.

In the context of the UK, the evidence clearly demonstrates that the development of religious broadcasting was also led by mainly individual personalities rather than the initiative of the Churches. The chief protagonist being Lord Reith himself and the preachers he brought to air like Dick Sheppard and W.H.Elliott, subsequently William Temple and George Macleod and in their time the Directors of Religious Broadcasting like Stobart, Iremonger, Welch and House. The impact and influence of these men cannot be overstated with the mainstream churches just following their lead.

Recognition has also to be given the Central Religious Advisory Committee (CRAC) and its regional counterparts, which Reith brought into existence in order to provide the necessary representation of the mainstream churches and advise on suitable people to broadcast on the BBC and decide how the BBC could best represent the nature of Christianity in the UK. Their contribution being vital during this period.

The Government too had a role to play through its various Committees and Reports and demonstrated an awareness that religious broadcasting needed to be a vital element within the output of the BBC and took serious note of the submissions, not only made by Reith and his successors on this, but of the Directors of Religious Broadcasting and the different mainstream denominations. In addition sometimes handling quite voracious attacks by those who were not of the same mind over the key role of Christianity in this country.

In the period considered in this chapter, the audience figures also demonstrate the popularity of religious broadcasting on radio. Listening to religious broadcasts of some nature became a significant part of the British psyche and those who broadcast became household names in their own right, often leaving churches overflowing with supporters. The tradition, established by Reith was that the BBC must boost Christianity as the 'official religion' of the country.

Eventually the value and credibility of religious broadcasting merited a dedicated Department and Director in the BBC and this Department made considerable contributions to bringing major national events to the listening public with a strong religious element always featured, whether that be in Coronations, in the time of War, Funerals or National Celebrations.

The unfolding story of religious broadcasting at the BBC shows a level of evolution rather revolution, moving from the very strict Sabbatarian outlook of Reith himself, with programming limiting the microphone to only certain contributors, to accepting controversy and debate on religious issues in a tolerant way, whilst still hoping that the personal faith of listeners would be encouraged and deepened.

Whether it be America or Britain we see in these formative years the strategic role that both on-air or off-air personalities made not only in birthing religious broadcasting and establishing it as key component of the broadcasting landscape of the time, but in crafting its development so that it had a significant impact on the social milieu of the era, both inside and outside of the Church.

CHAPTER 2 GOD IS MARCHING ON

NOTES

1. Howe, D. W., *What God Hath Wrought: The Transformation of America 1815-1848* (New York: Oxford University Press, 2007), p.1.

2. Pohlman, M. E., *Broadcasting the Faith: Protestant Religious Radio a Theology in America 1920-1950*. (PhD). Southern Baptist Theological Seminary (2011), p.1.

3. Bruce, S., *Pray TV: Televangelism in America* (London: Routledge, 1990), p.2.

4. Erickson, H., *Religious Radio and Television in the United States 1921 – 1991: The Programs and Personalities* (Jefferson: McFarland & Co. 1992), p.10.

5. Ibid., p.2.

6. Lochte, B., *Christian Radio: The Growth of a Mainstream Broadcasting Force* (Jefferson: McFarland & Co.2006), p. 26-27.

7. Hangen, T. J., *Redeeming the Dial: Radio Religion and Popular Culture in America* (Chapel Hill: University of North Carolina Press, 2002), p.57.

8. Armstrong, B., *The Electric Church* (Nashville: Thomas Nelson, 1979), p.27.

9. Knock Jr., S. F., *The Development of Network Religious Broadcasting in the United States 1923-1948*. (Masters). American University (1959), p.9.

10. Ellens, J. H., *Models of Religious Broadcasting* (Grand Rapids: W. B. Eerdmans, 1974), p.16.

11. Ward, S. M., *Air of Salvation: The Story of Christian Broadcasting* (Grand Rapids: Baker Books, 1994), p.204.

12. Sterling, C. H. and Kittross, J. M., *Stay Tuned: A Concise history of American Broadcasting*. 3rd edition (New Jersey: Edward Arnold, 2002), p.102.

13. Benjamin, L.M., *Freedom of the Air and the Public Interest: First Amendment Rights in Broadcasting to 1935* (Carbondale: Southern Illinois University Press, 1998), p.221.

14. Caldwell, L.G., The Standard of Public Interest: Convenience or Necessity as Used in the Radio Act of 1927 (*Air Law Review*, 1927),p.10-11.

15. Elvy, P., *Buying Time: The Foundations of the Electronic Church* (Great Wakering: McCrimmons, 1986), p.36.

16. Ibid., p.36.

17. Ward, S.M. (1994), p.204.

18. Lochte, B. (2006), p.22.

19. Schultze, Q. J., *Televangelism and American Culture: The Business of Popular Religion* (Grand Rapids: Baker Book House, 1991), p.31.

20. Lochte, B. (2006), p.28.

21. Armstrong, B. (1979), p.39.

22. Hangen, T.J. (2002), p.12-23.

23. Ibid., p.26.

24. Ward, S.M. (1994), p.234.

25. Bruce, S., (1990), p.28-29.

26. Melton, J. G., Lucas, P. C. and Stone, J. R., *Prime Time Religion: An Encyclopaedia of Religious Broadcasting*. (Phoenix: Oryx Press, 1997), p.387.

27. Ward, S.M. (1994), p.56.

28. Armstrong, B. (1979), p.178-180.

29. Ward, S.M. (1994), p.69-70.

30. Lochte, B. (2006), p.39.

31. Dubourdieu, W. J., 1933. *Religious Broadcasting in the United States*. Unpublished. (PhD). Northwestern University (1933), p.10.

32. National Broadcasting Company, *Broadcasting in the Public Interest*. (New York: NBC, 1939), p.57.

33. Loveless, W. P., *Manual of Gospel Broadcasting*. (Illinois: Moody Press, 1946), p.13.

34. Johnstone, R. L., Who Listens to Religious Broadcasts Anymore? *Journal of Broadcasting*, 16 (1) 1971: 120.

35. Bruce, S. (1990), p.29.

36. Armstrong, B. (1979), p.60.

37. Rosenthal, M., *Protestants and TV in the 1950s: Responses to a New Medium*. (New York: Macmillan, 2007), p.43-4.

38. Ward, S.M. (1994), p.76-81.

39. Ellens, J.H. (1974), p.88-90.

40. Editorial, America's Television Bishop. *Yorkshire Post and Leeds Mercury*. 4th April, (1953), p.5.

41. Rosenthal, M. (2007), p.44-45.

42. Hoover, S. M., 1988. *Mass Media Religion: The Social Sources of the Electronic Church*. (Newbury Park: Sage, 1988), p.52.

43. Bruce, S. (1990), p.35.

44. Ibid., p.37.

45. Lochte, B. (2005), p.27.

46. Matelski, M. J., *Vatican Radio: Propagation by the Airways*. (Westport: Praegar, 1995), p.20.

47. Bowman, E. G., *Eyes Beyond the Horizon* (Nashville: Thomas Nelson,1991), p.174.

48. Ibid., p.179.

49. Freed, P., *Towers to Eternity*. (Waco: Word, 1968), p.89.

50. Ibid., p.99.

51. Shurick, E. P. J., *The First Quarter of American Broadcasting* (Kansas City: Midland Publishing, 1946), p.310.

52. Paulu, B., *Television and Radio in the United Kingdom* (London: MacMillan,1981), p.274.

53. Cooper, B. G., *Religious Broadcasting in Britain 1922-1939*. Unpublished. (PhD). Oxford University (1962), p.45-46.

54. Clericus, *BBC Religion* (London: Watts & Co.1942), p.10.

55. Higgins, C., *This New Noise*. (London: Guardian Books, 2015), p.15.

56. Editorial, Broadcast Religion. *Radio Magazine*. June (1934), p.49.

57. Wolfe, K. M., *The Churches and the British Broadcasting Corporation 1922-1956. The Politics of Broadcast Religion*. (London: SCM, 1984), p.5.

58. Wallis, R., *Looking on Glass*. Unpublished. (Masters). Exeter University (1987), p.20.

59. Dinwiddie, M., *Religion by Radio: Its Place in British Broadcasting* (London: George Allen & Unwin Ltd. 1968), p.31.

60. Quicke, A. and Quicke, J., *Hidden Agendas: The Politics of Religious Broadcasting in Britain 1987 – 1991*. (Virginia Beach: Dominion Kings Grant Publications, 1992), p.32-54.

61. Cooper, B.G. (1962), p.27.

62. Dinwiddie, M. (1968), p.46.

63. Correspondent, Largest Pulpit in the World. *Radio Magazine*. 14th November (1934), p.49.

64. Editorial, Religion that is Broadcast. *Radio Times*. 6th February (1925), p.1.

65. Editorial, The World We Listen In. *Radio Times*. 20th May (1932), p.466.

66. BBC Handbook (1932), p.216.

67. Sheppard, H. R. L., Wider Scope than Wesley's. *The Radio Times*. 2nd March (1928), p.430.

68. Lischer, R., *Theories of Preaching*. (Durham: Labyrinth Press, 1987), p.81.

69. Taylor, C., The Church and Radio. *St.Martin's Review* (1947), p.146-150.

70. Cooper, B.G. (1962), p.101.

71. Grayston, K., Religious Broadcasting in Great Britain. *World Dominion*, January/February (1951), p.51.

72. Briggs, A., *The History of Broadcasting in the United Kingdom*. Vol. 11: *The Golden Age of Wireless* (Oxford: Oxford University Press, 1965), p.211.

73. BBC Handbook (1933), p.27.

74. in Allighan, G., *Sir John Reith*. London: Stanley Paul and Co.1938), p.230.

75. Eckersley, R., *The BBC and All That*. London: Samson Law Marston & Co.1946), p.123, 162-164.

76. Briggs, A. (1965), p.48ff.

77. Ibid., p.218-219.

78. Church of England's Convocation Report (1931), p.3.

79. Wolfe, K.M. (1984), p.33-35.

80. Editorial, Religion and the BBC. *The Times*. June 24th (1931), p.13.

81. Davidson, R., Broadcasting as a National Service. *Radio Times*. 17th December (1926), p.669.

82. Cooper, B.G. (1962), p.84.

83. BBC Handbook (1934), p.91.

84. Wolfe, K.M. (1984), p.14.

85. BBC Handbook (1928), p.131.

86. BBC, *Religious Broadcasting: History and Current Practice*.The First 10 Years 1922–1932. (London: 1943), BBC WAC. File Ref: R34/815/2, p.1.

87. Eckersley, P. P., *The Power behind the Microphone* (London: Jonathan Cape,1941), p.100.

88. Briggs, A. (1965), p.230.

89. Wolfe, K.M. (1984), p.146.

90. Welch, J. W., Religious Broadcasting. *St Martin's Review*. (1944), p.25.

91. Noonan, C., The Production of Religious Broadcasting: the Case of the BBC. (PhD). Glasgow University (2009), p.69.

92. Wolfe, K.M. (1984), p.205.

93. Dinwiddie, M. (1968), p.179.

94. Wolfe. K. M., *Religious Broadcasting Now: British Religious Broadcasting in Perspective* (London: IBA, 1983), p.10.

95. Haley, W., *Moral Values in Broadcasting* (London: British Council of Churches, 1948), p.6.

96. Wolfe, K.M. (1984), p.174.

97. Fortner, R. S., *Radio, Morality and Culture* (Illinois: Southern Illinois University Press, 2005), p.192.

98. Dinwiddie, M. (1968), p.25.

99. Powell, A., *Letter to William Paton at the World Council of Churches*: 3rd December (1940), BBC WAC. File Ref: R4/72/1.

100. Temple, W. E., 1935. The Christian and the World Situation. *The Listener*. 4th September (1935), p.375-376.

101. Editorial, The Archbishop's Plea. *Radio Times*. 13th September (1935), p. 2.

102. Briggs, A., *The History of Broadcasting in the United Kingdom* Vol. 111: *The War of Words.* (London: Oxford University Press, 1970), p.622.

103. Wolfe, K.M. (1984), p.176.

104. Noonan, C. (2009), p.62.

105. CRAC Meeting (1941) *Minutes* BBC WAC.File Ref: R32/67/1.

106. CRAC Meeting, (1940) *Minutes* BBC WAC.File Ref.R34/814/1.

107. Briggs, A. (1970), p.630.

108. Ibid., p.633.

109. Briggs, A., *The BBC: The First Fifty Years.* (Oxford: Oxford University Press, 1985), p.217.

110. Dinwiddie, M. (1968), p.115.

111. Temple, W. E., *Citizen and Churchman*. (London: Eyre and Spottiswood, 1941), p.83.

112. Wallis, R. (1987), p.32.

113. Cooper, B.G (1962), p.99.

114. Ibid., p.100.

115. Noonan, C. (2009), p.65.

116. Dinwiddie, M. (1968), p.29.

117. Quicke, A. and Quicke, J. (1992), p.32.

118. House, F., *The Church on the Air: The Work of the Religious Broadcasting Department* (London: BBC, 1949), p.3.

119. House, F., *Confidential Paper Prepared for CRAC*. (London: 1948), BBC WAC. File Ref: R6/17/1.

120. Quicke, A., and Quicke, J. (1992), p.32.

121. Report of the Broadcasting Committee 1951, *(Beveridge Report)* Cmnd.8116. (London: HMSO), p.63-66.

122. Dinwiddie, M. (1968), p.29-30.

123. in Wolfe, K.M. (1984), p.356.

124. Briggs, A., *The History of Broadcasting in the United Kingdom*. Vol. V: *Competition* (Oxford: Oxford University Press, 1995), p.704.

125. in Wolfe, K.M. (1984), p.362.

126. British Council of Churches, *Christianity and Broadcasting* (London: 1950), Church of England Archive Centre. File Ref: BCC/10/5/29, p.68.

127. Ibid., p.39.

128. Briggs, A. (1995), p.710.

129. Reith, J. C. W., *Speech to the House of Lords*. 22nd May (1952), Hansard Col.1297.

130. Gorham, M.A.C., *Memo: To J. Welch.* 17th January (1946), BBC WAC. File Ref: R17/174/2.

131. House, F., *Religious Programmes on Television* (London: BBC, 1950), p.5.

132. Wolfe, K.M. (1984), p.404.

133. Beale, C., *Scope and Character of Religious Television* (London. BBC, 1952), p.1.

134. Ibid., p.3.

135. in Briggs (1995), p.713.

136. House, F., *Religious Broadcasting: 1945 – 1955.* Annual Conference of Religious Broadcasting Department (1955),BBC WAC. File Ref: T16/183/3, p.6

137. Correspondent, 1955. Morals without Religion. *The Times.* 20th January (1955), p.5.

138. Briggs, A, (1995), p.732.

139. Noonan, C. (2009), p.70-71.

140. in Shurick, E. P. J. (1946), p.94.

141. Pohlman, M. E., *Broadcasting the Faith: Protestant Religious Radio a Theology in America 1920-1950.* (PhD). Southern Baptist Theological Seminary (2011), p.4.

142. Berger. P., From the Crisis of Religion to the Crisis of Secularity. *In:* Douglas, M. and Tipton, S., *Religion and America: Spirituality in a Secular Age* (Boston: Beacon Press, 1982), p.16.

CHAPTER 3

NEW HORIZONS
The Expansion of Religious Television and Radio 1955-1995

The purpose of this chapter is to trace how the early experiments in religious television were catapulted into a significant media expansion both in the United States and Britain and how also in the breaking of the mould of the BBC monopoly, the commercial trends of America became prevalent in the UK both in television and radio, providing new horizons and opportunities for religious broadcasting.

1. The American Experience

The television medium began to captivate the entire nation in 1950, although less than 10% of all households held a TV set. But by 1955 most areas of the country had television stations and 65% of the nation's households owned a set. By the end of the decade television was nationwide and nine out of ten homes across the country had sets[1] and by the mid 1980s there were more than 8,400 radio stations, more than 980 commercial and non-commercial television stations in the country with 96% of homes with television sets and about 98.5% of American homes with at least one radio set.[2] What soon became obvious was that,

> the content of politics, religion, education and everything else that comprised public business would need to change and be recast in terms that were most suitable for television.[3]

In terms of religious programmes on television, these were not a new phenomenon and were part of the schedules since television began in the USA just as religious programmes, as we have seen, were part of the early broadcasts on radio. But as Hill pointed out "religious broadcasting was to become the most rapidly growing area of communications".[4] However such developments were not universally popular, some feeling that, "radio and television are powerful agents towards the further materialization of the minds of men.. They are part of a godless technocracy".[5]

The first regular television broadcasts had been made in 1939 and 1940 by the NBC network and in terms of religious broadcasting it was dominated by the three major faith groups: Roman Catholics, Protestants and Jews, but it was not really until 1947 that religious organisations really grasped the potential for television.[6] The practice of the networks was to deal primarily with these mainline religious groups. Catholics were represented by the National Council of Catholic Men, Jews by the Jewish Seminary of America and Protestants by the Federal Council of Churches of Christ and also the National Religious Broadcasters Association. These groups enjoyed working relationships with radio networks and when television emerged these relationships were extended into the new medium.[7]

It was the 1950s that became the heyday of network mainline religious programming (for clarity 'mainline' will be used in relation to the Roman Catholic Church and those Protestant Churches identified with the National Council of Churches. The terms "Evangelical", "Fundamentalist" and or "Conservative" will be used to identify those churches or broadcast groups affiliated with the National Religious Broadcasters or its parent body, National Association of Evangelicals). Programmes from the mainline denominations such as *Lamp unto My Feet* (CBS), *Directions* (ABC), *Frontiers of Faith* (NBC) and *Look up and Live* (CBS) all began production in this period.[8]

Television, like other new communications media before it, prompted a renewed hope for mass evangelism.[9] Both the Broadcast and Film Commission (BFC) and the National Religious Broadcasters (NRB) were founded out of the conviction that the preaching of the Gospel on the airwaves was significant for the nation as a public service and that it also needed to be protected. This conviction however was interpreted from completely different perspectives.[10] So when television arrived the more innovative of the independent Christian groups, who lacked free air-time and resources of the large mainline denominations, developed the structure and charisma for attracting substantial financial support from the viewing audience to enable them to purchase commercial air-time from stations. It was these independent, audience-supported evangelists who eventually took over the religious airwaves in the 1960s and 1970s and earned the nickname "televangelists" and became part of a movement that was dubbed the "electric church" originally by Ben Armstrong.

> The unprecedented linking of twentieth-century technology with Christ's commandment, *Go ye into all the world and preach the gospel to every creature*, has created a dynamic new phenomena that I call *the electric church*".[11]

Some have felt in the context of religious broadcasting that this Great Commission turned into the Great Commotion.[12] But there is no doubt that the "electronic church" as it also became known, had immense impact and was characterized by the strong personalities of its leaders. Its history and the use of mass communication to preach the gospel can be traced to the tradition of the revivalists of the 19th Century like Charles Finney, Dwight Moody and Billy Sunday.[13] In fact the circus-styled revivalism shaped the spirit and structure of American Protestantism, which in its wildest forms saw Protestant worship with staged healings, clownish preachers and cheering congregations.[14] But more than the mainline churches, these new broadcast ministries largely depended on the savvy, ability and fame of individual preachers, evangelists and revivalists. Like Hollywood or show business generally, televangelism relied extensively on public persona. John Corry writing in the *New York Times* reflected, "the preachers understand television and they use it very well. For one thing they entertain using their own personalities to comfort and inspire".[15]

Television made many of the televangelists 'stars' in their own right[16] and changed the standard conventions for proclaiming the gospel.[17] One critic however put it as starkly as this,

> on television, religion like everything else, is presented, quite simply and without apology as entertainment. Everything that makes religion an historic, profound and sacred human activity is stripped away; there is no ritual, no dogma, no tradition, no theology, and above all, no sense of spiritual transcendence. On these shows the preacher is tops. God comes out as a second banana.[18]

A similar assertion was made by Dennis Benson, a Presbyterian clergyman who had spent years exploring religious communications and commenting,

> I don't think religion can be broadcast. The lumpy nature of linear religious chunks thrown into most station formats causes media indigestion. The depth of the message is eroded by the inconsistent forms we use for the media presentation. The only place for the rigid programming is the Sunday morning ghetto. Here it reaches those who are already within the faith community.[19]

As a media phenomenon, certainly the electronic church was far more dependent upon charismatic leadership than the local church.[20] It is very clear from a detailed study of the audience for religious broadcasting in the 1950s that the most popular programmes were those which were structured around a single strong personality.[21] Televangelism reflects the American pre-occupation with stardom and celebrity status, matching what Barnouw described as "an image empire" (1970). Americans being not as much interested in ideas and perspectives, debates and dialogue, as they are in people and personality. Indeed the televangelist and message were so intertwined that even many regular viewers equate the ministry with the preacher, when in fact they were usually large organisations that carried on the multifaceted work of the typical TV ministry.[22]

In the United States televangelism was an outgrowth of commercial broadcasting. Both types of broadcasting were based on the modern concept of marketing, which insists that products and services should be tuned in to the wants and needs of consumers. Not all religious messages will sell in the competitive TV environment and the market shaped a televangelist's message and its presentation. The terrain illustrates,

> a global development of this religious market as a specialized genre and where the globalization of religion has led to a massive global trade in religious commodities.[23]

Writing in the *New York Times* Ernest Holsendolp also observed,

> Religious broadcasting is one of the fastest growing sectors in communication and to the consternation of many established churches. Paid religious broadcasting is big business with revenues often estimated to exceed 500 million dollars a year.[24]

By contrast the mainline Protestant and Roman Catholic broadcasters tried to avoid even the appearance of commercialism by refusing to solicit funds or shape programme content to be competitive in the commercial TV ratings race or exert TV viewers to seek personal salvation.[25]

If televangelism is any type of religious institution it is part of what has been called "the invisible church". It is a congregation without a real church – just a collection of believers tied together by their allegiance to a television ministry or its leader, similar to the case argued by Luckmann (1967). The leading lights in the 'electric church' do not represent actual church and indeed they do not occupy themselves with denominational concerns. With the exception of Robert Schuller and Mother Angelica they are clearly identified with the conservative or fundamentalist movements, which although were strong were nevertheless minorities within American Christendom. With only a few exceptions they owned or operated their own broadcasting networks, free from denominational control or investment.[26]

Changes in the relative structures of religious television began to occur in the 1960s. Religious Broadcasters were really faced with four options. They could operate their own stations at an enormous cost, or they could buy expensive blocks of time on existing networks. Or they could hope that stations would broadcast the public service announcements they sent or alternatively choose to buy advertising time.[27] Some argued that paid advertisements had certain advantages over full length programming and that these 'spots' could be used for worthwhile purposes. For example Edward Carnell of the Fuller Theological Seminary wrote,

> One of the most promising outlets that even a local church can sustain is to devise a tele-commercial, a sixty second drama from life which vividly advertises both the gospel and the church which preaches it. These dramas, carefully filmed, can be presented over and over, just as are advertisements for cigarettes. Through this means the gospel can repetitiously reach ears and eyes in the parlours of the nation. Furthermore such 'shorts' can be produced with a minimum of expertise.[28]

Overall there was a marked decrease in the broadcasting on sustaining time and the corresponding growth in both the nature and size of the independently syndicated evangelical programmes which were broadcast on purchased time.[29] So by 1977, 92% of religious television was on air-time that had been paid for.[30] Even the Pope Paul V1 in 1963 felt broadcasting was such an important opportunity in society as to warrant a Decree,

> Catholic programmes should be promoted in which listeners and viewers can be brought to share in the life of the Church and learn religious truths. An effort should also be made, where it maybe necessary, to set up Catholic stations. In such instances, however, care must be taken that their programmes are outstanding for their standards of excellent and achievement.[31]

It is important also to note also that in the context of religious broadcasting in America, the sheer size and vibrancy of US Pentecostalism particularly within the religious world was an important catalyst, as it accumulated resources, set up publishing houses, funded radio stations and created the platforms for some of the leading televangelists.[32] So during the 1960s and 70s the growth of the 'electric church' became spectacular.

Starting in Akron, Ohio, Rex Humbard (See Chapter 4) was one of the first evangelists (1952) to build a ministry that incorporated radio and television programming. In some way he was the prototype of the TV preachers and began his television ministry in 1953. Over the next 13 years he built up his programme *Cathedral of Tomorrow* until he was able to buy time regularly on 68 stations, rising to over 200 stations by 1973.[33]

Evangelists like Dr.Billy Graham and Oral Roberts (See Chapter 4) adapted tried and true approaches to this new medium and although Graham was not initially interested in broadcasting, Graham's *Hour of Decision* programme and television specials drew evangelical leaders to the potential of national-level broadcasting and became an early model for the electronic church,[34] making him one of the best known evangelists of his time and the voice of evangelical Christianity for millions around the world.[35]

Oral Roberts (See Chapter 4) made the transition from tent crusader as the "King of Faith Healers" into radio and television broadcasting. By 1955, Roberts was the national leader of paid religious television[36] and in the 1960s expanded his ministry into education with the Oral Roberts University (1963) and the City of Faith Hospital and Research Centre.[37] His tolerance for theological diversity led him to work with a wide range of Christian groups and his upbeat message of hope was combined with promises of health, happiness and prosperity.

Robert Schuller is one of the only televangelists from a mainline denomination. His programme *Hour of Power,* broadcast from his all glass church called the Crystal Cathedral, vied with Oral Roberts for the most watched televangelist. But by 1994 the programme was so rated, being seen in 44 foreign countries by an estimated 20 million viewers with special foreign language versions.[38] Starting in 1960 independent evangelical organisations also began to purchase and establish their own television stations and to develop their own programming networks. By 1978 there were approximately 30 religious television stations with another 30 applications for a television licence by religious groups before the Federal Communications Committee (FCC).[39]

There is no single reason for the rise of the 'electronic church' but by far the greatest boost it had came from what William Fore describes as the "spirit of de-regulation",[40] when in 1960 the FCC released a statement transforming religious broadcasting and opening the door for televangelists. The statement made it clear that the FCC would make no distinction between paid-time programmes and sustaining-time programmes when evaluating a station's performance in the public interest.[41] The 1960 FCC decision effectively broke the broadcast oligopoly of mainline church organisations by opening religious broadcasting to all who could afford to pay for it. It encouraged the development of many 'electric church' congregations that existed only via broadcasting and were financially self-perpetuating. Radio had seen a few of these, but television was to foster even more.[42] As quoted, just before the FCC ruling too, in effect only 53% of all religious broadcasting was paid time. But by 1977, paid time religious broadcasting had risen to 92%. Since the mid-1970s religious broadcasting has been firmly in the hands of the televangelists.[43] For as Fore points out, the mainline churches simply failed to understand and meet the needs of a significant number of people in their communities, people who were searching for a satisfying religious experience but who had not found it in the mainline churches, but found their solace in the ministries of the electronic church.[44]

This new seed-bed was a boost to existing TV broadcasters, but it became a golden opportunity for people like Pat Robertson, host of the *700 Club* programme and head of the first religious TV station Christian Broadcasting Network (See Chapter 4), plus a whole host of others like Jim Bakker and his wife Tammy Faye with their PTL Network (See Chapter 7), which developed into a multi million-dollar television ministry composed of a cable network and a real estate venture known as Heritage USA and Jimmy Swaggart who led one of the largest tele-ministries in the United States with an estimated $141 million dollar worldwide organisation and 8 million viewers per week[45] – one of the highest-rated religious telecasts in America (See Chapter 4). In addition Jerry Falwell's *Old Time Gospel Hour* and *Listen America* radio broadcasts from his church in Lynchburg Virginia, was to be the launch pad of a very powerful political lobby known as the Moral Majority (1979) which was to unite thousands of Christians on issues like abortion, pornography, homosexuality and moral and family values, in effect "the electronic church created a new counter culture. Its goals were restorative. To restore morality to America and to restore dignity to the family".[46] This 'New Christian Right' many believed even had some influence on the election of Ronald Reagan as President in 1980.[47]

It needs to be remembered also that fund-raising became a critical task for these independent religious broadcasters with the sale of books, tapes, films, Bibles and other religious artefacts, as were on-air appeals in some cases with the promise of 'success and prosperity' as a reward in return for a monetary contribution.[48] *Time Magazine* commented, "the preachers fund-raising became the stuff of jokes and sometimes of scandal".[49]

The media ministries needed to create and sustain an impression of growth and momentum that would attract viewers, win their loyalty and enthusiasm and motivate them to provide a dependable financial base for the ministry.[50] The 1987 survey of top televangelists by *Christianity Today*,[51] found in fact that viewer donations were a prime source of funding (average gifts around $30) for the televangelists and on average they spent 11.7% of their income on fund-raising. In the 1970s the annual expenditure of TV ministries for air time went from around 50 million dollars to 600 million. By the end of the decade there were 30 religiously orientated TV stations, more than a thousand religious radio stations and 4 religious networks all of them supported by audience contributions.[52]

As Gentry points out,

> the evangelists however sincere in their vision of God's will, are also entrepreneurs, who must reach an audiences with

messages provocative enough that viewers will fund their broadcast ministries through contributions.[53]

In terms of leadership and persona these broadcasters were significant innovators in their own sphere and innovation has proved to be critical in the process of strategic competitiveness,[54] a key factor in the development of religious broadcasting generally and specifically with the 'electric church' in particular.

However the issue of financial mismanagement, as well as sexual scandals amongst some of the televangelists,[55] led to a major drop in income amongst the tele-ministries and most were forced to scale back their organisations and the amount of airtime they purchased, though with the development of cable in the 1980s this became a significant platform for the likes of the Christian Broadcasting Network (CBN), Mother Angelica's Eternal Word Network (See Chapter 4) and the Trinity Broadcasting Network[56] and other programme providers like the Salem Media Group (See Appendix 2).

Harold Ellens writing in the 1970s tried to encapsulate the different approaches of religious broadcasting in America. In his *Models of Religious Broadcasting* (1974) he analyses four main approaches. The 'pulpit model' where sermon and sermon-type formats are the focal point of religious broadcasting and the preacher is almost the programme.[57] The second is a development on that, which he calls the 'Mighty Acts of God', where preaching is important, but it is significant as part of a total spectacle like the famous Billy Graham Crusades.[58] The third type, Ellens calls 'the instructional model' where broadcasters believe the church should use radio and television to teach and see the camera and microphone as an extension of the lecture-hall podium, along the lines of Dr. M.R. De Hann's *Radio Bible Class*.[59] Finally he describes the 'leaven model' where religious reflections are inserted into regular programming which is not unlike a commercial advertisement in its format.[60]

One way or another through these different formats religious broadcasting continued to make a significant impact. Despite all the negative issues, by the 1980s it is estimated that approximately one in three adults (60 million) were watching religious television in any given month.[61] But how many people actually watched religious television we don't know, but we suspect the number is substantially less than the TV preachers and secular press claimed (See Chapter 6). Whatever the actual count, the number is large enough to alert us to the fact that we are talking about a significant social phenomena in American society,[62] though the study by Stacey and Shupe indicates that televangelism preaches to the converted, who are already predisposed or self-selected to seek out its message and are persons who are members of fundamentalist congregations and or persons with highly orthodox religious beliefs.[63] As Jacques Ellul explained the best propaganda is to tell the people what they already want to believe.[64]

For some, televangelism was more about the business of marketing than the task of ministry.[65] Oberdorfer points out that the renowned media theorist, William Schramm, believed that the electronic media will not by themselves effectively communicate or transport the essence of Christianity. The media may stir up, challenge, evoke introspective examination, create some degree of desire for change, entertain or even educate, but until the human component is added that communication effort is less than successful.[66]

However, what we had in the American 'electronic church' is a phenomenon that gained immense power, almost entirely through the use of radio and television. It was estimated, for example, that one in 10 of all radio stations was religious in nature, approximately 1600 in total and mushrooming into a three billion dollar industry.[67] The televangelists used this power to join forces with the political right seeking to bring about a nation more in conformity to the demands of Christianity.[68] But fast forwarding to 1995, television is no longer a new medium and we take it for granted we live in a media-saturated world. The Christian Right is not so new anymore and evangelicals are not scorned as 'fundamentalists' but rather now courted as potential voters and an important market segment and the decline of mainline Protestantism both in numbers and influence is readily apparent to all.[69]

Although some of the major denominations are still involved in religious broadcasting, American religious television is so obviously dominated by fundamentalists, evangelicals and Pentecostals that it requires a mental effort not to treat televangelism and religious television as synonyms.[70] Were one looking for near-monopolies, one would simply note that more than half the airings of religious programmes are accounted for by just ten programmes and they are all evangelical or fundamentalist.[71]

With few exceptions, most TV ministries in the United States were audience-supported, personality led, experientially validated, technologically sophisticated, entertainment-orientated and expansionary minded. These six characteristics both define the electronic church and distinguish it from the broader category of 'religious broadcasting'.[72] In America all this became possible because of a largely non-interventionist regime by Government.[73]

There was unquestionably a substantial expansion of religious broadcasting in the USA,

> through cable and satellite technology, Christian media enjoys more coverage than ever before. But this same technology by giving audiences vastly expanded choices, has fragmented the viewing public into small niches based upon individual interests. As syndication gave way to Christian networks, broadcasters faced the potential of being relegated to a 'religious channel ghetto' seen only by Christians. Their challenge was to find ways of using the media technologies now being developed to meet viewers needs and reach out to the broader public.[74]

Modern day religious broadcasters are likely to be part of a vast bureaucratic operation which has diversified into a range of supporting enterprises. In most cases, the expansion has been towards creating an alternative community, a sub-culture of evangelical and fundamentalist piety, or in the case of networks, towards developing technology which can support such a community.

As Hoover summarizes in his reflection of religious broadcasting,

> Religious broadcasting is first of all a religious activity, produced by people who share common symbols, values and a 'moral culture' they celebrate. Second, electronic church broadcasting is embedded in the wider neo-evangelical and fundamentalist revivals of recent years. As such, it is tied to both the conservativeand the more mainstream wings of American religion. Third, the electronic church is a form of broadcasting. It shares formal and informal elements with all broadcasting, and its meaning is partly shaped by that context. Fourth, religious broadcasting has its own institutional and political structure. The organisations that produce these programs have their own histories and politics, and we must try to understand them. Fifth, religious broadcasting has come to have an influence on all religious institutions in America, even outside its fundamentalist and evangelical roots. Finally, religious broadcasting has influence on American culture itself. Such religiously based revitalization movements have had social and political implications beyond their spiritual bases.[75]

2. The Mould is Broken in the UK

The year 1955 saw a marked change in the development of television in the UK. Not only did three million more people start to watch programmes, but after September 1955 those in the London area had the opportunity of choosing to view either the programmes transmitted by the BBC or that transmitted by the new commercial companies.[76]

The monopoly enjoyed by the BBC in television was threatened, even though under its rule television had grown beyond the stage of being a novelty with an expansion from seven thousand five hundred licences in 1946, to a quarter of a million by 1949 and to about 5 million by the end of 1955 with a coverage of about 90% of the country.[77] Despite the hopes of the Beveridge Committee (1950) to preserve the monopoly of the BBC, the monopoly game was over and the Television Act of 1954 paved the way for the creation of the Independent Television Authority (later in 1972 to be called the Independent Broadcasting Authority – IBA) and its programme services known in 1955 as Independent Television – ITV.[78]

When Parliament was debating the Television Act in the early 1950s, Anglican and other church leaders strongly opposed commercial television, probably fearing an import of the American model we have illustrated earlier. Garbett for example, who had Chaired CRAC, speaking to a conference in 1952 said he feared television becoming commercialised rather than remaining an exclusively public medium.[79] Certainly in comparison with the American product, British religious broadcasting seemed immensely staid. Where televangelists in the United States preached their distinctive gospel, criticized those who disagreed with them and attempted to recruit followers for their particular brand, British religious broadcasting early on established itself as ecumenical, denominational, tolerant and uncontroversial.

The BBC position was set out in their Handbook in this period,

> Religious broadcasting has had a place in BBC programmes from the very earliest days, and new varieties of religious radio and television programmes are to be heard or seen every year; but the fundamental principles of religious broadcasting have remained essentially unchanged. The first is that the content of these broadcasts should be what is actually taught and practised by the principal organised expressions of religious life in the country – the Christian Churches. The second is that these broadcasts should not be planned only for church-goers, but for all who wish to listen to them and view them. The third is that the standards of performance in religious broadcasting should be comparable to those demanded in other programmes.[80]

Given this background, it is not surprising that ITV made considerable efforts to establish a strong religious broadcasting structure and output that would have a wider appeal. They set up a consultative committee parallel to the BBC (CRAC), organised religious broadcasting workshops attended by representatives of various churches[81] and set up various nationwide consultations. From the very start of ITV, the programme companies demonstrated their readiness to produce a significantly greater number of religious programmes than might reasonably have been considered necessary by the 1954 Act's requirements to balance programmes.[82]

The period 1956 to 1976 saw considerable growth in religious broadcasting, especially in television, as the BBC and the new ITV programme makers expanded the range of religious television programmes. The BBC Religious Television Department producing the highly successful *Jesus of Nazareth* (1956) drama[83] and since 1957, ITV developed Sunday morning broadcasts of church services from all parts of the country with production centres outside London, creating programmes for their own viewers. For example Scottish Television produced its first Jewish series in 1976, with companies in Wales and Ulster turning out many programmes,[84] whilst ATV who had made the first regular weekly religious television programme called *About Religion* (1956), also later producing a special series for schools, with the purpose to "reveal the importance of religious belief in the development of man and to examine the role of Christianity in this context".[85] Meanwhile the ABC network made their own religious programmes *Living Your life* (1957) and the popular *Sunday Break* (1958) between 6.15pm and 7.00pm on Sundays, as well as a range of week-night Epilogues produced in the regions.

In the early days of television, religious broadcasting held a privileged position within both television channels, much to the dismay of critics like the National Secular Society stating "there is partiality in practice but an arrogant refusal to recognise impartiality in theory. This is religious broadcasting".[86] But despite such criticism both the BBC and ITV were indeed able to establish a 'protected hour' between 6.15pm and 7.25pm on Sundays (better known as the 'Closed Period'). Though in television "ecology" granting the religious broadcasters this time period kept such broadcasts away from the peak broadcasting slots.[87] Altogether the BBC Religious Broadcasting Department provided between two and three hours a week of religious television and about 9 hours of radio. By the 1970s ITV was also providing up to two to three hours of religious programming every Sunday, plus late-night weekday programmes as well.[88]

However it did not take long before the newly formed ITV was under serious scrutiny. The 1962 Pilkington Committee was critical of the ITV companies and also had some significant recommendations for religious broadcasting. The Committee stated that the objectives of religious broadcasting for both the BBC and ITV were to reflect the worship, thought and action of those churches which represented the mainstream of the Christian tradition in Britain, to stress what is most relevant in the Christian faith in the modern world and to try and reach those outside the churches.[89]

These aims were in part met by the broadcasts of conventional church services, both in sound and vision on Sunday mornings and a range of devotional radio programmes ranging from short inserts like *Lift Up Your Hearts* or *Pause for Thought* and ITV's *Epilogues* to the longer *Daily Service*. But in an attempt to reach a wider audience there developed in the late 60s and early 70s a variety of religious 'light entertainment' programmes such as the BBC's *Songs of Praise* and Yorkshire Television's *Stars on Sunday*, both with what might be termed a 'sacred concert' approach.

Songs of Praise, the brainchild of Donald Baverstock, began in 1961 in Wales. With its hymn singing format and celebrity presenters it broadcast from churches to cathedrals, stadiums to beaches. As producer Raymond Short reflected, "the point of the programme was to let the viewer share in the local community's celebration of its faith through the singing of well known hymns".[90]

Despite its growing popularity, at its inception it was grudgingly accepted as the responsibility of the religious broadcasting department.[91] In its first 50 years it had an array of famous personalities like Geoffrey Wheeler, Sally Magnusson, Roger Royle, Diane-Louise Jordon, Aled Jones, Alan Tichmarsh, Eamonn Holmes and Pam Rhodes to name but a few. Again, significantly personality driven. Another former producer John Forrest commented,

> I made no apology for bringing entertainment into the religious sphere. We worship God in many different ways and popular entertainment is one of them.[92]

Since the first *Songs of Praise* aired, the television landscape changed irrevocably. Then there were only two channels broadcasting in black and white to a population largely in awe of the new technology. Contrast that with hundreds of terrestrial and satellite stations from all over the world beamed into peoples homes twenty four hours a day by the 1990s.[93] Whatever else can be said *Songs of Praise* is a survivor. It has seen off or outlived rivals from *Stars on Sunday* to *Highway*. There have been many ingenious ideas for programmes to replace *Songs of Praise* but nothing has ever succeeded[94] and research in 1995/96 indicated that 40% of a 3000 sample tuned-in regularly to the programme.[95] Pam Rhodes, one of its presenters since 1987 commented,

> Songs of Praise has kept its place on prime-time television in the UK and many other countries for 57 years. Its success has been its hymns – both traditional and modern and since we started putting the words on the bottom of the screen, it has probably become the biggest karaoke in the world. Whether it be the hymns or the interspersed interviews, the Christian message told in this way is a welcome reflection of God's love and both an inspiration and comfort to millions.[96]

Stars on Sunday was conceived by Yorkshire Television's, Head of Children's Programmes, Jess Yates (See Chapter 7).Yates, an almost larger than life character himself, had had an enormous success with *Junior Showtime* but wanted to develop a programme for the over 65's and believed that such a programme would have to draw upon popular religious feeling. After an experimental series called *Choirs on Sunday*, *Stars on Sunday* was launched as a 13 part series in the autumn of 1969 with an almost show-business approach. The programme featured well-known personalities appearing singing popular songs or reading passages from the Bible as well as featuring up-and-coming talent, with Yates stamping his own personality on it eventually, as its host. The format was a huge success, after its first

7 years it had featured over 3,500 people, presented close on 5000 singers and readers, over 250 different soloists and taking almost 6000 minutes of air time and was attracting a regular viewing audience of between 15 and 17 million, making it the first religious programme to enter the viewing charts.[97] Despite its critics ranging from the ITA itself, to the national press, there was an acceptance of its popularity,

> its ratings and its appreciation indices remain as high as ever. The latest report from our Viewers Panel gives it an appreciation score higher even than Crossroads – very substantially higher amongst the oldest age group (55+), amongst the women and amongst the lower income group (DE). Few programmes seen by a statistically reliable number of this Panel receive a higher appreciation score. In the eyes of most beholders it is a highly satisfying programme.[98]

In essence Yates managed to capitalize on what might be termed 'popular religion'[99] and in doing so set a precedent in religious programming which drew only partly on orthodox religious assumptions.

Highway, already mentioned, was also an ITV production which started in 1983 presented by another nation's favourite Sir Harry Secombe, with a mixture of music and chat from across the UK. Secombe reflected on the programme,

> Highway was a great new concept for a programme. Each week probably for three days, we would visit a town and film its most interesting and attractive aspects. Then we would meet people connected with the town, either living or working there, or famous people who had been born there. I was to be the link man and I would sing both on my own and with local choirs and orchestras. However the most important thing was its 'religious' element. The programme aimed to show the goodness of ordinary people doing invaluable work in the community, people who showed their faith and beliefs through their way of life and actions.[100]

CHAPTER 3 NEW HORIZONS

Highway was originally conceived as a successor to *Stars on Sunday* and hence a direct competitor to *Songs of Praise*. However, it relied much more on secular metaphors and much less on comfortable religious imagery than its BBC counterpart. The underlying philosophy of *Highway* was that most people's world view is highly secularised and in consequence if they are to recognise something as 'religious' it must be clearly labelled as such.[101]

The Sunday evening religious television programmes were really imbedded in the DNA of UK viewers at this time and the IBA undertook to look at the attitudes to the two flagship programmes of *Highway* and *Songs of Praise*. Its survey showed that at least one third of the respondents claimed to have watched one of these programmes during the previous month and although *Highway* seemed to tip the viewing figures compared with *Songs of Praise*,[102] the reality was that both programmes attracted and held substantial audiences. In their heyday, it was estimated that *Highway* was reaching around 7.8 million viewers and *Songs of Praise* around 7 million.[103] A broader assessment on the viewers of religious broadcasting will be addressed in Chapter 6.

Apart from these particularly significant programmes, there were a range of others in this period on the BBC, like *Meeting Point, A Chance to Meet, The Question Why, The Sunday Debate, Viewpoint* and the occasional documentaries like *Something Beautiful for God* (portrait of Mother Theresa of Calcutta).The ITV religious output came mostly from the five major network companies, LWT, Thames, ATV, Granada and Yorkshire, programmes like ATV's *Beyond Belief*, Granada's *Seven Days* and *Adam Smith* and LWT's *Roundhouse*. Of the 104 ITV religious slots in the 1970s, the big four took 85 to 90 and the smaller regional companies between 10 and 15, including Tyne Tees Television who produced a programme series with the ever popular Cliff Richard retelling the Gospel parables.[104]

Religion, in some form or another, was becoming a significant player in UK television and although Richard Cawston produced a sixty minute BBC documentary in 1966 on the Billy Graham London Crusade *I'm Going to Ask You to Get Up Out of Your Seat*, there was no regular place in British television for 'televangelism' American style. Interestingly, in religious broadcasting, as in other types of broadcasting, there was an ever growing place for current affairs.[105] This fitted with the growing strands of opinion within the BBC and within CRAC, who were keen to see these changes in religious broadcasting. Three appointments in the 1970s helped to bring this about. At the advisory level Robert Runcie, the Bishop of St Albans (later to become Archbishop of Canterbury) was appointed Chairman of CRAC. At the BBC, Colin Morris was appointed Head of Religious Television and he introduced a strand of analytical documentary programmes like *Anno Domini* (1975) which examined third world problems. Morris also realised something of the dilemma for Christian communicators in Britain and for his Department,

> how can religious output of a public service broadcasting organisation and the response of the Churches be synchronised without a privileged relationship being set up which the BBC's Charter or the IBA's Act of Parliament would outlaw? Christian television stations of the American type have no such problems.[106]

When *Anno Domini* was replaced, the third key appointment was of Peter Armstrong who was to edit the *Everyman* series (1970s). Over at LWT another current affairs religious programme called *Credo* (1980s) was also introduced.[107]

The religious broadcasting landscape was rapidly changing, driven by the personalities involved, as Peter Armstrong reflected,

> We had young television professionals, not clerics. On the whole the producers of the 1950s and 1960s were retrained clergy, whereas I preferred to take young television professionals who were interested in religion and who would learn more about that.[108]

Part of that changing landscape was to see the demise of the 'closed period'. The Governors of the BBC commenting,

CHAPTER 3 NEW HORIZONS

> The closed period came to be regarded as a kind of ghetto for religious programmes, roping them off from other programmes, keeping them apart from the minds of many people from 'real' television.[109]

Support for this was clear as *The Daily Telegraph* asserted "the claustrophobia of the old 'closed period' has at last gone for good".[110]

So with this driving force *Everyman*, with its interest in stories pertaining in some way to religious or moral issues, was scheduled outside of the 'closed period' at 10.30pm on Sunday evenings. John Lang, Head of BBC Religious Broadcasting spoke of *Everyman* and its sister religious programme tackling moral dilemmas – *Heart of the Matter*,[111] as being strong plants that could be put outside in the garden of competitive scheduling.[112] This professionalizing of religious broadcasting was hailed by broadcasters and churchmen alike as qualitatively 'better television'. But a balance had to be maintained as Charles Curran, The Director General of the BBC, himself a practising Catholic, put it in an earlier decade,

> I suppose some people would like to see religious broadcasting as a kind of evangelical mission to the country, a sort of missionary call in the BBC to convert the whole country back, as people would say, to Christian belief and practice. Now I don't think that, as a practical matter we can say that, what we are doing, in my view, is responding to the need in the audience, as we respond to other needs, and the need is represented by that group of practicing believing Christians who expect to see in their broadcasting system a response to their belief and commitment, just as other groups expect to see similar responses in other fields.[113]

As David Winter a former Head of Religious Broadcasting also reflected,

> My role I felt, was to keep the rumour of God alive in a changing scene in society, the church and in the BBC. This was the beginning of the new era in broadcasting, one in which

religion had to sit alongside other philosophies of life and in which religious broadcasting had to compete on level terms with every other kind of programmes. There was still plenty of religious output, but probably for the first time I began to realise that the broadcasting environment was changing, even if for the present slowly and gently.[114]

But generally speaking it was ITV who was more willing to get away from traditional patterns in religious programming, remarking in its 1977 Handbook,

> until now it would have been reasonable for the viewer to assume that religious television in this country meant Christian television. Certainly, with a few exceptions, programmes in the past have related more or less obviously to the Christian tradition ... but now it would be arrogant for Christians to claim an exclusive right to religious broadcasting.[115]

Therefore ITV began to develop programmes for those with other rites and beliefs, other than Christian. Thus under the title *One Man's Faith,* London Weekend Television broadcast the views of an authority on Buddhism and also broadcast an Eastern Orthodox Service. The tide in religious broadcasting was beginning to change, but the softening of the traditional Christianizing objective and the general understanding of the aims of religious broadcasting under the new regimes were to come under scrutiny in the 1977 Annan Report.

The brief of the Annan Report was to:-

> consider the future of the broadcasting services in the United Kingdom, including the dissemination by wire of broadcast and other programmes and of television for public showing; to consider the implications for present or any recommended additional services of new techniques; and to propose what constitutional, organisational and financial arrangements and what conditions should apply to conduct of all these services.[116]

As with all such Commissions, petitions were sent to the Committee, in this case from nearly 750 organisations and individuals. One of the most thorough submissions from the religious community came from CRAC, which discussed at some length its own position as an advisory body, also offering the Committee alternative guidelines for the aims of religious broadcasting.

1. To seek to reflect the worship, thought and actions of the principal religious traditions represented in Britain recognising that these traditions are mainly though not exclusively Christian.

2. To seek to present to viewers and listeners those beliefs, ideas issues and experiences in the contemporary world which are related to a religious interpretation of life.

3. To seek also to meet the religious interests, concerns and needs of those on the fringe of, or outside, the organised life of the churches.[117]

The position of the Committee moved along similar lines in being as inclusive and wide-ranging as possible, in the recognition that religion permeates all areas of life in one way or another and should not be too compartmentalised, stating,

> There is no reason why religion should not be present as an influence in all programmes reminding the moralists of spiritual values and the social scientists of the inevitability of individual moral choice.[118]

The Annan Report still saw the BBC as arguably the single most cultural institution in the nation,[119] with religious broadcasting historically playing a significant part in its output. Hence eight pages of the Report (Chapter 20) discussed religious broadcasting in terms of the fact that although church attendance had declined, there still remained a considerable interest in religion which should be matched by broadcasters. In essence the Committee accepted the guidelines submitted by CRAC which had something of a movement away from the proselytizing approach of earlier years and was more geared to a 'reflection' of the Christian faith and beliefs, whilst in parallel giving recognition to those outside of the Christian community. However, one of the strong recommendations of the Committee in this sphere was that,

> the Broadcasting Authorities should consider whether the aims of religious broadcasting would be better served by widening the range of expertise in their religious broadcasting departments or by spreading the responsibility for religious programmes to other production departments while ensuring specifically religious services continue to be broadcasting.[120]

The broadcaster's response to the Report was probably less positive than the Committee might have hoped for. ITV didn't have self-contained religious broadcasting departments anyway, though agreed the best professional skills should be applied to religious broadcasting as to any other,[121] whilst the BBC maintained the strategic importance of a dedicated religious broadcasting department, "We continue to believe, however, that the Religious Broadcasting Departments in Television and Radio should keep custody of their main output".[122]

However both institutions were agreed on the rejection of the Committee's recommendation of changing the advisory structure and sought to retain the use of CRAC. This was the advice originally of a working group looking at the "quality place and function of religious television and which recommended that CRAC worked for ITV and the BBC".[123]

The IBA later commented,

> The Authority would not wish to abandon the advantages that come from having a forum which considers matters of concern to all religious broadcasting.[124]

The BBC also unequivocally stating,

CHAPTER 3 NEW HORIZONS

> We believe that CRAC should continue to advise both broadcasting authorities in the way it does at present ... we think it is a help. [125]

Indeed CRAC came to play and important valued role and model in the BBC from early days and eventually within the IBA. Cindy Kent, singer and broadcaster, became a member of the Committee and reflects,

> Religion like politics is a divisive subject and CRAC had the tough task of taking on board the whole range of opinions on religious broadcasting and making balanced recommendations to the BBC and IBA. I served on CRAC with Bishop Robert Runcie, destined to become Archbishop of Canterbury. During our time we faced a lot of challenges due to internal and external pressures on religious broadcasting, but what we were always seeking to do was to find new and creative ways of making religious broadcasting relevant to the audiences.[126]

But arguably and finally, the most notable legacy of the Annan Report was the setting up of legislation that permitted the introduction of a fourth television channel – Channel 4. In retrospect and in comparison, the Annan Report was not so significant for the development of religious broadcasting. However, in providing the structure for the launch of Channel 4, it was very crucial, because of the eventual relationships between the churches and religious broadcasters and Channel 4, as will be examined later.

3. A Radio Revolution

Any media futurologists in the post-war years would have probably predicted that with the growing commercialisation of the media in America, the tidal wave of this would probably come ashore in the UK, in terms of its effects on radio first. But deliberations here in the UK about radio had accepted the achievements and prestige of the BBC as an internationally admired radio service and this was accompanied by the belief that radio would decline and television would take the centre stage. So a serious radio debate never took place in those years in the UK and the momentum was rather building towards the introduction of Independent Television (ITV) in 1955. Uniquely in the developed world therefore, the UK had a commercially funded service of television before such a radio service.[127]

Even though the Pilkington Committee (1962) was geared as an enquiry into the future of sound and television broadcasting, in the end it paid little attention to the issue of 'sound'. But behind the façade of regulation there was a quiet revolution emerging, less to do with politics and more to do with youth culture, affluence and rock 'n' roll, which overturned the complacency of the BBC and ushered in a radio revolution.[128] There had been the appeal of stations since the 1930's, like Radio Luxembourg, but it was to be the phenomena of 'off-shore pirate radio' between 1964 and 1967 and the likes of Radio Caroline, with its appeal to young music listeners, that was to create the legend of the boats that 'rocked' British broadcasting. The man behind Radio Caroline was a 22 year old Irish business man Ronan O'Rahilly and in opening up the airwaves he was determined to smash both the monopoly of the record industry and the broadcasting media.[129] A Gallup Poll in 1964, after Caroline had been on air only one month, showed how of the potential of 20 million listeners aged 17, about an estimated 7 million had tuned to Radio Caroline broadcasts at one time or another.[130] The success was not only in listening figures, but in the personalities it created, like Tony Blackburn, who went on to play a key role in BBC's Radio One. Looking back on his time on Caroline he commented, "I am very pleased to have been part of that era, because we really did revolutionise the whole of the broadcasting system".[131]

Whilst the general public loved both the rebellion and the music of the stations, the Government's face was firmly set against their operations and the Marine & Broadcasting (Offences) Act in 1967 ended the era of offshore pirate radio and heralded first developments within the BBC like Radio One (1967) and Radio Two (1967) and a network of local radio stations [132] and secondly paved the way for a Sound Broadcasting Act (1972) and the creation of Independent Local Radio stations funded by advertising, rather than the free market model of the full-blown commercial radio of America, that was rejected in the early years of UK broadcasting.[133]

Despite the Government's attempt at almost protectionism, during this period there were stations outside of the British mainland, broadcasting on short wave across continents or medium wave from central Europe to the United Kingdom. Trans World Radio, for example, (See Appendix 2) which began broadcasting to Europe from transmitters near Tangier, Morocco in 1954 and from 1960 onwards used the enormous power of the Radio Monte Carlo AM transmitter to rebroadcast American preachers.[134] Even Radio Caroline, previously mentioned, in the 1960s played out programmes by US evangelists and the sustained use of short wave radio by religious broadcasters, beyond regulatory powers, continued in an attempt to reach worldwide audiences, with international religious broadcasting representing one of the most important missionary advances of the 20th Century.[135]

Independent Local Radio, established by the Sound Broadcasting Act (1972) began in the UK in 1973 with licences awarded to LBC and Capital Radio in London and Radio Clyde in Glasgow, with a further 16 licences before 1976 and by 1983 forty-three stations covering more than 80% of the population.[136] Religion was not required by statute but was regarded as part of the public service, [137] but the stations were not allowed to be owned and run by religious organisations. Typically the commercial stations of the period would include a Sunday morning music and chat show themed on religious topics, without being overtly evangelical.[138] Blair Crawford, the Religious Producer for Sheffield's Radio Hallam, which began in 1974, reflected,

> Reaching a largely non-church going audience with effective religious programming is always a challenge. Every week the station carried a pre-recorded *Thought for the Day* slot and on Sunday the main religious programme, *Sunday Spread*, contained the stations normal mix of current chart hits, golden oldies, news bulletins and commercials. To this we added a mix of faith-centred stories and features, augmented by the best in gospel and contemporary Christian music. The show proved

to be extremely popular and attracted a weekly audience in excess of 90,000 listeners.[139]

The requirement for stations to include religious programming in their output was later relaxed in the 'lighter touch' 1990 Broadcasting Act,[140] which opened up the regulatory framework of British commercial radio as the government of the day sought to "stimulate competition, increase efficiency and widen consumer choice".[141] It was actually from the 1980s a change of emphasis began, in part reflecting the gradual secularization of British society. The BBC still produced a number of hours of religious broadcasting, but under a broader definition of what constituted such output, so that programming was more representative of the nation's beliefs, "religious output by the BBC came to be more 'about' religion and less specifically religious".[142]

This programme content gap began to be filled by emerging Christian radio stations, for example, United Christian Broadcasters (See Appendix 1), who joined other established organisations attempting to reach the United Kingdom and in 1987 began leasing the transmitters of Manx Radio on the Isle of Man, beginning a long standing commitment to Christian broadcasting in Britain. Its current CEO David L'Herroux comments,

> As Christians in the past have used various ways to communicate the Christian gospel, radio is a route which is available 24/7. It is a friend in the room, able to comfort, inspire and challenge and we at UCB, through radio, wanted to be a part of that mission in supporting the Church to reach as many people as possible for Christ and encourage them in their faith.[143]

Also with the establishment in Britain in the 1990s of short-term Christian RSLs (Restricted Service Licences) on AM and FM like Radio Greenbelt, as well as the opening of low-powered FM community radio stations like Hope FM in Bournemouth or Cross Rhythms in Stoke-on-Trent, independent Christian broadcasters had opportunities to develop day-long schedules of Christian programming, culminating eventually in 1995 with the first licensed Christian radio station – Premier Christian Radio in London (See Appendix 1). To an extent some of the programming of these Christian stations in the United Kingdom reflected contemporary US styles, inclusive of preaching by well known personalities, as well as with the music played being predominantly contemporary Christian music.[144]

4. The Battles with Regulators, Broadcasters and Government

With the developments of television and independent local radio and the changing regimes of regulation and management, it was inevitable that there would be battles for religious broadcasters in their attempt to represent the churches and the Christian faith authentically on the air-waves and televisions of Britain.

As Jim McDonnell one of the leading Catholic commentators stated about the era,

> religion does not fit easily into the dominant world view of most contemporary broadcasters who are often ill prepared to deal with religion ... broadcasters face a real challenge in accommodating those religious views which challenge or confront dominant or pluralistic or secular assumptions.[145]

With such a backdrop the churches and religious broadcasters would face challenges with the established institutions and start a trend of independence which was not wholly supported across the Christian spectrum here in the UK.

a) The Approach of the Central Religious Advisory Committee (CRAC)

For the major Churches the consumer model of broadcasting was deeply threatening. Once religion had had an unquestioned place in the broadcasting system, now they feared that religion might be pushed out of the mainstream broadcasting altogether. They saw various broadcasters suggesting that they should set up their own channels and they feared a future in which they would be confined to narrow-cast religious ghettos. They became aware that cable and eventually satellite might change the existing public service landscape fundamentally, whilst looking nervously at the United States and the widespread assumption of the 'electronic church' and all that could bring to these shores.[146]

The Television Act (1954) did not directly oblige Independent Television to transmit any religious programmes; it provided however if religious programmes were transmitted they must have the ITA's prior approval and that the ITA in turn should have the assistance and advice of a committee representative of the main streams of religious thought in Britain. Such a committee, the Central Religious Advisory Committee (CRAC), already existed as one of the early BBC committees and the Authority arranged for CRAC to serve it also,[147] along with a Panel of Religious Advisers which met monthly representing the Church of England, the Free Churches, the Roman Catholic Church and the religious organisations in Scotland, Wales and Northern Ireland.

CRAC had already petitioned Government Broadcasting Committees like Annan, but in the 1980s CRAC waged rebellions against both the IBA and the BBC. The Minutes of CRAC meetings in this era reveal for example quite extensive opposition to IBA policy on such matters as proselytising and the dispute rumbled on with a Committee meeting in 1983 later noting,

> there should now be a fresh examination by CRAC, with the BBC and IBA of the nature of religious broadcasting, its aims and directions in the 1980s and to include in this examination our response to the Electronic Broadcast Church and whether one element of programmes should not be overtly concerned with proselytization.[148]

So in 1984 the IBA introduced a confidential policy document which suggested that religious faith could be dealt with in various ways,

1. What religious is – programmes of exposition, apologetic or argument.

2. How religious faith is awakened, celebrated and expressed – programmes of worship, meditation and reflection.

3. What the personal religious and social consequences are – documentaries, testimonies and dramas.

4. A complementary approach to look at the world through a religious lens. Could the truth behind an issue be seen by adopting a distinctive religious perspective? Here the approach could be secular and the approach was religious.[149]

This document is remarkable in that it demonstrates how far the IBA view of religious broadcasting had changed since 1977. Now too for the first time in British religious broadcasting history, there was no mention of 'Christian' anywhere in the document.[150] Time and space doesn't allow a full exposition of the document, but it is clear that CRAC didn't sign up to IBA's propositions and there was clearly a strained relationship between CRAC and the IBA. Equally the IBA struggled to assemble a position on religious broadcasting and programming that would match the potential audiences of churched and unchurched.

While CRAC was set up merely as an advisory body, in terms of both the BBC and IBA and had no legislative power, it certainly did exercise its voice loudly when necessary. For example, when proposals to end religious programmes on independent television channels in early Sunday evening schedules were presented by representatives of the ITV independent television companies, CRAC firmly rejected the move asserting that the scheduling of religious programming was a recognition by the public service channels of the strength of public interest in religion and the importance in people's lives. The Committee rather wanted the programme makers to find new and popular forms of religious programming, but not at the expense of the Sunday evening religious programming slots.[151]

Despite misgivings by some, over the role and value of CRAC, there is no doubt of the important contribution it made on the religious broadcasting landscape. In the deliberations by the IBA about a body to advise on religion, they were given some strong commendations in 1955 about CRAC from Grisewood, the Chief Assistant to the Director General of the BBC,

> CRAC has played an important part in the religious life in this country by presenting religious activities in Britain to the people free from harmful elements of dissension and in a way which that does encourage the modes of Christian worship which have become congenial to the British people. The incursion of broadcasting into the religious field could have been harmful in several ways – even while the best intentions were applied to it. For example, it could have become substitutional for churchgoing or it could have tended to weaken the attachment of Christians to their churches. From these harmful consequences we have been saved – the public has been saved – to a large extent by CRAC. It has acted as a consultative assembly on these and many other important matters and on several important occasions of great national concern, doing work which the Corporation as a secular body could not do. It has made vital decisions, such as the definition of the mainstream of historic Christianity, without which broadcasting about religious matters would have been confused and perhaps hurtful to our religious life. It has met with general and with ecclesiastical approval to a remarkable degree so that the BBC has never been challenged on the main line of its policy by the Churches. All this has proved of great value not only to the Corporation but to the religious life of the British community.[152]

Going forward into the 1980s and 1990s this profile continued to be of real significance on many different levels, as will be demonstrated.

b) Cable, Satellite and the Channel 4 Factor

In the 1980s expansion and de-regulation were significant elements of the era; Channel 4 was about to come on-stream and committees like Hunt and Peacock (See Appendix 3) were appointed to look into the commercial possibilities of cable and satellite developments.

The Government plans for the 1980s were encapsulated in the Broadcasting Act 1981 (See Appendix 4) but the references to religion were very few. The first one stated "except with the previous approval of the Authority, there shall not be included in any programme broadcast by the Authority any religious service or any propaganda related to matters of a religious nature".[153] The second required the IBA to approve or arrange for the assistance of a committee representative of the main streams of religious thought.[154] The third reference forbade advertisement "by or on behalf of any body whose objects are wholly or mainly of a religious nature and no advertisement shall be permitted which is directed towards any religious end".[155]

While regulators were setting down parameters; within the religious broadcasting community there was a good deal more anxiety that the new platforms of cable and satellite would open up the UK to the worse elements of the American Electronic Church believing that its religious programmes were "more emotive and manipulative than any other kind of programming".[156] The Church Information Committee wanted all religious groups to be excluded from the participation in cable operating companies and from the opportunity to lease religious channels.[157]

In contrast the Evangelical Alliance, purporting to represent a million Christians, in 1983 expressed their support for the religious ownership of electronic broadcasting systems and channels,

> we believe it is unjust to exclude Christians as Christians from the direct access to this future development of television.. To exclude religious bodies from direct access to this electronic communication would be in our contemporary culture as intolerable as it would have been centuries ago if they had been excluded from direct access to the printing press.[158]

The following year, the introduction of the Cable and Broadcasting Act 1984 (See Appendix 4) allowed significant liberty for religious groups with permission to own cable channels, though not a whole 'diffusion service' for an area. The Act also suggested that not all the channels in a diffusion service should be given over to religious groups producing the same style of programming.[159] As a result of the Act a new kind of religious broadcasting was introduced to Britain, freed from the shackles of CRAC, whose authority did not extend to the cable channels. This new type of religious broadcasting was more in the older Reithian and newer American mould: it talked Christianity rather than talked about religion.[160]

Taking up the opportunity of de-regulation, the first religious cable channel in the UK began in 1986 with Vision Broadcasting, led by Fran Wildish, providing Christian programming for a couple of hours a week on the Swindon Cable network, which was first Cable TV operation in the UK. Vision Broadcasting drew its sources from Britain and Europe and also re-edited material from American stations such as the Christian Broadcasting Network. By 1991 it was providing several cable stations with two to three hours religious broadcasting per week. It was a pioneering venture and as such had lots of battles with the likes of the ITC, but gained wide support including from Parliamentarians.[161]

In contrast to the output of Vision, some religious programming in the 1980s began to display a progressive shift in its implicit religious commitment and there arose a new strand of documentary programmes made by the new generation of sceptical and often agnostic television professionals. One platform for this was Channel 4 which began in November 1982. Many people within the churches had had a hope that the advent of Channel 4, with its statutory hour of religious broadcasting each week and 'alternative' approach, would mean a fresh impetus for religion on television. It was assumed that the new breed of programmes would reflect a wider interest and a more ideologically committed approach than the BBC and ITV companies had been permitting.[162]

Whatever the hopes there might have been for this dynamic new channel, the appointment of John Ranelagh as Commissioning Editor for religious programming was to dent the initial enthusiasm and many of the independent submissions from such religious producers as Good News Television in Manchester and Charles Cordle's Trinity Trust and Lella Production's *Jesus Then and Now* (1985) were rejected (though successfully broadcast on the Welsh Channel S4C). Ranelagh who described himself as an "enthusiastic agnostic", also expressed his dislike of CRAC and any advisory structure and so was able to pursue his own personal agenda without any effective challenge.[163] It seemed that religious broadcasting was largely in an era where it seemed to be losing ground fast, both in quality and quantity. Ranelagh commented,

> there are other religions than separate Christian sects in the UK. There are more Muslims than Methodists and eight hundred thousand non-Christians worship in England. The concern of religious broadcasting must reflect diversity.[164]

In this whole context, news came in 1983 of a proposed three-part Easter documentary series of religious programmes by Channel 4, in association London Weekend Television (LWT), with the working title, *Jesus: An Examination of the Evidence*, which would advocate theories that would undermine the reliability of the Gospels and suggested that Jesus indulged in witchcraft and even doubted his existence. The programmes were inspired by an article by John Whale, the *Sunday Times's* religious affairs correspondent, entitled *The Gospel of the Losers*.[165] The programme concept was shared with Julian Norridge, the editor of religious and education features, with the production and direction given to David W. Rolfe, known for his BAFTA award winning film on the *Shroud of Turin* (1977).

The scripts for the series were leaked and came into the hands of a number of the Christian organisations and Christian leaders, who were appalled by what they read in its lack of balance and its ignorance of serious Biblical scholarship. Responses were also taken up by Stephen Goddard, the editor of the evangelical magazine *Buzz*,

> Fasten your seatbelts this month for London Weekend Television's £400,000 attempt to undermine the Biblical view of Christ. Watch out for two-and-a-half hours worth of speculative

theology which attempts to reduce Christ to a deluded mystical maverick.[166]

Religious broadcasting in the UK had been no stranger to controversy over the years, but this was to begin a major campaign which was to include leading theologians, church leaders and organisations and moved the campaign from relative obscurity to national news, so that by the time that the programmes came to be broadcast, the series had become one of the most publicised that Channel 4 had aired.[167] Reflecting on the campaign Goddard comments,

> The advanced scripts of the series came into my possession from a concerned individual working on the production and I spent several weeks wondering what to do about them. We were astonished by the amount of time afforded to tendentious views of the historical Jesus, without corresponding balance from conservative scholarship. The series was to be aired on Channel 4, a public service broadcast medium where a balance of opposing views is deemed a prerequisite. We therefore campaigned solely for a more balanced approach. We were called naïve by some but we know for certain that subsequent series already in the pipeline and even more speculative and one-sided, were abandoned as a direct result of our action.[168]

Whatever the true impact was of *Jesus the Evidence;* there was certainly acrimony and furore, but also reasoned debate, which would not terminate with the programme, in what was to be a period of growing secularisation and a time of meteoric changes in both media structures and content, something which religious broadcasting would be unable escape.

However, the irony of this period was that in the same year as the broadcast of *Jesus the Evidence* was on our screens, the American Evangelist Billy Graham was seen running his Mission England 'Crusades'. These were extensively covered for television by the BBC in Birmingham, Anglia in Norwich and Tyne Tees Television in Sunderland. A previous documentary had been made by Richard Cawston on Billy Graham for the BBC in 1966 entitled; *I am Going to Ask you to Get Up Out of Your Seat.* But at this time of growing liberalism in religious broadcasting in the 1980s, it was amazing the freedom given by the BBC and ITV for Billy Graham to make his classic appeal to the stadium audiences and to the TV viewers, to make a commitment to Christ. This evangelical message was clearly being relayed into the homes of Britain, as it was later in 1989 when BBC Radio transmitted the whole of the address of Billy Graham from West Ham Football Club. Despite its very clear proselytizing nature, the IBA in 1984 and the BBC in 1989 permitted such broadcasts.[169] A battle had been won, but the war was not over.

c) The Battle for Freedoms

It would be no exaggeration to describe the United Kingdom system of broadcasting which obtained until 1988, as closed in access and centralised in control, in comparison to the American system which is open in access and diffuse in control. Indeed, in an attempt to control the danger of religious excesses threatening from America, new government legislation had verged on something of a protectionist policy.

But the Thatcher Government (1979-90) was keen to encourage media competition. A Radio Green Paper was produced, *"Radio Choices and Opportunities: a consultative document"* (1987). Basically the Government, in its expansionist policy, wanted to see a balance between the provisions of services by the public authorities, commercial operators and community or other voluntary groups.

The main decisions there were:

- To allow the BBC to continue, but with fewer radio channels.

- To permit three new national commercial radio services to compete with the BBC.

- To create a new regulatory authority to select and supervise the new commercial companies (the future Radio Authority).

- To permit BBC local radio and existing ILR stations to continue but freed from their public service obligations.

- To encourage new community radio stations throughout the UK.

The responses to the Green Paper were legion, including from religious broadcasting groups like CRAC who were worried by restrictions on stations,

> excluding from programmes all expressions of the views and opinions of the persons providing the service, on religious matters or on matters which are of political or industrial controversy or relate to current public policy.[170]

In fact CRAC had a number of concerns, including that the prospect of dropping the requirements of 'proper balance and a wide range of subject matter' would inevitably lead to 'narrowcasting' and with the prospect of US religious groups wanting to expand evangelical broadcasting into Europe, they felt this would provide the possibility of manipulating opinion and exploiting vulnerable listeners and therefore another reason why CRAC should be engaged with any new regulatory authority to provide advice and expertise in this area.[171]

Meanwhile Mrs Thatcher, the Prime Minister, in terms of television, had already asked the Peacock Committee (1985-6) to look into the possibilities for the BBC to carry advertising. But the Committee rejected this and moved to produce its deregulatory White Paper *Broadcasting in the 90s: Competition, Choice and Quality* (1988) which recommended some of the most radical changes to commercial broadcasting in Britain since 1955. Douglas Hurd, the Home Secretary recommended the document as "coherent, comprehensive and controversial",[172] whilst others felt it was guided by commercial rather cultural imperatives and a threat to Channel 3 (ITV) with an exaggerated interest in a fifth channel, as well as a yet a new highly commercial regulator to cope with, in terms of the Independent Television Commission (ITC) replacing the former IBA.

CHAPTER 3 NEW HORIZONS

Timothy Renton, the Minister of State with special responsibility for broadcasting at the Home Office captured succinctly the Government's thinking declaring,

> Broadcasting stands on the edge of a new era and the Government intends that the opportunities created by new technologies should be fully exploited by broadcasters and driven forward by consumer demand. The raison d'etre for the White Paper has been to free the broadcasting market. Our plans allow wider access to the airwaves for a greater number of programme providers.[173]

It was estimated that there were in excess of 3,000 responses to the White Paper including from organisations like Age Concern to Channel 4 and from British Telecom to the Evangelical Alliance who asserted,

> In the UK today any church may own its own building, publishing a parish magazine, print books or own a local of national newspaper. Yet that same church is denied the right to purchase time or own a radio of TV station. The White Paper fails to present any argument for such an illogical denial of basic human freedom.[174]

The vast majority of respondents noted their concern that quality and minority interests would be sacrificed in a wake of franchise auctions.

Despite the reservations about the White Paper, it led on to the 1990 Broadcasting Act (See Appendix 4). It was a highly complicated legal document of 291 pages in length. Earl Ferrers, Minister of State at the Home Office, described it as "enormous", covering a "huge and complicated area".[175] The Bill with its 'lighter touch' regulatory approach was conceived at a time when the concept of the market was accorded almost a 'theological' importance – the Government believing that market forces could rule in the media industry as in any other field and in some respects the Act carried the aspiration of liberalising the regulatory regime into religious broadcasting.[176]

It would be true to say that many religious groups and their sympathizers believed that although there was a climate of opportunity and choice being built into the broadcasting framework through the Bill, there was a subversive discrimination against religious broadcasting. There were many speeches in regard to this as the Bill was going through its various stages, for example Kenneth Hind (MP for Lancashire West),

> I speak on behalf of thousands and millions of Christians in Britain. Our leaders espouse the ethos of Christianity and it is one of the major planks of everyday life, philosophy and beliefs, but one section of society is to be prevented from benefiting from the greater diversity of media stations provided by the Bill – religious groups especially the Christian churches.[177]

Other notable Parliamentarians took up the case in a similar vein, like Michael Alison MP and Lord Orr-Ewing and outside of Parliament the campaign about religious restrictions was wide-ranging and intense, with petitions from the National Council for Christian Standards led by Gareth Littler, John Q. Davis leading another group called the Christian Broadcasting Council, as well as CRAC, who took a completely different approach having the view that religious bodies should not be allowed to hold a television or Radio Authority licence.[178] But the campaign against the restrictions raged further and bigger because of the involvement of the Evangelical Alliance and their ability to harness the support of millions of Christians, as their Communications Secretary Peter Meadows recalls,

> The potential for religious groups to have the same broadcasting opportunities as every other segment of society was great news. However, our battles were mostly with the Church establishment – which wrongly imagined it would create an influx of American-style religious broadcasting. Our campaign, under the theme 'Don't let them gag the Church', gained momentous support among local churches and individual Christians, with MPs mailboxes full of letters from those arguing for Christians to have the same opportunities in broadcasting as anyone else.[179]

CHAPTER 3 NEW HORIZONS

As a result of numerous responses in and outside Parliament and various amendments,[180] there were some radical turn-arounds in some areas, including religious broadcasting. The Act had originally made all religious bodies 'disqualified persons' for the purpose of holding a licence to broadcast, now at the discretion of the Radio Authority (RA) and the Independent Television Commission (ITC) certain types of licence could be granted e.g. local analogue radio licences, satellite TV and radio licences and cable TV and radio licences.[181] So in the end the Act in its final form, made major concessions to religious broadcasters in terms of ownership, provided they stay within the rules on programme content outlined by the Radio Authority and ITC, making sure that broadcasting on religious matters was 'responsible not exploitative'.

The move to establish Restrictive Service Licences, as part of the Bill, which ran for a short time and on low power, also paved the way for religious broadcasters. Christmas 1991 saw a major Christian project – Radio Cracker, led by Steve Chalke, which set up 100 stations around the country for a month aimed at raising money for the Third World. Other groups took advantage of this provision in terms of the Christian Arts Festival – Greenbelt, as well town-based RSLs like Hope FM in Bournemouth. Windows of opportunity were beginning to open and credibility given to existing UK Christian broadcasters like UCB in Stoke on Trent and Vision Broadcasting in Swindon.

Prior to the Broadcasting Act of 1990 the situation amongst the commercial networks was disappointing for religious broadcasting. Out of the then 110 commercial stations many had dropped their religious programmes and within a very short time regular religious programmes were available only on a handful of stations. At the local level the future for local religious programmes seem to lay with the continuing health of the BBC local radio network.[182]

But a shift came, in terms of religious independent broadcasters, when a consortium known as London Christian Radio applied for a Medium Wave Licence for London and Greater London. The station was launched under the name Premier Christian Radio and commenced broadcasting on 10th June 1995. The launch party in

Battersea Park attracted thousands of people who for nearly 5 years had worked to capitalize on the opportunity of ownership that had been provided in the 1990 Broadcasting Bill. It was the first Christian terrestrial radio station in the UK. David Heron its former Chairman commented,

> The period running up to the launch of Premier Christian Radio on the 10th June 1995 was exciting and the culmination of years of hard word by a talented team of people. The crowds at Battersea Park were enthusiastic to hear this first Christian Radio Station in the UK – a real milestone in broadcasting.[183]

Premier is 100% owned by the registered charity, the Christian Media Trust and the charity funds the broadcasting production activities of Premier through the gifts its receives largely through the station's listeners. It is a model which had been seen in the context of the American stations and broadcasters and now applied here in the UK.

5. Summary

The era is a classic demonstration of the power of personality to shape events and movements in religious broadcasting. Whether that be the likes of Dr.Billy Graham and Pat Robertson in America, or such presenters as Jess Yates or the nation's favourites like Harry Secombe or Aled Jones in the UK. The personalities become synonymous with ministries and programmes and elicited devotion and following in the public arena of television and radio. But also, as has been seen, behind the scenes were those who were driving initiatives and campaigns who also became legends in their own right.

It also significant to recognise that in terms of religious broadcasting in this period in the UK, the Central Religious Advisory Committee (CRAC) continued to play a significant role firstly in regard to the BBC and then from 1955 with the IBA, in representing the views of most religious bodies. However in the 80s and 90s it was a turbulent time for CRAC, with internal wrangling's amongst its membership and confrontation with many evangelical bodies, who felt they were

CHAPTER 3 NEW HORIZONS

compromising the rights of independent religious broadcasters to be heard.

There is no doubt that in terms of America, this was the 'golden age' of those who came to be known as 'televangelists', with television as well as radio becoming the twin pulpits of the Electronic Church. The freedoms of Americans in religious broadcasting led to a very clear proselytizing approach in the media, whereas this period illustrates the struggles in the UK amongst broadcasters, regulators and Government to agree on the aims of religious broadcasting and the Codes of Practice they should adhere to.

Many of the freedoms for religious broadcasters in the American system stem from the fact most of them had moved into an avenue of 'buying time' on existing stations or setting up their own. This gave them control over the messaging and their methods. The contrast with Britain was that religious broadcasters had to work within the institutions of either the BBC or ITV, who had total control of both their status and their output. However, in view of broadcasting's many and highly valued religious programmes no one could accuse the BBC or ITV of having deserted Christianity.[184]

Driven by a Conservative Government, the last two decades of the 20th Century saw radical changes in broadcasting for both radio and television. Changes in the law were aimed to stimulate competition, increase efficiency and widen consumer choice. In the wake of this, religious broadcasters feared that public service broadcasting would be undermined and the privileged position that broadcast religion had enjoyed, would be eroded. At the same time there were hopes that the new freedoms would bring opportunities for independent broadcasters and media ownership.

The 1990 Broadcasting Act is crucial in this story. It highlighted the tensions between religious bodies who were seeking media platforms and the campaigning zeal of those who felt that the historic Christian faith of Britain should have a significant role to play on the television and radio sets of the UK. Until the 1990 Broadcasting Act religious institutions were disallowed from owning any radio stations in the

UK. The Act now allowed religious groups to own religious stations as well as satellite and cable stations.[185]

But continuing the contrast between the USA and the UK, looking over this period, Asa Briggs points out,

> The religious programmes of the UK were as different from religious programmes in the United States as its popular music programmes were from such American programmes.[186]

A former head of BBC Religious Broadcasting pointing out too that, the character of religious broadcasting in Britain had been moulded by three main forces, historical to do with the way broadcasting had developed, structural because of the properties of broadcasting as a medium and theological reflected in British society's religious profile and the traditions evolved by successive generations of religious broadcasters.[187]

Viewing this dynamic era in broadcasting, Horsfield expanded on the challenge there was for religious broadcasters,

> the implications of new media developments for groups in Christianity, therefore, lie not only in how to adapt to new models of communicating but also how to align themselves with new political conditions, new cultural perspectives, new intellectual perspectives, new economic arrangements and new industry requirements associated with the media shifts.[188]

Despite the changing political and social environment religious broadcasting continued to make a significant impact both here and in the USA, but to talk in terms of 'success' is a hard task, as a former Director General of the BBC emphasized, with a view as applicable to the USA as to the UK,

> no one in religious broadcasting would claim to be satisfied with what has been done; most would say simply that within the options open to them and given their position in the nation's communications structure, they have tried to find a

CHAPTER 3 NEW HORIZONS

genuinely Christian approach to broadcasting. Others must decide whether and how far they have succeeded.[188]

What is clear in this era is that the thread of the influence and impact of charismatic religious broadcasters that was there through the crucial radio years of 1921-1955, continued and was magnified in the television age. They were a huge element within the American broadcasting scene and created a powerful political lobby at the same time. In the UK their significance was far more controlled because of the broadcasting institutions and legislation, nevertheless they continued to play a major role on television and radio through a variety of programmes which were hugely popular because of the celebrities who became integral to their presentation. For this reason in the chapter that follows we examine some of the key individuals at the heart of the story of religious broadcasting in the USA and UK respectively.

NOTES

1. Lichty, L. W. and Topping, M.C., *American Broadcasting* (New York: Hastings House, 1975), p.522-523.

2. Oberdorfer, D. N., *Electronic Christianity: Myth or Ministry* (Taylor Falls: John L. Brekk & Sons.1982), p.13.

3. Postman, N., *Amusing Ourselves to Death* (London: Methuen, 1985), p.8.

4. Hill, D. G. H. and Davis, L., *Religious Broadcasting: A Selected Annotated Bibliography* (New York: Garland Publishers 1984), p.xi.

5. Grisewood, H., *Christian Communication – Word and Image* (Geneva: World Council of Churches, 1956), p.22.

6. Bruce, S., *Pray TV: Televangelism in America* (London: Routledge, 1990), p.29.

7. Horsfield, P. G., *Religious Television: the American Experience* (New York: Longmans, 1984,) p.3.

8. Ibid., p.5.

9. Czitrom, D. J., *Media and the American Mind: From Morse to McLuhan* (Chapel Hill: University of North Carolina Press, 1982), p.9-11.

10. Rosenthal, M., *Protestants and TV in the 1950s: Responses to a New Medium* (New York: Macmillan, 2007), p.78.

11. Armstrong, B., *The Electric Church* (Nashville: Thomas Nelson, 1979), p.8.

12. Engel, J. F., Great Commission or Great Commotion. *Christianity Today*. 20th April (1984), p.52.

13. Frankl, R., *Televangelism* (Carbondale: Southern Illinois University Press, 1987), p.4.

14. Stringfellow, W., *A Simplicity of Faith.* (Nashville: Abingdon, 1982), p.88-90.

15. Corry, J., Preachers Mastery of the Medium. *New York Times.* 2nd April (1987), p.26.

16. Hoover, S. M., *The Electronic Giant: A Critique of the Telecommunications Revolution from a Christian Perspective* (Elgin: The Brethren Press, 1982), p.123.

17. Hatch, N. O., *The Democratisation of American Christianity*. (New Haven: Yale University Press, 1989), p.216-217

18. Postman, N. (1985), p.119.

19. Benson, D. C., *Electric Evangelism* (Nashville: Abingdon Press, 1973), p.14-15.

20. Schultze, Q. J., *American Evangelicals and the Mass Media* (Grand Rapids: Academic Books, 1990), p.48.

21. Parker, E. C., Barry, D. W. and Smythe, D.W., *The Television/Radio Audience and Religion* (New York: Harper Brothers Publishers, 1955), p.63.

22. Schultze, Q. J., *Televangelism and American Culture: The Business of Popular Religion* (Grand Rapids: Baker Book House, 1991), p.32.

23. Pradip, T., Selling God/Saving Souls. *Global Media and Communication*, 5 (1) 2009:76.

24. Holsendolp, E., Religious Broadcasting Brings Rising Revenues and Creates Rivalries. *New York Times*. 2nd December (1979), p.1.

25. Mann, J., The Mainline Churches Strike Back. *US News & World Report*. 6th August (1982), p.60.

26. Elvy, P., *Buying Time: The Foundations of the Electronic Church* (Great Wakering: McCrimmons, 1986), p.28.

27. Ferre, J. P., *Channels of Belief: Religion and American Commercial Television* (Ames: Iowa State University Press, 1990), p.80-81.

28. Carnell, E. J., *Television: Servant or Master?* (Grand Rapids: W.B. Eerdmans, 1950), p.93.

29. Horsefield, P.G. (1984), p.10.

30. Elvy, P, (1986), p.38.

31. Pope Paul V1, Inter Mirifica (1963), Decree on the Means of Social Communication.

32. Kay, W. K., 2009. Pentecostalism and Religious Broadcasting. *Journal of Beliefs and Values*, 30 (3) 2009: 247.

33. Bruce, S. (1990), p.36-37.

34. Hoover, S. M., *Mass Media Religion: The Social Sources of the Electronic Church* (Newbury Park: Sage, 1988), p.57.

35. Swatos, W. H. Jr., *Encyclopaedia of Religion and Society* (Walnut Creek: Altamira Press, 1998), p.369.

36. Frankl, R. (1987), p.74.

37. Harrell Jr. D. E., *Oral Roberts: An American Life* (Bloomington: Indiana University Press, 1985), p.448.

38. Swatos, W.H.Jr. (1998), p.514.

39. Fore, W. F., The Unknown History of Televangelism. *Journal of the World Association of Christian Communication*, 54 (1) 2007:47.

40. Fore, W. F., Media, Religion and the Church's Task. *A Journal of Scholarly Reflection for Ministry*, 9 (4) 1988: 8.

41. Federal Communications Commission, *Report and Statement of Policy Research* (Washington. FCC, 1960), p.2315.

42. Neuendorf, K.A., *The Public Trust versus the Almighty Dollar in Religious Television: Controversies and Conclusions*. (Norwood: Ablex Publishing, 1990), p.78.

43. Fore, W.F. (2007), p.46.

44. Fore, W.F., *Television and Religion: the shaping of faith, values, and culture*. (Minneapolis: Augsburg Publishing, 1987), p.101.

45. Poloma, M., *The Assemblies of God at the Crossroads* (Knoxville: University of Tennessee Press, 1989), p.222.

46. Hadden, J. K. and Swann, C. E., *Prime Time Preachers: The Rising Power of Televangelism* (Reading: Addison Wesley Publishing, 1981), p.85.

47. Bruce, S., The Inevitable Failure of the Christian Right. *Sociology of Religion*, 55 (3) 1994:233; Beal, T., *Religion in America: A Very Short Introduction* (Oxford: Oxford University Press, 2008), p.55.

48. Morris, J., *The Preachers* (New York: St. Martin's Press, 1973), p.22.

49. Editorial, Gospel TV: Religion Politics and Money. *Time Magazine*. 17th February (1986), p.23.

50. Martin, W., *Perennial Problems of Prime-Time Preachers*. (Waco. Baylor University, 1987).

51. Editorial, Survey of Top TV Preachers. *Christianity Magazine*. 16th October (1987), p.46-49.

52. Fitzgerald, F., A Disciplined Charging Army. *New Yorker Magazine*. 18th May (1981), p.54.

53. Gentry, R. H., Broadcast Religion: When Does its Raise Fairness Doctrine Issues? *Journal of Broadcasting*, 28 (3)1984: 269.

54. Fritz, D. A., and Ibrahim, N. A., The Impact of Leadership Longevity in Innovation in a Religious Organisation. *Journal of Business Ethics*, 96 (2) 2010: 223.

55. Bruce, S. (1990), p.198-212.

56. Neuendorf, K.A. (1990), p.81.

57. Ellens, J. H., *Models of Religious Broadcasting* (Grand Rapids: W. B. Eerdmans, 1974), p.45-67.

58. Ibid., p.70.

59. Ibid., p.96-7.

60. Ibid., p.124.

61. Frankl, R., and Hadden, J.K., A Critical Review of the Religion and Television Research Report. *Review of Religious Research*, 29 (2), 1987:111-124.

62. Suman, M., *Religion and Prime Time Television* (Westport: Praeger Publishers, 1997), p.23.

63. Stacey, W. and Shupe, A., 1982. Correlates of Support for the Electronic Church. *Journal for the Scientific Study of Religion*, 21 (4) 1982: 299.

64. Ellul, J., *Propaganda: The Formation of Men's Attitude* (New York: Vintage Books, 1973), p.287.

65. Oberdorfer, D, N. (1982), p.112.

66. Ibid., p.85-6.

67. Everitt, A., *New Voices: An Update* (London: Radio Authority, 2003), p.22.

68. Fore, W.F. (2007), p.48.

69. Rosenthal, M. (2007), p.109.

70. Bruce, S. (1990), p.40.

71. Ibid., p.31.

72. Schultze, Q.J. (1991), p.28.

73. Leigh, I., Regulating Religious Broadcasting. *Ecclesiastical Law Journal*, 2 (10) 1992: 292.

74. Ward, S. M., *Air of Salvation: The Story of Christian Broadcasting* (Grand Rapids: Baker Books, 1994), p.208.

75. Hoover, S.M. (1988), p.21.

76. Beale, C., *Television and Religion* (Wallington: Religious Education Press, 1956), p.5.

77. Ibid., p.8.

78. Paulu, B., *Television and Radio in the United Kingdom* (London: MacMillan, 1981), p.57.

79. Correspondent, The Church and Television. *Coventry Evening Telegraph*. 6th November (1952), p.7.

80. BBC Handbook (1955), p.57.

81. Correspondent, Bishops Take Up Television Course. *The Times*. 17th April (1959), p.6.

82. Independent Television Authority, *Religious Programmes on Independent Television* (London: ITA, 1962), p.8.

83. Quicke, A. and Quicke, J., *Hidden Agendas: The Politics of Religious Broadcasting in Britain 1987 – 1991* (Virginia Beach: Dominion Kings Grant Publications, 1992), p.3.

84. Independent Broadcasting Authority, *Television and Radio Handbook* (London: IBA, 1976), p.103.

85. Paulu, B. (1981), p.284.

86. Tribe, D., *The Scandal of Religious Broadcasting* (London: National Secular Society. 1967), p.2.

87. Harrison, J., A Review of Religious Broadcasting on British Television. *Modern Believing*, 41 (4) 2000: 6.

88. Quicke, A., *Tomorrow's Television*. (Berkhamstead: Lion Publishing, 1976), p.119.

89. Report of the Broadcasting Committee 1962, (*Pilkington Report*) Cmnd.1753. (London: HMSO), p.16.

90. Short, R., Songs of Praise. *The Radio Times*. 15th April (1976), p.1.

91. Barnes, T., *Celebrating Songs of Praise: 50 Years* (Oxford: Lion, 2011), p.30.

92. Ibid., p.85.

93. Ibid., p.110.

94. Barr, A., Songs *of Praise: The Nation's Favourite* (Oxford: Lion, 2001), p.108.

95. BBC Research Department, *Songs of Praise*. (London: 1995/96), BBC WAC. File Ref: R9/1920/1, p.2-3.

96. Interview 5th July (2018)

97. Max-Wilson, P., *Stars on Sunday* (Pinner: Pentagon, 1976), p.34.

98. Sendall, B. C., *Stars on Sunday* (1972), IBA Collection File Ref: A/X/0009/5., Par.5

99. Knott, K., *Media Portrayals of Religion and their Reception*. (Leeds: Leeds University, 1982), p.3.

100. Secombe, H., *Harry Secombe's Highway* (London: Robson Books, 1985), p.7-9.

101. Simpson, N. A., *A Study of Religious Television Programmes in the UK*. (PhD), Edinburgh University (1989), p.206-207.

102. Gunter, B., *The Audience & Religious TV* (London: IBA Research Report, 1984), p.15.

103. Hunt, S., Transformations in British Religious Broadcasting. *In*: Bailey, M. and Redden, G., *Mediating Faiths and Religion and Socio-Cultural Change in Twenty-First Century* (Burlington: Ashgate, 2011), p.27-28.

104. Quicke, A. (1976), p.120-122.

105. Briggs, A., *The History of Broadcasting in the United Kingdom*. Vol. V: *Competition* (Oxford: Oxford University Press, 1995), p.581-582.

106. Morris, C., *God-in-a-Box: Christian strategy in the Television Age*. (London: Hodder and Stoughton, 1984), p.128.

107. Quicke, A. and Quicke, J. (1992). p.40.

108. Ibid., p.43.

109. BBC., *What Do You Think of it So Far?* (London: BBC. 1977), p.45.

110. Knight, P., Giving More Scope to Religion. *Daily Telegraph*. 29th August (1977), p.5.

111. Bakewell, J., *The Heart of the Matter: A Memoir* (London: BBC Books, 1996), p.9.

112. Lang, J., BBC Religious Programmes. *Daily Telegraph*. 29th August (1977), p.5

113. Curran, C., Shooting Arrows into the Air: The Function of Religious Broadcasting? *The Listener*. 29th August (1974), p.262.

114. Interview: 5th September (2018).

115. IBA Handbook (1977), p.43.

116. Report of the Broadcasting Committee 1977 (*Annan Report*) Cmnd.6753. (London. HMSO), p.3.

117. Ibid., Par.20.11.

118. Ibid., Par.20.18.

119. Ibid., p.79, 114.

120. Ibid., Par.20.18.

121. Independent Broadcasting Authority, Reponses by the Authority to the Annan Report. *Independent Broadcasting*, 12, 1977: 36.

122. BBC, *The BBC Response to the Annan Report* (London: BBC, 1977), p.38.

123. Independent Broadcasting Authority, *Television and Radio Handbook* (London: IBA, 1977), p.1.

124. Ibid., p.36.

125. BBC, (1977), p.38.

126. Interview: 12th October (2018).

127. Stoller, T., *Sounds of Your Life: The History of Independent Radio in the UK* (New Barnet: John Libbey Publishing Ltd., 2010) p.16-17.

128. Ibid., p.17.

129. Baron, M., *Independent Radio: The Story of Commercial Radio in the UK* (Lavenham: Terence Dalton, 1975), p.37.

130. Leonard, M., *The Story behind the 60's 'Pirate Radio Stations'*. (Heswall: Forest Press, 2004), p.13.

131. Henry, S. and Joel, M. V., *Pirate Radio: Then and Now* (Poole: Blandford Press, 1984), p.7.

132. Crisell, A., *An Introductory History of British Broadcasting*. 2nd edition (London: Routledge, 2002), p.144-146.

133. Paulu, B. (1981), p.165.

134. Kay, W. K. (2009), 248.

135. Stoneman, T. H. B., Preparing the Soil for Global Revival Station HCJBs Radio Circle 1949-59. *Church History: Studies in Christianity and Culture*, 76 (1) 2007: 115.

136. Crisell, A. (2002), p.196.

137. Leigh, I., Regulating Religious Broadcasting. *Ecclesiastical Law Journal*, 2 (10), 1992: 289.

138. Cooper, M., and Macaulay, M., Contemporary Christian Radio in Britain: A New Genre on the National Dial. *The Radio Journal – International Studies in Broadcast and Audio Media*, 13 (1/2), 2015: 77.

139. Interview: June 1st (2018).

140. McDonnell. J., From Certainty to Diversity: The Evolution of Religious Broadcasting Since 1990. *In*: Geybels, H., Mels, S. and Walrave, M., *Faith & Media: Analysis of Faith and Media* (Brussels: P. I. E. Peter Lang, 2009), p.154.

141. Crisell, A. (2002), p.226.

142. Hunt, S., Transformations in British Religious Broadcasting. *In*: Bailey, M. and Redden, G., *Mediating Faiths and Religion and Socio-Cultural Change in Twenty-First Century*. (Burlington: Ashgate, 2011), p.29.

143. Interview: 10th March (2019)

144. Cooper, M. and Macauley, M. (2015), p.79.

145. McDonnell, J., Religious Education and the Communication of Values. *In:* Arthur, C., *Religion and Media: An Introductory Reader* (Cardiff: University of Wales Press, 1993), p.92.

146. McDonnell, J. (2009), p.153.

147. Wolfe, K. M., *The Churches and the British Broadcasting Corporation 1922-1956. The Politics of Broadcast Religion.* (London: SCM, 1984), p.515; Briggs, A., *The History of Broadcasting in the United Kingdom.* Vol. V: *Competition.* (Oxford: Oxford University Press, 1995), p.722-733.

148. Central Religious Advisory Committee, Minutes (London: 1984), BBC WAC File Ref: R78/811/1

149. Independent Broadcasting Authority, 1984. *Religious Broadcasting Policy on Independent Television and Independent Local Radio.* (London: IBA, 1984), p.4.

150. Quicke, A. and Quicke, J. (1992), p.50.

151. Longley, C., The True Art of Teaching Religion. *The Times*. 24th September (1988), p.12.

152. Grisewood, H., *Christian Communication – Word and Image* (Geneva: World Council of Churches, 1955), p.3.

CHAPTER 3 NEW HORIZONS

153. Broadcasting Act 1981, Section 4(5) a).

154. Ibid., Section 16 (2) a).

155. Ibid., Section 2 (8).

156. Report of the Broadcasting Committee 1982, (*Hunt Report*) Cmnd.8866. (London. HMSO).

157. General Synod, *Cable Television*. (London: Church Information Office, 1983), p.12.

158. Evangelical Alliance, *Evidence to the Home Office on Cable and Satellite*. (London: Evangelical Alliance, 1983).

159. Cable and Broadcasting Act 1984, Section 11 Ptl: B9.

160. Quicke, A. and Quicke, J. (1992), p.60.

161. Ibid., p.60-61.

162. Wallis, R., *Looking on Glass*. Unpublished. (Masters). Exeter University (1987), p.66.

163. Quicke, A. and Quicke, J. (1992), p.63.

164. Ranalagh, J., Broadcasting for Breadth. *The Times*. 5th November (1983),p.10.

165. Whale, J., The Gospel of the Losers. *The Sunday Times*. 2nd December (1979), p.17.

166. Goddard, S., Jesus the Evidence. *Buzz*. April (1984), p.20-25.

167. Wallis, R., Channel 4 and the declining influence of organised religion on UK television. The case of Jesus: The Evidence. *Historical Journal of Film, Radio and Television*, 36 (4) 2016: 677.

168. Interview: 3rd July (2018).

169. Quicke, A and Quicke, J. (1992), p.65-67.

170. Green Paper: *Radio Choices and Opportunities: a consultative document* 1987, Cmnd.92. p.32 7.7(ii). (London: HMSO).

171. Quicke, A. and Quicke, J. (1992), p.80-83.

172. Editorial, 1990 Broadcasting Bill. *Broadcast Magazine*, 14th October, (1988), p13-14.

173. Editorial, 1988 White Paper on Broadcasting. *Broadcast Magazine*, 7th December (1988), p.7-8.

174. Evangelical Alliance, *Tele-Evangelists Cloud Broadcast Debate*. (London: Evangelical Alliance, 1989).

175. in Reville, N., *Broadcasting – The New Law.* (London: Butterworths, 1991), p.5.

176. Leigh, I. (1992), p.303.

177. Hind. K., *Commons Standing Committee F*. 25th January (1990), Hansard Col.322, 323.

178. Shegog, E., Godwatching. *Sunday Telegraph*. 26th November (1989), p.15.

179. Interview: 16th August (2018)

180. Quicke, A. and Quicke, J. (1982) Chapters 8-20.

181. Broadcasting Act 1990, 38 & 39 Eliz. 11, c.42.

182. McDonnell. J., From Certainty to Diversity: The Evolution of Religious Broadcasting Since 1990. *In:* Geybels, H., Mels, S. and Walrave, M., *Faith & Media: Analysis of Faith and Media* (Brussels: P. I. E. Peter Lang, 2009), p.154.

183. Interview: 21st June (2018).

184. General Synod Commission, *Broadcasting Society and the Church* (London. Church Information Office, 1973), p.8.

185. Coyer, K., *Its Not Just Radio: Models of Community Broadcasting in Britain and the United States*. (PhD). Goldsmith's College, London (2009), p.142.

186. Briggs, A., *The BBC: The First Fifty Years* (Oxford: Oxford University Press, 1985), p.130.

187. Morris, C., *Wrestling with an Angel* (London. Collins Fount, 1990), p.150.

188. Horsfield, P.G., *From Jesus to the Internet: A History of Christianity and Media* (London: Blackwell, 2015), p.288.

189. Curran, C., (1975), p.11.

CHAPTER 4

THE HALL OF FAME
The Champions of Religious Broadcasting

1. A Spectrum of Significance

It was historian and philosopher Thomas Carlyle who said, "The history of the world is but the biography of great men".[1] Certainly biography has had a long history going back more than two thousand years, though in recent years has been seen as something of a correction to much "woolly" history.[2] But biography was for a long time regarded by the academic world with scepticism, with many scholars who thought of tackling the field of biography not knowing how to encompass it[3] and others viewing it as merely "diffuse and journalistic".[4]

Even as early as 1915, Carl Van Doren commented "It is a pity that biography should go unstudied when other forms of literature have specialists in dozens.[5] But about a quarter of a century ago a greater interest did grow in the importance that personal background could contribute to the story of history. Across the world a number of centres devoted to biography have been established at universities, especially in Europe and there has been a trend to view biography as something of a 'micro history'[6] or 'life stories',[7] able not only to represent an entire character, but able to speak beyond that to the greater picture of their society, an important point that media historian David Hendy makes in asserting that biography is the "nexus through which larger structures might be revealed and understood".[8]

In addition, as Nigel Hamilton suggests, "biography's purpose is to discover for us and for those who follow us, as much as possible of the unvarnished, unromanticised, uncompromising truth about real lives".[9] Biography is therefore a significant platform to reflect the lives of those involved in the realms of broadcasting. Indeed, broadcasting is not just a random selection of sounds or words floating about in the ether, it is about people in places making their own particular proclamation. So it is very appropriate in chronicling the story of religious broadcasting to feature those unique personalities who made a significant contribution to its development, both here in the UK and in America.

As we have noted previously, Thomas Carlyle and Ralph Waldo Emerson in the 19th Century talked of 'heroes' – people who were distinctive and significantly important individuals. Max Weber (1864-1920) developed his concept of 'charisma' related to exceptional individuals too. Weber's work is incisive as a means with which to understand how human history is replete with charismatic individuals who have achieved considerable political, cultural and religious sway and whose power has been perceived to be almost 'mystical' or 'spiritual'[10] and who as a result received adulation and worship from their followers[11] and achieved a significant status in society. But this then morphs into a more modern context where the 'heroic' figures are less the focus and commentary and a current concept of 'celebrity' takes over.[12] To Boorstin, "the hero was distinguished by his achievements, the celebrity by his image or trademark ... the hero was a big man, the celebrity a big name".[13]

The whole concept of celebrity is a multi-faceted term whose Oxford English Dictionary definitions cite as being 'extolled' or 'famousness' or 'notoriety'. Chris Rojek author of the influential book *Celebrity* indicated the Latin root of the word celebrity is *celebren* which has connotations with both 'fame' and 'being thronged'.[14] However it is not just Latin from which 'celebrity' has emerged, as Rojek argues, it is also related to the French word célèbre which translates as 'famous' or 'well known in public'.[15]

As Fred Inglis argues, "the history of celebrity demands a kind of history which is largely missing on the shelves",[16] it is "everywhere acknowledged but never understood".[17] Equally, there is also common assumption that celebrity is a contemporary social phenomenon, but actually it is not so clear cut. Whereas celebrity is closely associated with the rise of technologies of mass communication, the desire to stand out from the social mass has been deeply embedded within human civilization for thousands of years.[18] So celebrity is a term that could be rightly applied to a number of historical figures. But as Inglis further argues, there is no doubt that with the development of communication media from the mid-18th Century, the specific concept of 'celebrity' replaced the more general process of 'renown' – a status typically linked with acts of 'high accomplishment' and civic acts which brought honour not to the individual but to the role which they inhabited.[19] So although the roots of fame and the active desire for fame are traceable to ancient civilizations and the more contemporary concept of celebrity emerged in the European sphere in the middle of the 18th Century, it certainly became more developed and shaped by the dominant forces of modernity, industrialization and urbanization. These processes were then accelerated and intensified by the mass circulation of newspapers (with an increasing focus on the lives of the famous) and the major modes of mass communications that would subsequently follow.

Marshall best summarizes this construction in terms of the nature, relevance and characteristics of celebrity:-

1. The celebrity is the epitome of the individual for identification and idealization in society.

2. The celebrity is not wholly determined by the culture industries and is therefore somewhat created and constructed by the audience's reading of dominant cultural representations.

3. The celebrity is a commodity and therefore expresses a form of valorization of the individual and personality that is coherent with capitalism and the associated consumer culture.[20]

Further, in modern celebrity culture it is true that the condition of celebrity status is convertible to a wide variety of domains. Thus the power of celebrity status appears in business, politics, artistic communities and yes religion and operates as a way of providing distinctions and definitions of success within those domains. Celebrity status also confers on the person a certain discursive power: within society, the celebrity is a voice above others, a voice that is channeled into the media systems as being legitimately significant,[21] albeit sometimes a transient one[22] and sometimes even a vacuous one.[23] So despite other commentaries on society, the individual continues to feature as a major force in modern day culture [24] with some achieving fame, celebrity and the pinnacle in terms of 'stardom', with all its trappings.[25]

So whether it is Carlyle and Emerson talking about 'heroes'; Weber and 'charismatic' personalities; Boorstin, Inglis, Rojek and Marshall with 'celebrities' or Dyer with 'stars', what we have identified is something of a synergy, demonstrating the emergence of powerful individuals, with what we have called a 'spectrum of significance', not all wielding identical power and influence, but all making an impact in their own spheres in their own unique way.

This backdrop serves us well in creating the context and understanding in which religious broadcasters operated particularly in the USA, but also to some extent in the UK. With 'celebrity' and 'personality' in recent years becoming interchangeable in our language, [26] it is interesting to see how the commentary outlined applies in the realms of religion and religious broadcasting.

Lofton in her study on *"Religion and the American Celebrity"* (2011) underlines the interconnectedness in America of ideas about religious institutions and ideas about celebrity success, with the links between the media of celebrity formation and propulsion and the media of religious missions and organizational development. In the American context the rise of the celebrity/personality makes their commodification and the dynamics of modern religion inextricable.[27]

Examples of this commingling can be seen in this chapter in terms of the religious broadcasting charismatic celebrities/personalities that took to the national and international stage carrying with them vast adoring and loyal audiences which re-enforced their 'celebrity' or 'star' status. As Loften goes on to say, this celebrity culture informs the religious imaginations of its consumers and the consumption of celebrity increasingly formats expectations of religious leadership and its distribution and communication.[28]

Therefore their audiences are seen as 'consumers' and the celebrities/personalities in the raw seen as 'commodities', creating what Marshall also called an "audience-subjectiveness", where the genre of the celebrity provides avenues for the development of audience meaning through the identification of the individual celebrity's subjectivity.[29] This in simple terms is what we see with the dynamic and charismatic religious broadcasting icons of America which featured in the radio and television media in this era, developing vast powerful 'industries' (to them 'ministries') with a Christian 'product' and audiences 'consumers' who form a community of dedicated, faithful supporters 'fans', who ensure the continuity and power of the celebrity/personality on the public stage.

This is very much a reflection of America and the religious broadcasting experience there. The UK is a significant contrast. The cradle of the public service broadcasting system of the BBC, which we have chronicled earlier, discouraged any personality 'cult' in terms of religious broadcasting, probably fearing it would mirror America. Despite this in terms of our 'spectrum of significance', certain individuals in the UK made a real impact through religious broadcasting both on and off-air and became household names both on radio and later on television.

The chapter here attempts to demonstrate from the US and the UK contexts, some of those key men and women who were the 'heroes', 'personalities', 'celebrities', 'stars' of religious broadcasting. They had a sense of calling from a higher being and a single-minded commitment to a cause[30] and were able to use the platforms of radio and television to bring the Christian message to countless millions of people in their own homes and make an impact far beyond what had ever been achieved before in terms of Christian communication.

2. The Key Personalities

a) John C.W. Reith (1889-1971)

Although John Reith was not a broadcaster himself, as the first General Manager (1922) and then Director General (1927) of the BBC, he was the key protagonist for introducing religious broadcasting into the early BBC programming. Reith was the youngest of seven children, born to a Scottish Presbyterian minister from the small Scottish town of Stonehaven. His early education in Glasgow and then Norfolk eventually led him to London in 1914 and engineering work at the Royal Albert Dock. But war was to take him away, with roles in the 5th Scottish Rifles, Royal Marine Engineers and finally, in 1919, as a Captain in the Royal Engineers.[31]

Despite having no broadcasting experience, he managed to apply for and land the job of General Manager at the newly created British Broadcasting Company (1922). As was said, "Nothing ever pleased him more than to be given sole command and presented with a blank sheet of paper.[32] But eventually being surrounded by technicians, artists, composers, playwrights, manufacturers and regulations and everything else in between, his task was to fit the whole complex puzzle together, to ensure the success of this new innovative form of mass media.

When at the age of 33, Reith took up his appointment at the BBC; he saw it more than just a job. In line with his strict religious background, he saw it as a 'calling'; a vocation for which he had been commissioned by God. His inherited Calvinism was both his sense of destiny to such a work and his driving ambition.[33] Broadcasting to him was to be a "drawn sword parting the darkness of ignorance"[34] and in order to fulfil this ideal he believed there should be only one broadcasting service, independent of the State and free from the need to make profits.

Reith was intimately concerned with the creation of programming policy and so the British Broadcasting Company made its first religious broadcast on Christmas Eve 1922, given by Rev. J.O. Mayo, Rector of Whitechapel, just 6 weeks after beginning regular daily operations and several weeks before receiving its first Licence on 18th January 1923. From then on, as the BBC developed, so did religious broadcasting with the introduction of a regular Sunday Service. Reith was convinced that broadcast religious services were of great value not only to the godly, but also to the men and women who would never darken a church door if they could avoid it,

> There are tens of thousands who would not go to any sort of church but to whom are now brought the influence of a straight-forward and manly religion. I know that even the singing of once familiar hymns has brought back the remembrance of happier and better days. There is no telling the effect when, for this brief period in a busy week, the lamps are lit before the Lord and the message and music of eternity move through the infinities of the ether.[35]

Reith's approach to religious broadcasting was very broad in scope and non-denominational. In 1924, Reith wrote in his *Broadcast Over Britain,* that from the outset British broadcasting had "a definite, though restrained association with religion in general, and with the Christian religion in particular".[36] The kind of Christianity that Reith wanted the BBC to reflect was 'thorough-going and optimistic', unconcerned with 'the narrow interpretation of dogma', and centred on 'the application of teaching of Christ to everyday life'. In order to achieve this Reith needed the advice and support of the churches in the 'main stream' of historic Christianity, as to whom they would accept as suitable speakers. A meeting with Archbishop Davidson led to the formation of the 'Sunday Committee' to provide this pipeline – a committee destined, in 1926, to become the Central Religious Advisory Committee (CRAC). Equally there was fastidiousness about Reith's choice of ecclesiastical advisors, Frederick Iremonger, William Temple, Cyril Garbett and Dick Sheppard, which combined with his Scottish hard-headedness, preserved him from the temptation of developing religious broadcasting along the parallel lines to that on the other side of the Atlantic.[37] But as Wolfe concluded in talking about Reith and his faith and the environment at the time,

> his Christianity was unrealistic but lyrical; the harsh poetry of his Presbyterian origins embraced personal piety enmeshed in notions of duty ... but it was a Christianity impatient with the churches.[38]

Therefore it is not surprising he took the initiatives and under his leadership, "by 1929 the place of religion in broadcast programmes had increased enormously; Sunday services, weekly evensong from Westminster Abbey and a daily service".[39] Unfortunately not everyone favoured the style of the Reithian Sunday which caused more controversy than did any other programme policy. As Quicke illustrates,

> on a typical Sunday in 1935, the programming consisted of good music and improving talks. The diet included Bach's St Matthew's Passion, Sheridan's The Rivals, classical music, Treasures of the Bible, Heroes of the Free Churches, a talk on How to Read an Epistle' and the first of three half-hour talks by Canon Charles Raven on 'The Way to God'.[40]

Whatever effect such scheduling may have had on religious belief in Britain, there is no doubt that it drove half the audience to powerful commercial stations like Radio Luxembourg and Radio Normandy, whose programmes of light music with advertising, were easily receivable in most of the United Kingdom.[41]

Although religious broadcasting in Britain was indeed supremely Reith's creation, that was only a segment of his vision for the BBC, which he saw as to inform, educate and entertain – a concept which would shape the development of public service broadcasting in Britain ever after[42] and remains part of the BBC's Mission Statement today. Reith saw the policy of the Company to bring the best of everything into the greatest number of homes.[43] In addition by 1924, Reith's book *Broadcast Over Britain*, had already laid out some of those abiding principles of the forthcoming Corporation.[44] But it was the General Strike of 1926 which was to see Reith at his best, making the most of the potential of radio to bring the immediate news of this industrial dispute to the nation, with what was to become its characteristic impartiality.

When the BBC received its Royal Charter in 1927, to become the British Broadcasting Corporation, Reith became its first Director General and as reward for his public service he was also knighted in the same year to become Lord Reith. His reign at the BBC, was considered autocratic and idiosyncratic and reflected his complex character, which gave rise to a management style and philosophical approach which was termed *Reithian* – an adjective, whether what it represents was admired or spurned. Siepmann comments,

> Sir John Reith was so certain he was right that no research seemed necessary. Regardless of its actual affects, for him his policy stood self-justified. Secure in his personal conviction of what was right and wrong, he imposed upon a nation the imprint of his personality.[45]

When he retired in 1938 he had spent sixteen years of his life in creating, "one of the most distinctive and impressive of modern British Institutions".[46] On leaving the BBC, Reith took charge of British Imperial Airways, but the war came before he was able to develop his role there. In 1940 The Prime Minister Neville Chamberlain appointed him as the Minister of Information, but then the new Prime Minister, Winston Churchill transferred him to the Ministry of Transport, but dropped him from the Cabinet in 1942. He had longed for a task of great responsibility during the war, but was to remain disappointed.

A later Director General of the BBC, William Haley (1942-52) commented on Reith's disposition at this time, "the middle aged man was convinced that the material and moral salvation of Britain in war and in peace would have been more assured had he been Prime Minister".[47] But after the war Reith became Chairman of the Commonwealth Communications Board and in 1948 the BBC inaugurated the *Reith Lectures* in his honour. In his later years he held a number of Directorships and also became Lord Rector of Glasgow University from 1965-1968.

Summarizing the life and impact of Reith is a monumental challenge, but maybe it is best captured in the words of the Moderator of the General Assembly of the Church of Scotland at Reith's Memorial Service in 1971,

> A man who established a kingdom, yet in his heart wanted to build a shrine...A man of vision who complained that he had never been given a big enough job to do. [48]

Reith's two books *Broadcast over Britain* (1924) and *Into the Wind* (1949) remain classic volumes of this titan of the 20th Century.

b) Rev.Dick Sheppard (1880-1937)

In terms of the development of religious broadcasting in the UK, Dick Sheppard, as he was commonly known, was the right man in the right place at the right time. He was dubbed "the Vicar of the BBC", the "People's Padre".[49]

Born in Windsor to one of the clergy of the Royal Chapel there, Hugh Richard Lawrie Sheppard had a privileged education at Marlborough College and then Trinity Hall Cambridge, but then spent a few years working with the poor in the East End of London, before becoming the secretary to Cosmo Lang, the then Bishop of Stepney. When the war came in 1914 he served as chaplain to a military hospital in France before returning to take up the fashionable position as Vicar of St. Martin-in-the-Fields. There he stayed for 12 years and "pioneered broadcasting and popular religious journalism and made the church one of the most famous centres of social work in London, with people queueing to come inside and sit on the chancel steps to hear him preach".[50] St. Martin's, in Trafalgar Square, was for Sheppard on arrival rather dark and unlovely with a small congregation, though frequented by a number of rich people and including the Prime Minister, Mr

Gladstone. However Sheppard was a visionary and declared, "I saw a great church standing in the greatest square in the greatest city of the world. And I stood on the west steps and I saw what this church would be to the life of the people".[51] As Northcott, points out...

> Gradually the public began to be aware that a man had arrived in the heart of London with an exceptional personality. He was not a crank or a snob or an old woman, but a much alive person with a devotion of an Anglo Catholic and the common sense of a Kingsley. This was the estimate of his character that created his popularity and made him and his church famous.[52]

Sheppard's influence on London grew from strength to strength, as his biographer Richard Ellis Roberts claims, "hundreds of thousands of men for whom religion had meant routine, boredom, mumbo-jumbo, something desiccated and dead, found it moving, helpful and alive".[53]

Meanwhile Sheppard had married Alison Lennox, who more than once had to nurse him and support him through his bouts of exhaustion and illness which would characterise much of his adult life and ministry. But despite his handicaps Sheppard was an astute man in many areas and sought to turn things of worldliness into advantage for the Church. So in 1924 he was exploiting two powerful instruments of communications. One was broadcasting, considered blasphemous by some. The other, the parish magazine, which many in the clergy thought was of little effect. However St. Martin's *Messenger* was turned into the *St. Martin's Review* and by 1924 sales of the magazine was averaging nearly six thousand and had subscribers in over forty different countries.[54]

Broadcasting had begun in 1922 and John Reith, its first Managing Director, knew of Sheppard's reputation and invited him to join the Religious Advisory Board. It was Sheppard Reith eulogised, asserting that his preaching "was the work of a man who understood profoundly the needs and sorrows and fears of humanity. The subtle mingling of humour and sharp visual imagery and sincerity has an aptness and reality which more complex sermons would have lacked entirely".[55]

Not surprisingly therefore Sheppard was asked to provide the first regular church service ever to be broadcast on the BBC which took place at St. Martin's on the evening of 6th January 1924 and for many marked the real beginning of religious broadcasting in Britain.[56] Sheppard was a perfect broadcaster who could appeal to the individual listener, as if he were talking not to a vast audience but to each member of it alone.[57] Sheppard wrote in the *St. Martin-in-the-Fields Calling*, "you must neither read nor preach your broadcast sermon, but just talk it".[58]

Sheppard's broadcast sermons gave him national fame in what he called his 'cry in the dark to over two hundred thousand people'.[59] As a result of one broadcast sermon Sheppard received nearly three thousand letters,[60] though it is true to say not all of them complimentary. But the vast majority showed the power of Sheppard's broadcasts, as the one he quotes in the *St. Martin's Review*... "I have fitted up a set for my mother of 84, it has put new life into her as she can't make the journey to church".[61] However another breakdown and acute asthma led to Sheppard's resignation from St. Martin's in 1926.

Sheppard had become a keen pacifist, writing and speaking considerably on the subject and later in 1936 set up the Peace Pledge Union. Rose Macaulay commented that for Sheppard "pacifism was an ardent adventure, a crusade. It might not work yet, he would admit, but it was worth a throw".[62] It was for him a great passion, as was the Church. He laid his heart bare in articulating his revolutionary vision of the Church in his book *The Impatience of a Parson*, feeling that "it is conceivable that Christ could be orthodox within any church today".[63] Sometimes even being cutting in his criticism, feeling there is often more real fellowship in the public house than in the Christian Church.[64] Despite the outspoken nature of his writing, the book became a popular publication in bookshops all over the country selling an estimated 100,000 copies. But thinking at this point his parish ministry was at an end; out of the blue in 1929 he was summoned to Downing Street and offered the appointment as Dean of Canterbury Cathedral. Despite huge audiences for his preaching at Canterbury, once again illness took its toll and he had to step down in 1931.

After leaving Canterbury he planned to write his autobiography, but despite starting the task, inevitably it was never to be finished. He did however return to London and engaged in numbers of activities, often up at five in the morning and working through until seven at night, sometimes even eighteen hour days and for a man plagued with ill health, pushed himself to the limits out of enthusiasm. One Sunday's appointments reveal his desire for service …

6.00am	Letter Writing
7.30am	Celebration Charing Cross Hospital
8.15am	Assist at St.Martin's
9.00am	Three ward services at the hospital
10.15am	Assist at St.Martin's
1.00pm	Sandwich lunch with friend
2.30pm	Two personal interviews
3.30pm	Christening
4.00pm	Four ward services at the hospital
7.30pm	Dinner at the Bath Club
9.00pm	Visiting the Crypt
10.15pm	BBC Epilogue
11.00pm	Letter writing until the early hours [65]

His latter years were to be spent as a Canon at St Paul's Cathedral, often dubbed the 'Parish Church of the City'. Sheppard felt the cold atmosphere of St. Paul's declaring, "Wren did a wonderful job, but he left one thing out. He didn't give it a soul and nobody knows how to remedy the omission".[66] He died alone in his canon's house at St. Paul's Cathedral, at odds with the Church leaders and broken hearted because his wife Alison had left him.

Dick Sheppard was a complex man. His Dean called him four or five characters in one, at once practical and mystical, gay and sad, popular and reticent, an autocrat and a democrat, struggling within himself and yet sublimely confident. One of his friends Arthur Wragg described him as "great in mind, great in humility, great in achievement and great in fun".[67]

After his death his coffin laid in state at St. Martin-in-the-Fields. It was estimated that one hundred thousand people passed by to pay their respects. His funeral took place at St. Paul's Cathedral. Crowds four deep lined the streets, men with their hats off and women in tears. Police held up traffic as a hundred clergy followed the hearse up Ludgate Hill to St Paul's where the Cathedral was crowded to the doors with people standing in the courtyard.[68] Sheppard was eventually buried, as he had requested, in the cloisters of Canterbury Cathedral.[69]

In terms of legacy, however eminent may be the theologians, however eloquent the preachers, however finished the services from cathedrals and churches throughout the country, it was in large measure the vision, the courage, the eager personality and the passionate sincerity of H.R.L. Sheppard which gave religion its established place in the broadcasting service.[70]

c) Rev.W.H. Elliott (1884-1957)

The man, who gained the reputation in the UK as the 'radio chaplain', was christened Wallace Harold Elliott (apparently he always hated his Christian names) and brought up in Horsham in East Sussex. His family were not very well off and at the age of 5 he developed meningitis and almost died. Maybe that was the spur for him to minister to others as a parson, an ambition he never seemed to swerve from as he expressed in his autobiography, "from early childhood I had it in mind that I should be a parson".[71] He was educated at the local Collyene School, but was often away ill with bouts of tonsillitis. Despite this he managed to win a place at

Brasenose College, Oxford, to study Theology. Not always an enjoyable experience for the young Elliott, who however was drawn to the music of Christ Church, New College and Magdalen. He left Oxford with a 2nd Class Degree in Theology and went to Ripon Clergy College and eventually was ordained in York Minister in 1907.[72]

He started a curacy in Guisborough in North Yorkshire, a once small market town expanded to accommodate miners, who Elliott felt suffered under such bad working conditions and when they went on strike ran a soup kitchen for them and their families.[73] Sadly ill health was to plague him again and he accepted an invitation to help at Leeds Parish Church, but the four to six weeks turned into five years, eventually becoming curate and deputizing for the vicar when he left to be a canon of Canterbury.

Elliott's popularity grew and the church was attracting big congregations. In 1918 he married Edith Evelyn Plantowe, but also became ill again and needed several months rest. Once he recovered he was on the move, this time to Holy Trinity, Folkestone where he stayed for 11 years, still struggling with his ill health. However after a short time at the canonry at St Pauls, it was the invitation to central London's St. Michael's Chester Square in 1930 that was to be the crucial appointment in his ministry.

Writing in the Parish Magazine soon after his arrival he said,

> Let me say at once I am amazed at all the work that is going on and the magnificent spirit of all those who night by night are giving freely of their time and energy for the benefit of St. Michaels ... I think that the congregation knows already that I am not contemplating any drastic changes in our services or ways of working. At the back of my mind there is the strange feeling that I am "on approval" at St. Michael's.[74]

He must have had premonition, as he described his first year as 'hell' and maybe he should have not taken up the appointment.[75] There were many arguments, but he sought consolation in developing a large choir with boys recruited from the church school. Despite the stumbling blocks in his early ministry at St. Michael's, he had much in his favour – good looks, a winning manner and a forceful delivery.[76]

His preaching gained him a growing reputation, which sparked the attention of Sir John Reith, Director General of the BBC, who invited him to talk about the possibility of broadcasting a late midweek service from the Church.[77] Broadcasting was still in its infancy and religious broadcasting not yet out of its cradle. A six week trial schedule of Tuesday evenings was arranged, which involved the congregation, but with a very homely six to seven minute address by Elliott. When the trial was coming to an end Elliott solicited his listeners and asked them to send postcards to the BBC if they wished the broadcasts to continue. Over 10,000 postcards were received. The services continued moving to Thursday evenings and continued for another eight years and became a national institution and Elliott a household name.[78]

Elliott was aware of the early suspicions some church leaders had about broadcasting, but in his second Christmas at St. Michael's, Elliott wrote to balance that in their *Parish Record Magazine*,

> Most of us are interested in Broadcasting. Few people have been able to resist the appeal of this new invention, which has made the world one great whispering gallery. Yet another link has been added to those chains which are making the world one. Like all inventions it has potentialities for good or for evil. Man can do with it what he will.[79]

Elliott recognised and exploited the peculiar advantages of broadcasting. His approach was highly personal stating,

> A broadcaster must be able, without any self-consciousness, to talk to the microphone as an old friend. He must never think of the millions listening and address himself to them. That is always fatal. If there is any image in his mind at all, it must be of one person.[80]

What Elliott did with it was to draw people through his Thursday night broadcasts from their parlours to the pews. As many as 500 people joined the congregation for the broadcasts, with attendances on Sunday at St. Michael's reaching nearly 2000, often with people still queuing outside. The newspapers picked this up, describing it as "the most remarkable and cosmopolitan congregation in the world"[81] and a unique phenomenon. Elliott also expressed his preaching philosophy to the Press,

> only by radio can one man talk as man to man and though really addressing millions, give the effect of helping and talking direct to the listener by the fireside.[82]

One listener responding to Elliott's broadcasts, expressed it in these terms,

> It is always a pleasure and privilege to listen to Mr. Elliott. Some parsons seem to live in the clouds and have no idea of realistic life as lived by common folk. Mr Elliott seems to have the gift of understanding and sympathy. His talks have been an inspiration to me.[83]

However despite his popularity not everyone was pleased with Elliott's broadcasting success. F.A. Iremonger, the BBC's Head of Religious Broadcasting complained that the addresses offered only comfort, with no challenge. There was no analysis of the desperate social crisis facing the nation.[84] The hymns being sentimental and often tear-jerking and Elliott was "talking about crocuses when the world is going up in flames".[85] However Elliott was supported by Reith and the favourite of King George V and Queen Mary, but with the war years, changes within BBC religious broadcasting, especially pressure from Welch the new Head of Religious Broadcasting[86] and his ill health, meant that the broadcasts were to draw to a close.[87] Something he lamented very much.[88]

Following a collapse he had a thyroid operation and spent two years recovering in Banbury. But the shocking news of the death of his 16 year old son Robin, in a road accident, seemed to shake him out of his malaise and he took up the invitation as Precentor, Deputy Clerk and Sub-Almoner at the Chapels Royal, serving as Sub-Dean from 1945-1948. For many years Elliott struggled against great physical disabilities and in 1948 felt he needed a lower key ministry and moved to the Collegiate Church of St. Mary in Warwick.[89] This one time Cathedral was not really downsizing, but he stayed for 18 months during which time he also became an honorary canon of Coventry Cathedral, until he retired back to Compton in Sussex where he continued to write. His total output of books, which included many collections of broadcast addresses, was nearly 50, including his autobiography *Undiscovered Ends* (1951) which did not win literary acclaim, but like his broadcasts proved popular with many, so much so that the book required reprinting just a month after its publication. Elliott died in 1957.[90]

d) Aimee Semple Mcpherson (1890-1944)

Long before the television preaching of Oral Roberts, Billy Graham and Pat Robertson there was Aimee Semple McPherson. "The first megastar evangelist of the media age".[91] She was born in Ontario in Canada to a mother who worked with the Salvation Army and a father who was a Methodist. But despite her religious background, by her teenage years she was into novels, movies and dances and had ambitions to be an actress – all things disapproved of by her family. But the call of God on her life proved too strong and at 17 she met and married a Pentecostal preacher, Robert Semple – both then travelling to China to do missionary work. Sadly Robert died of malaria one month before Aimee gave birth to her daughter Roberta and Aimee ended up moving back to America to live with her mother until, at 21, she married Harold McPherson and gave birth to her second and last child, Rolf.[92]

Aimee was a complex and controversial character, in many ways like John Reith. She suffered many ailments and serious bouts of depression and eventually ended up abandoning her husband and touring the country delivering sermons in barns, tents and open fields, until in 1922 when she was officially ordained as a Baptist minister. Her reputation grew as a powerfully persuasive speaker, a convincing faith healer and a trouble-shooter, who could be counted on to improve attendance in failing churches. In 1923 she went on to form the 5,300 seater International Church of the Four Square Gospel in Santa Monica California, named the Angelus Temple which was filled to capacity three times a day, seven days a week. Aimee in her autobiography *This is That* comments "The Temple seats still continue to be filled with people, but also with the glory of the Lord".[93]

It is said that the tabernacle more closely resembled a vaudeville theatre than a house of worship and Sister Aimee gave the best show in town, with exotic costumes, bizarre props and brassy music to pack 'em in.[94] A 36-piece orchestra would accompany enormous choirs. Elaborate pageants depicting Bible stories were staged complete with animals borrowed from farmers or, when it was in town, the circus. Aimee never did anything by halves. It is said that Charlie Chaplin said to Aimee, "Half your success is due to your magnetic appeal and half due to the props and lights".[95]

In her day McPherson became a unique force in American society.[96] She was the first woman to preach a sermon on the radio, to own and operate a radio station and she was the first woman to have a broadcast licence issued from the Federal Radio Commission. In 1924 using the communities who were connected to her via print, she had raised money to put KFSG (Kalling Four Square Gospel) on the air. The station was an instant success and it soon made Aimee's voice "one of the most familiar voices in America ... and enabled her to come into the homes of her followers any time of day or night, greatly augmenting her influence".[97] She stands at the cutting edge of the communication revolution taking place, as radio stations and receiver sets spread across the national landscape. As she said at the outset of her broadcasting career, "It has now become possible to stand in the pulpit and speaking in a normal voice, reach hundreds of thousands of listeners".[98]

The station earned a niche in the early history of broadcasting in America, but was one of the stations which had disputes with the authorities over a number of issues. The Secretary of State, Herbert Hoover in 1927 warned McPherson not to keep changing the dial frequency on her station whenever she felt like it. Aimee in typical fashion gave him a robust response via telegram which read ...

> Please order your minions of Satan to leave my station alone (Stop). You cannot expect the Almighty to abide by your wavelength nonsense (Stop). When I offer my prayers to Him I must fit into His wave reception (Stop). Open this station at once.[99]

Radio made McPherson's reputation and in the 1920's she continued to travel and preach, using the radio, the newspapers and her magazine *The Bridal Call* to communicate with those who had been touched by her message. But it was an event in 1926 that was to threaten her image. She disappeared while swimming off the Californian coast and first reports were that she had drowned. Her mother even posted a reward of $25,000 dollars for any information about her disappearance. But she showed up a few days later wandering around in the desert, claiming that she had been kidnapped. Though it is widely believed that her disappearance was actually a 'lovers' rendezvous with former KFSG radio technician Kenneth Ormiston.[100]

The abduction story was disputed and she ended up as the central figure in a trial for fraud, but it was deduced that her subterfuge had not been concocted to financially defraud anyone and so the charges were dropped. As they say the only thing better than death, career-wise, is resurrection. She returned to her Temple in triumph and if it hadn't exactly enhanced her reputation, the scandal had raised her profile even further and donations from relieved supporters flowed in as never before.

Brown, in his tongue-in-cheek article called the *Canadian Comeback Kid*, comments..

> Aimee was an extra sexy evangelist, a superstar of the Roaring Twenties. A sort of holy Salome, she not only outshone most

movie stars – at a time when cinema was still considered improper – but toured the entire North American continent to massive crowds and massive hysteria. Then, at the absolute pinnacle of her career, when she had her own widely successful radio station and a 'Temple' in Los Angeles that put Chartres cathedral to shame, she attempted a now-you-see-me publicity stunt that was so incredible it almost defies imagining.[101]

But in the 1930's McPherson suffered a number of setbacks, including a slump in listeners, a bout with alcohol, a foredoomed third marriage and an estrangement with her mother and Aimee's daughter from her first marriage. She staged a comeback in 1939 and within five years was drawing up plans for conquering the new electronic pulpit of television. But she was ravaged by insomnia and became dependent on sedatives to sleep and died of what was to be termed an accidental overdose in 1944 at the age of 53.[102]

After her death her church leaders brought the body back to Los Angeles, where it lay in state at the Angelus Temple for three days. According to the *Los Angeles Times*

> forty-five thousand people waited in long lines, some until two in the morning to file past the evangelists' bier… At the three-hour funeral service at the Temple, six thousand parishioners and an estimated fifty thousand dollars worth of flowers filled the Temple, with another two thousand people listening in from the Church's overflow auditorium.[103]

McPherson is buried in Forest Lawn Memorial Park Cemetery in Glendale California.

There have been many interpretations and evaluations of Aimee Semple McPherson and her approach to ministry. Blumhofer wrote that McPherson,

> was less an innovator than a populariser. She exploited the ideas and techniques of others – from the Salvation Army to the writers of Broadway spectacles, to capture the attention

of people and direct that attention from simple entertainment towards eternal concerns.[104]

She tended to focus listeners on issues like the importance of fanning faith to life, seeking the filling of the Holy Spirit and instilling a sense on those who came under her teaching that they were beautiful and worthy of God's blessings. But she also believed this spiritual awareness needed to be turned outwards, modelling the Christian life for people by reaching across cultural divides and encouraging people to action. She reached out to the black community, inviting them to preach at her church and she took over the Los Angeles free school lunch programme when the city dropped it. It is said that the Angelus Temple assisted more family units than any other public or private institutions in the city.

Brown comments that this was,

> A carefully calibrated programme of corporate social responsibility. Aimee welcomed the world-weary, housed the indigent, fed the hungry, healed the sick and saved souls like there was no tomorrow.[105]

This along with her "America Awake" campaign to bring politics, social action and communities in America back to its Christian heritage, was seen by McPherson simply as faith in action. She proclaimed, "Whether we be Republican or Democrat, Jew or Gentile, Catholic or Protestant we are made of the same clay, worship the same God and swear allegiance to the same country".[106] She trusted that if Christianity occupied a central place in national life, everything else would work out.

McPherson's chosen form of Christianity, known as Pentecostalism, had only emerged in America a few years before she encountered it and was still largely seen as a fringe division of Protestant Christianity. But Maddux maintains, "McPherson downplayed the controversial elements of the Pentecostal movement and instead took a moderate position that facilitated broad alliances".[107] She explicitly tried to build a ministry that would unify rather than divide Christians, although she was not unaware of her critics. Much of that criticism was because of what was termed her feminized Gospel, evident in her dramatic emotional and embodied performance of faith, something that is discussed at great length in Maddux's paper, *The Feminized Gospel: Aimee Semple McPherson and the Gendered Performance of Christianity*. McPherson argued, "Sex has nothing to do with the pulpit and pants don't make preachers".[108]

Aimee's powerful persona raised interest outside of the Christian community. For example her legend appeared in the television dramatization of Aimee's "kidnapping" starring Faye Dunaway as Aimee and Bette Davis as her mother. Aimee was also Frank Capra's *The Miracle Woman* (1931) starring Barbara Stanwyck, with what amounted to a brilliant McPherson imitation.[109] It is thought too that the character Sharon Falconer in Sinclair Lewis's *Elmer Gantry* was based on McPherson.[110] At her death she led a church of thousands in Los Angeles and was the head of a growing denomination. Today this denomination – the International Church of the Foursquare Gospel (ICFG) boasts a world wide membership of 8 million in more than 60,000 churches in 144 nations.[111]

Hart summarizes well in stating,

> McPherson remains a controversial figure even today, with mystery, criticism and admiration surrounding her memory. While her constant search for publicity became a double edged sword in her scandal-ridden life, her efforts to incorporate modern presentation style and advertising techniques into an emerging Pentecostal religion catapulted Pentecostalism into one of America's fastest growing religions.[112]

History is packed full of fascinating figures. Many were raised for greatness like John F. Kennedy or Queen Elizabeth II, but some came from nowhere and nothing but still rose to great prominence. Such indeed was Aimee Semple McPherson, the preacher and evangelist who reigned as America's best-known woman for much of her life.

e) Father Charles Coughlin (1891-1979)

Father Charles Coughlin, as he was better known, became the 'radio priest' of the 1930s and a man who in the eyes of many sceptics made religious broadcasting and demagoguery synonymous. Despite reaching up to thirty million listeners tuning into his weekly broadcasts, this Canadian-American Roman Catholic priest was destined to become one of the most controversial figures in the United States in the 1930s and early 1940s.[113]

Coughlin was born in Hamilton Ontario in 1891. His early education brought him into the fold of the Congregation of St. Basil, a society of priests dedicated to education. Therefore it wasn't surprising that Coughlin himself felt called to the priesthood and subsequently was Ordained in 1916. He eventually joined the Detroit diocese in 1923 and was granted his own ministry at the Shrine of the Little Flower in Royal Oak Michigan,[114] a town then under the thumb of the Ku Klux Clan. Normally associated with racial bigotry, particularly with black people, the Klan were also very anti-Catholic and just two weeks after the Shrine of the Little Flower was completed, the Klan burned a cross on its front lawn. But Coughlin only responded with a message of love, forgiveness and tolerance.[115]

Despite the small Catholic congregation, in what was largely a Protestant suburban community, Coughlin's powerful preaching soon attracted more people to his parish Services and also attracted the attention of Dick Richards, owner of the Detroit radio station WJR who invited him to speak on air on October 17th, 1926. As Brinkley points out Coughlin "was startled by his sudden popularity, but wasted little time in capitalizing on it".[116] He began to build up his own network of affiliate stations, among them Cincinnati's WLW and Chicago's WMAQ and in 1930 going national on CBS. Coughlin conducted his activities from the Little Flower Church for almost four decades, adding his famous tower to the building in 1928. By 1938, 46 radio stations across the country were taking Father Coughlin's Sunday afternoon broadcasts.[117]

Until the beginning of the Depression, Coughlin mainly covered religious topics in his weekly broadcasts. He told one reporter, "We avoid prejudicial subjects, all controversy and especially bigotry. We all believe in God".[118] But during the 1930's he increasingly addressed political topics and by 1934 Coughlin was perhaps the most prominent Roman Catholic speaker on political and financial issues, with a radio audience that reached tens of millions of people every week. It was claimed "by 1934 he was receiving more than 10,000 letters every day and his clerical staff numbered more than a hundred".[119] Some even claimed by the mid-1930s Coughlin received more mail than anyone in the world having compiled a mailing list that included two million contributors.[120] *Fortune Magazine* called him at that time "the biggest thing that ever happened to radio".[121]

Father Coughlin served up a heady brew of 'social justice' (the name of the weekly paper he launched in 1936) and fervent anti-Communism, a one-two punch guaranteed to appeal to lower-middle-class listeners living through the Great Depression. If fact Coughlin assumed the role of what Carpenter calls a "surrogate spokesman" for those who were economically traumatized by the Depression.[122] But he moved from being just a spokesman when his preaching became even more vehement, attacking the likes of Herbert Hoover, whom he called the bankers friend, the Holy Ghost of the rich, the protective angel of Wall Street.[123] These outbursts brought Coughlin to the attention of Franklin Roosevelt who was echoing Coughlin's rhetoric calling for "social justice through social action". Although an early supporter of Roosevelt and the New Deal – coining the phrase "Roosevelt or Ruin", his message turned later turned to "Roosevelt and Ruin".[124] Coughlin's eventual opposition to Roosevelt led him to found the National Union for Social Justice (NUSJ) in 1934 as a lobbying group, almost becoming a third political party. In presenting the NUSJ programme to his listening audience, Coughlin noted that it was their privilege "to reject or to accept my beliefs, to follow me or repudiate me", thereby making the proposed programme intricately identifiable with its proposer. The NUSJ was Coughlin; Coughlin was the NUSJ.[125]

Already by 1933 he had initiated contact with Mussolini and Hitler cherishing the Nazi's and Fascists as allies against communism and by 1938 the priest had also migrated to the fringes of the far right and openly espoused anti-Semitism influenced by the writings of the Irish theologian Father Denis Fahey.[126] It seemed no one was to easily escape his outrageous views and therefore it is not surprising that one of his biographers Donald Warren dubbed him the "Father of Hate Radio", in a book that was highly critical of Coughlin (1996). However, by 1940 Coughlin was forced off the air by a restrictive new broadcasting code that made it difficult to sell time to individuals with controversial views. Equally his Archbishop presented an ultimatum to the prelate: he would have to leave politics or the priesthood.[127] Coughlin responded in a way no one expected. He seemingly (some think he had no choice) went quietly into the night. He remained a parish priest, rarely in the news, until his retirement in 1966. In a rare interview during his declining years a journalist asked Coughlin whether there was anything he would do differently if he had his life to live over again. "There is nothing I would do the same", he replied.[128] He died in Michigan in 1979 at the age of 88.

In political terms, Marcus, one of Coughlin's biographers has argued that the priest was a blending of both the 'Left' and 'Right',

> An analysis of his career can help trace the ideological antecedents of McCarthyism in the 1950s and the Radical Right of the 1960s and the early 1970s. They too shared a strong belief that the federal government was not dealing properly with the internal and external problems facing the country.[129]

However, in addition an overview of Coughlin's career also provides insights into the role of religion in America and the combustible combination of religion and politics. He ushered in a revolution in American mass media by his dramatic ability to blend religion, politics and entertainment into a powerful brew whose impact is still being felt.[130] But Father Coughlin was certainly no saint. He was a gifted speaker, but used his talents to lash out at scapegoats such as Jews and he pilloried the Roosevelt administration. He fraternized with Fascist Italy and Nazi Germany and speculated on the stock market with money sent him for religious purposes, some estimate at around half a million dollars a year.[131] At his death he was worth nearly a million dollars.[132]

Coughlin might have less in common with his successors, the televangelists of the 1970s and 1980s, than a superficial comparison suggests. They were all empire builders and most were hungry for dollars. Yet few, if any, of the better-known televangelists, spewed venom with the velocity of Coughlin. Most were Protestant evangelists interested in converting lost sheep. Coughlin was not an evangelist in the historical Protestant tradition. Of the later preachers, only Jerry Falwell and Pat Robertson were comparably political, but their style was less inflammatory. Some of the televangelists, most notably Jimmy Swaggart and Jim Bakker were dethroned by sensational sex scandals.[133] But all of them used mass media to expand their scope and their impact, but whatever the complexities of Father Charles Coughlin, this 'radio priest' remains one of the most compelling human interest stories of 1930's America.[134]

f) Mother Mary Angelica (1923-2016)

'The Abbess of the Airwaves'.[135] Mother Angelica, as she was known, was born Rita Antoinette Rizzo in a squalid, crime ridden section of Canton, Ohio, an industrial hamlet an hour or so outside of Cleveland. Rita was ostracized by her predominantly Catholic peer group, not because of her poverty but because her parents had been divorced after her father abandoned them, when she was still only 5 years old. Her mother suffered from chronic depression, so by the age of 11, she was virtually on her own working all day driving a car from job to home to earn enough money to eat and with little interest in school. In addition while a schoolgirl, she was knocked over by a heavy power waxing machine which damaged her spine and forced her to wear leg braces for several years.[136] Rita's health was not good. She also suffered from severe abdominal pains, but found relief in the form of a woman named Rhoda Wise who was hailed as a mystic and someone who was alleged to be marked with the stigmata of Christ (bleeding on the palm of the hands). Rhoda Wise used prayer to counteract Rita's ailments and Rita felt God had performed a miracle, as her pain and abdominal lump causing it, had vanished.[137] In response to this the young girl decided to give her life to the church and entered a Franciscan Order in Cleveland, becoming a nun and in 1946, joined several other sisters to open the Sancta Clara monastery in Canton Ohio and became known as Sister Mary Angelica of the Annunciation. Sadly, misfortune bombarded her again when she severely injured her leg while scrubbing floors. Once more applying the power of prayer Sister Angelica promised God if she recovered, she would repay the favour by opening a monastery in the Protestant dominated deep South, where Catholics were not always welcome. She recovered, although from then on she could only walk by using a brace and cane, but with her circle of nuns she established Our Lady of the Angels in Birmingham, Alabama in 1961.[138] She and the other nuns engaged in various community projects to raise funds for the ministry and began both publishing books on Catholic issues and also recording her talks for sale. After an interview at Chicago's religious UHF channel WCFC-TV in 1978 she decided television was the place to be. She taped her first series of talks called *Our Hermitage* that same year for Pat Robertson's Christian Broadcasting Network (CBN), becoming a regular guest and the first Roman Catholic ever to appear on such a Protestant dominated channel.[139] But in 1980 because of a dispute with the Birmingham television station that provided videotape facilities for Mother Angelica, with no dedicated funds, no business plan and no hesitation, Angelica faithfully leapt into independent television production. "Unless you are willing to do the ridiculous, God will not do the miraculous" was her motto.[140] So she decided to set up makeshift studio in the garage of her monastery and sought to build a independent television service, without the sanction of her church and with second hand equipment and a low cost satellite dish. Her not-for-profit Eternal Word Television Network (EWTN) was born – the first denominational cable TV service to be licensed by the FCC. EWTN became the voice for American conservative and traditional Catholics on religious and social issues, helped with advice from priests, theologians, deacons and lay people to keep it in line the mainstream teachings of the Roman Catholic Church.[141]

CHAPTER 4 THE HALL OF FAME

In 1983, EWTN was reaching one million households and by 1984 had got a new fully modern studio. The station was running 24 hours daily by 1990 with a staff of 95. Although the network carried some syndicated religious programmes, EWTN produced 60% of its own material including *Mother Angelica Live*. The network was to exist solely on the contributions of viewers. There would be no advertising, no shilling for funds and no toll-free donation lines. She believed that people would be inspired by God to give without her asking.[142] According to EWTN, their networks, including the radio channel WEWN formed in 1992, now reach 250 million households in 140 countries.[143] In 1999 Mother Angelica visited Columbia where she claimed to have a vision to build a temple in honour of the child Jesus. Private donors contributed $48.6 million dollars and she opened the Shrine of the Most Blessed Sacrament in Hanceville in that same year.

As with many of her Protestant counterparts, Mother Angelica did not find universal favour with her parent church. Nonetheless the mainstream National Catholic Association for Broadcasters awarded her the prestigious Gabriel Award for excellence in broadcasting and in 2009 she was the recipient of the Pro Ecclesia et Pontifice Award granted by Pope Benedict XV1 for services to the Catholic Church.[144]

Mother Angelica hosted shows on EWTN until 2001 when she had a stroke. She continued to live in the monastery at Hanceville until her death at the age of 92 on Easter Sunday 2016. On news of her death the *New York Times* reflected that Mother Angelica, the "zinging nun" as she was nicknamed, was "an improbable superstar of religious broadcasting and arguably the most influential Roman Catholic woman in America".[145]

On a visit to the Vatican, Pope John Paul 11 called Mother Angelica a strong woman, a courageous woman and above all a charismatic woman. But in her own words, "Faith is what gets you really started. Hope is what keeps you going. Love is what brings you to the end".[146]

g) Dr.Billy Graham (1918-2018)

For virtually every year since the 1950s, Dr.Billy Graham was a fixture on the list of the ten most admired people in America and the world. It is claimed that Graham preached the Christian Gospel to as many as 215 million people in live audiences in 185 countries and credited with preaching to more individuals than anyone else in history, not counting at least one billion he addressed through radio, television and the written word.[147]

Born near Charlotte, North Carolina, in 1918, he was brought up on the family farm in a Scottish Presbyterian tradition, with strict observance of moral values and with a strong work ethic. After high school Graham moved to Tennessee to enrol in a Christian school, the Bob Jones College, but found it very rigid and moved to the Florida Bible Institute and then on to Wheaton College, where he also met Ruth McCue Bell, the daughter of a medical missionary. Married in 1943, they would eventually raise five children together.[148]

Graham briefly pastored the First Baptist Church in Western Springs, Illinois, before joining Youth for Christ International, an evangelical missionary group which spoke to returning servicemen and young people about God. In this role he toured the United States, Great Britain and much of Europe, eventually moving on to host his own revival meetings in many US cities starting with Los Angeles in 1949, which were promoted by the newspapers of William Randolph Hearst who reportedly told his editors to "puff Graham",[149] though a more accurate investigation shows it was really a Christian advertising man Walter Bennett who convinced Graham that national radio and television was the way to go in the late 1940s and thus gave impetus to the crusade movement and to Graham's 'superstar' status.[150]

Sociologically it is believed that Graham's success was directly related to the cultural climate of post–Second World War in America, Graham speaking out against Communism and binding together a vulnerable nation through religious revival. Although he tried to remain uninvolved in politics, Graham was befriended by several Presidents of the United States and was consulted by various international leaders at times when US relations were strained. It established him as the acknowledged standard-bearer for evangelical Christianity in America and beyond.[151]

Graham and his colleagues eventually formed the Billy Graham Evangelistic Association (BGEA) and Theodore Elsner, the President of the National Religious Broadcasters, offered Graham his own network radio show on ABC called *The Hour of Decision*. Graham in his autobiography recounts the conversation "Billy, you must go on national radio ... you're the man God could use to touch America through radio".[152] The programme initially was transmitted to 150 stations and at its peak reached 1,200 stations across America. The radio and television versions ran successfully on a weekly basis until 1954, when Graham decided to retain only the radio show, reserving his television appearances for the yearly crusades that remained top international ratings-grabbers for half a century.

With Graham's success the BGEA opened numerous international offices and started publishing periodicals like *Christianity Today* in 1956 and *Decision Magazine* in 1960 as well as producing records, tapes and films. Additionally Graham himself authored numerous books including *Angels: God's Secret Agents* (1975), *How to Be Born Again* (1979), *Death and the Life After* (1994), as well as his autobiography *Just as I am* (1997). Graham also accepted invitations from Christian groups around the world to hold evangelical "crusades", including London in 1954, when by its end he had spoken to 2 million people, delivering seventy-two major addresses in twelve weeks at Haringey Arena.[153]

Ann Temple columnist noted in the *Daily Mail*, "There is a rustle of awareness in this country that something has happened. The complacency of religion has been profoundly disturbed".[154] This was reflected in much of the media buzz at the time and despite the natural reluctance about an American preaching on British soil, with all the marketing strategy that the Graham "crusade" brought with it, the obvious fact was that here was a religion that worked and engendered huge responses which seemed to sway many of the sceptics.[155]

However, perhaps the best commendation is the one recounted by Graham's official biographer John Pollock, who tells of a private letter written on behalf of the Queen Mother to Dr.Graham saying,

> the immediate response to your addresses and the increasing number of those who are anxious to hear them, testify both to your own sincerity and to the eagerness with which the great host of the people of this country welcome the opportunity to fortify their religious belief and to reaffirm the principles which you proclaim.[156]

At such a royal level, this probably best expressed the feeling in the country to Graham's visit and ministry in the UK.

But despite the success of the London campaign and others in America, Graham was not everyone's favourite. He was pilloried by some conservative preachers in the 1960s for supporting the civil rights movements, fundamentalists wrote him off when he condemned violence perpetrated by an anti-abortion group and also felt his co-operation with churches affiliated with the World Council of Churches signalled a compromise with the corrupting forces of modernism. President Truman called him a "counterfeit"[157] and theologians like Niebuhr felt he was "simplistic".[158] However by the 1990s Graham was firmly established as the most respected conservative religious leader in America, the American literary critic Harold Bloom calling Graham "the Pope of Protestant America".[159]

Sensing the influence he had, Graham was determined to help evangelicalism have a greater impact beyond America, so the Billy Graham Evangelistic Association (BGEA) sponsored several major international conferences like the World Congress on Evangelism (Berlin 1966), the International Congress on World Evangelisation (Lausanne 1994) and two similar ones in Amsterdam (1983 and 1986). In addition beginning in 1978 Graham visited virtually every Soviet-controlled country, a privilege that no other religious leader received, with a platform to preach, encourage local Christians, as well as to explain to Communist leaders that their restriction of religious freedom was counter-productive.[160]

His life and ministry have been honoured with many international accolades including being honoured by the Queen with the insignia as Honorary Knight Commander of the Most Excellent Order of the British Empire (2001). In America in 1996 Congress resolved unanimously to confer the Congressional Gold Medal, the highest award the legislature could give, on Billy and Ruth Graham. At the ceremony Vice President Al Gore, said in his speech: "Few individuals have left such lasting impact on our national life. In presenting this Gold Medal, the United States of America makes a powerful statement about what is really important in our national life".[161] His stature was earlier increased also when in an era when financial scandals were blighting some of his fellow televangelists, Graham established the Evangelical Council for Financial Accounting (1979) to bring transparency and accountability to Christians in ministry. He set up the Billy Graham Training Centre in North Carolina to help Christians in their faith and few people other than Presidents and Kings can claim to have a Library (The Billy Graham Library, 2007) and an Archive Centre (The Billy Graham Center, 1980), established in recognition of their accomplishments.[162] Dr.Graham lived in the mountains of North Carolina, but in 1992 when it was announced he had Parkinson's disease, he handed over the running of the BGEA to his son William Franklin Graham 111.

It is perhaps finally appropriate to combine the perspective of the UK and the US on Billy Graham, through the words of the former British Ambassador in Washington, Sir Christopher Meyer in 2001 when he said,

> Dr.Graham has made an incalculable contribution to civic and religious life over 60 years. He has pursued his calling with a straightforward passion and faithfulness. Along the way he has left us an extraordinary legacy. Billy Graham has preached the Gospel to more people in live audiences than anyone else in history. His ministry has been truly international. Millions of people throughout the world have found his message inspirational. Lives have been deeply touched and changed. In the furthest corners of the world, Billy Graham has blazed a remarkable trail of Christian commitment, marked by tolerance

and respect for others and Dr.Graham's vision has kindled the continuing work of many thousands of others.[163]

When asked if he could live his life over again would he do anything different, Graham replied, "I would speak less and study more, and I would spend more time with my family ... I would also spend more time in spiritual nurture, seeking to grow closer to God so I could become more like Christ".[164] However, in the final chapter of his autobiography *Just as I am* he says, "About one thing I have absolutely no regrets however, it is my commitment many years ago to accept God's calling to serve him as an evangelist of the Gospel of Christ".[165]

Billy Graham died on February 21st 2018 at his home in Montreat. He was 99. The Pastor that filled stadiums and counselled Presidents became only the fourth private citizen to lie in state in the Capital's Rotunda.[166]

President Trump tweeted, "There was nobody like him, he will be missed by Christians and all religions. A very special man".[167]

h) Oral Roberts (1918-2009)

Oral Roberts, it is claimed, was one of the most influential religious leaders in the world in the 20th Century and influenced the course of modern Christianity as profoundly as any religious leader.[168]

Granville Oral Roberts was born into a deeply religious family in Oklahoma. His father was a farmer who preached the gospel and established Pentecostal Holiness churches having earlier broken away from the Methodist Church because of their lack of appreciation of charismatic gifts like speaking in tongues.[169] His mother regularly prayed for the sick and led people to Christ. A chronic stutterer as a boy Roberts also suffered a dangerous bout of tuberculosis and nearly died at the age of 17. In later life, he would credit the healing ministry of a Pentecostal pastor for the renewal of his health and the overcoming of his speech impediment. After high school he studied for a while at the Phillips Baptist College in Oklahoma, but left before graduating to establish his own travelling tent revival ministry. A tent reputed to hold 3000 people which he exchanged to increase the capacity to 12,000, enabling Roberts to be completely independent and away from the influence of other church leaders in the Pentecostal Holiness Church.[170]

1947 was a turning point in his life when he believed God was directing him to heal the sick. He set up the Oral Roberts Evangelistic Association (OREA) and from then on he held faith healing and evangelistic crusades across America. His divine healing ministry called for prayer to heal the whole person – body, mind and spirit. Through the years he conducted more than 300 crusades on six continents and personally laid hands in prayer on more than 2 million people.[171] His ministry had a profound influence on the conservative Protestant culture in America, probably second only to Billy Graham.

Apart from his crusades Roberts went into broadcasting in 1947. One of his biggest fans was Lee Braxton, a banker and former mayor of Miami, who taught Roberts how to combine financial acumen with showmanship. Braxton worked with Roberts as the preacher's right-hand-man for the next four decades.[172] Through his radio work and his first magazine *Healing Waters*, Oral Roberts became a nationally recognised leader of the post-war revival movement and in 1954 extended his ministry through television. From appearing on just 9 stations in 1954, his television ministry grew to a line up of 136 Channels in 1958. His television programme *The Abundant Life* was already reaching 80% of the United States by 1957 and it is estimated his *Thanksgiving Special* of 1970 reached over 27 million people.[173] As Harrell points out in his much acclaimed and detailed biography of Roberts,

> he literally took his healing message to Hollywood, escaped the Sunday morning religious ghetto, discarded the traditional preaching format and prepared the way for the modern electronic church.[174]

In his autobiography, *The Call*, Roberts recounts the early days of his television broadcasting,

> The first program filmed direct during the crusade was aired in February, 1955. It created a national controversy. At our office in Tulsa we were flooded with calls and television stations through North America were totally unprepared for the response they received. Their switchboards were jammed; their mail unprecedented... Millions were excited by our program and wanted it shown on their favourite stations.[175]

In four years 1954-1958 the Roberts organisation also created a telephone prayer request service, as well as several more house magazines, including a religious comic book, *Oral Roberts' True Stories*. His radio career thrived, although it was challenged by the Federal Communication Commission which was sensitive to complaints about the undocumented "miracles" recorded on Roberts' programmes.[176]

Roberts lived a lavish lifestyle which mirrored his *Seed Faith* philosophy expressed fully in his book *The Miracle of Seed Faith* (1970) that was to become the hallmark of his theology. His preached belief was that the more money one offers in the name of God, the more that person will be rewarded both on earth and in the hereafter – a forerunner of what eventually was to be known as the "prosperity gospel".[177] Whatever the spiritual insights behind this, Roberts was an astute operator on many fronts, he even surprised his followers in 1968 by re-joining the Methodist Church, claiming that his allegiance to a mainstream denomination allowed him to broaden his audience and save new souls. But one of his most significant developments was in 1963 to establish the Oral Roberts University in Tulsa, Oklahoma. As befits a Christian foundation, students were required to sign an honour code pledging not to drink, smoke or engage in premarital sexual activities. Roberts also placed special importance to the Prayer Tower in the centre of the campus. At the University Dedication Ceremony in 1967, the evangelist Dr.Billy Graham was the keynote speaker and the Oral Roberts University still remains one of the largest and most influential Christian liberal arts universities in the world.[178] Added to all this Roberts re-booted his television presence with a mainstream programme with sophisticated production and prominent celebrity guests and in the 1970s *Oral Roberts and You* became the highest rated television religious programme in the nation.[179]

In addition to the University development, in 1977 Roberts claimed to have had vision of a 900 ft. tall Jesus who told him to build the City of Faith Medical Research Centre which opened in 1981, but which operated for only eight years, closing in 1989. Not surprising these claims attracted a lot of criticism even from the religious leaders like the Rev. Carl McIntire stating, "Oral Roberts I'm afraid has gone berserk on these visions of his".[180] His outrageous claims continued, when he said that God would let him die unless he was able to raise $8 million dollars to save his university and church. But as Professor Quentin Schultze comments,

> you've got to see it in the context of a man who had a tremendous amount of pressure on him. He was at the top of an organisation that had to bring in millions of dollars each year to keep things going.[181]

However, the extravagances and controversies continued throughout the 1970s and 80s as did many crises for the Roberts family. Their daughter Rebecca and son-in-law Marshall were killed in a plane crash. Their son Ronnie struggled with depression after serving in Vietnam and also declaring himself gay. He grew despondent after losing his job and committed suicide and Richard Roberts got a divorce.[182]

Despite these setbacks, at its peak in the early 1980s, Roberts was the leader of a $120 million dollars a year organisation, employing 2,300 people inclusive of the university, hospital and medical school, as well as buildings on 50 acres south of Tulsa valued at $500 million dollars. Roberts retired in 1993 at the age of 75 and moved to California. The Oklahoma Senate honoured the life of Oral Roberts and the Oklahoma Association of Broadcasters elected Roberts to the OAB Hall of Fame.[183]

Oral Roberts' legacy is a mixed one. Roberts brought the truth of God's healing to the public in a way that few others accomplished in his lifetime. However, his financial and personal issues and increasingly extravagant claims eventually brought his ministry into disrepute. In his defence he once told a friend he was forced to,

> wear thirty two different hats in his life, including author, television personality, educator, developer, publisher, civic leader and a man who knows his way through financial nightmares![184]

Whatever the criticisms, it is commonly agreed that Oral Roberts paved the way for all the charismatic televangelists and faith healers who were to dominate religious television. He did more than anyone in the early Pentecostal movement to influence mainstream evangelicalism. He parlayed his television programmes into a vast empire that has left a deep mark on the church worldwide.[185]

i) Pat Robertson (1930 –)

Pat Robertson turned out to be one of the premier religious entrepreneurs of the age and unlike many televangelists, Marion G. "Pat" Robertson was not reared in poverty or reduced circumstances, he was born in 1930 in Lexington, Virginia into the family of a wealthy and influential Senator, Willis Robertson. It is reputed he got his nickname "Pat" from his six year old brother who enjoyed patting him as a baby and in later life Robertson preferred the nickname, to the more effeminate Marion.[186]

The first two decades of Robertson's life were filled with the usual privileged trappings of prep school, college (Yale University Law School) and sports (he was a Golden Gloves Boxing Champion). After serving as a Marine in Korea he returned to the United States in 1952 gaining a promotion to first lieutenant. However, not long after his University graduation, Robertson underwent a religious conversion and decided against a career in law, instead attended a Biblical Seminary in New York. Under the influence of a family friend,

CHAPTER 4 THE HALL OF FAME

Robertson, like many before him, took to the road as an itinerant Pentecostal preacher, ending up with several difficult years in New York City.[187] He was given the opportunity to speak on a failing UHF television in Portsmouth, Virginia and ended up buying the station and converting it into the launch pad for his Christian Broadcasting Network (CBN) in 1960.[188] Pat Robertson and CBN came to typify a prototype of the electric church for many observers.[189]

While struggling to keep CBN on the air Pat Robertson conducted a nightly television telethon appealing to viewers to send in $10 dollars a month. As the story goes the first 700 viewers who responded enabled CBN to square its debts. The telethon thereupon became a formalized programme under the title *The 700 Club*.[190] Robertson hosted the programme from its inception, glad-handing with guests with the skill of a commercial TV talk show host, with a format re-shaped by Robertson employee Jim Bakker, a move which upped the ratings by 20,000 people by 1966. Charismatic co-hosts joined, like Ben Kinchlow and Danuta Rulko Soderman and celebrity guests also helped to keep the *The 700 Club* moving, people like the boxer George Foreman, onetime Nixon aid Charles Colson, western stars like Roy Rogers and Dale Evans and the inimitable Galloping Gourmet – Graham Kerr.[191]

Robertson's approach was to

> present our program in as simple and direct style as appropriate ... However to maintain standards in our industry and to be effective in the marketplace, a degree of entertainment and showmanship is necessary. Communication by mass media is not the same as the direct personal contact between the pulpit and the pew.[192]

But whatever Robertson's ethos over this, the programme was certainly outspoken for its day, as Hoover points out in his analysis in *Mass Media Religion*,

> The programme has opposed abortion and has favoured prayer in schools, capital punishment, banking reform, a

strong defence policy, censorship of pornographic and violent media and has opposed the women's movement on some key issues including the Equal Rights Amendment and urged a more isolationist foreign policy.[193]

Certainly during his tenure as host of CBN's *The 700 Club* Robertson established himself as the premiere voice for the Charismatic movement. Even the theologically minded *Christian Century* named him their 1987 *Religious Newsmaker of the Year*.[194] But in terms of his own theological approach he developed his Kingdom Faith Principle which had elements of the Oral Roberts' *Seed Faith* policy. The Kingdom Principle stated that contributions made by home viewers towards the maintenance of the Robertson operation would be multiplied many times over in terms of prosperity on earth and security in the 'afterlife'.[195]

The operation had started humbler than humble with one camera, one studio and ancient equipment. Ben Armstrong in visiting the facility commented "the studio looked like something put together with coat hangers".[196] But CBN grew over the next decade, with changed formats and occupying a sumptuous new international headquarters in Virginia Beach. By 1975 it was estimated that CBN had in excess of 110 million viewers. Today CBN remains a major syndication and cable service estimated to be in 180 countries and broadcast in 71 languages. Its development turned Robertson in full circle from austerity to wealth and political influence.[197]

In the vein of Oral Roberts, Robertson also set up a University on his Virginia Beach campus, which was re-named Regent University in 1989. But his real surprise was to announce in 1986 his intention to seek the Republican nomination for the President of the United States. His qualification to that was that he would only stand if three million people volunteered for his campaign. He got his wish and raised millions of dollars for his campaign fund. Robertson skilfully altered his image so that he was now less of a televangelist and more a businessman and a captain of industry.[198] Despite the strong start to his campaign against George W. Bush, his position weakened and he ended his campaign and told supporters to cast their votes for

Bush, the eventual Republican nominee and Presidential winner. Notwithstanding his huge popularity, in the end his campaign suffered from three major flaws – an inadequate electoral base, a lack of campaign resources and a complex nomination process.[199] After his unsuccessful campaign Robertson started in 1989 the Christian Coalition, a million plus member Christian right organisation that campaigned for conservative candidates.[200] But Robertson left the Coalition in 2001.

After his political demise, Robertson turned his attention back to CBN and his related ministries, encompassing The Family Channel cable network with nearly sixty million subscribers, two radio news networks, a motion picture company, the university, an international relief agency, a national political education movement and a public service law centre.[201] The sale of his cable network (The Family Channel) to Fox in 1997 for nearly two billion dollars has ensured the future of his various interests.

Over the years Robertson had frequently used his platforms to express extreme views. He has compared gay people to Nazis, asserted that God punishes communities that displease Him with hurricanes, tornadoes and possibly even meteors and even blamed the federal courts and civil liberties groups for the 9/11 attacks, saying that it was divine retribution towards America, insisting that his consciousness of the nations cultural sinfulness was no different from Abraham Lincoln's belief that divine wrath had brought the horror of Civil War.[202]

Robert Boston in his book *The Most Dangerous Man in America? Pat Robertson and the Rise of the Christian Coalition,* further expands Robertson's extreme views when he had suggested that US forces assassinated Hugo Chavez, the President of Venezuela, that residents of Dover Pennsylvania could no longer expect God's protection after they removed creationists from the school board, that Israeli Prime Minister Ariel Sharon's stroke was punishment from God for giving Gaza to the Palestinians and that Muslims are crazed fanatics.[203]

Not many significant people or subjects escaped comments by Robertson in his heyday. But whatever negative column inches he attracted, millions of people followed and supported his ministries and aligned themselves with the sort of nationalism he once expressed on *The 700 Club*,

> America wasn't built on Hinduism, America wasn't built on Islam, America wasn't built on Buddhism, America and our democratic institutions were built on the Christian faith. There is no question about it.[204]

Robertson stepped down as Chief Executive of CBN in 2007 and was succeeded by his son Gordon. He has authored or co-authored 25 books including his autobiography *Shout it from the Housetops* (1972) and his 1991 book *The New World Order* which became a *New York Times* best seller.

Robertson was another man who was in the right place at the right time. He rode the rising tide of the charismatic revival and of religious television to his extraordinary place of leadership in the mid-1980s. The emergence of what came to be called the 'electronic church' was made possible by the technological breakthroughs in cable and television, but the adaptability of the charismatic religious experience ignited the explosive growth of the electronic church. No one contributed more to that moulding of a religious message to the medium of television than Robertson.[205]

j) Jerry Falwell (1933-2007)

Jerry Laman Falwell Sr. was dubbed "God's Right Hand"[206] and the "The Preacher Who Put God into Politics".[207] Falwell was an American Southern Baptist pastor, televangelist and conservative activist. He was the founding pastor of the Thomas Road Baptist Church, a megachurch in Lynchburg, Virginia and founded the Liberty University in 1971 and co-founded in 1979 the political organisation known as the Moral Majority.

Falwell lived one of the most consequential lives of any American in the last half of the 20th Century. Falwell was not the most popular televangelist, but he was one of a handful who in the 1970s had developed a nationwide audience and had been bringing in over thirty million dollars a year in contributions from that audience.[208] For some Falwell became the face of televangelism. It is also true that some men and a few women had more direct influence on the nation's politics, though while there is some debate about whether President Reagan could have won his election (1980) without the millions of voters Falwell energized and organised, there is no doubt that the moral concerns that mattered to Falwell and his voters became an integral part of the Reagan revolution. Others began colleges and universities in the second half of the 20th Century, but none grew faster than Falwell's Liberty University. Many people affected the culture in myriad ways but Jerry Falwell changed what it meant to be a Christian in America.[209] Under his leadership and allied preachers, millions of inerrant Bible believers broke old taboos constraining their interactions with outsiders, claimed new cultural territory and refashioned themselves in church services, Bible studies, books and pamphlets, classrooms, families, daily life and the public arena. In this process they altered what it meant to be a fundamentalist and reconfigured the larger fellowship of born-again Christians.[210]

Falwell was born in Lynchburg in central Virginia by the James River, in a countryside of small farms and wooded rolling hills at the foot of the Blue Ridge Mountains. A small city of just 67,000 in the 1980s, far from any major urban centre, though several large American corporations had plants there and its nearly 200 small factories turned out a great variety of goods including paper products, medical supplies, children's clothing and shoes. Because of the diversity of its manufacturers business, journals used it for a 'middletown' or a model of the national economy as a whole. Lynchburg called itself a city, but it was really a collection of suburbs with its population spread out over 50 square miles.[211] In many ways it mirrored the growth pattern of America's leading industrial cities of the era.[212]

According to his testimony, Falwell's mother was a devout Christian and his father Carey was an agnostic, an alcoholic, a bootlegger, but a successful small businessman. Falwell became a Christian when he was just 18, an experience he recounts in his autobiography, "in that simple act of confession and belief God forgave my sinfulness. I didn't doubt it then and I haven't doubted it to this day".[213]

Soon after, Falwell felt called by God to preach and trained at the Baptist Bible College in Springfield, Missouri and at the age of just 22 in 1956, he founded the Thomas Road Baptist Church in his hometown, with just 35 members, though in a year his congregation went from 35 to 864.[214] The congregation's original meeting place was a small factory that was used for bottling soft drinks that carried the trademark Donald Duck. So the neighbourhood children nicknamed it the "Donald Duck Church".[215] The Thomas Road Baptist Church however, was eventually to become a prototype for the modern Megachurch and in the 1980s claimed a membership of twenty thousand and a weekly attendance of eight thousand at its five regular services.

In 1956 he also began the *Old-Time Gospel Hour* (a recording of the 11am Service in the Thomas Road Baptist Church with some editing and extra material occasionally added) a nationwide syndicated radio programme which by 1971 was on 300 stations and within a few more years was on 900 stations. This morphed into a television version reaching an estimated audience of 18 million viewers all over the country,[216] paralleled by magazines, books, newsletters and pamphlets. He was the only preacher in Lynchburg who had a television programme, a medium that nationally known evangelists such as Oral Roberts and Dr.Billy Graham had only recently adopted.[217] In addition its multifaceted direct-mail fundraising appeals reached millions of conservative Christians and raised hundreds of millions of dollars during the 1980s. He was neither the first nor the most popular televangelist but he was certainly one of the most prominent,[218] making multiple appearances on ABC's late night news show *Nightline* and regular guesting on the *Phil Donohue Show*. This was all part of marketing himself to a larger audience, being cognizant of his role as an evangelical entrepreneur rather than merely a small town pastor.[219]

In 1958 he had married his wife Macel and they had two sons (Jerry Jr and Jonathan) and a daughter (Jeanie). Family life was important to Falwell and Macel supported him throughout his career. Falwell joked, "Macel and I have never considered divorce. Murder maybe, but never divorce" ... "we have had a million fights and she's won them all".[220] Macel's own book *Jerry Falwell: His Life and Legacy* (2008) provides a totally different perspective of the life of a man that many had opinions of, largely shaped by the media. She writes, "in fact he was the polar opposite of his public persona".[221] Something that was also reflected by one of his arch enemies, Larry Flynt, the publisher of *Hustler* magazine,

> the more I got to know Falwell, the more I began to see that his public portrayals were caricatures of himself. There was a dichotomy between the real Falwell and the one he showed the public ... the ultimate insult though was one I never expected, we became friends.[222]

The Falwells were married nearly fifty years until his death in 2007 at the age of 73.

Education was also important to Falwell and became part of the wider ministry of Thomas Road Baptist Church. Falwell became Chancellor of Liberty Baptist College and Seminary which became Liberty University, growing from a one room Bible class originally inside the church, to a 4,400 acre campus with 9,558 residential students,[223] a project he had undertaken with Elmer L. Towns. But his educational system also included the Lynchburg Christian Academy (a Christian day school), the Liberty Bible Institute, the Liberty Home Bible Institute (a national correspondence course) and the Liberty University School of Lifelong Learning (a national external degree programme).

On behalf of his many ministries Falwell travelled extensively during the 1980s, claiming to travel three thousand miles a week in his private white Israeli-made jet. Jerry Falwell loved his jet. In 1980 it was no small thing for a preacher to have one, even if he was a preacher with a TV show.[224] On his journeys he delivered hundreds of sermons and talks in churches, public gatherings and private meetings throughout America every year. He made countless remarks at press conferences, luncheons and dinners and spoke at dozens of annual conferences of preachers, church leaders and Christian broadcasters.[225] As Winters points out,

> Falwell used his plane, his fax machine, his email and any other technological advance to get his message out. He was a master communicator in the pulpit and saw almost every new technology as a pulpit too.[226]

But it was for his political initiatives that Farwell's notoriety grew. He really became politicized following the US Supreme Court ruling in *Roe v Wade* (1973) which legalized abortion and first came to prominence with his *"Listen America"* rallies during the nation's bicentennial in 1976, urging Americans to turn from what he viewed as their moral laxity and to embrace truth and virtue.[227] His approach was reflected in his book of the same name (1980). He was greatly influenced by Francis Schaeffer, then the intellectual guru of religious fundamentalism, Falwell following his advice to use his ministry broadcasts to address such issues from a moral perspective. The favourable reception of those messages led to the creation of the Moral Majority, the origin of the name coming from a meeting with the New Right leader Paul Weyrich and others, who convinced Falwell to create an organisation by that name.[228] As Falwell declared, "the moralists in America have had enough, we are joining hands together for the changing and the rejuvenating of our nation".[229]

The Moral Majority was an outgrowth of, or result of, the modern conservative movement of its time and largely Republican in orientation.[230] Essentially it was a lobbying group that sought to pressure legislators to vote in socially conservative ways. Falwell sought influence not control.[231] The Moral Majority's message in essence was that the country was chopping off the Judeo-Christian roots that had nourished its political and legal vitality and those roots needed to be grown back if the country was to survive.[232] Practically it meant they were against abortion, gay rights, the women's liberation movement, pornography, legalised gambling and 'porn rock'. It was for school prayer, free enterprise, fiscal conservativism, a strong military and the defence of Israel. Falwell claimed that his organisation was responsible for sending 3 to 4 million newly registered voters to the polls in 1980, enabling Ronal Reagan's election as President. He personally was a voice for many Americans of the time whose main concern about moral issues led to demands for a re-affirmation of Judeo-Christian values and traditions.[233]

Commentators have often asked why the Religious Right and the Moral Majority gained so much traction at this time. Robert Sandon addressed that in pinpointing four factors to account for its novelty and effectiveness. One was the independence of television evangelists who need no accountability; secondly the links between the Religious Right and the political right; thirdly a pragmatic 'reverse ecumenism' that allowed fundamentalists to work with Roman Catholics, Mormons and Jews on common concerns and finally the rapid rise of Christian academies which fuelled knowledge sympathetic to the principles of the Moral Majority.[234] Others have pointed out,

> the moral majority kicked or tumbled over a cultural trip, alerting us to a much more fundamental change in modern society – the collapse of the 200 year legacy of the secular Enlightenment in Western culture.[235]

Neuhaus was a Lutheran pastor and very critical of the Moral Majority, but had to admit,

> what is clear on both the philosophical level in the rough and tumble of politics, is that the Falwell's of the nation and their increasingly militant and devoted flock are a phenomenon that cannot be dismissed or ignored.[236]

The Moral Majority in essence served as a bridge between the evangelical and fundamental churches and the Republican Party. The Conservative caucus and other right wing groups came to be served well by the Reagan administration that they helped to elect. Their appetite for power had been wetted and they did come to expect more from the White House than was reasonably possible. The separation of Church and State however still remained a cardinal principle of the US Constitution, but there is no doubt that that the Moral Majority had an effect on elections and legislatures. It was even reported that Falwell claimed, "We have a President who agrees with every position the Moral Majority represents"[237] and as *Time Magazine* reflected "they have moved into the center of America's cultural stage and their reach extends now to the highest office in the land".[238]

However, the Moral Majority disbanded in 1989 following the negative public reaction to several televangelism scandals in the 1980s (involving such prominent figures as Jim Bakker and Jimmy Swaggart). In the midst of the crisis of Bakker's PTL ministry he had requested Falwell to take over as the head of the PTL ministerial complex. But after only a few weeks Bakker levelled charges that Falwell had stolen the ministry. The media dubbed the ensuing battle between Bakker and Falwell for the control of the ministry as the 'Holy Wars', Falwell even airing his own position and outlook in the conflict on the PTL network, in a strategic programme called *From the Pastor's Study* on 30th April 1987.[239] Falwell's apologia was intended to demonstrate his expertise in both secular and spiritual matters and marked a shift in the nature of televangelistic rhetoric aiming to restore credibility and confidence that had so obviously been undermined in this period.[240] Unfortunately donations to PTL declined in the wake of the Bakker scandal and despite raising 20 million dollars to keep PTL solvent, Falwell was unable to bring the ministry out of bankruptcy and he resigned in October 1987.[241]

Many remember Falwell for his inflammatory statements, for which his wife Macel commented "he was receiving death threats on a daily basis".[242] He once said Aids was God's punishment for the 'sinful behaviour' of homosexuality. In 1999, he raised alarm by charging that the children's television character Tinky Winky was cast as a homosexual and communicated a gay message and urged parents to boycott the *Teletubbies* programme on which the character appeared. Perhaps his most controversial comment came in the aftermath of 9/11 when he blamed the terrorist attacks as a result of the forces of secularism in America, including the American Civil Liberties Union, People for the American Way, pagans, abortionists, feminists, gays and lesbians. To his critics Falwell could be a bully, lacking in Christian charity.[243]

After the demise of the Moral Majority the organisation was essentially replaced by Pat Robertson's Christian Coalition, though Falwell did try unsuccessfully to revive the Moral Majority as the Faith and Values Coalition. After his death he was succeeded by his sons Jerry Falwell Jr. who took on the role as President of Liberty University and Jonathan Falwell who became the senior pastor of Thomas Road Baptist Church.[244]

Falwell's legacy is a mixed one. He did have many critics but behind the controversies was a shrewd, savvy operator with an original vision for effecting political and moral change. He rallied religious conservatives to the political arena at a time when most fundamentalists and other conservative religious leaders were inclined to stay away and he helped pulled off what had once seemed an impossible task, uniting religious conservatives from many faiths and doctrines, by emphasizing what they had in common.[245]

His manner was patient and affable, his sermons having none of the air of white-hot Pentecostal menace of contemporaries like Jimmy Swaggart, for instance. He shared podiums with Senator Kennedy, appeared at hostile college campuses and in 1984 spent an evening before a crowd full of hecklers at a Town Hall in New York, probably not changing many minds but sometimes convincing skeptics of his good will. He never entirely left the public eye, whether in his role of trying to rescue the foundering PTL ministry of Jim Bakker in the late 1980s, or pursuing a libel suit against Larry Flynt, the publisher of Hustler magazine, all the way to the Supreme Court, or describing President Bill Clinton as an "ungodly liar".[246]

In a sense he remade the fundamentalist church, leading his people during the 1980s towards a more open-minded engagement with American society culture and politics and helped make that worldly engagement part of the definition of a true Bible-believing Christian[247] The Moral Majority may not have represented the views of the majority of Americans, but its views have had a lasting impact on the

American political dialogue and the changes he wrought continue to shape the culture in which Americans live today.

In the course of the history of 20th Century American religious history there have been few figures that were as polarizing as Jerry Falwell. Revered by his followers and considered zealous and egregious by his opponents, Falwell was a key figurehead in the revival of political intervention in the late 20th Century and created a name for himself by a rhetorical and polemical style of his own.[248] But as Winters writes,

> In the end it is impossible to avoid a frank admiration for Falwell's gifts, his perseverance, his sheer energy that he brought to his task, even if one also experiences ambivalence or even disdain about his career and its consequences. Few Americans can say they have achieved the profound impact on their times and country that Falwell could rightly claim.[249]

The founding father and long public face of the religious right left behind a university, a megachurch and the values of a movement that still continues his legacy.

3. Summary

The panorama here of this disparate group of people reveals something of the colourful nature of the early days of religious broadcasting. It illustrates "the spectrum of significance" in both American and British contexts.

If truth be told there were thousands of people who took to the microphone and screen, in an attempt to share their faith and ministry through modern media. But these were a pioneering core who in their different ways and for one reason or another hit the headlines becoming significant 'personalities' 'celebrities' or 'stars' in the field of religious broadcasting.

So why the choice? It would have been really useful if there had been an independent poll of the most significant religious broadcasters in this era. Sadly no such poll exists. However, the people featured here do seem to have wide recognition by those who worked in the religious broadcasting area or still do. Therefore it possible to justify the choices. Reith because as the first Director General of the BBC he created the environment and had the determination to make religious broadcasting a key component of the BBC's output and set a precedent for its relevance. Dick Sheppard and W.H.Elliott because as the chosen broadcasters of Reith they helped marry the Established Church with media and demonstrated how radio broadcasts could convey the Christian message to thousands of people all over the country and help attract people back to church and faith. Aimee Semple McPherson because she was the first female pioneer in Christian broadcasting and was able to excite her listeners with her own unique brand of the newly emerging Pentecostalism. Father Charles Coughlin, because he made his mark as the Catholic priest who was able to build a vast congregation of millions and used that platform for a political and social agenda. Mother Mary Angelica, because who against all odds with the Catholic Church and as a person from a religious order, was able to create a very influential Catholic television network. Dr.Billy Graham because who through his radio and television broadcasts and crusade meetings became the most well known Christian leader on the planet. Oral Roberts because he created the transition from church to media with a significant emphasis and message about Christian healing and prosperity. Finally Pat Robertson and Jerry Falwell who created a synergy between evangelical/fundamentalist Christians and the Republican Party using their radio and television broadcasts and preaching, with one even standing for President and the other creating a powerful political lobby.

What we can observe is that they had certain things in common.

Firstly, they lived at a time of technological advancement, when firstly through radio and then through television, they had a platform to speak directly to countless thousands of people they could never engage with in any other way. This gave them fame, power, privilege and popularity beyond their wildest dreams. Secondly, as John Donne wrote, "no man is an island", [250] for all of them involved in broadcasting needed teams of people to get them and keep them on air and in many cases huge finances, which for some of them was either their downfall or a real stumbling block for their critics. Thirdly, their broadcasting was centred in some established religious affiliation, whether in America that was Baptist or Pentecostal or in Britain it was Presbyterianism or Anglican. This shaped their thinking and provided the context from which they operated, even if on some occasions they did not have the wholesale backing of their denominations. Fourthly, although their listeners and viewers largely connected with them through media, broadcasting became a portal to draw thousands of people to rallies and ultimately into the churches, where numbers exploded in a way not previously seen for many years. Lives were changed through religious broadcasting and its celebrities and societies were transformed in many areas of the world even in the face of a growing secularism.

But recognition needs to be given to the fact that although religious broadcasting made a big impact in both America and in Britain; the developments in the USA were of a different level to the UK. Firstly, the commercial channels and the largely open access in America provided the means for entrepreneurial individuals to build empires through broadcasting in a way not possible in the UK because of the regulatory platforms, firstly through the BBC and then through the later commercial networks. Secondly, neither did we see the role of women in religious broadcasting evolve in the UK as in America, even though in non-religious programming that was a significant development in this period. Thirdly the biographies provide a clue to the fact that what was experienced were two parallel universes in terms of structure, even though eventually through technology the means to access what became a cross fertilization of content on a international plain, opened up. Finally, what we can observe is that in America religious broadcasting had grown from merely an appendage of commercial broadcasting to a major, multimillion-dollar industry in its own right, with people who became celebrities and household names even to those who had no religious affiliation. While in the UK, it remained fairly marginalised on terrestrial channels, featured on some satellite outlets and struggling to get expansion without the sort of networks and opportunities that existed in America and featuring mainly those who had come out of church-based contexts, who became well known personalities but on the 'spectrum of significance' not in the same league as their American counterparts.

In summary, these key players on the world stage of religious broadcasting helped make their own history, but they did not make it under self-selected circumstances but rather within the social, political and religious contexts of their day (the latter point amplified in the next chapter). But they were pioneers in their own right and created what was almost a cult following to their message and leadership and used the powerful tools of radio and television to that end.

NOTES

1. Carlyle, T., *On Heroes, Hero Worship and the Heroic in History* (New York: Appleton & Co. 1841), p.16.

2. Renders, H. and Haan, B., *Theoretical Discussions of Biography: Approaches from History, Micro history and Life Writing* (Leiden: Brill, 2014),p.ix.

3. Rollyson, C., *Biography: An Annotated Bibliography* (Chicago: Pasadena & Englewood Cliffs, 1992), p.8.

4. Novarr, D., *The Lines of Life: Theories of Biography 1880-1970* (West Lafayette: Purdue University Press, 1986),p.xiv.

5. Van Doren, C., *Biography as a Literary Form* (New York: Columbia University Press, 1915), p.180-185.

6. Ginsburg, C. and Poni, C., *Microhistory and the Lost Peoples of Europe* (Baltimore: John Hopkins University Press, 1991), p.181-190.

7. Bertaux, D., *Biography and Society: The Life History Approach to the Social Sciences.* (Beverley Hills: Sage, 1981).

8. Hendy, D., Biography and the Emotions as the Missing 'Narrative' in Media History. *Media History*, 18 (3-4) 2012: 375.

9. in Renders, H. and Haan, B. (2014), p.232.

10. Barron, L., *Celebrity Cultures* (London. Sage, 2015), p.29.

11. Weber, M. K. E., *The Theory of Social & Economic Organisations*. Trans. Parsons, T. 1947. (New York: Free Press, 1915), p.242.

12. Boorstin, D., From Hero to Celebrity: The Human Pseudo-Event. *In:* Marshall, P. D., *The Celebrity Culture Reader*. (London: Routledge, 2006), p.77.

13. Ibid., p.81.

14. Rojek, C., *Celebrity* (London: Reaktion Books, 2001), p.9.

15. Ibid., p.9.

16. Inglis, F., *A Short History of Celebrity* (Princeton: Princeton University Press, 2010), p.19.

CHAPTER 4 THE HALL OF FAME

17. Ibid., p.4.

18. Barron, L. (2015), p.11.

19. Inglis, F. (2010), p.4.

20. Marshall, P. D., *Celebrity and Power* (Minneapolis: University of Minnesota Press, 1997), p.19.

21. Ibid., p.x.

22. Barnes, R. D., 2010. *Outrageous Invasions: Celebrities' Private Lives, Media, and the Law.* (Oxford: Oxford University Press, 2010), p.14.

23. Goldsmith. B., The Meaning of Celebrity. *New York Times.* 4th December (1983), p. 75-76.

24. Dyer. R., *Heavenly Bodies: Film Stars and Society* (Basingstoke: MacMillan, 1987), p.10.

25. Dyer, R., *Stars* (London: British Film Institute, 1982), p.43.

26. Goldsmith, B. (1983), p.75.

27. Lofton. K., Religion and the American Celebrity. *Social Compass*, 58 (3) 2011:349.

28. Ibid., p.349.

29. Marshall, P.D. (1997), p.242.

30. Aberbach, D., *Charisma in Politics Religion and the Media: Private Trauma Public Ideals* (Basingstoke: Macmillan, 1996), p.37.

31. Higgins, C., *This New Noise.* (London: Guardian Books, 2015), p.3-5; Boyle, A., *Only the Wind will Listen*: Reith of the BBC (London: Hutchinson, 1972), p.80.

32. McIntyre, I., *The Expense of Glory: A Life of John Reith* (London: Harper Collins, 1993), p.119.

33. Boyle, A. (1972), p.34.

34. Quicke, A., *Tomorrow's Television* (Berkhamstead: Lion Publishing, 1976), p.26.

35. Reith, J. C. W., *Broadcast over Britain* (London: Hodder and Stoughton, 1924), p.198-199.

36. Ibid., p.191.

37. Morris, C., *God-in-a-Box: Christian strategy in the Television Age* (London: Hodder and Stoughton, 1984), p.97.

38. Wolfe, K. M., *The Churches and the British Broadcasting Corporation 1922-1956. The Politics of Broadcast Religion* (London: SCM, 1984), p.4.

39. Ibid., p.13.

40. Quicke, A. (1992), p.26.

41. Paulu, B., *Television and Radio in the United Kingdom* (London: MacMillan, 1981), p.282.

42. Street, S., *Historical Dictionary of British Radio* (Plymouth: Rowman & Littlefield, 2015), p.287.

43. Reith, J.C.W. (1924), p.147.

44. Higgins, C. (2015), p.14.

45. Siepmann, C. A., *Radio, Television and Society* (New York: Oxford University Press, 1950), p.129-130.

46. Briggs, A., *The History of Broadcasting in the United Kingdom. Vol. V: Competition* (Oxford: Oxford University Press, 1995), p.3.

47. Haley, W., John Reith: A Man for One Season. *American Scholar*, 45 (4) 1976: 562.

48. in McIntyre, I. (1993), p.402.

49. Paxton, W., *Dick Sheppard: An Apostle of Brotherhood* (London: Chapman & Hall, 1938), p.99.

50. Scott, C., *Dick Sheppard* (London: Hodder & Stoughton, 1977), p.13.

51. Luccock, H. E., *The Best of Dick Sheppard* (New York: Harper Brothers, 1951), p.44.

52. Northcott, R. J., *Dick Sheppard and St. Martin's* (London: Longmans Green & Co. 1937), p.85.

53. Roberts, R. E., *H. R. L. Sheppard* (London: John Murray, 1942), p.92-93.

54. Scott, C. (1977), p.123.

55. Marshall, H., *Dick Sheppard by His Friends* (London: Hodder & Stoughton, 1938), p.8.

56. Quicke, A. (1992), p.28.

57. Briggs, A. (1995), p.212.

58. Sheppard, H. R. L., *Sermon. St. Martin-in-the-Fields Calling* (London: Athenaeum Press, 1932), p.32.

59. Luccock, H.E. (1951), p. 27.

60. Northcott, R.J. (1937), p.101.

61. Sheppard, H. R. L., Responses to Broadcasts. *St.Martin's Review* (1925), p.303.

62. Marshall, H. (1938), p.180.

63. Sheppard, H. R. L., *The Impatience of a Parson* (London: Hodder and Stoughton, 1927), p.71.

64. Luccock, H.E. (1951), p.162.

65. Scott, C. (1977), p.198.

66. Ibid., p.213.

67. Marshall, H. (1938), p.166.

68. Roberts, R.E. (1942), p.311-312.

69. Ibid., p.315-316.

70. Marshall, H. (1938), p.11-16.

71. Elliott, W. H., *Undiscovered Ends* (London: Peter Davis, 1951), p.41.

72. Beeson, T., The Canons (London: SCM Press, 2006), p.137-138.

73. Ibid., p.138.

74. Elliott, W. H., Vicars Letter. *St. Michael's Parish Magazine.* November (1930), p.2.

75. Elliott, W.H. (1951), p.145-147.

76. Obituary, Canon W.H. Elliott. *The Times.* 7th March (1951), p.12.

77. Elliott, W.H. (1951), p.153.

78. Wolfe, K.M. (1984), p.61.

79. Elliott, W. H., Christmas Address. *St. Michael's Parish Record.* 10th December (1931), p.233.

80. Elliott, W.H. (1951), p.169.

81. Knox, C., A Man Who Preaches. *Daily Mail.* 4th December (1933), p.3.

82. Elliott, W. H., Religion on Air. *Daily Mail.* 6th December (1930), p.5.

83. BBC, Listener *Research Report: Religious Broadcasting* (London: Listener Research Department, 1941), BBC WAC. File Ref: R9/66/1.

84. Wolfe, K.M.(1984), p.82.

85. Iremonger, F.A., *Report to Sir Cecil Graves.* 7th May (1936), BBC WAC.File Ref: R4/72/1.

86. Wolfe, K.M. (1984), p.154-157.

87. Beeson, T. (2006), p.143.

88. Elliott, W.H. (1951), p.198.

89. Ibid., p.144-145.

90. Beeson, T. (2006), p.145.

91. D'Antonio, M., Aimee Semple McPherson. *Biography*, 2 (9) 1998: 47.

92. Ellens, J. H., *Models of Religious Broadcasting* (Grand Rapids: W. B. Eerdmans, 1974), p.70-71.

93. McPherson, A. S., *This is That* (Los Angeles: Foursquare Publications, 1996), p.591.

CHAPTER 4 THE HALL OF FAME

94. Erickson, H., *Religious Radio and Television in the United States 1921 – 1991: The Programs and Personalities* (Jefferson: McFarland & Co. 1992), p.126.

95. Sutton, M. A., *Aimee Semple McPherson and the Resurrection of Christian America* (Cambridge Mass.: Harvard University Press, 2007), p.76.

96. Underation, C., Sending the Vision: Symbolic Convergence Theory and Aimee Semple McPherson. *Atlantic Journal of Communications*, 20 (5) 2012: 277.

97. Blumhofer, E., *Aimee Semple McPherson: Everybody's Sister* (Grand Rapids: Eerdman's, 1993), p.267 – 268.

98. McPherson, A.S., Radio Opportunities. *Four Square*. December (1923), p.24.

99. Erickson, H. (1992), p.127.

100. Maddux, K., The Feminized Gospel: Aimee Semple McPherson and the Gendered Performance of Christianity. *Women's Studies in Communication*, 35 (1) 2012: 292.

101. Brown, S., The Canadian Comeback Kid. *In: Fail Better in Stumbling to Success in Sales & Marketing, 25 Remarkable Renegades Show How* (London: Marshall Cavendish/ Cyan, 2008), p.73.

102. Ibid., p.78.

103. Correspondent, Attended by Throngs. *Los Angeles Times*.10th October (1944), p.13.

104. Blumhofer, E. (1993), p.8.

105. Brown, S. (2008), p.77.

106. Sutton, M. A., Clutching to 'Christian' America. *The Journal of Policy History*, 17 (3) 2005: 321.

107. Maddux, K., 2011. The Foursquare Gospel of Aimee Semple McPherson. *Rhetoric and Public Affairs*, 14 (2) 2011: 301.

108. in Sutton, M.A. (2005), p.319.

109. Richard, K, Frank Capra's Miracle Woman. *Christianity Today*, 13th December (2011), p.18.

110. Bering-Jenson, H., 1993. Sister Aimee: The Life of Aimee Semple McPherson. *Insight on the News*, 9 (14) 1993: 22.

111. www.foursquare.org/about/stats

112. Hart, A., *Gods and Gurus in the City of Angels: Aimee Semple McPherson, Swami Paramananda and Los Angeles in the 1920s*. (Masters). California Polytechnic State University (2015), p.42.

113. Eesinoun, B., Reflections of a Radio Priest. *Focus Midwest*. February (1963) p.8-10.

114. Athans, M. C., 1987. A New Perspective on Father Charles E. Coughlin. *Church History*, 56 (2) 1987:227.

115. Ellens, J.H. (1974), p.56.

116. Brinkley, A., *Voices of Protest: Huey long, Father Coughlin and the Great Depression*. (New York: Alfred A. Knopf Publishing, 1983), p.91.

117. Hoar, T. F. X., *Religious Broadcasting 1920-1980: Four Religious Pioneers and the Process of Evangelisation*. (PhD). Salve Regina University (2011), p. 98.

118. in Brinkley, A. (1983), p.91.

119. Ibid., p.119.

120. Jeansonne, G., 2012. The Priest and the President: Father Coughlin, FDR, and the 1930s America. *Midwest Quarterly*, 53 (4) 2012: 362.

121. in Ellens, J.H. (1974), p.57.

122. Carpenter, R. H., *Father Charles E. Coughlin: Surrogate Spokesman for the Disaffected*. (Westport: Greenwood Press, 1998).

123. Teachout, T., 1996. Founding Father. *National Review*, 48 (15) 1996: 53.

124. Krebs, A., Charles Coughlin 30s Radio Priest. *New York Times*. 28th October (1979), p.2.

125. Sayer, J. E., Father Charles Coughlin: Ideologue and Demagogue of the Depression. *Northwest Communication Association*, 15 (1) 1983:21.

126. Athans, M.C. (1987), p. 224.

127. Lipset, S.M. and Raab, E., *The Policies of Unreason: Right-wing Extremism in America, 1790-1977* (Chicago: University of Chicago Press, 1978), p.150-208.

128. in Jeansonne, G. (2012), p.371.

129. Marcus, S., *Father Coughlin: The Tumultuous Life of the Priest of the Little Flower* (Boston: Little Brown, 1973), p.231.

130. Warren, D., *Radio Priest: Charles Coughlin the Father of Hate Radio* (New York The Free Press, 1996), p.2.

131. Lochte, B., *Christian Radio: The Growth of a Mainstream Broadcasting Force* (Jefferson: McFarland & Co. 2005), p.31.

132. Jeansonne, G. (2012), p.362.

133. Ibid., p.372.

134. Jenson, R.J., Father Charles E. Coughlin: Surrogate Spokesman for the Disaffected. *Rhetoric and Public Affairs* 2 (3) 1999:522.

135. Arroyo, R., *Mother Angelica: The Remarkable Story of a Nun, Her Nerve and a Network of Miracles* (New York: Doubleday, 2005), p.192.

136. Davison, P., 2016. Mother Mary Angelica. *The Herald*. 5th April (2016), p.12.

137. Arroyo, R. (2005), p.30-32.

138. Erickson, H. (1992), p.122-123.

139. Elson, J., Mother Knows Best. *Time Magazine*. 7th August (1995), p.58.

140. in Arroyo, R. (2005), p.146.

141. Elvy, P., *Buying Time: The Foundations of the Electronic Church* (Great Wakering: McCrimmons, 1986), p.104-5.

142. Arroyo, R. (2005), p.162.

143. Obituary, Mother Angelica: Television Nun. *The Telegraph*. 29th March (2016), p.16.

144. Fox, M., Mother Mary Angelica. *International New York Times*. 29th March (2016), p.10.

145. Vitello, P., *Mary Mother Angelica*, Popular TV Host, Dies at 92. *New York Times*. 27th March (2016), p.10.

146. EWTN in *National Catholic Register* (2016).

147. Woodward, K. L., Dr. Christian. *Commonweal*, 145 (6) 2018: 20-23.

148. McLoughlin, W. G., *Billy Graham: Revivalist in a Secular Age.* (New York: Ronald Press, 1960), p.25-35.

149. Erickson, H. (1992), p.87.

150. Editorial, Mass Media Evangelism: Bennett's Gift to Graham. *Christianity Today*. 13th January (1981), p.13.

151. Aikman, D., Killing Communism with Kindness. *Christianity Today*. 12th April (2018), p.72-75.

152. Graham, B., *Just as I am: The Autobiography of Billy Graham* (London: Harper Collins, 1997), p.177.

153. Wyland, D., Reverend Billy Graham: Ordinary Man, Extraordinary Call. *inspirationalChristians.org* (2013), p.5.

154. Temple, A., Billy Graham at Harringay. *Daily Mail*. 21st May (1954), p.4.

155. Harris, A., and Spence, M., Disturbing the Complacency of Religion. The Evangelical Crusades of Dr Billy Graham and Father Patrick Peyton in Britain 1951-54. *Twentieth Century British History*, 8 (4) 2007:481-513.

156. Pollock, J., *The Billy Graham Story* (Grand Rapids: Zondervan, 1985), p.75.

157. Rankin, S., Confessor-in-Chief. *Christian History*. www.christianhistoryinstitute.org (2014), Issue # 111.

158. Campbell, D., The Legacy of Billy Graham. *Theology in Scotland*, 15 (2) 2008:77.

159. Barnes, D., The Most Influential Evangelist of our Time. *Christianity*. 21st February (2018), p.34-45.

160. Aikman, D., *Christianity Today* (2018), p.72-75.

161. in Pollock, J., (1985) p.277.

162. Wyland, D. (2013), p.5.

163. in Pollock, J. (1985), p.291.

164. in Wyland, D. (2013), p.11.

165. Graham, B. (1997), p.724.

166. Stolberg, S.G., and Shear M.G., Billy Graham Lies in Honour at US. *New York Times*, 28th February (2018), p.14.

167. Trump, D., *The Great Billy Graham is Dead*. in @realDonaldTrump, February 21st (2018).

168. Harrell Jr. D. E., *Oral Roberts: An American Life* (Bloomington: Indiana University Press, 1985), p.vii.

169. Ellens, J.H. (1974), p.80.

170. Hadden, J. K. and Swann, C. E., *Prime Time Preachers: The Rising Power of Televangelism* (Reading: Addison Wesley Publishing, 1981), p.23.

171. Schneider, D., 2009. Oral Roberts: Fiery Preacher Dies at 91. *New York Times*. 15th December (2009), p.1.

172. Erickson, H. (1992), p.153.

173. Ellens, J.H. (1974), p.87.

174. Harrell Jr. D.E. (1985), p.viii.

175. Roberts, O., *The Call: An Autobiography* (New York: Doubleday, 1972), p.180.

176. Barnouw, E., *Tube of Plenty: The Evolution of American Television*. 2nd edition (New York: Oxford University Press, 1990), p.198-199.

177. Juozapavicius, J., Oral Roberts, 91. A Trailblazer Televangelist. *The Star* 16th December (2009).

178. Schneider, D., Oral Roberts: Fiery Preacher Dies at 91. *New York Times*. 15th December (2009), p.1.

179. Ward, S. M., *Air of Salvation: The Story of Christian Broadcasting* (Grand Rapids: Baker Books, 1994), p.241.

180. McIntire, R. C., Oral Roberts. *Boston Globe*. 30th November (1980), p.13.

181. Schultze, Q. J., 1987. Fund-Raising: Did Oral Roberts Go Too Far? *Christianity Today*, 15th February (1987), p.215.

182. Roberts, R., *He's the God of the Second Chance* (Tulsa: Oral Roberts Evangelistic Association, 1985), p.30.

183. Harrell, Jr.D.E. (1985), p.307.

184. Roberts, O., Holiness. *Pentecostal Holiness Advocate*. 27th May (1948), p.3.

185. Fiske, E. B., 1973. The Oral Roberts Empire. *New York Times*. 22nd April (1973, p.216.

186. www.patrobertson.com

187. Ward, S.M. (1994), p.242.

188. Ibid., p.97-99.

189. Hoover, S. M., *Mass Media Religion: The Social Sources of the Electronic Church* (Newbury Park: Sage, 1988), p.73

190. Bruce, S., *Pray TV: Televangelism in America* (London: Routledge, 1990), p.39.

191. Haddon, J.K. and Swann, C.E. (1981), p.210.

192. Peck, J., *The Gods of Televangelism: The Crisis of Meaning and the Appeal of Religious Television* (New Jersey: Hampton Press, 1993), p.1.

193. Hoover, S.M. (1988), p.77.

194. Wall, J., Religious Newsmaker. *Christian Century*, January 6-13 (1988), p.3.

195. Marley, D. J., *Pat Robertson: An American Life* (Lanham: Rowman & Littlefield, 2007), p.32.

196. Armstrong, B., *The Electric Church* (Nashville: Thomas Nelson, 1979), p.101.

197. Erickson, H. (1992), p.157.

198. Bruce, S., *The Rise and Fall of the New Christian Right: Conservative Protestant Politics in America 1978-1988* (Oxford: Clarendon Press, 1988), p.129-30.

199. Green, J. C., Pat Robertson and the Latest Crusade: Religious Resources and the 1988 Presidential Campaign. *Social Science Quarterly*, 74 (1) 1993: 157-168.

200. Fisher, R. and Tamarkin, S., Right Wing Organisations Do This Too: The Case of the Christian Coalition. *Journal of Community Practice*, 19 (4) 2011: 407.

201. Ward, S.M. (1994), p.242.

202. Harrell Jr. D. E., *Pat Robertson: A Life and Legacy* (Grand Rapids: Eerdmans, 2010), p.299).

203. Boston, R., The End of the Line for Pat Robertson. *Humanist*, 66 (3) 2006:37-38.

204. *700 Club* March 13th (2006).

205. Harrell. Jr.D.E. (2010), p.68.

206. Winters, M. S., *God Right Hand: How Jerry Falwell made God a Republican and Baptized the American Right* (New York: Harper One, 2012).

207. Gilgoff, D., The Preacher Who Put God into Politics. *US News and World Report*, 142 (19) 2007:16-17.

208. Fitzgerald, F., A Disciplined Charging Army. *New Yorker Magazine*. 18th May (1981), p.54.

209. Winters, M.S. (2012), p.5.

210. Harding, S. F., *The Book of Jerry Falwell: Fundamentalist Language and Politics* (Princeton: Princeton University Press, 2000), p.11.

211. Fitzgerald, F. (1981), p.64.

212. Williams, D. K., Jerry Falwell's Sunbelt Politics: The Regional Origins of the Moral Majority. *The Journal of Political History*, 22 (2) 2010: 129.

213. Falwell, J., *Strength for the Journey: An Autobiography* (New York: Simon & Schuster, 1987), p.122-123

214. Fitzgerald, F. (1981), p.82.

215. Young, P. D., *God's Bullies: Native Reflections on Preachers and Politics* (New York: Holt, Rineheart and Winston, 1982), p.210.

216. Woodward, K. L., Fineman, H., Mayer, A.J. and Lindsay, J., 1980. A Tide of Born Again Politics. *Newsweek*. 15th September (1980), p.28.

217. Williams, D. K. (2010), p.130

218. Winters, S.M. (2012), p.10,

219. Williams D.K. (2010), p.133.

220. Falwell, J. (1987), p.155.

221. Falwell, M., *Jerry Falwell: His Life and Legacy*. (New York: Howard Books, 2008), p.7

222. Flynt, L., My Friend, Jerry Falwell. *Los Angeles Times*. 20th May (2007), p.16.

223. Smillie, D., Prophets of Boom. *Forbes*. 18th September (2006), p.119

224. Fineman, H., The Face of the Moral Majority. *Newsweek*. 29th April (2007), p.14.

225. Harding, S.F. (2000), p.15.

226. Winters, S.M. (2012), p.10.

227. FitzGerald, F. (1981), p.122.

228. Falwell, J. (1987), p.359.

229. Woodward, K. L., et.al (1980), p.28-36.

230. Goodman Jr., W. R. and Price, J. J. H., *Jerry Falwell: An Unauthorized Profile* (Lynchburg: Paris & Associates, 1981), p.29.

231. Woodward, K.L., et al. *Newsweek* 15th September (1980), p.36.

232. Minnery, T., The Man behind the Mask. *Christianity Today*. 4th September (1981), p.28-29.

233. D'Souza, D., *Falwell before the Millennium: A Critical Biography* (Chicago: Regency Gateway, 1984), p.194.

234. Sandon, R., Religious Piety and Political Reaction. *Public Policy*. 6 (2) 1981: 609.

235. Neuhaus in D'Souza, D. (1984), p.196.

236. in Woodward, K.L. et al. (1980), p.36.

237. *National Issues Survey* (1985).

238. Oastling. R.N.L., Russell, B. and Gregory, H., Legions Seek to Remake Church and Society. *Time Magazine*. 2nd September (1985), p.48.

239. Brown, G., Jerry Falwell and the PTL: The Rhetoric of Apologia. *The Journal of Communications and Religion*, 14 (1) 1990: 9.

240. Ibid., p.16.

241. Correspondent, Falwell Quits Warning PTL Ministry May End. *New York Times*. 9th October (1987), p.14.

242. Falwell, M. (2008), p.166.

243. Fineman, H., *Newsweek* (2007), p.14.

244. Applebome, P., Jerry Falwell: Moral Majority Founder Dies at 73. *New York Times*. 16th May (2007), p.11.

245. Marus, R., Falwell Leaves a Complex Legacy. *Christian Century*, 124 (12) 2007: 10-11.

246. Applebone, P., *New York Times* (2007), p.11

247. Harding, S.F. (2000), p.28.

248. Bell, A., 2008. *Radical Religious Rebels: The Rise and Fall of Jerry Falwell and the Moral Majority*. (Masters). East Tennessee State University (2008), p.55.

249. Winters, S.M. (2012), p.5-6

250. Donne, J., *Devotion upon Emergent Occasions. Meditation XV11* (1624) (Montana: Kessinger Publishing, 2010).

CHAPTER 5

OPPORTUNITY KNOCKS
The Relationship between the Churches and Broadcasting

The focus of this chapter is to examine the relationship between the churches of the USA and UK and their relevant broadcasting institutions and how it was not only the 'on-air' celebrities that were significant for religious broadcasting, but also a stream of key personalities who were the driving forces to bring about significant developments, on behalf of and within the churches in the religious broadcasting arena.

Much of the material will centre on the clusters of churches within the Federal Council of Churches of Christ of America (eventually re-named the National Council of Churches) and the National Religious Broadcasters' network in America and in the UK with the British Council of Churches and its participant members, as well as key religious advisory committees like the Central Religious Advisory Committee (CRAC).

The systems under which religious broadcasting operated differed greatly from country to country in the 20th Century and the relationship between churches and the broadcasting agencies was largely conditional on the national set-up, as will be demonstrated with the examples of the USA and the UK.

Finally the chapter looks briefly at how the Church and clergy were portrayed through drama and humour on the television networks of the USA and the UK in the latter half of the 20th Century.

1. An American Dynamic

The American system of broadcasting, privately owned and operated as it was in a context of limited governmental control, permitted broadcasters a greater measure of freedom of programming that was not available in any other country. This latitude in programming may be seen clearly in the area of religious broadcasting.[1]

As has been noted in previous chapters, religion was surprisingly prominent in radio broadcasting from the start. At first, the predominant form was local religious broadcasts by local churches. Indeed many churches managed to own their own stations in those early days. By 1925 there were approximately 600 radio stations operating in the country, 63 of them church owned.[2] But by the beginning of the 1930s most churches found it necessary to sell their radio stations to commercial interests because of the onset of the Depression and "the use of radio by religious bodies became almost wholly at the discretion of the commercial broadcasters in control of stations and network facilities".[3] However, what we also can observe is that the advent of radio found American Protestantism in the middle of its greatest internal conflict, a religious battle between the forces of Liberalism-Modernism and Conservativism-Fundamentalism.[4] For our purposes here, we will call them the Traditionalists and the Evangelicals.

a) The Traditionalists

Early in the history of religious broadcasting, there were also co-operative and interdenominational efforts as well as local ones. The Federal Council of Churches of Christ was originally formed in 1908 under the leadership of the Rev. William H. Roberts and by 1923 represented about 25 denominations and encouraged councils of churches in local communities throughout the nation to develop cooperative broadcasting. The idea caught on in most major cities and "no activity was more closely identified in the popular mind with the Federal Council than religious radio".[5] But despite the enthusiasm of the leadership there were some misgivings, as the FCCC Report of the Commission on Evangelism noted,

CHAPTER 5 OPPORTUNITY KNOCKS

> The radio is a mighty instrument for good or evil. It is estimated twenty million listeners constitute the audience. Some however are questioning the spiritual value of the radio. This is a matter to be settled by actual experience and we shall be glad to know what the results of this new form of the proclamation of the truth really are.[6]

A similar reflection was made by the *Christian Century* publication,

> wisely used, the possibilities of radio are beyond imagination, but abused may lead quickly to a popular reaction that will dramatically curtail the outreach of this form service.[7]

The industry also had a view on this, as reflected by *Radio Broadcast* magazine..

> radio has placed before the Church an opportunity for usefulness greater than any other single one in all its long history. However, the Church so far has failed to make the most of this opportunity, not because technical facilities are underdeveloped, but because it has not chosen to adapt itself to the new opportunity.[8]

Whatever the reservations, developments did get underway and by the beginning of 1923 Frank C. Goodman broadcast three weekly religious programmes on New York stations with FCCC encouragement. By 1924 the Greater New York Federation of Churches had begun the weekly broadcast, *National Pulpit Radio*, with Dr.S.Parkes Cadman preaching on the station WEAF. That station became WNBC in 1926 and the NBC network was born.[9]

Once its network operations were established NBC turned to the FCCC for co-operation in religious programming. NBC wanted the FCCC to be the sole source of Protestant programming. Moreover, such a cooperative arrangement took care of the problem of having to satisfy numerous denominations with 'equal time'. The FCCC was delighted with the arrangement and its General Secretary Charles S. MacFarland was appointed by NBC to its National Religious Advisory

Council in 1928.[10] The cooperative arrangement between NBC and the FCCC was permanently to shape the history of religious broadcasting in crucial ways and broadcasting by local churches, as well as independent and denominational religious broadcasting feeling the influence of the practices devised and policies hammered out in New York.[11] NBC allocated its free public service time or 'sustaining time' exclusively to FCCC programmes, leaving its local affiliate stations with a limited amount of public service time for local religious programmes. By the 1940s the FCCC was claiming "religious broadcasting is the great modern power for indirect evangelism offered to the church".[12]

However, eventually, because of the FCCC's monopoly in terms of structure and programming, a conviction arose that the FCCC broadcast ministry was in effect imprisoned by NBC and the FCCC was accused of being the network's handmaiden, with stronger allegiance to NBC and its free public service programming opportunities, rather than to Christian distinctiveness and creativity. This situation heralded the end of unified religious broadcasting and independent broadcasting by all segments of the major faiths became more common, with most of American denominations undertaking some type of broadcast ministry with some achieving significant national scope.[13]

The United Presbyterian Church, for example, considered a radio ministry as early as the 1930s and its main efforts were with the FCCC. When reviewing its broadcast policy in the 1940s it rejected the new trend of independent broadcasting but did join Everett Parker's newly formed Joint Religious Radio Committee (JRRC) which included Congregational, Methodist, Presbyterian USA, Evangelical and Reformed denominations and the United Church of Canada. The Presbyterian Church US began in radio in 1945 with the Southern Religious Radio Conference (SRRC) under the leadership of Dr. John Alexander who produced a programme called *The Protestant Hour*. Meanwhile the Southern Baptists established a Radio Committee in 1938 climaxing a long history of local broadcasting by individual congregations and groups of churches. In 1941 the *Southern Baptist Hour* was initiated using a preaching format on network public service time. For 4 years the Baptists remained members of the SRRC until 1949 when all their broadcasting activities were moved to Fort Worth. That move, established a permanent pattern of independent broadcasting for the Southern Baptists culminating in its Radio and Television Commission (RTC) spearheaded by Paul M. Stevens.[14]

The national broadcasting ministry of the Protestant Episcopal Church began in 1945 when *The Living People* was broadcast for Lent with an innovative format. A religious situation was dramatized by leading actors and the programme privately syndicated to local stations. The Episcopalians also broadcast *Great Scenes from Great Plays*, a series of dramatic radio excerpts from well known dramas. This was religious programming "without sermons, Bible readings or hymn singing".[15]

Lutheran efforts at broadcasting began early with Dr. Walter A. Maier (See Chapter 2) in 1924 and by 1929 *The Lutheran Hour* was initiated as a denominational programme of the Lutheran Church. In 1930 the programme gained national exposure on CBS. *The Lutheran Hour* is still the only national radio broadcast of the Missouri Synod Lutherans. Its full story is well documented in Paul L. Maier's *"A Man Spoke, A World Listened"* (1963). The Lutheran Church in America has a national radio ministry with historical roots that go back to 1931 with a strong early preaching format. The enterprise was carried out under the auspices of the FCCC and broadcast over NBC.[16]

The United Methodist Church joined the SRRC in 1946 after some attempts at privately syndicated denominational broadcasting; it remained with SRRC until 1963 but continued its private syndications also. Many of its programmes were also organised by the Upper Room Radio Parish and by 1952 there were 600 radio stations carrying the programmes and its *Family Week* series was carried by 1200 stations.[17]

The Roman Catholics also had a role within this mix. As Soukup points out, the Catholic Church, has seldom hesitated to speak about communication and the means of communication and has tended to address serious issues in a fairly competent manner.[18]

Their stance on media is reflected through Papal encyclicals and documents produced by Vatican Councils asserting that it was a useful instrument,

> to enlighten and instruct men and to direct their minds and hearts towards higher and spiritual things[19] and not to be at the service of error or the squares of vice but may prove to be rather a help to educate and train men and recall them to their higher state.[20]

But in the early part of the 20th Century there had been reservations.[21] As Jim McDonnell the former Head of the Catholic Communications Centre reflected,

> there had been a growing apprehension about the press with a preoccupation with a hostile anti-clerical press criticising the position and authority of the Pope. There was a push for Catholic press and media to defend and promote the Church's teaching and rally the faithful and this background informs the Church's reaction to film and radio.[22]

Eventually a more positive approach did emerge,

> decent radio and television programs should be effectively supported, especially those suited to the family. Ample encouragement should be given to Catholic transmissions which invite listeners and viewers to share in the life of the Church and which convey religious truths.[23]

The Catholic Church came to adopt the view that religious broadcasting was an "indispensable means of evangelism"[24] and needed to engage with its potential to pursue the goals of the Catholic Church and "could not afford to ignore such opportunities"[25] and so began to produce programmes concerned with proclamation (the assurance of faith) and the symbolic communication of the content of faith, in terms of broadcasts of the Mass on television.[26] Also in America some of the most impressive work in religious 'spot' broadcasting was done by the Franciscan Order under the direction of Father Emery Tang who gained the nickname as "the world's most turned-on monk".[27] Tang saw the religious 'spot' as not so much a modern parable as a mini-morality play. More than 750 stations in the United States, nearly 300 in Canada and about 50 in Australia carried the Franciscan spots which were not really geared to proselytize, rather they called humans to think and reflect. One New York television station ran a single Franciscan spot more than forty times.[28]

One of the great success stories also in religious broadcast history was *Faith for Today*, since 1950 the international television ministry of the Seventh-Day Adventists. Its star was the skilled and adaptable William A. Fagal. *Faith for Today* was the first network television programme sponsored by any denomination. Although the denomination was not generally considered to represent neither mainstream Protestantism nor American ecclesiastical power, the programme was broadcast over 200 hundred television stations in the United States with an international ministry equally as impressive.[29]

The United Church of Christ also had its roots in national broadcasting, interwoven with the ministry of Everett C. Parker. In 1944 when Parker became the prime mover in establishing the JRRC, he was a member of the Congregational Christian Church and head of the denomination's radio committee. Parker's initiatives led him to be the new head of the Protestant Radio Commission of the FCCC.[30] With rare exception the radio programming was on free public service time both in network distribution and private syndication, also with the onset of television the FCCC began to seek "a positive service that was non-competitive with traditional worship, an ever important factor in its rationale for radio broadcasting".[31] The Southern Baptists declaring at their Convention, "in a matter of months Southern Baptists must face the opportunities of this new open door for the propagation of the gospel".[32] The Lutherans under Walter Maier also hailed television as a new medium for preaching and Everett Parker joined the challenge commenting,

We have the opportunity to start from scratch in the development of a great new communication art. We must divorce ourselves from all preconceived ideas of conventional methods of the religious message and experiment with various programme formats. We must avoid the mistakes of religious radio which concentrated on one format and diversify our programmes.[33]

The first national religious television came in late 1949 through the Protestant Radio Commission of the FCCC; ABC-TV presented a series called *I Believe...* with noted theologians discussing religion as it affected every day life. The same year a television puppet series began dramatizing well-known biblical stories – the Good Samaritan, the Prodigal Son, the Lost Sheep and the Ten Talents.[34] As the commercial scope and sophistication of television broadcasting grew, so did the ecclesiastical interest and its unusual potentials for religion engaging with variety and sophistication. As in the history of religious radio, so applicable also in the history of religious television, strong voices called for the church to use maximum creativity in programming technique and to keep pace with all things media.[35]

JRRC's influence was so significant that in 1948, the Protestant Radio Commission of the FCCC merged with the JRRC and in 1950 the old FCCC re – formed as the National Council of Churches of Christ in the USA (NCC). The NCC became "the legal, doctrinal, ecclesiological and scholastic successor of the Federal Council of Churches".[36] Under its first President the Rev. Henry Knox Sherrill, the NCC became the largest ecumenical body in America with around 33 of the 200 denominations in America with around 51 million people in more than 140,000 congregations.[37] The memorial record of the opening ceremony on November 28th 1950 for the founding of the NCC, called *Christian Faith in Action,* makes the point,

> religious bodies take media very seriously. The National Council of Churches (formerly the FCCC) has maintained a dialogue with the media industry on the issue of ethics in communication, concentrating on film early on but quickly branching out into areas of broadcasting and other technologies.[38]

For Sherrill the motivation and vision was clear, "the Council marks a new determination that the American way will be increasingly the Christian way for such is our heritage".[39] In a way making their mission to align with the fact that America was built on the faith of the founding fathers and the country was needing to regain that inheritance.

The National Council of Churches (NCC) went on to establish a special study commission on *"The Role of Radio, Television and Films in Religion"*[40] and reported,

> In spite of the fact that radio, television and films have added a new dimension to life, they remain an appendage to the life of the church. No real attempt has been made to assess the influence on the Christian community. No long range planning has been done towards a positive integration of these media into the total effort of the church to fulfil its mission in society … We recognise that a relatively new and pervasive influence has come into our culture.. These new communications media deeply influence all levels of life.. The role of interpreting the meaning of life once was largely carried by the church… Now, even though unintentionally, nevertheless inevitably, the mass media of communication participate in this function. The church must make its resources for this interpretive role available, critically and constructively, to the media of communication so that this function is responsibly fulfilled.[41]

In line with the case of this study, it is clear that once again all these developments were driven by strong minded and innovative personalities like Charles MacFlarland and Rev. William H. Roberts at the FCCC; Dr John Alexander with the United Presbyterian Church; Walter Maier with the Lutherans, Paul Stevens with the Southern Baptists; William A. Fagal with the Seventh-Day Adventists, Everett C. Parker with his formation of new bodies like the JRRC and the Rev. Henry Knox Sherrill with the NCC. These men were key players in an unfolding drama that was to be the early religious broadcasting story within the traditional churches.

b) The Evangelicals

In the United States, evangelicalism is an umbrella group of Protestant Christians who believe in the necessity of being born again, emphasize the importance of evangelism and affirm traditional Protestant teachings on the authority and the historicity of the Bible (as described in Chapter 1, Section 3).

The evangelical tradition is in fact older than the United States itself and no other faith has so powerfully shaped the nation's course, from the American Revolution through the sectional crisis and all the way up to the Religious Right. Yale's Jon Butler pinpointed an 'evangelical paradigm' as "the single most powerful explanatory device adopted by academic historians to account for the distinctive features of American culture, society and identity".[42]

The history of evangelical communication is impressive, but the American context is highly significant. The United States has been a creative laboratory in which evangelicals have been able to experiment with every imaginable form and medium of communication and pioneered one form of mass communication after another. The Christian church was a communicating church and the evangelicals were the pilgrims in the new media lands.[43] The evangelist William Foulkes expressed it so well,

> there is something so uncanny and far-reaching in the persuasiveness of the radio waves to a Christian, it might well become another Pentecost – a potential Pentecost.[44]

A sentiment echoed by Ben Armstrong (an eventual Executive Director of National Religious Broadcasters) speaking of the "awesome technology of broadcasting" as one of the "major miracles of modern times" which "restored conditions remarkably similar to the early church".[45] The church in relationship with broadcasting had found a significant ally. Therefore, as Murch put it,

> Evangelicals were in the forefront of religion which recognised radio broadcasting as an effective means of propaganda. Radio

CHAPTER 5 OPPORTUNITY KNOCKS

reached out everywhere; it carried its messages at a speed of 186,000 miles a second; it leaped over boundaries, penetrated walls and touched people never before accessible to the Gospel.[47]

But part of the challenge for evangelicals in their desire for access to the radio airwaves was that their opponents, the liberals, were organised and they were not. Because so many fundamentalist, evangelical and Pentecostal churches were independent or part of loosely structured denominations, it was almost impossible to form a conservative counterpart to the National Council of Churches (NCC). In the 1940s the Mutual Radio Network, which had been a home for evangelical broadcasters when they were beginning to feel they had been driven off the airwaves, began to have second thoughts about its policy that permitted paid religion; so many Christian radio broadcasters saw a need to mount an organised effort to maintain their presence in broadcasting.[47]

Pioneered by the fundamentalist preacher Carl McIntire a convention was called in St. Louis, the result of which was the formation of the National Association of Evangelicals for United Action (now the NAE). This group was the first to address the plight of Christian radio broadcasters and the discriminatory policies of the FCCC and the commercial broadcasting industry. Its aim was to protect the rights of Christian radio broadcasters to preach whatever the speakers deemed appropriate, to purchase time to do so and to share the free sustaining time with liberals.[48] In his keynote address evangelical Boston pastor Harold Ockenga said, "Evangelicals have been so frozen out ... the hour calls for a united front for evangelical action".[49] A Report of their Policy Committee therefore recommended the establishment of a radio committee "to help their goal of securing a fair and equal opportunity for the use of radio facilities by evangelical groups or individuals".[50]

Two years later some NAE members invited about 150 Christian radio broadcasters to a conference in Columbus, Ohio, to form a separate organisation for their benefit. On April 12th 1944 the conference attendees founded the National Religious Broadcasters (NRB). With the respected theologian William Ward Ayer as its first chairman, NRB moved quickly to establish a Code of Ethics that governed programme content, technical quality and financial disclosure and sought to distance NRB members from the "charlatans, con artists and hucksters who existed on the fringes of Christian radio".[51]

Certainly the NRB took credit for 'saving' the network airwaves from the hands of the liberal Protestants. Glenwood Blackmore on behalf of *United Evangelical Action* claimed that "there would not be a single evangelical biblical broadcast of the Gospel on the air in America today had the NRB not won that battle for the airwaves during the 1940s".[52] The reality was very different than the spin, but it is true they played an important role as evangelicals in protesting against the liberal 'conspiracy' to keep evangelical programmes off the air. It was reported that when MacFarland of the National Council of Churches was asked whether his expectation was that the NCC should control all religious broadcasts, making it impossible for denominational congregations to get on the air and for pastors to broadcast, Dr.MacFarland responded "precisely, the Council feels this to be a wise policy".[53] The Advisory Policy Statement of the National Council of Churches (1956) which encapsulated this approach and advised against commercial religious time for radio and television, created a serious backlash. The NRB President Eugene Bertermann called it a "colossal blunder for mainstream Protestants".[54] The statement from the NRB was unequivocal,

> We cannot agree with the recent declaration of the Broadcasting and Film Commission of the National Council of Churches relative to its recommendation of the elimination of paid time for religious broadcasting, because the National Council of Churches of Christ does not speak for all Christians in America. For instance factually there are more than twenty million members of various Protestant Churches who are not affiliated with the NCC.[55]

Also evangelicals were not alone in their condemnation; *Broadcasting Magazine* (the major trade journal) chided the restrictive approach and defended the policy of selling religious air time.[56] Times were changing with television and FM and AM radio stations vying for advertising revenue, commercial religious broadcasts were welcomed and evangelicals were increasingly recognised as making up the significant proportion of America's Protestants. So as the NRB Annual Report of the time stated, "the radio picture for NRB is the brightest in its history".[57]

As with the traditionalists the evangelicals had their heroes, those within the Christian community who saw the vision, had the skills and charisma to birth new opportunities in religious broadcasting, sometimes against all the odds. The evangelicals included some of the most distinguished names in religious broadcasting. People like Carl McIntyre with the National Association of Evangelicals and William Ward Ayer, Eugene R. Bertermann and later Ben Armstrong of the National Religious Broadcasters, who were to take the 'new voice' to be the 'predominant voice'. With leadership like this the NRB (the broadcasting arm of the National Association of Evangelicals) became the nucleus of a vibrant media sub-culture both serving the growing evangelical movement and popularizing its worldview.[58] As the NRB brochure declared,

> the National Religious Broadcasters unites the influences and activity of many individual broadcasters, large and small, to help preserve free and complete access to the radio and television lanes of America for the broadcasting of the Gospel of the Lord Jesus Christ.[59]

But the reality was that the divisions within the churches undermined what could have been a greater influence for them. Equally undermining was their initial fear that broadcasting would reduce the numbers of people attending church, as Bishop Stearly of the Episcopal Church wrote,

> why would you go to your parish church when you can sit at ease in your parlour and hear the heavenly music of a capable choir and be charmed by the fervid eloquence of a magnetic preacher.[60]

The reaction to this was a sort of self protection with every denomination, Roman Catholics, Lutherans, Presbyterians, Methods, Baptists and many more beginning radio worship services, indicating that whatever the differences within the churches (and there were many) the one thing that the churches did agree on was that religion did belong on the airwaves and that access therefore had to be protected.[61] Despite the conflicts within the churches and the whole television experience, there was in the end a great deal of religious programming.[62] As Schultze reflects,

> History shows a dynamic relationship between evangelical broadcasting and local congregations. Instead of one driving out the other, they adjusted to each other; where possible, each took advantage of the other, so that neither was the same afterward.[63]

As a result of their involvement, the main radio networks all invited representatives from the churches to sit on their advisory boards, within their governing structures. But missing in the approach of both wings of Protestants, as well as that of the Roman Catholics, was a concern beyond religious broadcasting to the developing federal policies governing broadcasting, the rise and dominance of commercial networks and the intrusive character of advertising and the consequent social effects of this new medium of communication.[64] There is little evidence that the churches gave broadcasting much thought in their ecclesiastical assemblies (apart from over internal disputes) and the end result was that they had very little effect on the creation of general public policy on broadcasting, in an era when the nature of broadcasting was being shaped in America.[65]

2. The British Reserve

Alan Bookbinder, a former Head of Religion and Ethics at the BBC, gave a Beckley Lecture on *"Religious Broadcasting Challenges the Churches"* (2003). In it he reflected the challenge that was there for churches at the inception of radio in the UK,

> Religion on the BBC offers religious communities a chance to use the power and privilege that the airwaves offer. To address

the big questions of morality and mortality that are the very stuff of religion. To tell stories that fill this great public space with hope and to find the confidence to be heard in a noisy impatient world.[66]

Writing in the *Montrose & Arbroath Review* in the early years of television, one minister expressed this same strategic point.

We within the church dare not let the potential of broadcasting escape our notice. In these facilities we enjoy for broadcasting the Christian message in this country, we have a tremendous instrument for good.[67]

Indeed an important opportunity and ministry which the Church was to pursue in various ways.

a) A New Ministry Door Opens

So far as the trajectory of British religion is concerned there can be few more interesting issues than the relationship of the Church to broadcasting. The medium of broadcasting was uniquely powerful and its advent almost comparable to the invention of printing. The opportunity (as some saw it) was the evangelisation of England. The threat was the provision of programmes which would draw people away from Church to listen at home passively and intermittently.[68]

As we have previously noted at some length in Chapter 2 and Chapter 4 and was re-asserted by the Central Religious Advisory Committee (CRAC) in its important document *"Review of the Aims and Achievements of Religious Broadcasting 1923-1948,* "the Corporation (the BBC) in the person of Mr. John Reith himself took the initiative to arouse the interest of the churches in broadcasting".[69]

This brief but important statement is almost inadequate to capture the strength of the motivation of Reith (an ardent Presbyterian) to see religious broadcasting as part of the output of the BBC, but as also an instrument of almost social reform through the proclamation of the Christian faith over the airwaves. Although Reith himself was never really a committed 'churchman', as mentioned previously, he was committed to the promulgation of 'dynamic' Christianity in national and personal life and Sunday was the one institution which he believed belonged to the maintenance of a Christian presence.[70]

But the beginnings of religious broadcasting were tentative and very cautious. The original desire and drive for religious broadcasting was coming from Reith and the BBC, but the Church seemed to meet the opportunities with either apathy or opposition generally at first, much to the frustration of Reith who stated,

> Religion by radio – probably relatively the most ineffectual or anyhow most inefficient of all sectional activities of broadcasting. Here millions of pounds worth of advertising has been done for the church for free.. greater than any protest or petition by the churches could have secured.[71]

He almost implied it might be too late..."if the church had followed up there might have been a national revival on a scale hitherto unimagined".[72]

What Reith did however, in March 1923, was to approach the Archbishop of Canterbury personally on this matter, who was very interested when he knew there were 100,000 listeners in London alone. The Archbishop, Randall Davidson, recognised at once the possibilities of the new medium in the service of religion and cordially approved Reith's basic principle of no transmission during the hours of public worship and a religious address every Sunday evening. What Davidson arranged were representatives of the Church of England, the free churches and the Church of Rome to confer about religious broadcasting. At this meeting on May 1st in his room in House of Lords, the representatives asked Archbishop to appoint a Chairman.[73] That Chairman turned out to be the powerful personality of Cyril Forster Garbett, the Bishop of Southwark. This Religious Advisory Committee (or Sunday Committee as it was called then) consisted of six members. The Church of England was represented by Canon C.S. Woodward, Vicar of St.Peter's Cranley Gardens and by the Rev.H.R.L. Sheppard, Vicar of St. Martin-in-the-Fields. The Free

CHAPTER 5 OPPORTUNITY KNOCKS

Church representative was the Rev.Thomas Nightingale, Secretary to the Free Church Federal Council. Dr.R.C.Gillie represented the Presbyterians in England and Mr Herbert Ward recommended by the Westminster Cathedral authorities, represented the Roman Catholics. As the work of religious broadcasting developed and expanded, the church membership of the Central Religious Advisory Committee (CRAC) was enlarged and Regional Committees were also established.[74]

Garbett's leadership of this committee until 1945 was really significant. His biographer Charles Smyth commented,

> with modesty of demeanour, he combined great natural dignity; people did not want to argue with him. Moreover, such was his influence that from those present he generally elicited agreement with his own views on points of principle and policy.[75]

In his own words Garbett reflected,

> It has been a delightful Committee to preside over. We have discussed most frankly the various problems which have arisen, but there has been remarkable agreement among its members and as far as I remember no vote has ever been taken on an important issue on which there was a difference of opinion, for after debate we have always reached a common mind.[76]

Garbett was both confident and influential with this strategic committee. He never attempted any bias in favour of the Church of England, or showed any partiality, conscious or unconscious for broadcasters of his own persuasion. What he was clear about was that that the BBC, in terms of religious broadcasting, should not stray into fields outside religion and that the religion that was broadcast would be what the listener would recognise as Christianity. His conviction was clear on the potential of this new medium for the Church,

> Broadcasting is one of the greatest discoveries of our time ... We ought to be especially grateful for the way in which religious

addresses and services are broadcast on Sundays. To broadcast an address means speaking to a great mission congregation, it is in my opinion one of the greatest evangelistic opportunities the Church has ever been given: the Gospel in this way enters into innumerable homes where the door is closed to clergymen and ministers.[77]

Through all the years of his service, Garbett's wise and powerful counsel and impartial judgement saved the BBC from making many mistakes in religious broadcasting and from taking decisions which it might subsequently have had reason to regret.[78] It is difficult to estimate the full measure of what religious broadcasting owes to Cyril Garbett as the first Chairman of the Religious Advisory Committee, but certainly British religious broadcasting might have been very different had it not been for his guiding hand.[79]

This positive view of the leadership of Garbett and people like him was reflected later by Cyril Taylor writing in the *St. Martin's Review*,

Broadcasting: the use of the microphone is one part of the work of the Church. The BBC first offered the use of the microphone to the Church: the Church did not ask to be allowed to use it. In fact in the early days the Church showed considerable hesitation in accepting the invitation and it is something for which we may be profoundly thankful that amongst the churchman called to advise the BBC there were men who boldly decided that the church must use this new medium of communication, which seemed certain to become as unique a power in the nation's life.[80]

As a result of the Central Religious Advisory Committee representing the churches and them feeling stakeholders in this new medium, momentum and interest grew especially concerning the way that religious services broadcast were having an impact. The Church's Convocation of Canterbury through Canon E.G. Selywn moved that a committee be appointed to "consider the religious value of broadcast services and their bearing on public worship and to report".[81]

CHAPTER 5 OPPORTUNITY KNOCKS

In 1931, the committee's report was presented to the Convocation by the Bishop of Ely, Dr. White-Thomson. The report addressed concerns expressed two years earlier as follows:

- "there was little evidence of people being brought by the wireless to church and to church life and fellowship".[82]

- "the Report did not suggest the introduction of controversial subjects. Broadcast services must usually be more or less simple and general in character. Yet the message, surely, be distinct and definitely Christian".[83]

- "the last note of the Report was one of thankfulness for the amazing reception of religious facilities. Within a month of the introduction of the 10.15 service 8,000 letters of appreciation had reached Savoy Hill and there was not doubt that one of the most 'popular' items of the whole week was the Epilogue at 10.30pm on Sunday evening".[84]

The reality was that the struggle for the Church to come to terms with radio was inevitable. Radio increased the stakes for the Church, made it more necessary for the Church to pay attention to its 'attractiveness' – to the incisiveness of its arguments, the uprightness of its clergy, the image of its community, the vitality of its preaching and the quality of its music.[85] In a world where radio was so closely interwoven into the lives of men and women, the Church had duties far beyond providing speakers for wireless services and talks. The Church had much to learn from its ways of speech, its use of music and drama and of discussion.[86]

What was true for the Established Church was also increasingly true for the Roman Catholic Church who sought and fought to gain its place in the broadcasting arena in the UK as McDonnell again reflects,

> since the 19th century Catholics had been seen as something of a threat by the Established Church, but the Catholic Church wanted to take what opportunity they had with broadcasting seriously and were willing to fight their corner within the

establishment set-up. So they encouraged some of their best writers and speakers to take up the mantle. People like the Jesuit's Martin Darcy, Cyril Martindale, Fr.Ronald Knox and later the Franciscan (later Bishop) Agnellus Andrew, who was a consummate diplomat and trusted by the BBC and advanced the cause of Catholics in broadcasting through avenues like the establishment of the Catholic Centre for Mass Media in Hatch End, which aimed to give the highest level of training to those carrying the cause of Catholicism into the media.[87]

Whatever the tensions (and there were many) a Church of England Report, *"Towards the Conversion of England"* (1945) made an important statement,

> religious broadcasting is recognised as the work of the Church. Those responsible for religious broadcasting are the servants of the Church in Broadcasting House. Religious broadcasting with immense resources and annihilation of space is able to take the Gospel into every home in the land.[88]

They saw that religious broadcasting was for the Church the greatest power for indirect evangelism offered and although this Report came from the Church of England, a similar approach was matched by the significant Report from the British Council of Churches (BCC) *Christianity and Broadcasting* (1950), which took up this point and extended it declaring, "what the BBC does is to provide the Church with an immense congregation"[89] though as the BCC submission to the Beveridge Report makes plain,

> the object of religious broadcasting shall be concerned not as that of seeking converts to one particular church, but as that of maintaining the common elements in all religious bodies.[90]

But the BCC under the dynamic leadership of the Bishop of Bristol also tried to promote the Church's involvement in broadcasting generally and not just religious broadcasting, saying that, "the contribution of Christianity to broadcasting is not exhausted by worship and exposition"[91] ... "our main concern is not with religious broadcasting alone but with the proper place and influence of Christian thought in broadcasting as whole".[92] In terms of the Church, the BCC Report was an immensely influential document and much cited. It talked about the threat of secularism, the important contribution of the BBC (including its Religious Broadcasting Department) and the need for it to have freedom from external interference. Its recommendations are important to mention:-

1. That those responsible for programmes which are broadly educational should examine more closely the meaning and character of education in a period of revolutionary change such as our own, in order to discover how the BBC can better enable listeners at various levels to respond to the challenge of the times.

2. That the objective of the Religious Broadcasting Department should be to reach the listener who is outside the Christian Churches at least as much as to cater for the Church-goers and that therefore the Department should be encouraged to experiment in methods of presentation outside the range of services and more particularly, in religious drama.

3. That the scope of religious broadcasting should be recognised as touching all matters involved in the right ordering of society and that whatever the Christian mind has a contribution to make, that contribution should be heard.

4. That the Churches while repudiating any right to an official veto or censorship should stimulate in Christian public opinion a vigorous alertness to the quality and standards of secular programmes.

5. That the churches should recognise the need for fostering amongst their members an intelligent critical interest in broadcasting, both as a means of fulfilling their own responsibilities and of assisting the Corporation in its work.

6. That the experiments in controversial religious discussion should be continued and extended to cover a wider range of listeners.

7. That the present system of monopoly broadcasting under public corporation or some modification of it, be continued as better designed to ensure freedom and initiatives in broadcasting than either government control or commercial broadcasting.

This was a strategic and influential document coming out of the church's representative body in terms of the British Council of Churches in the post-war years, in an attempt to unify the church's relationship with broadcasting. But as we have seen right from the earliest days things were not straightforward or sweetness and light. Reith had had to go directly to the Church of England for advice about selecting speakers.[93] The Religious Advisory Committee too had decided that Communion Services would not be broadcast and that Christian Science or Rationalist (Humanist) talks should not be admitted to the Sunday evening programme[94] or broadcasting of 'spiritualism' and 'faith healing' were also excluded.[95] Already efforts were underway to 'separate the sheep from the goats' insofar as religious services was concerned.[96]

To add to this earlier there was the external pressure that the majority of the listening public were not attracted by the Reithian Sunday style of programmes and began to tune-in to foreign stations like Radio Luxembourg.[97] This was a challenge to the churches and the BBC to produce more relevant and attractive programming, to win back listeners and undoubtedly this was in the minds of those behind the British Council of Churches Report.

But despite high aspirations about presenting the Christian faith in a powerful, positive and united way, what would emerge in the UK was similar to the squabbles between Traditionalists and Evangelicals in America, but here it was between Catholics and Protestants. The Catholics complaining about the BBC's 'censorship' of priests, with some Protestants writing letters protesting about the inclusion of Catholic religious services altogether [98] or at the least the amount of Roman Catholic services proportionate to the Romish population.[99] These disputes, along with others, pitted one self-proclaimed 'defender of the faith' against those who would threaten his or her particular view.

Despite such difficulties, during the first thirty-four years until the coming of Independent Television, the mainstream churches were keen to uphold their right to a privileged place within the broadcasting output. The Church invited 'inside' by Britain's monopoly broadcaster did not want to lose its influence, even if that was defined by the Corporation. However, during those years too, broadcasting would reveal aspects of Christian belief running the gauntlet of a social and intellectual revolution. It would challenge those images of a Christian culture shared particularly by churchmen, which suggested that a vast majority of people were still favourably disposed towards the churches in general and Christian belief in particular. To their cost the churches fought hard throughout the period to avoid any questioning of the Christian faith on the air.[100]

The result of the various Reports, Conferences and Committees indicated that for many of these early years the Church remained somewhat reserved and equivocal about the impact of broadcasting – at once fearful of its power to damage faith or reduce congregations, but also desirous to use it to build up that faith, recognising that this new means of communication would have significant cultural impacts, which the Church could not ignore.

b) A Whole New World

In the post-war years religious broadcasting was still a major preoccupation of the broadcasters[101] and also of the churches. Though, with some arrogance, the BBC seemed to feel "increasingly religious broadcasting seems to do what the churches cannot do".[102] For many within the Church though,

> the work of religious broadcasting was regarded as supplementary to and not a substitute for what the churches do. Quite simply religious broadcasting is an ally of the churches.[103]

So, the engagement of the Church continued through its Central Religious Advisory Committee (CRAC) maintaining its manifesto in 1948 on behalf of the churches with regard to religious broadcasting,

> to reflect and proclaim "the faith of the Church" as it is actually found in the Bible and in the living traditions and liturgical life and preaching of the visible Christian churches. Religious broadcasting must of necessity concentrate on those fundamental doctrines of Faith which are embodied in the creeds and held in common by all churches "within the mainstream of historic Christianity". There should be the utmost charity in references to conflicting interpretations of the Faith and actual sectarian controversy should not normally find a place "on the air", but room should be found from time to time for representatives of different Christian traditions to make positive statements of their distinctive convictions, and broadcasters should be constantly on their guard against fostering a kind of 'disembodied Christianity' or 'radio religion'.[104]

The Roman Catholic Church in a similar vein, but in a much later submission to the Annan Report also made a very strong plea for robust religious broadcasting,

> the place of religious broadcasting in the general services requires no special pleading. Since its initiation, broadcasting has opened up whole new areas of experience for listeners and viewers.. Religious broadcasting has awakened or renewed an interest in religion among many who have not the habit of attending church.[105]

It also went on to point that against the half a million or so who attend football matches , ten times as many (approximately five million people) attend church on Sunday. This alone making a big potential audience for religious broadcasting. But equally the Roman Catholic Church maintained that,

> the Church should also be actively concerned with the secular media and especially with the shaping of media policy. Christians

CHAPTER 5 OPPORTUNITY KNOCKS

have the responsibility to make their voice heard in all the media and not confined to giving out just Church news.[106]

But with the onset of television came a whole new agenda for the churches, one which some critics felt was too much,

> the church took centuries to learn the value of the printed word, it has hardly begun to understand the implications of the spoken word on TV.[107]

A similar reflection was made by Reindorp in the *Daily Mirror* in 1958 hoping "that the church should make better use of television than it made of radio in the early days of broadcasting".[108] Many people inside the television service also persisted in the belief that religion did not make 'good television' anyway.[109] But as television developed, the BBC insisted to the churches, "the fundamental religious policy of the BBC is the same for television as for sound broadcasting".[110] So the approach of the British Council of Churches was that, "if the door for religious programmes was wide open, the door must be entered".[111] Though in reality it took a long time for the BBC, supported by CRAC, to get round to television church services. But between 1956 and 1976 there was considerable growth in religious broadcasting in radio and more particularly in television, as the BBC and the newly established independent/commercial ITV programme makers expanded the range of religious television programmes. Until then religious television was a small and underfunded part of BBC broadcasting until the birth of Independent Television in 1955. At first, the BBC broadcast a monthly rather than weekly Sunday morning service from selected churches, but because of the high cost of outside broadcasts, Epilogues in the studio were cheaper to produce and these were plentiful.[112]

This time proved too to be a whole new opportunity for the churches as its Central Religious Advisory Committee (CRAC) expanded its duties significantly with the arrival of ITV. Interestingly despite tensions in other spheres, when the ITA was formed there was favourable co-operation between the BBC and the ITA and the Church, through CRAC.[113] Under the spur of genuine competition between differing contracting companies there were now new initiatives in religious broadcasting, including ATV's *About Religion* (1956) the first regular weekly religious television programme to be produced in Britain. But Sendall from the ITA was right to conclude,

> when it comes to the point, the majestic and in some respects Reithian Central Religious Advisory Committee, took a puckish delight in treating the new Independent Television as of equal status and importance with the BBC.[114]

The 66th Meeting of CRAC on 6th March 1956 welcomed a representative from the Independent Television Authority for the first time. The Authority in its policies set aside time on Sunday every week for religious programmes, not because it felt pressured by the churches, but because it was providing the audience with an element that they recognised and were glad to have. In their later assessments they reflected,

> We have a television service with a strong religious content established by the nature of public control provision and partly because providers think that it is good for viewers.[115]

They also felt, "the touch with the churches has been particularly close"[116] and the relationship between CRAC and the regulatory body for Independent Television continued when independent radio was introduced and the ITA became the IBA (Independent Broadcasting Authority) in 1973. The 1981 Broadcasting Act required the IBA by statute to have a religious advisory body, a role which CRAC took on and although the 1990 Broadcasting Act withdrew the requirement for a statutory advisory body, when the Independent Television Commission (ITC) and the Radio Authority took over the duties of the IBA in December 1990, CRAC was retained as its official though no longer statutory, religious advisory body.[117]

Another broadcasting challenge and opportunity for the Church was that of local radio. The popularity of pirate radio (discussed in Chapter 3) brought something of a mind-shift in the management of the BBC. So apart from the creation of Radio 1 to meet the demands of a growing youth culture, the BBC also launched BBC Local Radio stations in the late 60s and early 70s.[118] Soon after, from 1973 Independent Local Radio (ILR) also emerged with an initial 19 stations. The local radio dynamic demanded special programming geared to the local area and that included religious broadcasting. As the ITA commented in its Annual Report,

> as new stations came on air, they each began doing their own religious broadcasting with various arrangements in different cities in co-operation with local church radio committees.[119]

This raised the issue of churches putting forward people to fulfil this opportunity. This was a big challenge as few ministers or parishioners had any experience of radio and so there was an important development to support them in the creation in 1967 of the Churches Advisory Council for Local Broadcasting (CACLB), backed by the British Council of Churches, the Evangelical Alliance, the Roman Catholic Church and the World Association for Christian Broadcasting. Its first Director, Jeff Bonser, commented on the challenge,

> it started because of the huge growth in media, especially local media. So you can imagine all those stations looking for people to present their religious radio programmes. Also the churches needed a body to be in touch with the broadcasting authorities, government and the churches, so it brought the denominations and broadcasters together, supporting them with training and conferences to help make an impact in the local broadcasting situations.[120]

Despite all the excellent efforts made in local religious broadcasting, some observers remained very critical commenting that "the failure of the churches to get their radio act together is not just a pity it is an oversight of stunning proportions".[121] For some the impact was less than the potential.

Another big challenge for the churches was that the explosion of television and the emergence especially of commercial television and radio which brought an opportunity also brought with it a move towards de-regulation. As the 1980s unfolded there were radical transformations in broadcasting in the UK (See Chapter 3) as Sir Brian Young outlined in his 1983 lecture pointing out that the public service tradition of British Broadcasting was under threat[122] a point re-iterated by Hendy stating,

> the public service model had been challenged almost everywhere as state regulation or national monopoly had been cut back, new commercial competitors entered the arena and the number of available channels multiplied exponentially.[123]

The basic assumption that public service ideals should extend across the whole range of broadcasting output was being seriously challenged. These traditions had been set out as early as 1924 by C.A. Lewis, the BBC's organiser of programmes. They were:

1. To cater for the majority of the time to the majority of the public, though without forgetting the needs of the 'minorities'.

2. To keep programming on the 'upper side' of public taste and to avoid giving 'offence'.

3. To provide a forum for public debate which would be impartial and free from governmental interference.

4. To provide religious broadcasts which were both non-sectarian and non-dogmatic.[124]

But the changes which began in the 1980s, as stated, were concomitant with new technological developments, a growing competitive environment and an ever advancing culture of pluralism, secularity, the consumerist society and widening expressions of religiosity in Britain.[125]

For the major Churches a 'consumer model' of broadcasting was deeply threatening as they feared that the clear provisions in public service broadcasting would be lost if it was undermined and religion that had a certain and unquestioned place in the broadcasting system, might be pushed out of mainstream broadcasting altogether,[126] as support for religious broadcasting declined from its peaks of the 1970s. Clifford Longley, writing in the *Times* an important article in the 1980s, reflected that the Church of England remained resolute in its defence of public service broadcasting and the strategic role of the BBC. The nub of the Anglican case being summed up in these terms,

> Our concern is that the British people should have available to them the best and widest range of programmes that can be made. The standard set by the regulated British broadcasting industry is envied all over the world; conversely deregulated broadcasting in other countries has had deleterious consequences.[127]

Simultaneously the Roman Catholic Church also warned that deregulation could open the door to American style media evangelism and urged the government to stand against this and even to ban ownership of radio and TV stations by religious bodies. Their concern was that,

> all that had been uniquely built in the UK through regulation and practice, should not be lost and that the Churches should be engaged in the debate to promote a public service broadcasting and religious broadcasting which would be for the common good and not any sectarian agenda.[128]

Eventually the whole march of de-regulation culminated in the formation and passing of the 1990 Broadcasting Act (discussed previously in Chapter 3). The passing of the Act did not however end arguments among Churches and religious broadcasters about the future direction of religious broadcasting. A sharp debate continued within the Churches about the extent to which new possibilities for religious advertising and religious ownership would be beneficial. Many evangelical Christians were enthusiastic about the possibilities for a more evangelistic style of religious programming. They and some within other denominations too saw the new possibilities for religious advertising as generally beneficial, though the lifting of religious advertising restrictions had a relatively limited take up. More controversially supporters of private religious broadcasters wanted to bring the rules about on-air fund-raising on radio and television into question. Their argument was that Christian groups were being denied basic human rights and freedoms in that they were being forbidden to ask for money on air, engage in recruitment or proselytise.[129]

The Catholic Church, the Church of England the Church of Scotland and the Methodists generally took the opposite position, these churches saw more dangers than opportunities in allowing religious groups the freedom to ask for money and to proselytise. In a multi-cultural society they felt that such activities could be possible sources of offence and feared that they would set the cause back of better inter-faith dialogue. Secondly lurid reports of televangelism in the US [130] were a constant reminder of the considerable possibilities for financial abuse and scandal. For these reasons the Churches generally favoured a restrictive, regulatory policy and were not in favour of changing the law.

Neither the Catholic Church nor the other major denominations sought to own their own radio stations or television channels. In their estimation the costs of running such enterprises would be too great for the Churches to sustain, they believe it was better to concentrate on sustaining and improving the considerable amount of ecumenical programming already produced by the BBC and commercial television rather than competing with each other.[131]

Finally, in terms of the relationship between the Church and religious broadcasting in the UK, it seems that the churches on their side regarded the BBC as a distinctly establishment institution and expected that it would do as it was told or at least advised. Hence the complex disputes between the mainstream Christian churches and the BBC from 1922 until 1956, was really a struggle for supremacy.[132]

Initially, as seen in previous chapters, many individual churchmen regarded broadcasting as a triviality which belonged chiefly to technically minded enthusiasts, thinking it was none of their business, which is hardly surprising as they had been raised on the printed word.[133] However, by 1956 with regard to both radio and television, many of the most eminent church leaders were taking broadcasting seriously, as by then the foundations of religious policy in public service were firmly in place thanks to the leadership of people like F.A.Cockin, the Bishop of Bristol and others and the successive teams of the Central Religious Advisory Committees (CRAC). But as time moved on and society and broadcasting changed Wallis rightly concludes,

> these changes resulted in an escalating sense of disentitlement on the part of the Christian churches, which had been slow to welcome or appreciate their initial advantages and were then slow to understand their altering circumstances, generally lacking the initiative, the coordination or the strategies to engage with changing times.[134]

So guided by significant personalities during the first thirty-four years until the coming of independent television, the mainstream churches managed to assert their special rights, both to a place within the broadcasting output and to protection from what they regarded as unwelcome innovations by broadcasters; but with the advent of independent local radio and television and later cable and satellite there were now alternative styles of broadcast religion which no matter how innovative its policies were, would be associated with a consumer model of broadcasting and commercial interests.[135]

3. The Church on Television

While a number of books feature the phenomenon of televangelism, religious broadcasters or religious themes in general on secular television, few have focussed specifically on a study of representations of ecclesiastics on prime television shows.[136] It is therefore appropriate to recognise with the onset of television, how various writers and producers in both the USA and the UK sought the opportunity to weave religion, the Church and the clergy into the dramas of everyday life, in their respective cultures, with various degrees of success.

a) An American Trilogy

In terms of America there were three trends in which television depicted the Church. The shows of the 1960s/70s tended to focus on the internal conflicts in the Church, the 1980s and early 90s illustrate the Church's struggle for relevance in the modern world and finally those of the 90s onwards, portray the Church in a more family context.

The era of conflict focussed on the Catholic Church, which is not surprising as in the 1960s and 1970s Catholicism was receiving lots of attention for wide ranging reforms instituted by the Vatican. A series of programmes featured the disputes between the younger, more liberal clergy who welcomed these reforms and their more conservative and older counterparts who resisted them.[137] This trend included programmes from the earliest church-set drama, *Going My Way* (1962-1963), to the situation comedy and occasional musical, *The Flying Nun* (1967-70) and finally the rather short-lived *In the Beginning* (1978), which centred on a clash between an older, conservative priest and a younger liberal nun.

The next category arose in the 1980s when church leaders were attempting to remain relevant in the contemporary society of the day. *Sarge* (1971-1972) focussed on a former policeman turned Catholic cleric who used his investigatory skills to serve the rather worldly needs of his community. Another classic was *Hell Town* (1985) where an ex-con turned priest, together with a selection of street-wise nuns serve a congregation of orphans and city-slickers and help them survive life in the inner city. A similar treatment was *Sister Kate* (1989-1990), though her ministry was to the children of a suburban orphanage. Finally probably the most well-known programme in this period would be the *Father Dowling Mysteries* (1989-1991) which featured a tradition-minded priest who enlists a progressive ex-con nun to help him solve his parish's criminal, if not spiritual problems.[138]

An age of family centred programmes followed with an emphasis more on leaders of the Protestant faiths rather than Catholic. *Family Holvak* (1975) for example followed the everyday life of a Tennessee minister during the Depression. *Amen* (1986-91) focussed on the family and church life of the parish's most outspoken deacon. Not only was this the most successful Protestant-set programme, it was also one of the first programmes to highlight an African-American congregation. Other programmes followed like *Good News* (1997-1998), *Amazing Grace* (1995) and *Soul Man* (1997-1998), but the most successful programme in this category was *7th Heaven* (1996-2007), a programme about a pastor and his ever growing family. The show was destined to become one of the longest-running family dramas in television history.[139]

Woven into these dramas a number of themes emerged – issues of ecumenism, clerical celibacy and sexuality, the question of vocation and increasingly race and gender and how the Church responded to all these. However, what seems apparent was that the most successful programmes of these eras were the ones which took a light-hearted approach to depicting the Church, whereas those which focussed on controversy – no matter how realistic or relevant, fared poorly by television's standards of success, such as ratings and longevity.[140] What is clear is that the Church in the 20th Century was a fixture in television's version of America's cultural landscape.

b) Religion on Screen: Made in Britain.

As with America, it is interesting to see how from the 1950s the Church has been viewed through the lens of British television. Although it is true that the Church now in the 21st Century may have a dwindling influence and a shrinking number of worshippers in some areas, nevertheless in the second half of the 20th Century it was a compelling source for drama and human interest, reflected through the small screen.

In the early days of television in the UK the Church and leading Anglican churchmen, like Archbishops Fisher and Garbett, were influential in providing both ethical and philosophical advice to the broadcasting institutions and their programme makers and especially through significant events like the 1953 Coronation of the Queen.[141] But eventually, although the Church remained a productive object of attention for writers, producers and executives, it lost a great deal of its mainstream influence over broadcasting[142] and a more fictional portrayal was to emerge where the Church was probed, mocked, satirised and sometimes lampooned when it was used for dramatic purposes.

In the early 50s there had been some literary adaptations like Hugh Walpole's *The Cathedral* (1952), but it was not long before programme makers found that the clergy could be a significant source of humour. However, the BBC's early attempts at comedy focussing on the Church ran into difficulty because the writers made the mistake of thinking that the Church was intrinsically funny and that it was enough to say someone was a vicar for everyone to fall about laughing.[143] As a result of criticisms, the BBC initially retreated from ecclesiastical comedy and ITV's Associated Rediffusion took up the mantle with *Our Man at St.Mark's* (1963-1966), a sitcom following the exploits of the somewhat eccentric Rev. Andrew Parker, as he wove in and out of the lives of the parishioners of the village of Felgate. The programme established and maintained its popularity with audiences and two years into its run was still in the top 20 programmes for network television.[144]

All Gas and Gaiters was the second ecclesiastical comedy of the 1960s (1966-1971), this time produced by the BBC. It was an instant success and suddenly large audiences were watching actors in the roles of senior clergy lusting after women, hitting the sherry bottle and wandering around a palace in their pyjamas.[145] While the series was a broad comedy, much of the humour depended upon the audience recognising the institutional structures and ecclesiastical politics of the Church of England[146] and although it initially caused controversy within religious institutions of the day, the nation's clergy soon became the show's greatest fans.

These landmark programmes moved the roles of the clergy from behind the scenes to in front of the cameras within a comedy context. However, although there were not many such series in the chronology of television, there were 'ecclesiastical elements' throughout British television, in shows like *That Was The Week That's Was* (1962-1963), *Yes*

CHAPTER 5 OPPORTUNITY KNOCKS

Prime Minister (1980-1988), *Dad's Army* (1966-1977), *The Two Ronnies* (1971-1987) and *Black Adder* (1983-1989), to name but a few.

But the BBC was eventually to start a regeneration of Church-based sitcoms in the form of the highly successful *Vicar of Dibley*. The show was originally aired on the BBC in 1994 and set in a small fictional Oxfordshire village. A new vicar had been requested. What they got was Geraldine Granger, a non-traditional, chocolate loving, rock n' roll playing vicar. That's not what gets the citizens of Dibley in an uproar though. It's because she was a woman. The writer Richard Curtis picking up on the decision by the Church of England in 1992 to allow women to be ordained as priests.[147] The comedy of the Church's divisions being registered in Dibley, with the series directly confronting the tone and content of much real-life opposition to women priests. An oft-quoted line from the first episode has the new vicar declaring, 'You were expecting a bloke. Beard, bible, bad breath and instead you got a babe with a bob cut and a magnificent bosom'.[148] However, the story-line continually demonstrated Geraldine's determination to show her worthiness to the village. Some commentators within the Anglican Church even credited the show with both normalising female ministry and promoting ordination as an attractive option for women.[149] Nevertheless, in total contrast the BBC's 21st Century drama *Rev* (2010-2014) was to move from the rural to the urban, with the Rev.Adam Smallbone of St Saviour's Hackney East London, juggling the demands of married life, a parish of genuine believers, people on the streets and drug addicts along with the management of a declining church congregation and internal Church of England politics.[150]

But hot on the heels of the *Vicar of Dibley* was Channel 4's Irish-set sitcom Father Ted (1995–1998), providing an irreverent satire of Catholic belief and practice. It was the show that took viewers to the remote Craggy Island and the three priests who lived there: Father Ted Crilly himself, the permanently sozzled Father Jack and the permanently bewildered Father Dougal with Ted trying to bring stability to his congregation as well as the surreal townspeople of Craggy Island. So humour and the Church were never far from the television screens, but a new element began to be introduced in the form of a generation of programmes where clergy were involved in fighting crime.

Father Brown, for example, was a British television detective period drama set in the mid-50s, which began airing on BBC One on 14 January 2013. Brown was a fictional character based on Father John O'Connor who was born in 1870 and died in 1952. He was a parish priest in Bradford who was involved in the conversion of novelist G.K.Chesterton to Catholicism in 1922. Father Brown went on to feature in 51 detective short stories by Chesterton, which were adapted into productions for television, film and radio.[151] Father Brown of St. Mary's Catholic Church used the distinctive skills of his close friends, as well as his own wits to solve crimes, occasionally to the neglect of his more mundane parish duties, but delightfully defended the depths of Christian answers to human problems against the vain arrogance of both the modern enlightenment and post modern superstition.[152] Eventually, the programme became one of the longest running daytime detective dramas on the BBC, though it is also interesting that other popular detective serious such as *Midsomer Murders* (1997–) *Inspector Morse* (1987–2000) and *Grantchester* (2014–) all showcased vicars, rectors or college chaplains in their narratives.

The programmes featured here, both American and British locate the Church in different communities rural and urban, committed and indifferent and highlight through entertaining humour and drama, the challenges faced by the institution and its clergy.[153]

4. Summary

The Church in the USA, apart from a few exceptions, was generally accepting and creative with the potential of religious broadcasting in both radio and television. By comparison in the UK, apart from a few individuals, the Church was initially very reticent and reserved and even fearful of what religious broadcasting might do to church attendance or even take away its role with it simply becoming the 'church of the air'.

However, disputes between the 'traditionalists' and the 'evangelicals' in America really undermined the potential united front there could have been in religious broadcasting. It was inevitable that over time one of these forces would predominate. In the end the evangelical coalition mastery of mass communication some have seen as a matter of survival and success. In an age of sight and sound evangelicals used the reality of communication, utilizing the force of mainstream media to convince themselves and many others that they were a real presence in public life.[154]

In terms of the UK, the Church of England undoubtedly was the key platform relating to the newly formed BBC in 1922. From that point onwards the Central Religious Advisory Committee (CRAC) played a crucial and interdenominational role in trying to keep religious broadcasting in line with what the churches felt was authentic Christianity. Despite the internal tensions within the Church, the external pressures of a growing secularisation and the demands of the broadcasting institutions and legislation that developed, for many years the Church had a golden opportunity to reach millions of people across the UK with the Christian message. However, if the history of religion in broadcasting in the UK had been less protectionist, more imaginative, open-ended, self-critical and flexible, it might have had more impact on the life of the nation than it did.

Finally the chapter examines the spectacle of how the Church and clergy were featured on US and UK television, especially in the dramas and sitcoms throughout the second half of the 20th Century. Significantly it demonstrates that the Church, which exists in every community in one form or another, was source material both for humour, controversy and drama, often portrayed through particular charismatic individuals who were front of stage on the small screen, many of whom became household names through the programmes.

In conclusion the chapter demonstrates that it was wasn't just the relationship between the Church as an institution and religious broadcasting in abstract, rather it was the life's work of leading Church people both here and America who played a strategic role within denominations and religious institutions to create and take the opportunities of religious broadcasting and support the charismatic personalities who took to the airwaves working within the religious and media landscape that pertained in each country. These people were not the 'celebrities' or 'stars' that made the headlines, but in terms of the 'spectrum of significance' they were vitally important in the sphere of the development of religious broadcasting throughout the 20th Century and helped create the environment which provided the large audiences which would be attracted to both religious radio and television programmes.

CHAPTER 5 OPPORTUNITY KNOCKS

NOTES

1. Saunders, L. S., *The National Religious Broadcasters and the Availability of Commercial Radio Time*. (PhD). University of Illinois (1968), p.1.

2. Rodgers, W. W., Broadcasting Church Services. *Radio Broadcast*. August (1922), p.321.

3. Jennings, R. M., *Policies and Practices of Selected National Religious Bodies as Related to Broadcasting in the Public Interest 1920-1950*. (PhD). New York University (1968), p.3.

4. Vanderlaan, E. C., *Fundamentalism versus Modernism* (New York: H.W.Wilson and Co. 1925), p.31.

5. Hutchinson, J. A., *We Are Not Divided: A Critical Historical Study of the Federal Council of the Churches of Christ in America* (New York: Round Table Press, 1941), p.285.

6. FCCC, Report on Evangelism (1924), p.110.

7. Editorial, Radio Preaching and Its Problems. *Christian Century*. October (1924), p.1654.

8. Editorial, Religious Broadcasting. *Radio Broadcast*. November (1925), p.34.

9. Ellens, J. H., *Models of Religious Broadcasting*. (Grand Rapids: W. B. Eerdmans, 1974), p.17.

10. Ibid., p.28.

11. Rosenthal, M., *Protestants and TV in the 1950s: Responses to a New Medium* (New York: Macmillan, 2007), p.41-43.

12. Federal Council of Churches, *Biennial Report*. (New York: FCCC, 1946), p.105, 149.

13. Ellens, J.H. (1974), p.20.

14. Ibid., p.20-21.

15. Jennings, R. M. (1968), p.467ff.

16. Spence, H., The Man of the Lutheran Hour. *Saturday Evening Post*. 19th June (1948), p.17-20.

17. Jennings, R.M. (1968), p.433-434.

18. Soukup, P. A., 1993. Church Documents and the Media. *Concilium*, 6, 1993:71.

19. Miranda Prorsus, Encyclical Letter of Pope Pius X11 on Motion Pictures, Radio and television (1957), p.20 (See also Appendix 6).

20. Ibid., p.28.

21. Vigilanti Cura, Encyclical Letter of Pope Pius X1 on the Motion Picture (1936), p.5 (See also Appendix 6).

22. Interview: 3rd October (2019).

23. Inter Mirifica, Decree on the Means of Social Communication (1963), p.4 (See also Appendix 6)

24. Communio et Progressio, Pastoral Instruction on the Means of Social Communication by order of the Second Vatican Council (1971), Sec.163 (See also Appendix 6)

25. Ibid., Sec.50.

26. Fuchs, O., How the Church deals with the Media. *Concilium*, 6, 1993:84.

27. Ellens, J.H. (1974), p.131.

28. Finnigan, J., The Spiritual Soft Sell of Father Emery Tang. *TV Guide*. 18th March (1972), p.45.

29. Coon, R. W., *The Public Speaking of Dr. William A. Fagal of Faith for Today*. (PhD). Michigan State University (1970), p.129-13.

30. Lobsenz, N. M., Everett Parker's Broadcasting Crusade. *Columbia Journalism Review*, 8 (3) 1969: 30-36.

31. Jennings, R.M. (1968), p.117.

32. Southern Baptists, *Annual of the Southern Baptist Convention*. (Nashville: Southern Baptist Convention, 1947), p.294.

33. Parker,E.C., The Potential of Radio. *Religion News Service* January 3rd (1949).

34. Jennings, R.M. (1968), p.350.

35. Federal Council of Churches, *Broadcasting and the Public*. (New York. Abingdon, 1938), p.7.

36. Tulga, C. E., *The Case Against the National Council of Churches*. (Chicago: Conservative Baptist Association of America, 1951), p.60.

37. Linder, E.W., *Yearbook of American and Canadian Churches* (Nashville. Abingdon Press, 2007),p.76.

38. National Council of Churches, *Christian Faith in Action*. (New York: NCC, 1951), p.10

39. Ibid., p.11.

40. Rosenthal, M., 2001. This Nation under God: The Broadcasting and Film Commission of the National Council of Churches and the New Medium of Television. *The Communication Review*, 4 (3) 2001: 362-363.

41. NCC, *The Role of Radio, Television and Films in Religion* (1960), p.13-14.

42. in Fea, J., *Born Again History* (2008), usreligion.blogspot.com.

43. Schultze, Q. J., *American Evangelicals and the Mass Media*. (Grand Rapids: Academic Books, 1990), p.25-26.

44. Foulkes, W. H., *Radio Evangelism in The Message and Method of the New Evangelism*, edit Bader, J. M., (New York: Round Table Press, 1937), p.230.

45. Armstrong, B., *The Electric Church*. (Nashville: Thomas Nelson, 1979), p. 7, 9.

46. Murch, J. D. F., *Co-operation without Compromise: A History of the National Association of Evangelicals* (Grand Rapids: Eerdmans, 1956), p.72.

47. Ward, S. M., *Air of Salvation: The Story of Christian Broadcasting* (Grand Rapids: Baker Books, 1994), p.18-19.

48. Lochte, B., *Christian Radio: The Growth of a Mainstream Broadcasting Force* (Jefferson: McFarland & Co. 2005), p.38.

49. in Ward, S.M, (1994), p.59.

50. Murch, J.D.F. (1956), p.75.

51. Lochte, B. (2006), p.39.

52. Blackmore, G., *Shall the NCC Control Religious Broadcasting?* (Wheaton: United Evangelical Action, 1956), p.185.

53. in Murch, J.D.F. (1956), p.74.

54. Saunders, L. S., (1968), p.155.

55. National Religious Broadcasters, *NCC Advisory Council Policy Statement*. (Washington: NRB, 12th April, 1956).

56. Editorial, 1956. Time and Tolerance. *Broadcasting Magazine*. 3rd September (1956), p.102.

57. National Religious Broadcasters, *Annual Report*. (Wheaton. United Evangelical Action, 1950), p.17.

58. Hangen, T. J., *Redeeming the Dial: Radio Religion and Popular Culture in America* (Chapel Hill: University of North Carolina Press, 2002), p.141.

59. National Religious Broadcasters, *Ten Reasons Why You Should Join and Support the National Religious Broadcasters* (Washington: NRB, 1966).

60. Stearly, B., The Effects of Broadcasting on the Churches. *Radio Broadcast Magazine*. August (1923), p.273-274.

61. Fortner, R. S., *Radio, Morality and Culture* (Illinois: Southern Illinois University Press, 2005), p.112.

62. Bluem, A. W., 1969. *Religious Television Programming: A Study of Relevance* (New York: Hastings House, 1969), p.25.

63. Schultze, Q.J., The Wireless Gospel. *Christianity Today*. 18th January (1988), p.20.

64. Fortner, R.S. (2005),124-125.

65. Ibid., p.126-127.

66. Bookbinder, A., Religious Broadcasting: Challenge to the Churches. *Epworth Review*, 30 (4) 2003: 13.

67. Turner, D. M. R., The Church and Broadcasting. *Montrose and Arbroath Review*. September 18th (1952), p.4.

68. Martin, D., The Church and the British Broadcasting Corporation 1922-1956. The Politics of Broadcast Religion. *Religious Studies*, 22 (2) 1986: 283.

69. Central Religious Advisory Committee, *Review of the Aims and Achievement of Religious Broadcasting 1923-1948*. (London: 1948), Church of England Archive Centre, File Ref: BCC/7/1/9/5/1.

70. Wolfe, K. M., *The Churches and the British Broadcasting Corporation 1922-1956. The Politics of Broadcast Religion*. (London: SCM, 1984), p.5.

71. Dinwiddie, M., *Religion by Radio: Its Place in British Broadcasting*. London: George Allen & Unwin Ltd, 1968), p.9

72. Ibid., p.9.

73. Bell, G. K. A., *Randall Davidson: Archbishop of Canterbury*. 3rd edition (London: Oxford University Press, 1957), p.1210-1211.

74. Quicke, A. and Quicke, J., *Hidden Agendas: The Politics of Religious Broadcasting in Britain 1987 – 1991* (Virginia Beach: Dominion Kings Grant Publications, 1992), p.27-28.

75. Smyth, C., *Cyril Forster Garbett* (London: Hodder and Stoughton, 1959), p.202.

76. Ibid., p.201.

77. Garbett, C. F., Broadcasting. *Southwark Diocesan Gazette*. March (1925), p.22.

78. Smyth, C., 1959, p.210.

79. Ibid., p.212.

80. Taylor, C., The Church and Radio. *St.Martin's Review* (1947), p.146.

81. Convocation of Canterbury, *The Eighth Georgia v Regnante: Joint Committee*. Committees of the Lower House (London. SPCK, 1929), p.111.

82. Church of England, *The Religious Value of Broadcast Services and their Bearing on Public Worship*. (London: Church of England, 1931), p.17.

83. Ibid., p.18.

84. Ibid., p.20-21.

85. Fortner, R.S. (2005), p.48.

86. Independent Television Authority, *Religion in Britain and Northern Ireland* (London: ITA, 1970), p.43.

87. Interview: 3rd October (2019).

88. Church Assembly Board, *Towards the Conversion of England* (London: Church of England Commission on Evangelism, 1945), p.105.

89. British Council of Churches, *Christianity and Broadcasting*. (London: 1950), Church of England Archive Centre, File Ref: BCC/10/5/29, p.32.

90. Report of the Broadcasting Committee 1951, (*Beveridge Report*) Cmnd.8116 (London: HMSO), Chapter 1X p.60.

91. BCC Report (1950), p.21.

92. Ibid., p.25.

93. BBC, *Religious Broadcasting: History and Current Practice.The First 10 Years 1922-1932.*(London 1943), BBC WAC. File Ref: R34/815/2, p.1, 3.

94. Ibid., p.2.

95. Ibid., p.5.

96. Fortner, R.S. (2005), p.55.

97. Street, S., *A Concise History of British Radio 1922-2002* (Tiveton: Kelly Publications, 2002), p.41.

98. Whates, A. E., *Letter to Sir John Reith*, 8th January (1935), BBC WAC. File Ref: R41/179/1.

99. Wolfe, K. M. (1984), p.41.

100. Ibid., p. xxii-xxiii.

101. Briggs, A., *The History of Broadcasting in the United Kingdom*. Vol. V: *Competition* (Oxford: Oxford University Press, 1995), p.696.

102. BBC, *Controversy in Religious Broadcasting*. (London: 1947), Church of England Archive Centre, File Ref: BCC/7/1/9/5/2, p.40.

103. Richards, B. Rev., The Church Speaks. *Nelson Leader*. July 6th (1956), p.4.

104. Central Religious Advisory Committee, *Review of the Aims and Achievement of Religious Broadcasting 1923-1948*. (London: 1948), Church of England Archive Centre, File Ref: BCC/7/1/9/5/1, p. 8.

105. Roman Catholic Report to the Annan Committee (1975), p.11.

106. Aetatis Novae, Pastoral Instruction on Social Communications on the Anniversary of Communio et Progessio (1992), Sec.8.

107. Saxon, E., 1964. On Television. *Church Times*. 24th April (1954), p.7.

108. Reindorp, G. E., Unseen congregation. *Daily Mirror*, 19th June (1958), p.7.

109. Briggs, A. (1995), p.712.

110. BBC, 1947. *Controversy in Religious Broadcasting* (London: 1947), Church of England Archive Centre, File Ref: BCC/7/1/9/5/2.

111. BCC, (1950), p.40.

112. Quicke, A, and Quicke, J. (1992), p.37

113. Independent Television Authority, *Annual Report & Accounts* (London: ITA.1974/75), p. 27.

114. Sendall, B. C., *Independent Television in Britain*. Vol.1 (London: Macmillan, 1982), p.104.

115. Independent Television Authority, *Religious Programmes on Independent Television* (London: ITA, 1962), p.13.

116. Independent Television Authority, *Religion in Television* (London: ITA, 1964), p.11.

117. Quicke, A. and Quicke J. (1992), p.37.

118. Stoller, T., *Sounds of Your Life: The History of Independent Radio in the UK* (New Barnet: John Libbey Publishing Ltd. 2010), p.22.

119. Independent Television Authority, *Annual Report & Accounts* (London: ITA. 1974/75), p.39.

120. Interview: July 16th (2019).

121. Ward, T., The Churches and Local Radio. *Church Times*. 26th February (1988), p.12.

122. in McDonnell, J., *Public Service Broadcasting*. (London: Routledge, 1991),p.78.

123. Hendy, D., *Public Service Broadcasting*. (Basingstoke: Palgrave Macmillan, 2013), p.98.

124. Lewis, C.A., *Broadcasting From Within*. (London: George Newnes, 1924), p.48-50.

125. Hunt, S.,*Transformations in British Religious Broadcasting. In*: Bailey, M. and Redden, G., *Mediating Faiths and Religion and Socio-Cultural Change in Twenty-First Century*. (Burlington: Ashgate, 2011), p.25

126. McDonnell. J., *From Certainty to Diversity: The Evolution of Religious Broadcasting Since 1990. In*: Geybels, H., Mels, S. and Walrave, M., *Faith & Media: Analysis of Faith and Media*. (Brussels: P. I. E. Peter Lang, 2009)

127. Longley. C., Broadcasting as Challenge. *The Times*. 6th July (1987), p.12.

128. Interview: October 3th (2019).

129. McDonnell, J. (2009), p.155.

130. Editorial, 1986. Gospel TV: Religion Politics and Money. *Time Magazine*. 17th February (1096), p.23.

131. Quicke, A. and Quicke,J. (1992), p.86-87.

132. Wolfe, K.M. (1984), p.xxiii.

133. Ibid., p.xxi.

134. Wallis, R., Genesis of the Bible Documentary: the Development of Religious Broadcasting in the UK. *In*: Bond, H. K. and Adams, E., *The Bible on Television*. (London: T & T Clark, 2020), p. 28.

135. McDonnell, J. (2009), p.153.

136. Clark, S.H., Created in Whose Image? Religious Characters on Network Television. *Journal of Media and Religion*, 4: 2005: 137-153.

CHAPTER 5 OPPORTUNITY KNOCKS

137. Wolff, R., *The Church on TV* (New York: Continuum Books, 2010), p.7.

138. Ibid., p.7.

139. Ibid., p.8.

140. Ibid., p.8-9.

141. Harmes M., et.al *The Church on British Television* (London:Palgrave Macmillan,2020), p.20-21

142. Ibid., p.106

143. Apps, E. Pursued by Bishops: The Memoirs of Edwin Apps (London: Durand-Peyroles, 2013).

144. Editorial, Our Man at St.Marks, *Stage and Television Today*, July 22nd (1965), p.10.

145. Harmes, M., et.al. (2020), p.115.

146. Crome, A. "Wonderful, "Hot," "Good" Priests: Clergy on Contemporary British TV and the New Visibility of Religion Thesis. *Religions* 11(1) 2020: 1-15.

147. Sorenson, S., The Collar: Reading Christian Ministry in Fiction, Television and Film (Eugene: Cascade Books, 2014), p.194.

148. Harmes,M., et. al (2020), p.226.

149. Butt, R. The Vicar of Dibley Effect: More Women Ordained Than Men, *The Guardian* 14th November (2007), p.13.

150. Rev (www.comedy.co.uk/rev).

151. Correspondent, Father Brown. *Independent Catholic News*, 5th January (2015), p.6.

152. Burns, T. The Rationalism of Father Brown. *Perspectives on Political Science* 34(1) 2005: 42.

153. Harmes, M, et.al. (2020), p.230.

154. Carpenter, J. A., *Tuning the Gospel Fundamentalist Radio Broadcast and the Revival of Mass Religion 1939-1945* (Urbana: University of Illinois, 1985), p.15.

CHAPTER 6

AUDIENCE IS KING
An Assessment of the Significance of Audiences to Religious Broadcasting

The maxim "the audience is king"[1] or "sovereign"[2] are common expressions in the media industry, recognising the importance to broadcasters of the audience it serves and of the need to match content with the needs of those who view or listen. This principle is true in broadcasting, but also true in other spheres too. This chapter will aim to outline the principles behind this and especially in regard to religious broadcasting in the United States and Britain, where the issue of who and how many people are viewing and listening was seriously crucial for programme makers and in some cases for those whose responsibility was to create and manage the finances to keep ministries and programmes on air. As one observer remarked, "the Christian communicator must learn to tailor his messages to the audience at least as well as Proctor & Gamble".[3] This chapter is no mere appendage, the issue of audiences and their demographics were significantly important to the personalities featured in Chapter 4 and the Church networks and their leaders highlighted in Chapter 5, who all attempted to match their broadcasts and ministries to their audiences and potential audiences in order to make the maximum impact.

1. The Challenge of Research

When broadcasting began in 1920s, audience research was not at all widespread and broadcasters in the early days of radio in Britain and the United States knew remarkably little about their listeners and what they knew was often based on unreliable and misleading methods.

The first form of measurement used in the United States to guide programming was by counting the number of letters elicited by programmes. An apocryphal quote was that one letter was equivalent to a thousands listeners. Other measurements drew circles on maps of the area of the station, deducing how many listeners there might be. But in reality differences in transmitter power, local geography, station programming, wavelengths and other factors were known to influence the size of populations reached by each station.[4]

In Britain radio broadcasting began in 1922, no commercial broadcasting on television until 1955 and no commercial radio until 1973. In fact the BBC, for example, had no audience research for more than 10 years after its establishment, which was a concern to many like Val Gielgud, the BBC Productions Director,

> I cannot help feeling more and more strongly, that we are fundamentally ignorant as to how our various programmes are received and what their relative popularity is. It must be a considerable source of disquiet to many people bedsides myself, to think that it is quite possible that a very great deal of money and time and effort maybe expended on broadcasting into a void.[5]

Audience research was formally established within the BBC in 1936, serving as an instrument of public accountability as well as providing information for programme makers and management. In the United States the process was completely different. American radio was guided by one fundamental principle: people are attracted to listen if they get the programmes they want. All American audience measurement has derived from this basic marketing principle. Listeners and viewers choose what they listen to or watch. Advertisers choose where they will place their advertisements.[6] In the broadcasting world this is the difference between the public service broadcasting of the UK and the commercial broadcasting of the USA and it is reflected in the outlook and approach of the audience research.

Audience research can be used as a means of maximising the effectiveness of public advocacy campaigns and of improving and enhancing education and information for effective democracy and good government. Audience research is a means of providing essential information to aid the process of programme making. It can be used as a means of maximising the efficient and cost-effective use of limited resources or to increase awareness of a consumer brand.[7] The core issue is that research provides information and as Francis Bacon expressed, "knowledge is itself power".[8]

2. An American Review

Three main elements are important to consider here, the size and the characteristics of the audience and the motivation to listen and watch.

a) Size Matters

In the realm of religious broadcasting the image of success is seen and portrayed in the size of the audience to programmes/channels and really acts as almost an indication of God's blessing on the ministry enterprise. In addition when audience size has financial implications, the accuracy of measurement can be crucial to a range of different stakeholders, including investors, producers, performers, exhibitors and advertisers.[9]

Indeed of all the controversies that have surrounded religious broadcasting in America, the most heated and long standing debate has concerned the audience size. Spokespersons such as Ben Armstrong of the National Religious Broadcasters claimed the audience to be as large as 100 million, Jim Bakker figured his PTL audience to be over 20 million, Jerry Falwell estimated his television audience at 15 million. The *Wall Street Journal* produced the largest estimate of a total around 130 million.[10] On the other hand Dr.William Fore of the National Council of Churches (NCC) more realistically suggested the audience for all programmes to be in the region of 10 to 20 million regular viewers.[11]

The fear was that such overwhelming numbers may cause diminished attendance and contributions to the local church. Professor Martin E.

Marty of the University of Chicago noted, "televised religion may be weaning adherents away from the traditional local churches in droves and becoming a feared contemporary rival to church religion".[12]

This assertion was not agreed by everyone,[13] but whatever the fears, the reality is that estimates of audience size have been inconsistent and imprecise for a number of reasons, but one key factor is that most publicized studies of audience size have been based on polling data where there is no independent check on the reliability of the self-reports. Time and again opinion polls have found that 40% of Americans claim to be regular viewers. This figure however, cannot be supported by ratings data. Two analyses of audience size[14] based on available data from the two national ratings firms, suggested the audience to be in the range of 20 million.[15]

The most commonly used figures for estimating audience sizes are provided by the large survey companies, Nielsen and Arbitron. These two companies conduct continuous research on a carefully calculated, statistically representative basis into audiences of most broadcast programmes on a local, regional and national level. These audience figures are widely used by broadcasters and advertisers for the determination of a programme's popularity. Both survey companies include syndicated religious programmes in their regular audience research and figures provided by Nielsen in 1981 indicated the combined audience for all syndicated religious programmes was 21,751,000.[16] Earlier studies by Nielsen and Arbitron quoted by *Time Magazine*[17] provided a greater insight into the ratings of some individual Christian broadcasting ministries,

Ministry	*Audience*	
Pat Robertson	16.6 million	(daily)
Jimmy Swaggart	9.3 million	(weekly)
Robert Schuller	7.6 million	(weekly)
Jim Bakker	5.6 million	(daily)
Oral Roberts	5.6 million	(weekly)
Jerry Falwell	5.6 million	(weekly)

However, the inadequacy of both the Nielsen and Arbitron figures is that they do not measure the audience for cable programmes and a number of religious syndicators moved into cable and therefore that might indicate that audience figures would be greater. But the reality is that the picture is far from precise. The data agencies indicating that the combined audiences are less than 20 million per week, whilst the religious broadcasters themselves tend to inflate their audience statistics – "there is a fairly common suspicion that preachers sometimes count arms and legs instead of heads".[18]

According to Ferre, religious television demonstrated itself as a type of entrepreneurial individualism with a regular audience of no more than 20 million viewers, which is less than one tenth of the population of the United States.[19] However, the conclusion of this tortuous debate is that we are still some way from a definite estimate of the size of the audience for religious broadcasting and maybe have to agree with the research of Hadden and Shupe (1988)[20] that the weekly audience is not less than 13.3 and more likely to be around 15 million per week, which is sizable, but only 8% of the total viewing population and nothing like the inflated figures that have previously been published,[21] but still represents a number equal to the membership of the United Methodist, Presbyterian and Episcopal Churches combined.[22] Writing in the *New York Times* in 1989 Peter Applebome's assessment was that, "the public is deeply committed to religious broadcasting with a fifth of the population watching despite the scandals".[23]

To re-iterate, how many people watch religious television? We don't know, but we suspect that the number is substantially less than the TV preachers and the secular press have claimed. Whatever the actual count, the number is large enough to serve to alert us to the fact that we are talking about a significant social phenomenon in American society.[24]

b) The Characteristics of Religious Broadcasting Audiences

The issue of the size of the audience is of some consequence, but more relevant is the significance and demographics of the audience, which is related to broader issues such as policy, politics, society and culture.

1. *Women watch religious programmes more than men*

In most of the research generally the proportion of women to men is approximately two to one. Hadden and Swann report some Arbitron data on the viewers for the top ten programmes, where the percentage of watchers who are women ranges from a low of 60% to a high of 73%.[25] It is sometimes suggested that the main reason for this disparity is most programmes are broadcast when women are more available.[26] However these trends have been found in other studies of religious programming. Robinson in a 1964 study of the radio and television audience in seven cities found that women were greater consumers of religious programmes that men[27] and Buddenbaum in 1979 found that regular viewers of religious television programmes were twice as likely to be female as male.[28] Some however believe that the gender amplifications are almost certainly explained by the imbalance in television watching, with women watching significantly more day-time television than do men.[29]

2. *Viewing religious programmes increases with age*

The religious broadcasting audience has a fairly distinct age profile. Again the Hadden and Swann Arbitron data makes the point that all the syndicated programmes have audiences of which two-thirds to three-quarters are fifty years of age or over.[30] The older profile obviously matches with people too who are more infirm and find it harder to get to church and therefore benefit from viewing religious programmes. Equally some who are seriously ill for example would find great appeal in the healing ministries of televangelists, like Oral Roberts.

Dennis in his research in the Detroit area in 1962 found that while increasing age was not directly proportional to increasing viewing and listening, a significant shift occurred once the person reached 60.[31] Robinson in an analysis of seven US cities found that half of the respondents to his research who watched religious broadcasts regularly were over 60.[32] By contrast, research with adolescents and young adults showed that 67.2 % and 70.3% respectively reported they never watched religious programmes compared to 25.7% who said they sometimes watched.[33]

Finally, Tamney and Johnson's 1984 study on religious broadcasting viewing habits in Indiana suggests that the relationship between age, religiosity and viewing religious television, itself changes with age. Amongst the young, those who did not attend church also did not watch religious television. Amongst the old, those who did not attend church did watch religious television. Tamney and Johnson concluded that old people watch more religious television than young people, because they have greater trouble attending church and because they were generally more involved with all religious activities.[34]

3. Their income and education is of a lower status

The available evidence seems to show that viewers and listeners of religious broadcasting are less well educated than average. Robinson in his study (1964) found that people with the lowest levels of formal education were much more likely to listen or view religious programmes regularly. He found that only 30% of those whose income was less than $13,000 dollars were non-viewers of religious programmes compared to 67% of those whose income was greater than $16,000 dollars[35] Buddenbaum found that the regular audience for religious broadcasting comprised mainly blue collar workers and 'others', which included housewives and non-classifiable employed persons. Only 5.3% of the professionals identified by the study reported that they watched religious programmes regularly compared to 30.4% of blue collar workers and 25.3% of others.[36] Not surprisingly therefore the socio-economic status of the religious broadcasting audience, as measured by occupation, both reflects and amplifies the education bias.[37]

An interesting study by Thomas suggests that religion and religious broadcasting far from being the 'opiate of the masses', in a Marxian sense, reveals also that religious programmes are subject to social class variations. Taking a sample of 23 broadcasts, she found that 14 were orientated towards the working-class ego (*Rex Humbard*), 6 towards the middle-class ego (*The Old Time Gospel Hour*) and 3 towards the upwardly mobile (*700 Club*). Within the first group, piety and devotion were stressed above professional accomplishment, the same principle of 'social functionality' extending up the ladder so that the upwardly-mobile received views designed to rationalise their social position.[38]

4. Geography is relevant

In considering the American scene, recognition needs to be made that the country is vast and its culture varied, so regional variations related to the religious broadcasting audience could be significant. Though all the major religious programmes are broadcast in every major part of the country, the make-up of their audiences show a distinct bias towards the southern and mid-western states, regions which are the highest church attendance in the country.[39] This is supported by the Dennis study (1962) showing that having ones birthplace in one of the southern states was a significant factor in distinguishing audience from non-audience of religious programmes.[40]

Indeed while the eastern states contain 22.5% of the total population of the country the major religious broadcasters draw only between 10.3% and 14.7% of their audiences from that area.[41] But of all the major televangelists only Robert Schuller, the one preacher who is a minister of a mainstream denomination (the Reformed Church), is the exception with 24% of his audience from the eastern states and is equally popular in the east, the mid-west and the south.[42]

5. The audience has a high religious interest and church affiliation

The major proportion of the audience of religious broadcasting are people who indicate a high religious affiliation especially religious conservatism. The largest group of viewers are independent fundamentalist Baptists (21%), second are Southern Baptists (19%). A group dubbed 'Charismatic Christians' is third at 10.5%, followed closely by Catholics (10%), United Methodists (8.3%) and other Methodists

(7.1%). Mainstream Presbyterians, Lutherans, Disciples of Christ, United Church of Christ and Episcopalians each make up less than 2% of the audience.[43]

From the national population sample in the 1978 Gallup Poll, the poll found that those who watch religious television programmes compared to those who don't watch religious television are more likely to have had a conversion experience, to believe that the Bible is free of mistakes, to believe in a personal devil, to read the Bible more often, to talk with others about their faith more often, to attend church services more frequently and to hold to or engage in beliefs and practice characteristic of evangelicals as a whole. The typical US evangelical was characterized as a white female southerner, aged 50 or over, with a high school education and modest income.[44]

So not only is the audience drawn disproportionately from a particularly conservative Protestant tradition, but within any denomination, it is the most conservative members who will be the most frequent watchers.[45]

A national investigation of religious radio programme audiences was done in 1971 by Johnstone, the Director of Research for the Lutheran Church and he concluded,

> religious broadcasting tends to reach those who already have been reached in the sense of already having formal association with religious institutions. The old, the church member, the regular attender these comprise the large majority of the listening audience for religious broadcasts.[46]

A further commentator concurred,

> in spite of their much-touted new formats, technological sophistication and prominence in the secular world, the audience for religious television today is older, less educated, more rural and more conventionally religious that its non-religious-viewing cohort. There is little reason to believe that many outside of the traditional audience are actually viewing.[47]

c) Why Do People Watch Particular Religious Television Programmes?

The research on the audience of religious broadcasting indicates that there is a correlation between the nature and content of a programme and the dominant characteristics of the audience it attracts. Halloran makes an important point in that,

> the TV message is not so much one single message ... but more like several messages ... and we need to know the potential of each vehicle with regard to all the relevant sub-cultures.[48]

1. The Evangelistic Content

People engage with the programming because they feel it is reaching outsiders with the message of the Christian faith with a view to converting them. 'To get the gospel out' seems a motive for watching and for supporting financially. Though as already been seen, broadcasters on the whole are not reaching outsiders, but insiders.[49]

2. Inspiration, Companionship and Support

When Engel surveyed those who had called Channel 38 in Chicago he found that for the majority of the respondents the most helpful role of the station and its programmes had been to help them grow spiritually.[50] In parallel Hilton's survey of the use of television worship services by Irvington Presbyterian Church, showed that the major uses made of the programmes were for personal inspiration and uplift and prayer.[51] The Christian Broadcasting Network's Counselling Centre in Boston for example in its first two years (1977-79) received only 2,724 calls for salvation but 36,497 requests for prayer.[52]

3. Leisure Time Activity

Why people watch religious programmes on television is derived from its use over an individual's life span.[53] In America, Bourgault in her small survey (an exclusively church-based sample) found most viewers could be profiled as 'religious entertainment seekers'.

However the only programme tested in this research was the *Praise the Lord Club* and also the work was limited to the small city of Nelsonville, Ohio (population 4,400). Only one respondent evidently looked to the programme primarily for inspiration and support rather than to the local church, the vast majority treating it as a source of diversion with a religious bent.[54]

Mostly television fulfils a more important role in the lives of older people than younger people. It is the predominant leisure time activity of older adults and older adults may watch more religious television simply by reason of the greater frequency of viewing. Religious programmes in this context seem to act as a source of information, a substitute for lost social activity and the ability to attend church.[55]

4. Self Awareness

Finally Buddenbaum in her 1979 study noted that religious television audience reported quite different needs from those of the general television audience. Television viewing as a whole has been found to be most useful in satisfying the need to be entertained, to kill time, to relax and release tension and to avoid the feelings of loneliness. While religious viewing correlates positively with the need to know oneself better and also correlates positively with the need to avoid feelings of loneliness.[56]

In concluding on the various surveys, Peck asserts,

> Although the general religious television audience shares certain general characteristics – predominantly female, over 50, rural, lower income and education, there are significant differences between audiences for particular programmes. The actual audience of religious programmes is fairly fragmented and those who do watch, do so for very specific reasons.[57]

Certainly, there is no doubt that the advanced technological competence of religious broadcasters, the extent of their organisations and corporations, the variety of their programming and the breadth and impact of their reach were being closely watched by partisan and non-partisan groups alike.[58]

3. A Very British Approach

a) Early Days

From the strength of its monopoly, the BBC focussed on building its credibility on its status and its programmes. However, as stated earlier, it is a remarkable feature of the early BBC that its broadcasters worked in almost complete ignorance of their audiences. None of those involved in making programmes for the British public had any systematic knowledge of the audiences for whom they were making these programmes, nor the reactions of those audiences to the programmes they had made.[59]

But eventually there were suggestions from various individuals and departments within the BBC that it would be a good idea to find out what people liked to listen to and why. They did not consider letters to the Programme Correspondence Section (which numbered about 50,000 items per year by 1927) or the *Radio Times* to be a sufficient approach. John Reith (the Director General), however was uneasy about systematic audience research, fearing it would influence programme planning and start a regime of chasing ratings in the pattern of America.[60]

But by 1936, fourteen years after the commencement of broadcasting by the BBC, its General Advisory Council voted to go ahead with a more structured approach and despite his lack of experience in broadcasting, R.J.E. Silvey a professional statistician from the London Press Exchange, began work as a Listener Research Assistant and built up the Listener Research (later Audience Research) Department and laid the groundwork for the methods of gathering and analysing data.[61] As Gorham, a former post-war Director of BBC Television reflected,

> to study these figures, as we did, day by day, seven days a week, gave you a feeling of being in touch with your audience

and much more satisfying than depending on letters, which are often written by minorities, or by taking the opinions of the comparatively few people around London who you can meet yourself.[62]

In a 1956 lecture to the St.Pauls' Lecture Society on *Religion of the Air*, Silvey underlined the approach of his Department,

> it is for us to provide the facts and ensure that they are properly understood, but it is not for us to decide upon the policy that should be pursued in the light of them. It is for us to provide the most accurate charts for the navigator, but it is not for us to decide upon the ships course.[63]

In the same lecture he made some important reflections on what their research had shown regarding religious broadcasting,

> it is true that listening to religious broadcasts is much more common amongst churchgoers than non-church goers. It is certainly not true that religious broadcasts are ignored by all non-church goers. We found that a quarter of them listen to religious broadcasts frequently and a further quarter occasionally. It means that religious broadcasting is a means whereby the influence of Christian teaching and worship is brought to bear in some degree upon half of the people who are outside the church.[64]

The latter quote being significant in the mission of religious broadcasting, to reach out beyond the church and impact the lives of ordinary people.

b) The Scope of BBC Research

As the Audience Research Department developed, so did its brief,

> Audience Research is the systematic study of the public for broadcasting. Its function is to supply information. Whilst it is not by any means the only source of information available

to the Corporation, it is distinctive in that it supplies the scientific method, through the use of specialized techniques, to the collection and analysis of information. The Audience Research Department serves all departments concerned with 'domestic' sound and television broadcasting. It is not concerned with External Broadcasting.[65]

In detail the Department provided 4 keys functions:-

1. Providing estimates of *audience size* both in terms of networks and individual programmes for both television and radio services, whether national regional or local.

2. Establishing *what kind of people* (whether disproportionately the young or the elderly, the higher or lower socio-economic sections etc.) comprise these audiences.

3. and crucially how they *feel* about the programmes they come to see or hear whether stimulated or bored, enlightened or entertained.

4. Assisting the programme planners or producers at the *formative* stage of a programme, series or serial: early in the creative process to obtain some insight into whether the producer seems to be communicating the message or obtaining the responses that he or she intends.

5. Tackling the rather more tricky areas of 'social effects and mores' of broadcasting what is and what is not acceptable in terms of 'taste' (sex, violence and language being the traditional principal areas of concern).[66]

So the Department provided background information about the population, audience sizes, and research for programme production, general audience studies and particular audience studies. In the field of Religious Broadcasting, the department had a key role to provide information, identify trends and particularly to reflect feedback on specific programmes.

c) What Does The Audience Research Reveal?

1. Religious Affiliation

A survey by the department in 1939 (Special Report) [67] with 4000 listeners asked people what was their religion. The aim being to get a better understanding of the potential for religious broadcasting and craft programmes more appropriately. Of the respondents 60% said they were Church of England, 6% Church of Scotland, 9% Non-Conformist, 13% Catholic, other Christian groups 1%, Jewish 1%, Muslims 1%, Hindi/Sikh, 1%, Agnostic 1%, Atheists 2%, no religion 4% and not stated 1%.

All but a small minority (who said they are agnostic, atheists or have no religion) said they have a religious belief i.e. more than 4 out of 5 respondents identified themselves with a religion, though this does not necessarily imply that they were active participants in a religious group or institution. In fact by 1989 only 17% of the British public claimed to go to a place of worship regularly.[68]

2. Responses to Religious Broadcasting

The Listener Research Department was to canvas responses to the existing output of religious broadcasting in 1941.

The results show of the then 30 million civilian listening public, 5 million were enthusiastic towards broadcast religious services. Another 9 million were considered to be indifferent. Of the remainder, 5.5 million do not like broadcast religious services and 3 million are hostile to them. The 5 million 'very enthusiastic' maybe regarded as the nucleus of the broadcast religious service public. The 5 million consists of about 3.5 million women and 1.5 million men. Furthermore nearly half of the listeners are over 60 years of age, whereas in the whole listening population, listeners over 60 constitute less than a third. The average age of the listeners in the five million therefore is much higher than the average age of listeners as whole. When looking at the very popular programme *Lift up Your Hearts* the report points out that three-quarter of the average audience for this programme are favourably disposed towards broadcast religious services.[69]

3. Religious Broadcasting Preferences

Of all religious broadcasts the Sunday evening services are listened to the most. On average, one third of respondents in the 1942 Listener Research Survey (see all results below) listened to one or other of the evening services each Sunday. The Sunday morning services were usually listened to by rather over one fifth, the midweek services by nearly as many, while 15% usually listened to the Epilogue. No record of actual listening to the Daily Service is available, but 13% say they listened to it regularly and another 13% occasionally.

Services from places of worship are always listened to by greater numbers than studio services. The relative dislike of the studio service is more marked among working class than among middle class listeners.

Relatively speaking more working class than middle class respondents listen to the Sunday morning service, the evening services, the mid-week service, the children's services and the daily service. Relatively more middle class respondents listen to the Epilogue, to religious feature programmes, to *Melodies of Christendom* and to religious talks. It seems than amongst the English regions listening to nearly every type of religious programme is least in the London region and greatest in the West region.

By 1943 it was estimated that about 50% of the whole adult audience listened to one or more of the services and other religious items.[70] Clearly some programmes were hugely popular. The monthly Sunday evening services from St. Martin-in-the-Fields, which were broadcast on all wavelengths, were listened to by more people than to all alternative services taken together on other Sundays.[71]

Putting this in a comparative context, Cyril Taylor writing in the *St. Martin's Review* in 1947 pointed out,

> When *Sunday Half Hour* comes on the air something like six million people are listening. That is one million more people that would fill every seat in every cinema in the whole of this country.[72]

4. Religious Broadcasting and the Public

Silvey in his account of the BBC Audience Research Department, recounts an initiative regarding Religious Broadcasting,

> The Religious Broadcasting Department backed by what everyone knew as the Central Religious Advisory Committee, wanted to know the extent to which they were or were not preaching to the converted. So we devised a questionnaire about religious beliefs and practices and arranged for the fieldwork to be done by the Gallup Poll. The findings were printed for distribution to religious leaders and other interested parties as *Religious Broadcasting and the Public*.[73]

The Report focussed on 3 groups of roughly equal size. 'Frequent listeners' to religious broadcasting, 'occasional listeners' and 'non-listeners'. Compared to the population as a whole the frequent listeners included a larger proportion of women and older people and widowed and a smaller proportion of single persons. Conversely the non-listeners included a larger proportion of men, of young people and single persons and a smaller proportion of widows than does the population. In respect of social class the composition of the frequent listening and non-listening do not differ markedly. The major difference between frequent and non-listeners to religious broadcasts is in respect of church going. Results show that the more a person goes to church the more they are likely to listen. But about one in four of the frequent listener group were classified as non-churchgoers. Non-conformist affiliations are to be found more often, the Roman Catholics less often, than their numbers in the population warrant. It is inevitable that since frequent churchgoers constitute a much larger proportion of the frequent listening group than of the non-listeners, the opinions and beliefs of the frequent listeners are more orthodox than those of non-listeners and more than one person in four in the entire sample claimed that religious broadcasts had helped them in the past.

People's motives for listening are much more difficult to ascertain. As between the under and over 50s, for example, there is a markedly different emphasis placed on the teaching function of religious broadcasts, the under 50s laying greater stress on it. In the same way the under 50s laying more stress than their elders upon the help which religious broadcasts afforded them in coping with daily life. The common endorsement was that religious broadcasts are "a comfort".

The Report gives some indicators too about church going. Two-thirds of frequent churchgoers are women, whereas more than half the non-churchgoers are men. The single and the widowed go to church more than the married and with each step down the social scale non-churchgoing increases. Far more Roman Catholics than Protestants go to church frequently, though non-churchgoing is rarest amongst those who claim Non-conformist affiliations.

If the decline in churchgoing needed confirmation it contains it in this survey. Six out of ten non-churchgoers say they used to go, seven out of ten occasional churchgoers say they used to go more often and so do three out of ten frequent churchgoers. Though there is nothing to suggest this indicates any lack of their Christian beliefs, its momentum is rather more sociological where an earlier generation went to church because 'everybody' went. But conformity has now changed.[74]

By the end of the 1950s the BBC were estimating,

> on a typical day, 13 million seven hundred people watch one of more BBC television programmes, nearly 22 million hear one or more BBC sound programmes.[75]

So how does religious broadcasting fit into that context? In a speech to the St. Pauls Lecture Society, the then Head of BBC Religious Broadcasting, the Rev. Roy McKay, reflected on the *Religious Broadcasting and the Public Report* indicating that whilst there was a decline in church attendance there remained a strong interest in the BBC's religious programmes with,

> something like three million listening to *Lift up Your Hearts*, three hundred and sixty thousand to the *Daily Service*, three and a half million to *Five to Ten* and three and half million to the *People's Service*, seven hundred and fifty thousand to the 9.30 Sunday Morning Service and three hundred and sixty thousand to the *Sunday Evening Service*.[76]

He saw the aim of the Department to "support and extend the witness of the Church to the Christian Gospel" [77] and believed the figures revealed the significant work done by the BBC, as probably the only contact with Christianity for a vast number of non-churchgoers of all ages.

Francis House, a former head of BBC Religious Broadcasting writing in *The Times* stated,

> 12 million people listen to one religious broadcast on a Sunday and an estimated audience for all broadcasts was over 18 million. 40% of the audience are also uncommitted Christians.[78]

The official view by the BBC in their 1955 Handbook still showed a substantial audience stating,

> that nearly one third of the adult population hear one of the religious broadcasts on a Sunday and the majority of these listeners are believed to be men and women who are not regular churchgoers.[79]

5. Interest in Religious or Spiritual Matters

The 1984 BBC Audience Research survey really confirmed much of previous indicators. 41% of the population claimed to be interested in religious or spiritual matters. Women were more likely than men to say were interested – almost half of women compared with just over one third of men. Elderly people were more likely than average to be interested in religious matters, as were people who lived alone. A regional survey also showed that people in Scotland or the North of England were the least likely to be interested and people in Northern Ireland were the most likely to have said they were interested. Nothing of the survey indicated that interest in religion is a middle-class activity nor for those with less education.

Four out of five people who were interested in religious matters said they were interested in seeing religious or spiritual programmes on television. Again as one might expect elderly people were the most likely to be interested and heavy television viewers were more likely to be interested than light television viewers. Just under half of those interested in religious matters said they were interested in hearing religious or spiritual on radio (about 20% of the population as a whole interested in hearing religious programmes on radio). About three quarters of this group listened to some religious programmes on radio; men who claimed an interest were more likely than women to actually listen and elderly people more likely to do so than young adults.

Sunday was the programme heard by the largest number of people – 42% of this group listened to *Sunday* sometimes; about a quarter of the group listened to the *Daily Service* and *Morning Service* and just under one fifth ever listened to *Pause for Thought*. Smaller proportions listened to other religious programmes on the BBC network and local stations. About a quarter of who expressed an interest in hearing religious programmes on radio, but did not listen, said it was because they did not listen to radio very much at all and a further quarter said that religious programmes were transmitted at inconvenient times.

Nine out of ten listeners were Christians and about one third were frequent churchgoers. The audience included many long term and loyal listeners some listening to programmes for at least 10 years.[80]

4. A Commercial Perspective

As we have seen the BBC originally developed its Listener Research Department in the mid 1930s, which became strategic in the wartime years to assess its radio impact. The BBC used a Daily Survey to measure audience size both for radio and later television. In addition a panel evaluated programmes providing 'reaction' indices.

The second milestone, however, was the growth of a second television network founded in 1955, funded by advertising and the Independent Television channel, ITV, controlled by the Independent Television Authority (ITA). With the addition of a commercial radio network in the 1970s the ITA's responsibilities and title broadened to the Independent Broadcasting Authority (IBA). The Television Act 1964 required the IBA to "ascertain the state of public opinion concerning the programmes".[81] So the Independent Television Companies holding franchises from the then ITA, co-operated with the advertisers and agencies to form a Joint Industry Committee for Television Advertising Research (JICTAR), which commissioned its own audience size measurement from contractors who set up a metered diary system based on 2,600 homes nationwide. Hence sampling the nation was in fact more thoroughly done than in the US and sufficient in size to provide strategic information with the support of the ITA/IBA's own dedicated Research Department looking into issues of both size and quality.[82] Equally in terms of radio, since 1992 a jointly owned company, Radio Joint Audience Research Limited (RAJAR) has used a single methodology to carry out audience research that satisfies the competing interests of publically and privately owned broadcasting organisations and because of the broad consensus around its findings, the data produced has enjoyed the status of a 'gold standard'.[83]

As we have seen in previous chapters religious broadcasts formed part of the regular schedules of the two major networks in the United Kingdom (BBC 1 and ITV) since the very first days of their transmissions. On ITV for example, the first Epilogue was broadcast on its first day. The first Church Service was seen on this channel a few weeks later and within four months the first discussion programme *About*

Religion, also appeared. Thus a pattern of religious broadcasting was quickly established consisting of the Sunday morning service, Sunday evening features with discussion and later on, the nightly Epilogue and since the 1950s as television expanded, so the range of religious output exhibited considerable growth.[84]

But how many people are viewing, who are they and what is their interest, have all been on-going questions. As is the case with every kind of programme, the numbers of viewers can be an unreliable indicator of the popularity of religious programmes. Ratings depend heavily on scheduling factors, time of transmission, opposite programmes on the other channel, preceding and following programmes on the same and other channels. Further it cannot be asserted there is a 'natural' constituency of viewers who both want to and can view religious programmes, as the act of viewing depends on a range of circumstances including being at home and pleasing people who might have other preferences and so on.[85]

a) The Audience and Religious Television

There were four UK surveys carried out in 1961, 1968, 1970 and 1978 which set out to investigate the audience for religious broadcasting.

In 1961, the Independent Television Authority commissioned a survey into the impact of religious programmes on the people who watched ITV. The results showed that 55% of the audience for Sunday services claimed to make a special effort to watch them and it showed that religious programmes commanded about the same degree of interest as other 'serious' programmes such as *This Week* or *What the Papers Say*. One in ten people in the survey thought it was desirable to have religious programmes on television. 78% of all viewers claimed to be either keenly interested (23%) or fairly interested (55%). Half of these said they went to church once a month or more. Broadly speaking 3 in 10 claimed to attend religious services once a month or more.[86]

In 1968, in a sample of around 1000 adults, extensive details were obtained from respondents about their religious beliefs, attitudes, values and their viewing habits. It seems that only half of the respondents paid attention to religious programmes when they came on and a further quarter said they left the set on but only 16% of respondents in Britain and only 4% in N. Ireland claimed to switch off religious programmes. The findings also showed that women were more likely than men to pay attention to religious programmes and over 80% of those who said they were personally very religious claimed to pay attention to religious programmes while only 30 % of those who were not at all religious claimed to do so.

Researchers were also keen to know what religious television was perceived to be achieving, as this produces strategic information for programme makers. Three aims were mentioned most often – "to provide services for people who can't get to church" (Britain – 47%. N. Ireland 22%), "to make people stop and think" (Britain 34%, N. Ireland 30%), and "to link religion with everyday life" (Britain 31%, N. Ireland 22%). The first two of these aims were endorsed in almost equal numbers by religious and non-religious respondents; the third was endorsed more often by religious individuals.[87]

In 1970, the ITA conducted another survey on *Religion in Britain and Northern Ireland* which also looked into religious broadcasting. It concluded that the motive for religious broadcasting was, "to make people stop and think, to relate religious principles to every day life and to increase tolerance and understanding"[88] and that the real audience for religious broadcasting is "composed in Britain of predominantly pious and elderly female viewers".[89]

The 1978 study was carried out by the IBA's Audience Research Department with a representative sample of 500 people in the London area. It was found that religious output on radio and television appealed more to those with strong religious beliefs and there was some evidence too that church services were used rather more often by lonely people, for whom the religious broadcasts provided companionship.

In summary, several main findings emerge in this era on the public's attitudes to religious broadcasting,

1. Survey research with representative or selective samples, together with experimental research have indicated that religious programmes tend to be liked best by those who are committed to a religion, or who perceive themselves in a general sense to be religious.

2. There is a preference among religious and non-religious individuals for broadcasts which indicate the relevance or the role of religion in everyday life, rather than for programmes which simply depict the formal, ritualized practices of the established churches.

3. Religious people who are viewers of programmes which focus on formal acts of worship do perceive such programmes serve a number of useful functions for themselves and for others e.g. those unable to attend church due to infirmity.[90]

b) *Godwatching*

In the 1980s the IBA commissioned further research into religious broadcasting ending in a published Report known as *Godwatching* (1988).

The Report highlighted a number of issues which included a scrutiny of audience trends. In terms of audience information obtained from standard industry sources like TAM, JICTAR and BARB from the 1960s to the 1980s, although actual numbers of people who watch religious programmes had increased since the early 1960s, in percentage terms, with the size of the growing and available television audience, it appeared there had been a decline since the early 1970s. Defenders of religious broadcasts argued this was due to scheduling effects especially with the effects of the relaxation over the 'closed period' where then religious programmes faced intense competition. However despite this trend, the research did indicate that still 62% of adults had seen one religious programme on the ITV network, BBC or Channel 4 and proved that where religious output was a regular, well-established part of the television menu – this was taken up by a majority of viewers on at least an occasional basis.[91]

The research also showed that in considering the numbers for Sunday religious programmes, which were not insignificant by any standards (as per the evidence quoted), there must be a clear distinction drawn between morning programmes, consisting of church services and the Sunday evening religious output which varied in content and seriousness of subject matter over the years. So by the 1980s on ITV, the pattern was common for a small audience for Sunday mornings e.g. 400,000 to 600,000 (typically a televised service) and a substantially larger audience for the evening period e.g. 8 million (typically a documentary style programme and a more celebratory programme of hymn singing or similar).[92]

What was clear at the time of the research was that the greater part of the religious broadcasting audience, approximately three quarters, could be attributed to *Highway* and *Songs of Praise*, the two flagship programmes of ITV and BBC respectively.

c) *Highway* and *Songs of Praise*

Given the very high status of these programmes on their networks, it seemed a logical task to look how the audience viewed and responded to these programmes.

Highway had hit the ITV screens in 1983 on Sunday evenings at 6.40pm. It was designed to compete with the highly successful *Songs of Praise* on the BBC. Whilst large audiences for programme makers are desirable – the audiences in their heyday for *Highway* was reaching 7.8 million and for *Songs of Praise* 6.9 million.[93] The 1984 research done by the IBA Research Department attempted to examine also what the audience thought or felt about the programmes, which might indicate the way viewers feel religion should be portrayed on television. The Research Department conducted weekly programme appreciation surveys on a regional basis within each major Independent Television region (of which there are 12). In this case additional questionnaires were given to respondents during the last weeks of February and May, which asked how many episodes of *Highway* and *Songs of Praise* they had seen over the month and what they thought about the content. Results showed that on average about one in three respondents had seen at least one edition of *Highway* or *Songs of Praise*. More women than men indicated that they had watched *Highway* or *Songs of Praise* and older respondents were more likely than younger respondents to have seen the programmes at least once in the previous month. In addition it would seem that heavy viewers of television are also more likely to have seen *Highway* or *Songs of Praise* at least once during the last month.

In regard to the content in terms of *Highway*, most respondents were happy with the format, but expressed the preference for more items about local activities especially showing the church helping ordinary people with their problems and about one in four wanted more music and singing outside church settings and more interviews talking about either their lives or their beliefs. Turning to opinions about *Songs of Praise*, the results were largely running parallel to those observed for *Highway*. Also a number of principle functions of religious television were identified. Entertainment, education and spiritual were all highlighted in both programmes as a positive contribution in religious broadcasting.[94]

From the later BARB/AGB Research in 1988, indications are that *Highway* and *Songs of Praise* maybe appealed to slightly different audiences, the former was a little different in terms of age, but was markedly more working class than the latter, although both had older profiles than the viewing population at large. In both cases younger viewers were unlikely to feature in the audience – older viewers over 45 and particularly over 55 were most likely to watch.[95]

d) *Seeing is Believing*

Seeing is Believing, became the title of one of the latest pieces of research done by the IBA into religious broadcasting in the 1990s. The two part research firstly involved qualitative research in which a series of focus groups were run with members of religious traditions, with those of little belief, atheists/agnostics and religious broadcasting professionals and secondly, a nationwide survey across the United Kingdom covering a representative sample of UK viewers with additional recruited respondents and satellite and cable viewers.[96]

In the main survey, more than one in five (22%) claimed to have no religious faith at all. More than seven in ten (73%) claimed to belong to a Christian denomination, most often either to the Anglican or Roman Catholic Church. Nearly one in ten Christians (9%) claimed to be 'born again' or evangelical Christians. Claimed attendance at church or place of worship was surprisingly high with more than one in five respondents in general saying they attended at least once per month (23%). The most regular attenders were Black Pentecostal and Muslim respondents, among whom more than eight in ten and six in ten respectively claimed at least weekly attendance, while more than a fifth of respondents (23%) claiming at least monthly church attendance with the strongest claims of personal religiosity being Black Pentecostal and Muslim respondents.[97]

From the survey it seemed that the general impression of religious programming held by the population at large is conceived quite narrowly in terms of church services, hymn singing and people talking about their beliefs. Hence televised religion was regarded as a substitute for real church going and a great help for those unable to get to church. The actively religious in the sample believed that religious programmes were tuned into them and additionally provided a vehicle for sharing Christianity with a wider audience. The middle ground group felt religious broadcasting was good for those who needed comfort and as a catalyst for raising moral and ethical issues. In addition religious television it was thought could broaden and enhance religious knowledge and understanding, teach about different religions and link religion with everyday life. All groups however expressed reservations about American style TV evangelism and felt there was a need to protect vulnerable groups like the children or elderly from predatory preaching or claims for healing.[98]

In summary, the Report indicated there is nothing in religious broadcasting as a genre which causes viewers to turn off. Programmes which meet a special need and worship programmes in particular, are accepted as an important part of television's social function. However a restricted definition of religious programming would seem to disenfranchise a large section of the potential audience. The audience is on the whole well disposed to religious programmes, but where there was dissatisfaction amongst some groups who might favour more charismatic output, it was likely that the new opportunities of cable and satellite might provide that more specialized programming.[99]

5. Summary

The analysis of audiences is a complex issue and Starkey makes a point that is as applicable to the USA as it is to the UK that,

> producing estimates of invisible consumption by audiences is one of an inexact science. The logic and mathematics of sampling orthodoxy may be sound, but the practice of sampling in audience surveys seems to produce telling inconsistences that demonstrably deny some audience research the legitimacy to which it aspires.[100]

The various estimates of audience sizes for religious broadcasting in America make confusing reading – Ben Armstrong (1978) over 100 million, Dr William Fore (1975) less than 10 million, Arbitron Research (1984) 13.3 million, Haddon and Swann (1981) 20.5 million and the largest of all the *Wall Street Journal* (1981) 130 million.[101] The most likely conclusion, taking on board the cable extension for religious broadcasting, is that a figure around 15 million to 20 million is nearer the mark.

Whatever the truth of the disputes over audience size (already detailed) certainly in the context of America, 'audience is king' to the religious broadcasters, because their size and demographics are crucially important as both a status symbol and as the fundamental source of income to religious programmes and networks which are 'listener-supported'.

The various studies, illustrated, sometimes concentrate on the different parts of the 'elephant' but a broad sweep of the American audiences for religious broadcasting show them comprising of older female Protestants, who are lower in socio-economic status and education and who live in rural areas of the South with their large families. Politically the audience tends to be Conservative whilst religiously more fundamentalist in belief.[102]

Seemingly the motivation for the audiences in America, ranges from wanting to see the Christian message heard by more people to enable their 'conversion', to helping them on their own spiritual journey in providing prayer and emotional support in times of loneliness, as well as those who have a more ritualised approach where it becomes just one form of entertainment.

In terms of evangelistic effectiveness the reality is that the landmark Annenberg study into religious broadcasting in the early 1980s found that a great many of religious viewers already had strong beliefs and religious broadcasts failed to reach large numbers of viewers who are not actively religious, nor did they make many converts.[103]

Here in the UK the BBC was slow to develop structured audience research, but the establishment of the Department in 1936 ensured more accurate details of listening and eventually viewing for generations to come.

In contrast to America, although the listening/viewing figures are naturally larger in the States because of population, the research seems to indicate a larger percentage of the potential British audience watch religious broadcasts. There is also a marked difference in terms of the style of American programmes which on the whole, though not exclusively, are preacher/personality focussed, compared with the UK, which tend to feature religious services, discussion programmes and documentaries.

In summary, whilst also being attracted by the strong charismatic broadcasting personalities all the research both in America and the UK indicates there is a substantial correlation between those who are religious and attend places of worship and listen or view religious broadcasting. Despite this, the evidence shows there is still an audience for religious broadcasting that is considerably larger than the number of people who are involved in church life. In the UK that might be because of the nostalgic fondness of the British for hymns more than the sense of an enduring and meaningful Christianity beyond the churches, whilst the audiences for televangelism in America really complement its institutional religion.[104] Whichever way the data is perceived one doesn't need to wake up Einstein to understand there was substantial demand in the listening and viewing marketplace for religious content, two specific examples of this being provided in the following Case Studies.

NOTES

1. Schubert, P., *The Electric Word: The Rise of Radio* (New York: Macmillan, 1928), p.310.

2. Hatch, N. O., *The Democratisation of American Christianity* (New Haven: Yale University Press, 1989), p.125-161.

3. Coleman, L. E. J., *Christian Communication in the 1970s. Review and Expositor: An International Baptist Journal*, 67 (1) 1970: 73.

4. Butsch. R., *The Making of American Audiences: From Stage to Television 1750-1990* (Cambridge: Cambridge University Press, 2000), p.196-197; Hurwitz, D., *Audience Research in American Broadcasting* (Mass Communication Annual Convention, Oregon, 1983), p.1-5.

5. Gielgud, V., *Letter to R.H. Eckersley*. 12th May (1930), BBC WAC. File Ref: R20/176/2.

6. Mytton, G., *Handbook on Radio and Television Research* (London: BBC, 1999), p.18.

7. Ibid., p.17.

8. Bacon, F., *Meditationes Sacrae and Human Philosophy* (1597) (Montanna: Kessinger Publishing, 1996).

9. Starkey, G., Estimating Audiences: Sampling in Television and Radio Audience Research. *Cultural Trends*, 13 (1) 2004: 4.

10. Hadden, J. K. and Swann, C. E., *Prime Time Preachers: The Rising Power of Televangelism* (Reading: Addison Wesley Publishing, 1981), p.7

11. Fore, W. F., Religion on the airwaves: In the public interest? *Christian Century*. September 17th (1975), p.782-783.

12. Graham, B., The Future of TV Evangelism. *TV Guide*. 4th October, (1983), p.6.

13. Pritchard, G. G. D., When Watching Religious TV is Like Attending Church. *Journal of Communication*, 35 (1) 1985: 123-131.

14. Hadden, J.K., Swann, C.E. and Martin, W., The Birth of a Media Myth. *New Yorker*. June (1981), p.7-16.

15. Hoover, S. M., *Mass Media Religion: The Social Sources of the Electronic Church* (Newbury Park: Sage, 1988), p.266.

16. Horsfield, P. G., *Religious Television: the American Experience* (New York: Longmans, 1984), p.108.

17. Editorial, Gospel TV: Religion Politics and Money. *Time Magazine*. 17th February (1986), p.67.

18. Martin, W. (1981), p.10.

19. Ferre, J. P., *Channels of Belief: Religion and American Commercial Television* (Ames: Iowa State University Press, 1990), p.xiii.

20. Hadden, J.K. and Shupe, A., *Televangelism: Power and Politics on God's Frontier* (New York: Henry Holt, 1988).

21. Bruce, S., *Pray TV: Televangelism in America* (London: Routledge, 1990), p.103.

22. Editorial, Gospel TV: Religion Politics and Money. *Time Magazine*. 17th February (1986), p.23.

23. Applebome, P., Scandals Aside TV Preachers Thrive. *New York Times*. 8th October (1989), p.24.

24. Suman, M., *Religion and Prime Time Television* (Westport: Praeger Publishers, 1997), p.23.

25. Haddon, J.K. and Swann.C.E. (1981), p.61-62.

26. Horsfield, P.G. (1984), p.112.

27. Robinson, H. W., *A Study of the Audience for Religious Radio and Television Broadcast in Seven Cities throughout the US*. (PhD). Illinois University (1964), p.127.

28. Buddenbaum, J. M., *The Audience for Religious Television Programmes*. (Masters). Indiana University (1979), p.55.

29. Bruce, S, (1990), p.108.

30. Hadden, J.K. and Swann, C.E. (1981), p.61.

31. Dennis, J. L., *An Analysis of the Audience of Religious Radio and Television Programmes in the Detroit Metropolitan Area*. (PhD). University of Michigan (1962), p.56.

32. Robinson, H.W. (1964), p.127.

33. Buddenbaum, J.M. (1979), p.54.

34. Tamney, J. B., and Johnson, S., Religious Television in Middletown. *Review of Religious Research*, 25 (4) 1984:303-313.

35. Robinson, H.W. (1964), p.127.

36. Buddenbaum, J.M. (1979), p.56-57.

37. Bruce, S. (1990), p.110.

38. Thomas, S., The Route to Redemption: Religion and Social Class. *Journal of Communication*, 35 (1) 1985: 113.

39. Hadden, J.K. and Swann, C.E. (1981), p.60-61.

40. Dennis J.L. (1962), p.68-70.

41. Horsfield, P.G. (1984), p.115.

42. Bruce, S. (1990), p.110.

43. Ibid., p.112.

44. Gallup Poll, *Evangelical Christianity* (Washington. Gallup, 1978), p.109-125.

45. Gaddy, G.D. and Pritchard, D., When Watching Religious TV is Like Attending Church. *Journal of Communications*, 35, 1985:123-131.

46. Johnstone, R. L., Who Listens to Religious Broadcasts Anymore? *Journal of Broadcasting*, 16 (1) 197:115.

47. Hoover, S.M. (1988), p.69.

48. Halloran, J.D., *Communication and Community* (Strasbourg: Council of Europe, 1975), p.6.

49. Horsfield, P.G. (1984), p.119.

50. Engel, J. F., *A Pilot Research Study of Channel 38, WCFC, Chicago*. (Wheaton: Wheaton College Graduate School, 1979), p.38-39.

51. Hilton, C. T., *The Influence of Television Worship Services on the Irvington Presbyterian Church*. (PhD). Drew University (1980), p.55-56.

52. Horsfield, P.G, (1984), p.120

53. Morrison, A.J., Mass Media Use by Adults. *American Behavioural Scientist*, 23 (1) 1979: 71-93.

54. Bourgault, L. M., The Electric Church: The PTL Club. *Journal of Religious Studies*, 12, 1985: 94.

55. Dennis, J.L. (1962), p.175.

56. Buddenbaum, J.M. (1979), p.60-85.

57. Peck, J., *The Gods of Televangelism: The Crisis of Meaning and the Appeal of Religious Television* (New Jersey: Hampton Press, 1993), p.140.

58. Abelman, R. I., Why Do People Watch Religious TV? A Uses and Gratification Approach. *Review of Religious Research*, 29 (I2) 1987:199.

59. Nicholas, S., *BBC Listener Research Department 1937-1950* (East Ardesley: Microform Academic Publishers, 2006), p.1.

60. Pegg, M., *British Radio Broadcasting and its Audience 1918-1939* (PhD). Oxford University (1980), p.270-271.

61. Nicholas, S. (2006), p.31.

62. Gorham, M. A. C., *Sound and Fury: 21 Years in the BBC* (London: Percival Marshall, 1948), p.166.

63. Silvey, R. J. E., 1956. *Religion of the Air: Audiences for Religious Broadcasting* (London. St Pauls Lecture Society, 1956), p.5.

64. Ibid., p.7.

65. BBC, *BBC Audience Research in the United Kingdom: Methods and Service* (London: BBC, 1970), p.3.

CHAPTER 6 AUDIENCE IS KING

66. BBC, *BBC Audience Research Findings*. (London: BBC Audience Research Department, 1978/79), p.7.

67. BBC, *Audiences for Religious Broadcasting*. (London. BBC Listener Research Department, 1939), BBC Written Archives Centre. File Ref: R9/9/3, p.1.

68. Jacobs,E. and Worcester,R., *We British: Britain Under the MORIscope* (London: Weidenfeld and Nicholson, 1990), p.22.

69. BBC, *Listener Research Report: Religious Broadcasting* (London: Listener Research Department, 1941), BBC WAC. File Ref: R9/66/1, p.8.

70. Dinwiddie, M., *Religion by Radio: Its Place in British Broadcasting* (London: George Allen & Unwin Ltd. 1968), p.115.

71. BBC, *Inquiry into Studio or OB Broadcasts* (London: Listener Research Department, 1942), BBC WAC. File Ref: R9/9/6, p.1-2.

72. Taylor, C., The Church and Radio. *St.Martin's Review* (1947), p.146-150.

73. BBC, *Religious Broadcasting and the Public* (London: Audience Research Department, 1955), BBC WAC. File Ref: R9/9/19, p.150-151.

74. Ibid., p.39-42.

75. BBC, *Consultation on Religious Broadcasting and Television* (London: BBC, 1958), BBC WAC. File Ref: R12/893/1, p.7.

76. McKay, R. Aims of Religious Broadcasting (London. St. Paul's Lecture Society, 1956), p.16.

77. Ibid., p.16.

78. House, F., Evangelise or Perish. *The Times*. 10th September (1952), p.7.

79. BBC Handbook (1955), p.59.

80. BBC, *Religious & Spiritual Programmes* (London.: BBC Audience Research Department, 1984), BBC WAC. Ref. File: R9/164/1, p.6-7.

81. Central Office of Information, *Broadcasting in Britain* (London. HMSO, 1973), p.33.

82. Wober, J. M., and Gunter, B., Television Audience Research at Britain's Independent Broadcasting Authority. *Journal of Broadcasting and Electronic Media*, 30 (1) 1986: 15-16.

83. Starkey, G., Radio Audience Research: Challenging the "Gold Standard". *Cultural Trends*. 12 (45) 2002: 44.

84. Gunter, B., *The Audience & Religious TV* (London: IBA Research Report, 1984), p.1-6.

85. Svennevig, M., Haldane. I., Spreis, S. and Gunter, B., *Godwatching: Viewers, Religion and Television* (London: John Libbey, 1988), p.9.

86. Independent Television Authority, *Religious Programmes on Independent Television* (London: ITA, 1962), p.51-56.

87. Gunter, B, (1984), p.22-26.

88. Independent Television Authority, *Religion in Britain and Northern Ireland* (London: ITA, 1970), p.50.

89. Ibid, p.50.

90. Haldane, I., *Who and what is Religious Broadcasting for?* (1978), IBA Collection: File Ref: A/R/1700/17 p.13-16.

91. Gunter, B. and Viney, R., *Seeing is Believing: Religion and Television in the 1990s* (London: John Libbey, 1994), p.2.

92. Svennevig, M. et al. (1988), p.10.

93. Ibid., p.11.

94. Gunter, B., *Attitudes to Sunday Evening Religious Broadcasts on Television: Highway and Songs of Praise Compared* (London. IBA Research Report, 1984), p.2.

95. Svennevig, M. et.al. (1988), p.14.

96. Gunter, B., and Viney, R. (1994), p.5.

97. Ibid., p.27-28.

98. Ibid., p.46-47, 73.

99. Ibid., p.123.

100. Starkey, G., Estimating Audiences: Sampling in Television and Radio Audience Research. *Cultural Trends*, 13 (1) 2004: 22.

101. Hoover, S. M., The Religious Television Audience: A Matter of Size of Significance. *Review of Religious Research*, 29 (2) 1987:135-136.

102. Litman, B.R. and Bain, E., The Viewership of Religious Programmes: A Multidisciplinary Analysis of Televangelism. *Review of Religious Research*, 30 (4) 1989: 334.

103. Wanner, C. N., *Transmitting the Word: A Cultural Analysis of Religious Broadcasting*. (PhD). University of Georgia (2016), p.180.

104. Bruce, S., *Religion in Modern Britain* (Oxford: Oxford University Press, 1995), p. 58.

CHAPTER 7

ON THE CASE
*A Comparative Study of a
USA and UK Religious Programme*

1. Introduction

The purpose of this chapter is to change the dynamic of looking at religious broadcasting in this era from the macro level to the micro level, moving from the extensive to the intensive, by using two programme case studies, one from the USA and one from the UK. Both these studies illustrating the strong personality dimension of religious broadcasting and demonstrating the impact they made as a result.

Case studies have been defined as "an empirical inquiry that investigates a contemporary phenomenon (the case) in depth and within its real world contexts".[1] Miles has argued that case studies are one of the most important research methods of sociology[2] and certainly case study research has grown in reputation as an effective qualitative methodology to investigate and understand complex issues in real world settings. Case study designs have been used across a number of disciplines, particularly the social sciences, education, business, law, and health, to address a wide range of research questions. Consequently, over the last 40 years, through the application of a variety of methodological approaches, case study research has undergone substantial development. Change and progress have stemmed from parallel influences from historical approaches to research and individual researcher's preferences, perspectives on and interpretations of case study research.[3] Equally, case studies often produce a special insight of those studied and expand the experience of the audience, showing them people and places which would otherwise remain invisible. Case studies also present information in a more familiar and interesting mode than extensive research can. These functions assist the final function of using the case study to create a more comprehensive analysis. Because of the richness and 'realness' of such case study research, it is more effective as a device.[4]

This is also a comparative study within two national broadcasting systems, with the case studies centred on two commercial networks. Comparative studies seem useful at addressing situations at both the macro and micro level and are valuable in understanding what lies behind the everyday social experience, the social structures and cultural institutions that dominate everyday life.[5]

So it is in these contexts that the chapter will look at the *PTL* (Praise the Lord) programme from America and *Stars on Sunday* from the UK. Both programmes strongly illustrating, though not exclusively, the case of religious broadcasting being 'personality' 'celebrity' driven. Others in this broadcasting genre made their mark, but the *PTL Club* and *Stars on Sunday* were the pinnacle of how a 'charismatic' character could make a huge impact and create a significant following to their programming.

2. The Cases

a) *PTL (Praise the Lord) Club*

The Country

The programme originated in the United States of America.

The Creators

The *PTL Club*, also known as *The Jim and Tammy Show*, was a Christian television programme that was first hosted by evangelists Jim and Tammy Faye Bakker. It ran from 1974 to 1989.

The Context

As was previously chronicled, during the 1970's a relatively new phenomenon appeared on the American religious scene. Sometimes termed 'the electric church',[6] the phenomenon referring to a group of superstar evangelists who used multi-million dollar budgets and state of the art technology to produce religious television programmes wrapped in entertainment formats.

The 1978 Gallup Survey indicated that 55% of women and 46% of men watched a least some religious television broadcasts. Regular churchgoers and persons who say religion was 'very important' in their lives each make up 62% of the religious television audience. Protestants (59%) were more likely to view than Catholics (34%) and the likelihood of a person viewing increases with age. The great majority of viewers were fundamentalists whose religious tradition embraced the conversion (born again) experience and the belief in the inerrancy of the Bible.[7]

The *'PTL Club'* was from this context. Known alternatively as the *'Praise the Lord Club'* or the *'People that Love Club'*, it was produced by the *PTL* Network, which operated a three-million-dollar broadcasting facility in Charlotte, North Carolina. The organisation was independent of any denominational affiliation and presented an extremely ecumenical view of Christianity. The two-hour programme was hosted by Jim Bakker, an ordained Assembly of God Minister and his wife Tammy Faye and co-hosted by Henry Harrison.[8]

Charlotte was an ideal location for Bakker's new venture. It had once been a centre of North Carolina's textile mills and the mill workers who had flocked to Charlotte's old-style Pentecostal churches. But it was becoming a booming financial centre that lured white-collar migrants to its businesses and banks and to its sprawling suburbs. These men and women – like millions of others – wanted a soothing, reassuring religion and Bakker and *PTL* supplied it hour after hour.[9] In addition, Charlotte's business leaders had close ties to the Full Gospel Business Men's Fellowship International (FGBMFI), the largest network of Christian business men in the world.[10] These men quickly allied with Jim to turn *PTL* into an ever expanding empire dedicated to positive thinking.

The Celebrities

Jim Bakker was one of the most important leaders of the Charismatic movement and a very influential televangelist of the 1980s.[11] He was born James Orsen Bakker in Muskegon, Michigan. It is said that his middle name was inspired by the famous film star Orson Wells and maybe this was what led the young Jim Bakker to pursue a show business career, including the staging of high school amateur theatricals.[12]

At 16, he seemed quite a reckless youth, but things turned full circle after he was involved in a motor accident in which he ran over a three year old boy. The remorse over this seems to have been what led him to a Christian commitment and a move to study as an Assemblies of God minister at the North Central Bible College of Minnesota. Bakker happened to see the 1960 revival conducted by Oral Roberts and was impressed by the similarities between show business and Bible ministry.[13]

While at the Bible School he met Tammy Faye La Velley and in 1961 they married. They left Bible College to become evangelists and for the first four years of their marriage they lived a hand-to-mouth existence touring their own evangelical puppet show. In 1965 they were spotted by Pat Robertson and hired into CBN, a move which greatly contributed to the growth and reshaping of the network and especially of the flagship *700 Club* which took on a Johnny Carson style talk variety hour. This in addition to presenting their own children's programme, *The Jim and Tammy Show,* a title they later adopted for their *PTL* network programme.[14]

But then in 1972 with a growing disquiet amongst the staff at the Bakkers more Pentecostalist approach and because of the subsequent increasing pressure on them, the Bakkers left CBN to go independent, forming their own corporation[15] and headed to California to join an old Assemblies of God associate Paul Crouch, a relationship that was a better match theologically for the Bakkers. The Crouch-Baker enterprise would take the name Trinity Broadcasting Network and combined Crouch's technical know-how and Bakker's on-camera appeal,[16] going on the air in 1973 with a daily inspirational talk show *Praise the Lord (PTL)*. But another split was to come after only one year and while it was agreed Paul Crouch would keep the Trinity Broadcasting name, Jim and Tammy would keep the initials *PTL* for their new network which they set up in Charlotte North Carolina, a place he declared was ripe for revival.[17]

Their show's popularity grew quickly, carried nationwide on 70 commercial stations and 20 cable services averaging over 12 million viewers. In 1976 Bakker expanded his empire with a massive theme park, the 'Disneyland for the devout'[18] – Heritage Village, in North Carolina. This soon expanded into Heritage USA which became the third most successful theme park in the USA and included time-share condominiums and an expensive facility for the handicapped.[19] They added to this a satellite system to distribute their network 24 hours a day across the country. All this supported by donations from viewers at a level of $1 million dollars per week. Indeed it cost, more than $100 million dollars to build and operate Heritage USA and Bakker's television ministry.[20]

From a UK perspective in the 1980s it was not easy to assess the level of significance and impact of the Bakkers and *PTL*, but commenting on the Bakker's empire Professor John Wigger explained,

> the Bakker's footprint in their subculture was very big. They had one of the first private satellite television networks, that was one of the many innovative things they did. They reached into 14 million American homes, so that was not insignificant. They broadcast twenty four hours a day and as some of their airtime was sold it brought in a great deal of money, which is how they became rich, subsequently broadcasting their programming into 40 nations around the world.[21]

Not surprisingly such significant activities attracted widespread interest and the local *Charlotte Observer* led by Charles E. Shepard, began investigations, after hearing rumours that money raised for the *PTL* ministry was actually used to support the Bakker's lavish lifestyle.[22] Overall they published a series of approximately 600 articles between 1984 and 1988 regarding *PTL* and the organisation's finances, which also showed that the Heritage USA's condominiums were not available to the Bakker's fans, as had been advertised and that the park's huge handicap facility housed but a single tenant.[23]

Previously in 1979 the FCC threatened to revoke Bakker's license for misrepresenting the purpose of his fundraising and by 1984 the IRS threatened to remove Bakker's tax-free status. Eventually in 1987 Bakker was forced to resign from *PTL* after the revelation that he had to pay $279,000 dollars silence monies to a Jessica Hahn who had claimed she was raped by Bakker, a claim that he denied, though not denying a consensual sexual encounter.[24]

Shepard's coverage of *PTL* led the newspaper to win the prestigious Pulitzer Prize in 1988 and in his book he reflects something of the irony of that *PTL* story,

> In the year of his disgrace, Jim Bakker secured the celebrity status he had coveted for so long. At the beginning of 1987, he had a position of prominence in the charismatic Christian world. His ministry claimed six hundred thousand supporters and revenues of $120 million dollars a year. Within three months, Bakker had become a recognised celebrity in tens of millions of households. He and his wife Tammy Faye seemed to be everywhere: in the headlines, on the cover of national magazines and on TV news shows.[25]

So the breakdown of *PTL* and everything that went with it was tragic and elevated *PTL* and Bakker to the front page of newspapers, for different reasons, across the United States, leading to his downfall and creating one of the most dramatic stories of the 1980s.[26]

Following Bakker's resignation in 1987 he was succeeded by Jerry Falwell, founder of the Moral Majority, who worked hard to keep the *PTL* ministry afloat. Originally it was an amicable arrangement coming as a plea for help by the Bakkers, but the severity of the situation turned it into a very hostile take-over with Falwell having very harsh words about Bakker's character, calling him "the greatest scab and cancer of Christianity in the past 200 years of church history".[27] Despite this Falwell expressed his belief that the Bakker scandal was a sobering lesson and therefore had strengthened broadcast evangelism and made Christianity stronger, more mature and more committed.[28] However, things were not so positive for Bakker as after a long investigation by the Federal grand jury, in 1988 he was indicted on eight counts of mail fraud, 15 counts of wire fraud and one count of conspiracy and sentenced to a grotesquely long prison term of 45 years and a $500,000 dollar fine.[29] Bakker writes of the experience.

> I was stunned. I felt as though a huge wrecking ball had dropped on top of me. Every bone in my body felt like it had been pulverized, yet I continued to stand expressionless before the judge. For a moment, I thought I might collapse right there in the front of the courtroom. The emotional pain was so intense, my body gradually slipped into a state of shock.[30]

His sentence even eclipsed what many killers and rapists received.[31] In his book *Jim Bakker: Miscarriage of Justice?* (1998) James Albert, an attorney himself, argues that Bakker's case was badly handled from every point of view with a notoriously tough judge – Judge Robert Potter (nicknamed 'maximum Bob') and had things been different, the end result might not have been the same. Undoubtedly these factors were brought into consideration when in 1992 Bakker' sentence was reviewed and reduced to 8 years, of which he did serve five.[32] Inmate 07407-058, one-time confidant of Presidents was reduced to being a convict. Adding to this tragedy, in the same year, he and Tammy were also divorced. A year later Tammy was to marry Roe Messner.[33]

Eventually after his release from prison, Bakker wrote his book *I was Wrong*, in which he back-tracked on much of his former teachings especially about a prosperity gospel,

> For years I had embraced and espoused a gospel that some sceptics had branded as a 'prosperity gospel'... I realised that I had helped propagate an imposter, not a true gospel.[34]

In 1998 he married Lori Beth Graham, herself a former televangelist and in 2003 started broadcasting the daily *Jim Bakker Show* with his new wife, in Branson Missouri. Still broadcasting to this day, his emphasis has turned to end time events and the Second Coming of Christ, outlined in his 2013 book *Time Has Come: How to Prepare Now for Epic Events Ahead*.[35]

The Content

The style of the Bakker's *PTL* show fitted perfectly into the emerging Charismatic movement. Charismatic publications had been preaching a message of success tied to the nuclear family ideal for years. The formula was simple. Individual success meant happy suburban family life. These publications were filled with stories telling how rebellious youth, drug addicts and radicals had given up an unfulfilling life for one of family security and economic prosperity. Embracing success and family was the solution to the alienation of modern society. This message reassured middle class husbands and wives who faced a stressful workplace and the challenge of fulfilment in the home. Through belief in God, believers could thrive in a competitive, narcissistic culture whilst maintaining an emotionally successful family life. It was part of a larger Charismatic narrative that emphasized the adaptability of Pentecostal practice.[36]

Although there was much of the narrative that was not dissimilar to the presentation of Robertson on the *700 Club*, Bakker was more of the tradition of preachers from Aimee Semple McPherson to Norman Vincent Peale, who emphasized God's desire for our prosperity, health, and spiritual wellness.[37] This 'prosperity gospel', as it came to be known, was one of the most significant religious messages in the post Second World War period. In many ways it shaped American religious culture across a wide spectrum of race class and religious groups.[38] The roots of the modern prosperity gospel are long and tangled,[39] but in essence the theology was that God will grant financial success and good health to all believers who have enough faith.[40] Bakker expressed it in his terms, "God wants you to be happy, God wants you to be rich, God wants you to prosper"[41] and American audiences came to make this gospel their own and it was to be the predominant message of the *PTL Club*.

The *PTL Club* was a very unique piece of American television. The daily show was the centrepiece of *PTL's* programming through the 1970s, broadcast 'live' and recorded on tape five days a week from 11am to 1pm in front of a studio audience.[42] The show opened with the song, *"Praise the Lord, see what we have done,"* and then Jim and Tammy would begin the show with fundraising offers. They encouraged viewers to become *PTL* members and offered 'gifts' for donations. Oftentimes, they would follow their appeals for contributions by bringing guests into the audience for informal discussions about their lives. Bakker would highlight how God had answered his followers' prayers and alleviated people's stress; with faith they were given wealth, health, and happiness. For Bakker these proclamations were a miraculous proof of God's blessing.[43]

Also Jim's personality and the format were crucial to the show's success. Unlike Robertson, who had a Yale-educated and seminary-trained background, Jim had the folksy charm of a friend sitting on the other side of a table. This informality was quite different from the vociferous and highly emotional evangelists that he had grown up with. It was more akin to turning on the *'Tonight Show'* and like Carson, Bakker would sit behind a desk in a suit and tie and invite people to join him. Bakker had a subtle feel for his core audience, but unlike other talk show hosts like Carson, who worked from a carefully prepared script of questions and jokes, Bakker never used a script and rarely pre-interviewed guests.[44] When he did interviews, he would task about how the guest had come to Christ and had witnessed the healing power of the Holy Spirit. The guests told stories about how their faith transformed their lives and had led to fulfilment and happiness. Often, the interviews were followed by appeals for money. Tammy frequently appeared on set, supplying an emotional response to the heart-warming stories of support.[45]

Bakker also differed from other emerging televangelists such as Jerry Fallwell who presented explicit political messages and preached sober sermons. Instead, the Bakkers employed entertainment and storytelling. This format was an instant success. Bakker understood that stern messages would not work for television. As he later recalled, "Preaching is to go to a large crowd, but when people are in their homes, I felt they (the audience) didn't always want somebody shouting in their ear." He told his staff to "look right at the camera lens and make believe he was speaking to one individual in the comfort of their living room." He also understood, as did Robertson, that middle class Charismatics didn't "want to watch hard religious programing hour after hour." Soon the Bakkers were local celebrities who became featured guests at local parades and within the community.[46]

Part of Bakker's appeal was his ability to invoke the methods of Pentecostal healers.[47] He would offer healing prayers to callers and some would call back and claim that Jim Bakker had cured their disease or injuries. He also emphasized how belief in Christ was central to a life of happiness and he realized that presenting viewers with a crisis was an effective way of winning pledges. He learned to exaggerate crises in order to attract funds. Over time, this tendency would become a staple part of his ministry and televangelism in general. He understood that viewers, if threatened with the loss of one of their shows, were much more apt to donate funds and to accept the station's use of repeated fundraising drives. He was also inclined to exaggerate the number of people who had called into the ministry and whom he had healed. For Bakker, however, fundraising meant growth and expansion. Such goals easily consumed him.[48]

Jim and Tammy had developed an immensely appealing style of performance that drew viewers to their shows and kept them entranced with their interviews, the singing and the personal revelations. Above all, however, the Bakkers had developed a religious message that promised a relationship with Christ while protecting the family and embracing consumption and prosperity. *PTL* dedicated itself to Bakker's Pentecostalism and prosperity theology. Bakker's ability to sell this message was vital to his success and he was directly responsible for this new form of Pentecostalism – transforming free-market ideas into a cultural movement which helped make the Assemblies of God the fastest growing denomination in the United States.[49]

As with his shows at CBN and TBN, the *PTL Club* was presented in a relaxed style of Christian television. Bakker wearing his flamboyant plaid jumpsuits and loud ties, usually entered from the back where he chatted with the audience on the way to the stage. The new version became an instant hit. As he had done at CBN, Bakker interviewed guests who described how their faith had led them to become happier and more successful. Increasingly, however, he highlighted economic success. He promised viewers that God would give them control over their lives despite their circumstances.[50] He presented upbeat, encouraging musical numbers that were accompanied by promises of an abundant life and reassurances that 'God loves you.' Then he would move to the mock living room set to banter with the support staff before introducing their guests. Much of the banter was about Jim and Tammy's family life. For example, in one episode Jim described Tammy Faye's obsession with wrapping gifts, while Tammy mocked Jim's unwillingness to wrap his own presents. On other episodes, their children – Jay and Sue Bakker – came on stage and the Bakkers would talk about their family vacations and their children's various interests or the latest flu bug that was going around the home. They projected an image of an idealized Christian family. They allowed the audience, of course, to see an ideal vision of a happy Christian home. They would also devote entire shows to celebrating the Bakkers' anniversaries, birthdays, and other familial events where they would put together montages of family scenes. During breaks, *PTL* would advertise other ministers who had shows on the network, as well other Christian authors. The Bakkers also created commercials that promoted giving to their ministry.[51]

As mentioned, in order to reinforce this relaxed style, Bakker interlaced the show with upbeat musical numbers. Many of these musical numbers were performed by Tammy and some by her daughter Tammy Sue. *PTL* band members also sang original songs and Christian hymns. Christian artists such as Pat Boone and David L. Cook were also featured. Nearly every song focused on overcoming fear and adversity, along with the importance of self-fulfilment. Some of Tammy Faye's most popular songs, were *"Don't Give Up"* or *"You Can Make it"*, performed in her emotional style that signalled to the audience that she understood their struggles, telling the audience that they were not alone and that things would get better if they trusted in the Lord.[52]

An important part of the show was Bakker's assistant Henry Harrison. Harrison had been with Bakker since his days at CBN, and they had become close friends. Bakker was best man at Harrison's 1972 wedding and Harrison rented a room from the increasingly wealthy Bakkers. Harrison also became Bakker's co-host, earning the title of the Ed McMahon of Christian television. He was a perfect match for Bakker, who loved the limelight, because Harrison was willing to play second fiddle.[53] His job on stage was primarily to tell jokes, give hugs and keep guests smiling, ensuring that the show never veered away from its positive message. His role, however, had other important aspects, Bakker often prompting him to give a folksy response to questions that provoked laughter.[54]

Along with musical numbers, the *PTL Club* included interviews with guests. These usually took on three common formats. One of the most common guests were evangelical Christians who had written books on evangelical family issues that focused on emotional difficulties surrounding marriage or raising children. Other guests were Charismatic preachers, some of whom had programmes during other timeslots on the *PTL* network. These included Robert Schuller, Oral Roberts, and Rex Humbard, and most were prosperity theology ministers. Famous evangelical Christians were also frequently on the show, these included people like Chuck Colson and Gary Paxton.[55] Invariably, they would describe how Christ had made their lives better or more prosperous. Bakker also interviewed less famous people who had stories about how Bakker's message had transformed their lives. Bakker also frequently featured phone banks on his show. Bakker had begun using these while at CBN but at that time he used them in the manner of a Pentecostal healer. Now they became a fundraising tool. During many broadcasts, the phones were to the right of the stage and staffed with 60 volunteers who managed viewer prayer requests and donations to the ministry.[56] As telephone counsellors recalled, individuals phoned in seeking help for a wide range of problems. Following these confessions, counsellors usually provided the callers with prayers and prompts for donations – along with promises that their wishes would be fulfilled. Bakker also used these phone calls to gather mailing lists so that he could promote his motivational materials. Bakker developed a series of tapes and books that promoted positive thinking and in this material, witnesses would testify how giving to Bakker's ministry had transformed their lives.[57]

On the air Bakker would highlight how God had answered his followers' prayers and alleviated people's stress; with faith they were given wealth, health, and happiness. For Bakker these proclamations were proof of God's blessing. Bakker even claimed the verse "Faith without works is dead" should not be used to hold Christians accountable for charitable acts, but rather to hold God accountable for the gifts he promised the faithful. Christians, he claimed, should not obey God based on blind faith. They should praise God for what he does for us, 'works' and not just on faith alone. The theme of every show was that anyone could be seen as a victim and everyone could overcome. In particular, Bakker suggested that the real victims of American society were middle-class men and women trying to enjoy God's prosperity.[58] Problems were usually personal and self-generated and were overcome by a new willingness to be happy and to undertake a life-long journey of self-discovery. Oftentimes, stories combined these psychological issues with economic troubles, in order to explain how trust in God and positive thinking had led to a life of wealth and happiness. Bakker explained on his television network he did not want to hear any bad news. He would not allow his staff to book a guest who was sick or having severe financial, emotional, or spiritual problems. If a guest had not come out on 'the victory side of life,' he or she was not asked to be on the air. He said he was not being cruel he just wanted everyone to praise the Lord and be happy.[59]

Various guests expounded on this message. For example, after Bakker reminded his audience to give to his ministry, one featured viewer Judy Chavez described how she had risen out of a childhood of hopelessness to a life of happiness and prosperity. She then declared that in a country where 'children were being discarded in garbage cans' the country desperately needed Jim and Tammy's uplifting message. Tammy followed by reminding the audience that she grew up in a family without much money, but through faith she had been able to overcome hardship and succeed. Tammy then sang her inspirational song *"You Can Make it."*[60] When Bakker interviewed guests, he often interjected to describe how he and Tammy had fared with similar problems. This combined a sense of intimacy with the show's emphasis on positive thinking. As always, Bakker invoked the narrative of a life he had constructed, he reminded the audience how he had grown from a shy, poor, insecure boy into a happy, successful preacher. He and Tammy also discussed their own problems and how changing their thinking had allowed them to overcome hurdles. This was a demonstration of struggle and triumph that could be displayed on a daily basis. In one case, a guest described his struggles with agoraphobia, which led nearly everyone on stage, including the Bakkers, to declare that they too had overcome this fear of leaving their house. Through these discussions they repeatedly demonstrated that although negativity, poverty, anxiety and fear abounded in American society, positivity and faith in God allowed people to overcome these roadblocks.[61]

Bakker repeatedly told his audience that God wished a life filled with prosperity and pleasure upon those who believe. For example, he usually explained how important God's gifts of prosperity were to his ministry and his vision of Christianity and followed by a declaration that through positive thinking his followers could have anything they desired. It was sinful, he insisted, to not accept that God gives prosperity to those who believe. He said, "God wants to give you good things, and forgive you if you turned away from the things of the world." He then lambasted ministers who talked of hell and not enough about God's gifts, declaring that this message made *PTL* special and unique. Other times he was even more specific, proclaiming to the audience that they should not settle for Chevys if they wanted Cadillacs. At *PTL*, he reminded them, the good life was available for anyone who absorbed his message.[62]

Bakker coupled his message of prosperity with the family-centred themes on his show. These had been part of his ministry from his earliest days at CBN and they merged easily with his prosperity message. Bakker described *PTL* as a family and told his viewers that their donations would allow them to join 'our family'. The Bakkers presented themselves as a happy, fulfilled, prosperous family whose faith in God allowed them to live an affluent life. Many guests also articulated these themes. Many had written 'how-to' books on raising happy Christian families and how the Bible could be a guide to successful relationships. Many of these books helped parents communicate with their children and emphasized the importance of character development and faith. Others wrote guidebooks on how to protect children from a dangerous and profane outside world. Marriages were also often book topics. Bakker hosted many authors who had written books on how to nurture successful Christian marriages by improving communication and relying on the Bible.[63] Along with his prosperity message, this created a thriving ministry.

The Conclusions:

PTL was a ministry and a programme very much in the mould of a new style of Pentecostalism, which was part of the whole charismatic movement sweeping the USA and many parts of the planet in the late 20th Century. In fact the Charismatic Churches became the fastest growing segment of Protestantism in the United States and the world.[64] *PTL* was carving out an alternative culture that was built on a vision of God that served believers' needs and aspirations. As *Christianity Today* noted, these ideas were rapidly replacing Bakker's earlier promotion of healing. This new type of Pentecostalism was replacing the beliefs of Bakker's youth, which he now described as a religion of 'can't'. Instead, Bakker had created a church that provided blessings, healed families and provided prosperity. He had integrated Pentecostalism with the 1970s and 80s middle-class Sunbelt culture.[65]

In essence the Bakkers became the quintessential model for prosperity in the 1980s and became part of a new generation of broadcasting personalities competing for the hearts and minds of evangelical parishioners. Many of these broadcasters including the Bakkers promoted this new variant of Pentecostal theology called the 'prosperity gospel', which promised believers that God would reward their faith – especially their faithful donations – with material blessings. These preachers quickly became the most influential voices of American religion, attracting millions of adherents who donated billions of dollars annually.[66]

Bakker was never as political a preacher as his counterparts, like Jerry Falwell or Pat Robertson, but his message through *PTL* taps into one of the core impulses of contemporary evangelicalism: the importance of status. Bakker was clearly the centre of attraction on his talk show. His entrance, like that of Oral Roberts, was preceded by a musical fanfare. Then while his co-host gave him a rousing introduction, Bakker descended a long lighted platform to a seating area which was surrounded by the audience on three sides.[67] All this staged to emphasize his celebrity status and as such Bakker personifies in both his presence and his preaching much about American evangelicalism in this era.[68]

But the story of *PTL* is a cautionary tale of success and failure and of how that power and celebrity can corrupt.[69] Undoubtedly the overriding driver of *PTL* was the personality of Jim Bakker and his wife. As John Wigger reflects "without his and Tammy's personalities on-air *PTL* would have never worked, they indeed became cultural celebrities".[70] Although many admired Bakker's entrepreneurial sale skills,[71] seen through his programmes, there remains much criticism of his theological prowess and his moral compass and the damage that did, at the time, to the reputation of evangelical Christianity in the United States.

As *Time Magazine* concluded in 1987,

"If Jim Bakker began with holy intentions, he eventually fell victim to his own substantial ego. Bolstered by adoring crowds and flush with donated cash, the evangelical lost sight of the Christian message he preached. The more *PTL* prospered, the more apparently the preacher believed he could do no wrong. Until through a combination of mismanagement, cupidity and earthly temptation, disaster finally struck".[72]

The end of the *PTL* Empire was indeed to be one of the most colourful episodes of American religious history.[7]

b) *Stars on Sunday*

The Country

The United Kingdom

The Creators

The programme was an Independent Television production created by the Yorkshire Television region, based in Leeds.

The Context

The programme was first shown in 1969 and was presented every week during the year apart from a break at Christmas. The regular audience achieved approximately 15 million viewers a week at its height and consistently appeared among the best liked programmes on ITV. The spread of popularity amongst viewers of all classes, age groups and both sexes remained both remarkably high and steady. It also attracted a request post bag of between two and three thousand letters every week.[74]

It was not mandatory commercial television networks to carry religious broadcasting, but the ITA were to ensure programmes 'contain a suitable proportion of matter calculated to appeal to the tastes and outlook of persons served by the station'.[75] It was therefore reasonable to suppose this would include religious broadcasting.

Beyond this, the Act only required that when religious programmes were produced, they be made in consultation with a religious advisory panel 'representative of the main streams of religious thought'.[76] Not surprisingly, therefore it was to the already established Central Religious Advisory Committee (CRAC) that the ITA turned.[77]

So Yorkshire Television made its major religious debut in August 1968 with *Choirs on Sunday*. The programme came nearer than most in achieving ITV's ambition to find a religious programme as a rival to the BBC's *Songs of Praise*. Yet there was obviously a limit to the number of programmes that could be made based on recordings of choral talent in Yorkshire. When therefore the following summer Yorkshire Television was due to provide the network with a second religious music series of programmes, Jess Yates (who had been responsible for several editions of the previous production) came to the Authority's Panel of Religious Advisors to propose, a 'spin-off' from it to be named, *Stars on Sunday*. The Panel accepted Yorkshire Television's proposal, with the proviso that Jess Yates should work closely with the station's religious advisors. So *Stars on Sunday* went on air and Jess Yates eventually became its public face.[78]

The Celebrities

Jesse Frederick Joseph Yates was born in Tyldesley, Manchester on the 20th December 1918. Yates moved with his family to North Wales and he became a cinema organist in Colwyn Bay at the age of 15. On leaving school, he took a job as organist at the then new Odeon cinema in Llandudno and when Rank took over the circuit, he played across the whole country. After serving in the Army for four years during the Second World War, based in Radcliff, in Lancashire, he went back to organ-playing on the Rank Circuit. Involved in the formation of the Children's Film Foundation as 'Uncle Jess', he also made singalong records for children's Odeon Cinema Clubs. In 1951 Yates formed the Littlewoods and Vernon girls's choirs for both of the pools organisations, moving to be a freelance designer for the BBC. He worked on the first *Sooty Show* in 1952 and the first three years of the long running musical-hall programme *The Good Old Days* – starting in 1953 at the celebrated City Varieties Theatre, Leeds – as well as *Come Dancing, Top Town* and the *Miss World Contest*.[79]

In 1955 Yates switched to producing and made *Out of the Blue*, presented by Tyrone Power and wrote and produced *A Boy Named Will*, as a celebration of Shakespeare's birthday and presented three series of programmes about the film world, *Behind the Scenes, Junior Picture Parade* and *Filmland,* moving to Wawick Films in 1957 he wrote and directed documentary shorts for screening on television.[80] In 1959, a year after his marriage to the former dancer and actress Heller Toren (nee Elaine Smith), he gave up show business to buy the Deganwy Castle Hotel in Llandudno. The couple had a daughter, Paula, who eventually became a successful television presenter and married the Band Aid organiser Bob Geldof (though in 1997, Hughie Green of *Opportunity Knocks* was revealed to be Paula Yates's biological father). But the Yate's marriage soon floundered and Yates sold his hotel business, first moving back to Warwick films, then making a feature film about the Second World War, before joining Yorkshire Television, which had become one of the new ITV franchise holders in 1968.[81]

As Head of Children's Programmes his first success was the puppet series *Diane's Magic Book*, which he wrote and produced. Other series masterminded by him included the children's dramas *The Flaxton Boys*, starring a young Peter Firth and *Boy Dominic* , featuring Richard Todd and Brian Blessed. He also created and presented *How We Used to Live*, the longest running schools programme and winner of a BAFTA award. One of his greatest succsses also was *Junior Showtime*, a talent show for children that launched the careers of Bonnie Langford, Joe Longthorne, Keith Chegwin. Mark Curry and Rosemary Ford.[82] Show business wasn't simply his job but rather his way of life. He would work 100 hour weeks, presenting, directing, writing and producing thousands of programmes all fully networked.[83]

Yet it was his religious programmes that were to bring him most notoriety, first *Choirs on Sunday* (1968) and then the hugely popular *Stars on Sunday* (from 1969) which Yates created and earned him the title 'the Bishop' by his colleagues.[84] However, after 5 years and more than a thousand programmes at Yorkshire Television, Yate's world came to a crashing end on the 7th July 1974 with the *News of the World's* salacious and hugely damaging revelation that he had been having a relationship with Anita Kay, an only daughter of a driving school owner and an actress, more than 30 years his junior. Although Yates was still married, he and his wife had been apart for 10 years, she was in Majorca with another man and Yates and Kay were not even living together, but this was hardly mentioned during the relentless campaign waged against him. The *News of the World* article focussed on Anita's side of the story where in the interview she stated,

> I suppose a lot of people are going to think our affair is sorded. That he wants me because I am a young woman and that I am using him to help my career. But nothing could be further from the truth. Jess is the most wonderful person in the world , I love him completely and he loves me.[85]

Following the *News of the World* exposure, the press coverage about the affair was considerable across all the major newspapers and became terminal. Yates was smuggled out of the YTV office in the boot of a car and he never really worked in front of the cameras again in the UK.[86] However, Stars on Sunday carried on for a further five years without him, eventually being replaced by *Your Hundred Best Hymns*. Although Yates never worked again on British television there were moves to re-launch his career again in America and he had several offers from television companies there, but nothing ever came of it.[87]

Yates was divorced from his wife by mutual consent a year after the scandal, lived with Anita Kay until they parted and she later marrying someone else. Serena Daroubakhsh lived with Yates the last 4 years of his life until his death by a stroke on 9th April 1993. She recalls, "he had amazing charisma and people naturally congregated around him wherever he was and whatever he was doing".[88]

CHAPTER 7 ON THE CASE

The Content

Stars on Sunday began from the audience's point of view on Sunday 17th August 1969. For Yorkshire Television it began in early June of that same year. Jess Yates who produced the *Choirs on Sunday* series suggested an extension of the *Choirs on Sunday* idea but balanced in favour of 'stars' rather than choirs. He had felt for some time that there should be a programme that was made especially for the older generations, which would contain the sort of musical material that held a particular appeal to them. He drafted out the basic idea for an actual edition. It would consist of a male singer, female singer, choral item, a song by a child or children and a Bible reading and possibly an instrumental item. The programme would also include requests from the viewers and a presenter would read out names of the people whose requests were included in the programme. Because the programme series would only be six weeks long, it was thought only a small nucleus of artists would be needed.[89]

When the first programme was transmitted on the 17th August the audience figures were around 4.5 million. This was quite an increase over the size of an audience that usually watched at 7pm on an August Sunday. The second edition increased the audience by about 2 million and by the 5th edition saw it rise to 10 million. Plus, letters and requests were pouring in at a rate of 2,500 per week, for a programme that only had above-the-line costs of about £1000 per programme, at a time when a typical variety show could cost £60,000.[90] But this early success was only the start.

Much to consternation of people working in the industry, the programme was a huge hit with the public and the audience figures attracted many celebrities. The people ready to appear with Yates began to read like a 'Who's Who' of the church, politics and show business including the Archbishops of York and Canterbury, the Prime Minister Edward Heath, Earl Mountbatten, Sir John Gielgud, Sir Ralph Richardson, Gracie Fields, Bing Crosby, Eartha Kitt, Shirley Bassey, Harry Secombe, Cliff Richard, Roy Orbison – the list goes on.[91] As Yates declared "I went for star names because they would persuade people to watch".[92] These stars were all willing and seemed to be queuing up for a slot on the programme, some it was said were even willing to accept the £49.00 minimum appearance fee.[93] Its success was tempting, as Archbishop Coggan expressed,

> I did not feel I could refuse the invitation to appear on a dozen *Stars on Sunday* programmes, though it was not my favourite series. But what an opportunity to get something across which one believes is worthwhile and sorely needed.[94]

The show hit a peak of 22 million viewers with the Remembrance Sunday Special in 1973 followed by the Christmas Special, just after the Queen's Speech, when Grace Kelly came out of retirement to be the guest star.[95] This was religion re-cast as light entertainment. As well as Bible readings from the great and the good and hymns sung by the stars, the programme also showcased young people who had never been on television and other up-and-coming talent.

Yates, was described by the *Daily Express* in 1971 as the portly and benevolent producer and presenter of the programme who was obviously a devout and emotional man, often moved by the music on the show, picking music that his mother might like to hear.[96] More critically Clive James in *The Sunday Observer* in 1974 described one episode as, "self-serving sentimental goo, a substance which spreads like a steaming fen in the diabolical *Stars on Sunday*".[97] But to the adoring fans of the programme all seemed sweetness and light but as the *Express* further reported "behind the scenes of this unashamedly coy and syrupy programme, an angry storm is threatening that might even take it off the screen altogether".[98]

Yates had devised a restful formula of music, not so much sacred as saccharine, interspersed with Bible readings by film stars and the occasional homily from a real-life bishop. But the show's kitsch blend of sentimentality, celebrities and cozy escapism attracted much ridicule.[99] The Government appointed Independent Television Authority, for example, expressed its concern over the content of the programme in its Annual Report saying, both the Authority's own panel of Religious Advisors and members of the Central Religious Advisory Council have faced in *Stars on Sunday* an uncomfortable dilemma. On the one hand they cannot help but acknowledge the embarrassment given by the sentimental and naively escapist elements in this programme to those for whom the Christian Gospel conveys a quite different message. On the other hand equally incontestable is the immense popular success and unprecedented nationwide appreciation of a series which unreservedly claims and proclaims its religious intentions. It is a dilemma that will not easily resolved.[100]

Yates was an experienced entertainer and producer and was not impervious to the sniping at his programme, but remained unrepentant about its style and content, obviously deriving consolation from the viewing figures and the size of his mailbag. In an interview with the Reginald Brace of the *Yorkshire Post* he responded by saying,

the programme has become a very personal thing and if it reflects a certain innocence and naiveté, that is how I must be. It is geared to old people, many of whom watch it alone. They don't want to be reminded of retribution and hellfire. Anyone who gets to 65 has experienced many hard years. They want the comfort and promise of the Gospel.[101]

What ensued, while the programme continued its popular run, was a hive of activity within the Independent Television Authority and religious advisory bodies and the introduction of a religious advisor recommended by the Archbishop of York, in the form of the Rev. Brandon Jackson. Jackson was an energetic vicar from Shipley in Yorkshire, who had the Biblical expertise that Yates lacked and was called in to help write the scripts and create a rather more muscular Christianity in the programme. He commented,

I got to know Jess well and I was able to script things he could say with integrity. But I wrote scripts too that could accommodate his limitations.[102]

The programme continued to come under a lot of scrutiny and involved some of the highest executives in the ITA like Bernard Sendall,[103] but the addition of Jackson to the team began to see changes, though the programme's format and underlying philosophy remained unchanged. As Yates pointed out,

> People don't think when they watch TV, they feel. Often watching TV they just get bad news. Ours is the only programme where people can be guaranteed a kind of comfort. There is nothing wrong in comfort.[104]

Despite the reassuring words, the tensions over the programme raged on within the Independent Television Authority, with the weight of opinion against *Stars on Sunday* calling it 'chocolate-box religion'. The ITA's Programme Schedule Committee reported in 1971,

> We have looked at Stars on Sunday and discussed it time and time again and the programme has its apologists. The comfort it brings to millions, its current firm audience of some fifteen million and its very high place in the Authority's appreciation indices amongst all classes of viewers, both sexes and a wide age-range is significant. They have also been able to point to the reassuring presence of Jess Yates himself at the organ as chief presenter and his readiness to speak words of religious comfort. The programme has moreover recently added the Archbishop of Canterbury to its roster of Bible readers; a high seal of ecclesiastical approval.[105]

Despite all this, the Authority's advisors remained doubtful about the programme's validity as a religious programme and their deliberations indicated that if they had been able to find a creditable alternative, the programme would have been dropped.[106] It seemed in the end that *Stars on Sunday* became a programme that was either loved or hated, though it never set out to be controversial as Yates himself reflected,

> We just felt it was an opportunity for those people who did not have a programme they could call their own. Just about

every other section of the community was catered for by some programme or other, but there was very little for the over 65s. All we have tried to do is to provide a programme for them and it is largely incidental that it has proved to hold appeal for other sections of the community as well. Religion comes into it because we felt that the period devoted to religious type programmes was the only really suitable time for a series of this kind. In any case the majority of people for whom we are catering sought warmth, comfort and peace from religion.[107]

After the scandal regarding Yates and Anita Kay broke and his subsequent withdrawal from the programme, Rev. Brandon Jackson commented, "*Stars on Sunday* limped along for another five years, but without any sparkle, Jess was the genius that had made the programme hugely popular".[108]

The Conclusions:

It is an incontrovertible fact that it was the charismatic genius of Jess Yates, the creator of *Stars on Sunday*, that was to make the show such a success. He became the 'star' of the show and through his experience and skill was able to bring other national and international 'stars' to the small screen. The whole thing was 'celerity' led, which was by the astonishing viewing figures, good for the audience, but from a church, industry and press point of view was to cause a real dilemma.

The Press hardly had an impartial point of view on the programme. Their coverage was full of sarcasm and ridicule, but they faced an uphill task in criticising a programme that was so popularist. Similarly, some in the church and certainly within the religious advisory bodies people felt that the programme was more 'light entertainment' than religious. But the evolving programme gained the addition of the much respected Rev. Brandon Jackson who acted as the main advisor to the programme and crafted the scripts so that the programme became very much more anchored in Biblical faith. The personalities that were featured in song or word were there to convey this content, in a way that could appeal to a wide audience.

What the programme also demonstrated is that it is possible to present important religious themes without compromise and entertain people at the same time. Though being realistic about *Stars on Sunday*, the demographic of the programme was purposely targeted at an older age group and only within that context was it successful. But any television company would be envious these days of any programme that would attract a weekly average audience of 15 million viewers.

The *Stars on Sunday* phenomenon did not end well. The relationship between Yates and Anita Kay became a national scandal and Yates was expelled from the programme. It meant a slow demise to a programme that had been one of the most successful religious programmes in UK broadcasting history. The programme still retained potential but the surrounding circumstances combined with the approach of Yorkshire Television Executives meant it had run its course.[109]

3. Summary

As stated, the purpose of this case study approach is to provide an in-depth examination of two particular religious programmes as models from the USA and the UK, which indicate all the characteristics of how religious broadcasting makes its greatest impact when it is personality led.

In terms of broadcasting, both programmes originate in the context of a commercial network, *PTL* as part of the Bakker's own satellite network which was able to distribute the programme both nationally and internationally and *Stars on Sunday* as one of the flagship religious programmes of the newly formed Independent Television. On this point, the key observation is the issue is about scale. The *PTL* operation and production was part of a multi-million dollar empire controlled by the Bakkers which just featured religious programming, whereas *Stars on Sunday*, by comparison, was merely one religious programme in the 'closed period' of Sunday broadcasts.

A further important point, despite the inequalities of scale, was that their environment gave then both a platform to speak to millions of people. Bakker was just one of many televangelists in the USA that were able to operate in an independent way, with little regulation to influence them. But Jim Bakker's own entrepreneurial skills and charismatic personality combined to attract millions of viewers to *PTL*, turning him and Tammy into national and international celebrities. Ironically, without the same level of resources and having to endure quite rigid regulation in the UK, Yates and his team were able to create a highly popularist programme that had a larger share of the potential viewing audience than even Bakker was able to achieve in America. That maybe because America had more choices for religious broadcasting, but however it still meant that Yates was presenting and producing one of the most successful programmes on British television and certainly became a celebrity in his own right.

In addition in many ways there was a commonality of style between the two shows. Both featuring Christian music, bible readings, celebrities and viewer engagement. One point of departure was that *PTL* was a listener supported ministry, as were many in the USA and as such every programme featured significant appeals for money and testimonies of people who had given substantial amounts of money to the ministry and been blessed as a result. *Stars on Sunday* operating under UK regulations, was funded by the network and no such money-raising appeals were allowed and therefore not surprisingly Yates would never reach the 'dizzy heights' of financial gain that Bakker experienced, even if he did have a similar notoriety in the UK context.

Another differing perspective is what we might call the 'theology' or 'philosophy' of the programmes. *PTL* was quite clearly grounded in a new type of Pentecostalism, preaching a 'prosperity gospel', believing if people give money to God's ministries they will be also rewarded with a prosperous and successful life. In contrast, if anything *Stars on Sunday* was considered by some lacking in serious theology and more like light entertainment and therefore Yates constantly was under review by religious advisors and the Independent Television Authority. By their loyalty however the audience disagreed, though it remained one of the most controversial programmes on British television.

Both the Bakkers and Yates had to endure high levels of public criticism. By the mid-80s the Bakkers were pulling in millions of dollars from their ministry. They had multiple houses, expensive cars and high-priced jewellery and this success and exorbitant spending brought not only scrutiny from the likes of the *Charlotte Observer* but criticism from many quarters, including elements of the Church. Yates also faced mocking from the Press, not initially for his lifestyle, but for a television production that was deemed saccharine and sentimental. Despite the weight of criticisms, both Bakker and Yates were able to overcome any negativity through the volume of supporters they could rely on, which made both men and their programmes giants of religious broadcasting in their respective countries. However, when both became involved in serious and much publicised scandals their careers were ruined and to some extent, for a time, the reputation of religious broadcasting.

Why are these case studies important in the context of the whole study? Firstly they demonstrably help provide a greater insight into the life and times of two very charismatic personalities who were able so effectively to use the platform of television and their programmes to convey the Christian message. Secondly in the choice of these two intensive studies it provides a more in-depth understanding of the greater and contrasting context of religious broadcasting in the USA and the UK, where religious broadcasters were operating under two very different environments, Bakker being typical in the USA able to function totally independently, whereas Yates as other religious broadcasters in the UK under the authority of broadcasting institutions and their advisors. Thirdly as already been alluded, the programmes are 'models' of differing theological approaches. They were created in very distinct and different religious environments and therefore to some extent products of their own national history and religion. Finally and importantly the programmes were portals by which many people not only learned about the Christian faith, but either through it became committed Christians or were helped in their Christian faith. The letter response to both programmes indicates how much they were valued because of what the viewers experienced. In that process Bakker and Yates, to the viewers, often became the embodiment of their experience of God and their personalities channels of heaven on earth.

NOTES

1. Yin, R. K., *Case Study Research Design and Methods*. 5th edition (Thousand Oaks: Sage, 2014), p.199.

2. Miles, A. P., Social Work and the Science of Society. *Society and Social Research*, 27 (6) 1943: 433-440.

3. Harrison, H., Birks, M., Franklin, R., and Mills. J., Case Study Research: Foundations and Methodological Orientations. *Forum: Qualitative Social Research*, 18 (1) 2017: 1.

4. Stoecker, R., Evaluating and Re-thinking the Case Study. *The Sociological Review*, 39 (1) 1991: 108.

5. Llobera. J., Historical Comparative Research. *In*: Searle, C., *Researching Culture and Society*. (London: Sage, 1998), p.80.

6. Armstrong, B. *The Electric Church* (Nashville: Thomas Nelson, 1979).

7. Gallup Poll, *Evangelical Christianity* (Washington: Gallup, 1978), p.109, 125.

8. Bourgault, L. M., The PTL Club and Protestant Viewers: An Ethnographic Study. *Journal of Communication*, 35 (1) 1985:134.

9. Weinberg, E. G., *Creating Heaven on Earth: Jim Bakker and the Birth of Sunbelt Pentecostalism*. (PhD). University of Kentucky (2012), p.89.

10. Fotherby, V., *The Awakening Giant: The Miraculous Story of the Full Gospel Business Men's Fellowship International*. (London: Marshall Pickering, 2000), p.xv, 179,185.

11. Schultze, Q. J., *Televangelism and American Culture: The Business of Popular Religion* (Grand Rapids: Baker Book House, 1991), p.78.

12. Shepard, C. E., Jim Bakkers Middle Name was Show Business. *Seattle Post Intelligencer*. 9th October (1989), p.1.

13. Erickson, H., 1992. *Religious Radio and Television in the United States 1921 – 1991: The Programs and Personalities* (Jefferson: McFarland & Co, 1992), p.32.

14. Schultze, Q.J. (1991), p.113.

15. Shepard, C. E., *Forgiven: The Rise and Fall of Jim Bakker and the PTL Ministry* (New York: Atlantic Monthly Press, 1989), p.42-47.

16. Ibid., p.58.

17. Editorial, 1975. Bakker Religious Show. *Florence Morning News*. 7th September (1975), p.5.

18. Weinberg, E.G. (2012), p.3.

19. Johnson, E., A Theme Park, a Scandal and the Faded Ruins of a Television Empire. *Religion & Politics*. 28th October (2014), https://religionandpolitics.org,

20. Albert, J. A., Jim Bakker: Miscarriage of Justice? (Chicago: Open Court, 1998), p.41.

21. Interview: 9th July (2019).

22. Shepard, C.E., The Bakkers Lavish Lifestyle. *Charlotte Observer* 26th January (1986), p.10.

23. Tidewell, G. L., *Anatomy of a Fraud: Inside the Finances of the PTL Ministries* (New York: John Wiley & Sons) (1993), p.4-7.

24. Shepard, C. E., 1987. Jim Bakker Resigns from PTL. *Charlotte Observer*. 20th March (1987), p.1.

25. Shepard, C.E. (1989), p.xiii.

26. Effron, L., Paparetta, A. and Taudte, J., The scandals that brought down the Bakkers, once among US's most famous televangelists. *ABC News*. 20th December (2019).

27. in Albert, J.A. (1998), p.8.

28. John, K.E., Television Evangelists Have Been Tarnished by Scandal. *Washington Post* June 1st (1987), p.37.

29. Applebome, P., Scandals Aside TV Preachers Thrive. *New York Times*. 8th October (1989), p.24.

30. Bakker, J., *I Was Wrong* (Nashville: Thomas Nelson, 1996), p.5.

31. Page, C., Jim Bakker's Sentence is Too Harsh. *Chicago Tribune*, 29th October (1989), p.10.

32. Harris, A., Jim Bakker Sentence Overturned. *Washington Post.* 13th February (1991), p.5.

33. Messner, T. F., *Telling it My Way* (New York: Villard, 1996), p.314.

34. Bakker, J. (1996), p. 532-533.

35. Funk, T., Fallen PTL Preacher Jim Bakker is Back with a New Message about the Apocalypse. *Charlotte Observer.* 17th February (2018), p. 2; Wigger, J. H., *PTL: The Rise and Fall of Jim and Tammy Faye Bakker's Evangelical Empire.* (New York: Oxford University Press, 2017), p.334-335.

36. Weinberg, E.G. (2012), p.72.

37. Matzko, P., What Jim Bakker Can Teach American Evangelicals Today. 13th April (2018), www.thegospelcoalition.org.

38. Wigger, J., Blessed: A History of the American Prosperity Gospel. *Fides et Historia,* 47 (2) 2015: 47.

39. Bowler, K., *A History of the American Prosperity Gospel* (Oxford: Oxford University Press, 2013), p.11.

40. Ibid, p.6.

41. Bakker, J., *Eight Keys to Success* (Manchester: New Leaf Press, 1980), p.2.

42. Wigger, J. H. (2017), p.52.

43. Harris, A. and Isikoff. M., The Bakker's Tumultuous Return. *Washington Post.* 12th June (1986), p.3.

44. McLendon, M.A., Jim Bakker Seen By Millions Known By Few. *The Saturday Evening Post*, April, (1981), p. 50-53.

45. Shepard, C.E. (1989), p.161.

46. Barnhart, J. E. and Winzenburg, S., *Jim and Tammy: Charismatic Intrigue inside PTL.* (Buffalo: Prometheus Books, 1988), p.39-47.

47. Shepard, C.E. (1989), p.41.

48. Allitt, P., *Religion in America since 1945* (New York: Columbia Press, 2003), p.192.

49. Blumhofer, E. W., *Restoring the Faith: The Assemblies of God, Pentecostalism and American Culture* (Urbana: University of Illinois Press, 1993), p.244.

50. Bakker, J., *Showers of Blessing* (Charlotte: PTL, 1986), p.25.

51. *PTL Club*, 7th January (1986).

52. *PTL Club*, 31st March (1986).

53. Harrison, H. and Dudley, C., *Second Fiddle* (Green Forest: New Leaf Press, 1979).

54. Weinberg, E.G. (2012), p.98.

55. Ibid., p.98-99.

56. Hadden, J. K. and Swann, C. E., *Prime Time Preachers: The Rising Power of Televangelism* (Reading: Addison Wesley Publishing, 1981), p.34.

57. Freedman, S. G., Ideas & Trends: How Bakker Widened the Eye of the Needle. *Washington Post*. 14th June 1987), p.26.

58. Harris, A. and Isikoff, M. (1987), p.3.

59. Bakker, J. and Abraham. K., 1998. *Prosperity and the Coming Apocalypse*. (Nashville: Thomas Nelson Publishers, 1998), p.8.

60. *PTL Club*, 21st April (1985).

61. *PTL Club*, November 4th-7th (1985).

62. *PTL Club*, 25th April (1986).

63. *PTL Club*, November 4th (1986).

64. Jacobsen, D. G., *The World Christians: Who They Are, Where They Are and How They Got There* (Malden: Wiley Blackwell, 2011), p.56-60.

65. Yancy, P., The Ironies and Impact of PTL. *Christianity Today*. 21st September (1979), p.28-33.

66. Hoover, S. M., *Mass Media Religion: The Social Sources of the Electronic Church* (Newbury Park: Sage, 1988), p.229.

67. Dickenson, S. H., Characterising the Message of the Electric Church. *Florida Communication Journal*, 11 (1) 1983: 22.

68. Matzko, P. (2018).

69. Carter, H. W., 2017. The Cautionary Tale of Jim and Tammy Faye Bakker. *Christianity Today*. 19th September (2017), p.12-13.

70. Interview: 9th July (2019)

71. Knight, G.R., Democratization of the American Church (1991), www.digitalcommons.andrews.edu. p.176.

72. Hull, J. D., The Rise and Fall of 'Holy Joe'. *Time Magazine* 3rd August (1987), p. 54-55.

73. James, H., *Smile Pretty and Say Jesus: The Last Great Days of PTL* (Athens: University of Georgia Press, 19193), p.ix.

74. Independent Television Authority, *Annual Report & Accounts* (London. HMSO, 1970/71), p.39-40.

75. Television Act (1954), 2 & 3 Eliz.11, c.55.

76. Report of the Broadcasting Committee 1977 (*Annan Report*) Cmnd.6753. (London. HMSO), p.322.

77. Wallis, R., Genesis of the Bible Documentary: the Development of Religious Broadcasting in the UK. *In*: Bond, H. K. and Adams, E., *The Bible on Television*. (London: T & T Clark 2020), p.11.

78. ITV (1970/71), p.4.

79. Hayward, A., Obituary: Jess *Yates. The Independent*. 12th April (1993), p.17.

80. Barfield, N., Obituary: Jess Yates. *The Guardian*. 16th April (1963), p. 7.

81. Hickling, M., A Life in Times and Pictures. *Yorkshire Post*. 10th August (2005), p.3.

82. Hayward, A. (1993), p.17.

83. Hickling,M. (2005), p.3.

CHAPTER 7 ON THE CASE

84. Massingberd, H., *The Daily Telegraph: Third Book of Obituaries: The Entertainers.* (London: Macmillan, 1997), p.290.

85. Botham, N., My Love for Jess. *News of the World.* 5th July (1993), p.5.

86. Davies, C., Yates Loses His Job. *Daily Mirror.* 9th July (1974), p.14.

87. Gilchrist, R., Jess Yates Plans a 'Stars on Sunday' Comeback on American TV. *Daily Mail,* 24th September (1974), p.3.

88. in Hickling, M. (2005), p.3.

89. Max-Wilson, P., *Stars on Sunday.* (Pinner: Pentagon, 1976), p.11-12.

90. Obituary, Jess Yates. *The Times.* 12th April (1993), p.17.

91. Barfield, N. *The Guardian* 16th April (1993), p.17.

92. in Massingberd, H. (1997), p.293.

93. Obituary, *The Times,* April 12th (1993), p.17.

94. Harmes, B., Harmes, M.K. and Harmes, M., The Church on British Television: From the Coronation to Coronation Street (London: Palgrave Macmillan, 2020), p.96.

95. Hickling, M. (2005), p.3.

96. Correspondent, How Much Light Do these Stars Give Us? *Daily Express.* 27th November (1971), p.21.

97. James, C., O Lord Preserve Us. *The Sunday Observer.* 19th May (1974), p.35.

98. Correspondent, How Much Light Do these Stars Give Us? *Daily Express.* 27th November (1971), p.21.

99. Massingberd, H. (1997), p.292.

100. ITA (1970/71), p.39.

101. Brace, R., Wandering Innocent Among the Stars. *Yorkshire Post.* 11th January (1972), p.4.

102. Interview: 16th July (2019).

103. Sendall, B. C., *Stars on Sunday* (1971), IBA Collection File Ref: A/X/0009/1; Sendall, B. C., *Stars on Sunday* (1972), IBA Collection File Ref: A/X/0009/5.

104. Correspondent, *Daily Express* 27th November (1971), p.21.

105. ITA, (1970/71), p.2.

106. Ibid., 1971, p.3.

107. Outlook, Never Set Out To Be Controversial. *Sheffield Morning Telegraph*. 25th April (1972), p.3.

108. Interview: 16th July (2019).

109. Ibid.

CHAPTER 8

CONCLUSION
Following the Evidence

1. The Panorama Portrayed

The sophistication, diversification and influence of religious broadcasting are greatly underappreciated dimensions of the global religious scene of the 20th Century, but as the book has chronicled, religious broadcasting profoundly influenced the Christian community and the secular public for much of this era. It trumpeted the gospel message, in it various forms, across the globe. It caused directly or proximately the rise of parachurch ministries especially in America, but also became a significant force in the UK broadcasting landscape and in both cases influenced social, political and religious life.[1]

In essence a vast parish of the air and screen was formed creating a fellowship without actual membership. Right from its outset in the 1920s visionary pioneers grasped the significance of radio for evangelism, teaching and reflecting the Christian faith and values and the onset of television in the early 1950s was to extend that potential substantially.

Speaking first of America, the study portrays how the initial explosion of Christian radio stations were moderated by the formation of the Federal Radio Commission in 1927. The stations that survived often evolving in the midst of a bitter conflict between Fundamentalism and Modernism, Modernists using their majority in the Federal Council of Churches of Christ in the 1930s to try to control religious broadcasting and convincing the major networks of NBC and CBS to stop selling airtime to any religious groups; instead offering free airtime – 'sustaining time', to mainline Protestant, Catholic and Jewish groups.[2] Fundamentalist ministers were limited to purchasing airtime on local stations or through the Mutual Broadcasting System created in the late 1930s. But adverse pressure on Mutual to stop selling airtime led to the formation of the National Association of Evangelicals (NAE) in 1942 and its broadcasting arm the National Religious Broadcasters (NRB) in 1944. After the Second World War, religious broadcasting also went international with stations like HCJB, the Far East Broadcasting Company and Trans World Radio.[3]

In the early 1950s television became the new medium and despite the efforts of the National Council of Churches of Christ (which succeeded the Federal Council of Churches of Christ in 1950), independent broadcasters took front-of-stage, developing large scale multi-million dollar ministries. Christian television in this age of the 'televangelists' also gave celebrity status to its leading figures which included Dr.Billy Graham, Oral Roberts, Bishop Fulton J. Sheen, Jim Bakker, Jimmy Swaggart, Pat Robertson and Jerry Falwell, the latter ones using their power to join forces with the political right to attempt to extend the influence of Christianity and specifically conservative Evangelicalism. It is important also to remember there actually were women in religious broadcasting like Aimee Semple McPherson and Mother Mary Angelica, but the radio and television personalities remained predominantly a male domain. By the end of the 20th Century there were approximately 1,600 Christian radio stations on the air and 250 TV stations which blanketed the nation with the Christian gospel.[4]

Turning to the UK, the book establishes that from its inception the BBC saw the coverage of religion as a vital part of broadcasting's social responsibility. Despite some churches seeing radio as a threat, there was a general consensus between those within and outside the BBC as to the direction this genre should evolve. The aim was to promote and protect the Christian faith and give a greater appreciation of faith and religious doctrine to listeners, combining education and proselytism within its mission.[5] A position, which the study highlights, was driven and supported by Lord Reith and exemplified by some of his chosen broadcasters like the Rev. Dick Sheppard and Rev. W.H. Elliott and in programming featuring church services, bible readings, religious talks and hymn singing. This early consensus was achieved through extensive consultation with religious leaders through the portal of the Central Religious Advisory Committee (CRAC), founded in its original form in 1923 by the BBC, but extended to advise the Independent Television Authority (ITA) and the independent television companies from the 1950s.[6] When television established itself in the 1950s much of the content was adapted from radio, but the study also traces the increasing divergent directions of the Churches and the BBC, with the Corporation attempting to widen the appeal of religious broadcasting, a discussion that was an ongoing tension[7] and also engaged the Government through the work of the Beveridge (1951), Pilkington (1962) and the Annan Reports (1977). Although religious broadcasting had remained in the context of the BBC monopoly, the development of Commercial Television in the 1950s brought its own style of religious programming with a wide variety of tastes in drama, music and song,[8] though for many years both occupied the dedicated 70 minute 'closed period' early on Sunday evenings, filling it with programmes like *Songs of Praise, Highway* and *Stars on Sunday*.[9] With the onset of Channel 4 in the 1980s, more controversial religious programmes like *Jesus the Evidence* were to appear.[10] The book examines these developments and the road to gain recognition for independent religious broadcasters through to the 1990 Broadcasting Act[11] and the establishment of new stations like Premier Christian Radio (1995).

Finally and most importantly, the research highlights the significant issue of the impact of 'personality', whether that was in relation to the historical perspective expressed by Carlyle (1841), the sociological slant of Weber (1915) or the more contemporary concept of Boostin's 'celebrity' (2006). Applied in the context of this study, there is the demonstration that whether it was Falwell in the USA or Reith in the UK, or the others featured in the book, it was the dominant personality of these charismatic broadcasters that was to enable religious broadcasting to become a core broadcasting element in the 20th Century and an indispensable instrument for sharing the Christian message.

2. The Implications of the History

Although looking through the lens of the 21st Century one might assume that religious broadcasting was a mere 'niche' in the broadcasting spectrum, the evidence from the previous century tells a different story.

Firstly, the American narrative shows how the Church agreed with one of David Sarnoff's reflective speeches believing "radio as one of the world's greatest social forces"[12] and therefore was willing to engage with the opportunity that radio could bring for the communication of the Christian gospel, within only a month of the first professional voice being broadcast in December 1920 in Pittsburgh.[13] That is why many of early stations – 63 in total of the 600 stations operating in 1925, were Church owned.[14] The point being that religious broadcasting in America was playing a significant role in the media landscape – seeking through broadcasting to influence the heart of the nation and becoming one of "the largest single enterprises on the air",[15] driven largely by powerful broadcasting 'personalities' with huge listeners and viewers amounting to almost a cult following.[16] Although the context of early broadcasting in the UK was very different, Reith, like America's Sarnoff and others believed that radio could be a "wonderful influence",[17] but more than that religious broadcasting in particular had great potential for the churches with "the message and music of eternity moving through the rough infinities of the ether"[18] and religious broadcasting establishing itself as a powerful missionary and teaching medium at the service of the Churches.[19] Reith ensured that, as with America, religious broadcasting was an integral part of the broadcasting panorama.[20]

The second important observation is not only was religious broadcasting a critical part of early broadcasting, comparing the UK to the USA the approach was totally different. Briggs comments, "the religious programmes of the BBC were as different from religious programmes in the United States, as its popular music programmes were from such American programmes".[21] Here religious broadcasting was initially part of the public service output, closely allied to the established churches, with policies advised by the Central Religious

Advisory Committee (CRAC) and largely attempting to match the culture of the day and maintaining an ethos to inform, educate and entertain through the years of both radio and television with the BBC and into the era of commercial broadcasting.[22] Contrasting substantially with this, America although it had church networks like the FCCC/NCC influencing broadcasting, what evolved eventually was rather a cultural phenomenon of a multiplicity of independent radio and television stations and programmes led by religious leaders who were largely evangelical or fundamentalist theologically and who built 'mega-ministries' off the back of their broadcasting[23] and in essence helped to transform American religion in the 20th Century.[24] What is clear is that the experience of America's free market religious broadcasting did very little to encourage a similar experiment in the United Kingdom.[25]

A third consideration is that the history of religious broadcasting did not flow without its critics both in the USA and the UK. Numbers of commentators noted America's scores of television evangelists and hundreds of preachers broadcasting day and night, preaching a "bogus religion whose story was a wild tale of the end of the world and whose values closely resembled the worldview of secular America, the value of winning, of wealth, of power and of being Number One".[26] Its message of personal salvation and the promise of health and wealth was prominent, but the naïve message that faith could solve all the problems of the world was seen as simplistic and avoiding the hard issues of the 20th Century. As Schultze bluntly points out, "the good and the bad, the extravagant and the simple, the authentic and the counterfeit, have always existed side by side in evangelical broadcasting".[27] Added to this are the moral and financial scandals or extravagances of many of those spearheading American religious broadcasting, which attracted a great deal of criticism and sometimes even legal investigations.[28] However, it is easy to be critical and forget that many of these broadcasters were actually not stirred by their financial statements, or the ratings of Neilson and Arbitron, but by their sense that God's hand was on their shoulders empowering and inspiring them.[29] Overall Britain's religious broadcasting was by comparison deemed more authentic in being guided by the orthodox churches,[30] though 'Reithian Sundays', the continued Christian monopoly, denominationalism and the issue of proselytizing were all matters of contention and debate by the broadcasting and church networks,[31] as reflected by both the BBC, IBA and CRAC archives examined in this study.

Finally what also has been reflected in the book is that during the 20th Century when broadcasting and specifically religious broadcasting was developing there was a progression of secularisation which was to threaten the Church's institutional power and cultural influence.[32] This is not to be seen in mere numerical terms, but in the wider way that religion was judged as an integral part of the DNA of nations. Going on from that the study indicates a clear distinction between what is seen as secularisation applicable to Western Europe (including Britain) and the experience of America – some people even considering whether secularisation was a phenomenon concentrated only in a small part of the world.[33] Whatever the international perspective, the research supports the contention that during the 20th Century that media, in the form of radio and television, moved to the centre stage of society exercising enormous political, economic, cultural and religious power and those religious broadcasters both in America and Britain used these platforms to extend the communication of the Christian gospel. It can be argued that had it not been for their presence and influence, the tide of secularisation might have diminished more the role of religion and especially Christianity in society, both in the USA and the UK.

3. The Proposition of the Book

The overall contention of the study and illustrated in the material surveyed, is that although governments, broadcasting institutions and the churches played an important role in religious broadcasting in the 20th Century, it was charismatic entrepreneurial personalities that made the most impact in driving forward this genre of broadcasting history.

In America the development of large Christian ministries led by individuals like Dr.Billy Graham, Pat Robertson, Jim Bakker, Jerry

Falwell and others broadcasting through radio and television and creating huge audiences and devotees, conferred star/celebrity status on these people who became household names not only in the Church, but throughout the nation and in some cases the world.[34] Schultze, a prolific writer on religious broadcasting reflects,

> American religious media has been personality orientated from the beginning, creating denomination-like tribes with their own charismatic leaders. Such leaders serve as the symbolic figureheads for audience members' personal connections with God and God's truth.[35]

The spectrum of significance in the UK might not have been as pronounced, but the role of Reith, his broadcasters Shepherd and Elliott and the leaders of BBC Religious Broadcasting were to make a major impact in the output of the BBC, with at least four million people by the 1950s listening to a single religious broadcast, probably twice as many people who were attending Church on Sundays, with approximately half of those listeners being non-churchgoers.[36] Furthermore in the main era of BBC and Commercial Television from the late 1950s, personality-led programmes like *Songs of Praise*, *Highway* and *Stars on Sunday* were to create audiences up to 15 million viewers per week and demonstrated that religious broadcasting was valued and important, as part of the overall broadcasting culture of the UK.[37] As McDonnell concludes,

> Although religious broadcasting in the UK was on a smaller scale to that of the United States, it arguably played a more central role in reflecting the culture and religious landscape of the nation. The achievements of British religious broadcasting depended upon the efforts of many notable and charismatic people of faith, who made a significant contribution both on and off air, above all, John Reith, who decisively and fundamentally shaped the character and culture of British religious broadcasting.[38]

So whether is was the USA or the UK, the rationale for the use of media (radio and television) was invariably that broadcasters could extend the range of the church's normal work and enable the church to motivate people whom the Church and its workers could not reach more directly.[39] As the book has demonstrated this took on a different characteristic approach in the UK compared to the USA, but commonly it was the pattern of elements of Carlyle's 'Great Man' (1841) and Weber's 'charismatic personality' (1915) that was reflected in those who took to a national and sometimes international stage to proclaim the Christian message through radio and television.

This book has sought uniquely to follow the evidence of how religious broadcasting was able to evolve and develop in the 20th Century, giving extensive recognition to its champions who by their charisma and enterprise were able to make a significant impact on both broadcasting, the Church and the world.

CHAPTER 8 CONCLUSION

NOTES

1. Bisset, T., Religious Broadcasting Comes of Age. *Christianity Today*. 4th September (1981), p.33.

2. Bruce, S., *Pray TV: Televangelism in America* (London: Routledge, 1990), p.26-27.

3. Stoneman, T., Global Radio Broadcasting and the Dynamics of American Evangelicalism. *Journal of American Studies*, 51 (4) 2017: 1139.

4. Fore, W. F., The Unknown History of Televangelism. *Journal of the World Association of Christian Communication*, 54 (1) 2007: 46-48.

5. Noonan, C., The Production of Religious Broadcasting: the Case of the BBC. (PhD). Glasgow University (2009), p.197.

6. Wolfe, K. M., *The Churches and the British Broadcasting Corporation 1922-1956. The Politics of Broadcast Religion* (London: SCM, 1984), p.13, 523.

7. Central Religious Advisory Committee, *Religious Programmes Policy* (London: 1977), BBC WAC File Ref: R78/810/1.

8. Central Information Office, *Broadcasting in Britain*. (London: HMSO, 1973), p.11.

9. Paulu, B., 1981. *Television and Radio in the United Kingdom*. (London: MacMillan, 1981), p.282-283.

10. Wallis, R., Channel 4 and the declining influence of organised religion on UK television. The Case of Jesus: The Evidence. *Historical Journal of Film, Radio and Television*, 36 (4) 2016: 674-684.

11. Quicke, A. and Quicke, J., *Hidden Agendas: The Politics of Religious Broadcasting in Britain 1987-1991*. (Virginia Beach: Dominion Kings Grant Publications, 1992), p.99-161.

12. Sarnoff, D., 1947. *The Past and the Future of Radio*. New York Speech. IEEE Vol.99 Issue 10 (2011).

13. Bruce, S. (1990), p.25.

14. Ellens, J. H., *Models of Religious Broadcasting* (Grand Rapids: W. B. Eerdmans, 1974), p.16.

15. Editorial, Religious Broadcasting. *Literary Digest*. June (1931), p.22.

16. Ellens, J.H. (1974), p.28.

17. Reith, J. C. W., *Broadcast over Britain* (London: Hodder and Stoughton, 1924), p.197.

18. Ibid., p.199.

19. Grayston, K., Religious Broadcasting in Great Britain. *World Dominion*, January/February (1951), p.49.

20. Ibid., p.47.

21. Briggs, A., *The BBC: The First Fifty Years*. (Oxford: Oxford University Press, 1985), p.130.

22. Beeson, T. R., *An Eye for an Ear*. (London: SCM Press, 1972), p.87.

23. Howley, K., Prey TV: Televangelism and Interpellation. *Journal of Film and Video*, 53 (2/3) 2001: 23-24.

24. Dickenson, S. H., Characterising the Message of the Electric Church. *Florida Communication Journal*, 11 (1) 1983: 16.

25. Leigh, I., Regulating Religious Broadcasting. *Ecclesiastical Law Journal*, 2 (10) 1992: 292.

26. Fore, W.F. (2007), p.47.

27. Schultze Q, J., Evangelicalism, *Christianity Today*, 18th February (2001), p.20.

28. Editorial, The State of Christian Broadcasting. *Christianity Today*. 20th March (1988), p.48-50.

29. Minnery, T., The Man behind the Mask. *Christianity Today*. 4th September (1981), p.28-29.

30. McDonnell. J., From Certainty to Diversity: The Evolution of Religious Broadcasting Since 1990. *In*: Geybels, H., Mels, S. and Walrave, M., *Faith & Media: Analysis of Faith and Media*. (Brussels: P. I. E. Peter Lang, 2009), p.151.

31. Noonan, C., Piety and Professionalism. *Media History*, 19 (2) 2013: 198.

32. Wallis, R., (2016) p. 669

33. Deller, R., *Faith in View: Religion and Spirituality in Factual British Television 2000-2009*. (PhD). Sheffield Hallam University (2012), p.26

34. Dickenson, S.H. (1983), p.21-22.

35. Concluding Statement: Schultze, March 10th (2020).

36. Grayston, K. (1951), p.51.

37. Gunter, B. and Viney, R., *Seeing is Believing: Religion and Television in the 1990s*. (London: John Libbey, 1994), p.45-46.

38. Concluding Statement: McDonnell, March 14th (2020).

39. Parker, E. C., Barry, D. W. and Smythe, D.W., *The Television/Radio Audience and Religion*. (New York: Harper Brothers Publishers, 1955), p.49.

A BRIEF MEDIA CHRONOLOGY
(with relevant highlights and religious broadcasting landmarks)

1901 AD   Marconi transmits message from Cornwall to Newfoundland.

1904 AD   British Wireless Telegraph Act.

1908 AD   **Federal Council of Churches of Christ (FCCC) formed.**

1912 AD   First American Radio Act.

1919 AD   Radio Corporation of America founded

1920 AD   First radio stations in U.S. and Canada.

1921 AD   **First religious broadcast from Calvary Episcopal Church, Pittsburgh on KDKA.**

1922 AD   The BBC (the British Broadcasting Company Ltd) formed.

   Rev. J.A. Mayo, Rector of Whitechapel, gives first religious talk on BBC.

   Paul Radar begins his radio broadcast ministry in America.

   Aimee Semple McPherson becomes first woman to preach over radio.

1923 AD   Sykes Committee.

   R.R. Brown hosts the *Radio Chapel Service* inAmerica.

A BRIEF MEDIA CHRONOLOGY

Radio Times begins.

America's *Time* magazine publishes.

Sunday Committee/Central Religious Advisory Committee (CRAC) formed at the BBC.

Rev. Dick Sheppard becomes Britain's first religious radio personality on the BBC.

1925 AD **The Moody Bible Institute sets up its own station WMBI in Chicago.**

1926 AD John Logie Baird demonstrates television transmissions.

Crawford Committee.

National Broadcasting Company (NBC) established.

1927 AD The British Broadcasting Corporation commences.

US Radio Act setting up Federal Radio Commission (FRC).

"*Jazz Singer*" – started vogue of talking pictures.

John Reith becomes the first Director General of the BBC.

1928 AD First Disney animated cartoon – *Mickey Mouse*.

Donald Grey Barnhouse buys airtime to broadcast on a major network in US.

Sound recording magnetic tape developed.

1929 AD BBC's *The Listener* publishes.

Federal Council of Churches of Christ' *National Radio Pulpit* **first broadcast in US.**

NBC offers free 'sustaining time' to religious organisations.

Columbia Broadcasting System (CBS) established.

1930 AD **Charles E. Coughlin, Catholic priest, has a weekly audience on radio of 30 million listeners in US.**

Walter Maier's *Lutheran Hour* **goes national in US.**

Bishop Fulton Sheen's *The Catholic Hour* **begins on NBC.**

1931 AD **The Roman Catholic Church broadcasts through Vatican Radio.**

HCJB Ecuador becomes first missionary radio station in world.

1933 AD **BBC's Religious Broadcasting Department Created.**

1934 AD Federal Communications Commission (FCC) takes over from FRC.

The Mutual Broadcasting System sells time to evangelists in US.

1935 AD Selsdon Committee.

Ullswater Committee.

1936 AD England is first country with regular TV broadcasts – BBC television.

1937 AD	**Charles Fuller hosts *The Old Fashioned Revival Hour* on Mutual Broadcasting System in US.**
1938 AD	Reith retires from the BBC.
1939 AD	Paperback book introduced to the US.
1941 AD	Commercial TV begins in the USA.
1943 AD	American Broadcasting Company (ABC) formed.
	The Mutual Broadcasting System limits sales to evangelists in US.
1944 AD	**National Religious Broadcasting (NRB) group formed in US.**
	Hankey Committee.
	William Haley becomes Director General of the BBC.
1946 AD	Television service restarts in London.
1948 AD	Cable television developed.
	***The Lutheran Hour* – first regular religious TV programme.**
	FEBC begins radio from Manila Philippines.
1949 AD	**ABC lifts its ban on sale of airtime to religious broadcasters in US.**
1950 AD	Beveridge Committee.
	Billy Graham starts broadcasts of his *Hour of Decision*.

The Federal Council of Churches of Christ becomes the National Council of Churches (NCC).

British Council of Churches produces a major report on religious broadcasting.

1952 AD   **Bishop Fulton Sheen telecasts *Life is Worth Living* in US.**

1953 AD   Press Council set up in Britain.

Rex Humbard goes on TV with the *Cathedral of Tomorrow* in US.

1954 AD   The Television Act.

Oral Roberts takes his healing ministry to TV in US.

Paul Freed establishes *The Voice of Tangiers* radio station.

Beginning of colour television.

1955 AD   Commercial Television introduced in UK.

1956 AD   **Jerry Falwell begins his radio and television ministry in US.**

1957 AD   **NBC and CBS lift ban on selling airtime to evangelists in US.**

Billy Graham's New York Crusade goes national on TV in US.

1958 AD   Videotape introduced.

1960 AD   **Trans World Radio begins in Monte Carlo.**

1962 AD   Pilkington Committee.

1961 AD   **Christian Broadcasting Network (CBN) founded in US by Pat Robertson.**

           Songs of Praise **first broadcasts on the BBC.**

1962 AD   Cassette tape invented by Phillips.

           First live television from the USA via Telstar satellite.

1964 AD   The Television Act.

           Pirate Radio (Radio Caroline) appears.

1966 AD   **Pat Robertson starts the TV *700 Club*.**

1967 AD   The Marine Broadcasting (Offences) Act.

           US Carnegie Commission makes recommendations on broadcasting.

           National Public Radio (NPR) created in the US.

           US Broadcasting Act establishes public radio and television.

           BBC Local Radio begins.

           Churches Advisory Council for Local Broadcasting (CACLB) established.

1969 AD   BBC and ITV start regular colour television broadcasts.

           Sony launches videotape cassettes.

           Stars on Sunday **launches on ITV.**

1970 AD	**Robert Schuller's *Hour of Power* first airs.**
1972 AD	The Sound Broadcasting Act.
	Email process developed.
1973 AD	The Independent Broadcasting Authority Act.
	Trinity Broadcasting Network (TBN) set up in US.
	The IBA – Independent Broadcasting Authority formed.
	First commercial radio station in the UK – LBC in London.
	First mobile phone launched.
1974 AD	**Commencement of the Bakkers *PTL Club***
1976 AD	Apple Corporation founded.
1977 AD	Annan Committee.
	Trinity Broadcasting goes 24 hours a day in US.
1979 AD	The Independent Broadcasting Act.
	Jerry Falwell's Moral Majority launches in US.
1980 AD	CNN first 24 hour news station debuts in US.
1981 AD	The Broadcasting Act.
	MTV launches.
	Mother Angelica launches *Eternal Word Television* in US.

A BRIEF MEDIA CHRONOLOGY

1982 AD   Hunt Committee.

                Channel 4 launches.

                Sky, the first European cable and satellite channel begins.

                Salem Communications established in US.

1983 AD   *Jesus the Evidence* **controversy on Channel 4.**

                Highway **starts on ITV presented by Harry Secombe.**

1984 AD   The Cable and Broadcasting Act.

                First Congress statute deregulating cable TV.

1985 AD   Microsoft Windows is introduced.

1986 AD   Peacock Committee.

                Vision Broadcasting – first Christian cable station in the UK.

                United Christian Broadcasters (UCB) starts in the UK.

1987 AD   **Jim Bakker of** *PTL Club* **resigns over sexual misconduct in US and the next year is indicted for fraud.**

1988 AD   ISDN launched (Integrated Services Digital Network).

                Sony introduces CD player.

                Evangelist Jimmy Swaggart confesses to sexual perversion in US.

                Pat Robertson is nominated for President of the US.

1989 AD	Compaq laptop computer is birthed.
1990 AD	BSkyB formed by merger of BSB and Sky.
	World Wide Web launches.
	Broadcasting Act allows religious groups to own radio stations.
1992 AD	Radio Joint Audience Research (RAJAR) established.
1995 AD	DVD created.
	Premier – the first licenced Christian Radio station starts to broadcast.

BIBLIOGRAPHY

BOOKS

Aberbach, D., 1996. *Charisma in Politics Religion and the Media: Private Trauma Public Ideals*. Basingstoke: Macmillan.

Abercrombie, N. and Warde, A., 2000. *Contemporary British Society*. 3rd edition. Cambridge: Polity.

Adjibolosoo, S. B. S., 2000. *The Human Factor in Shaping the Course of History and Development*. Lanham BD: University of America.

Albanese, C. L., 2011. Understanding Christian Diversity in America In: Brekus,C. A. and Gilpin, W. C., *American Christianities: A History of Dominance and Diversity*. Chapel Hill: University of North Carolina Press.

Albert, J. A., 1998. *Jim Bakker: Miscarriage of Justice?* Chicago: Open Court.

Allighan, G., 1938. *Sir John Reith*. London: Stanley Paul and Co.

Allitt, P., 2003. *Religion in America since 1945*. New York: Columbia Press.

Apps, E., 2013. *Pursued by Bishops: The Memoirs of Edwin Apps*. London: Durand-Peyroles.

Argyle, M., 1965. *Religious Behaviour*. London: Routledge & Kegan Paul.

Armstrong, B., 1979. *The Electric Church*. Nashville: Thomas Nelson.

Arroyo, R., 2005. *Mother Angelica: The Remarkable Story of a Nun, Her Nerve and a Network of Miracles.* New York: Doubleday.

Arthur, C., 1993. *Religion and the Media: An Introductory Reader.* Cardiff: University of Wales.

Austin, A., 1980. *Aimee Semple McPherson.* Don Mills: Fitzhenry & Whiteside.

Bachman, J. W., 1960. *The Church in the World of Radio & Television.* New York: National Board of Young Christian's Associations.

Bacon, F., 1597. *Meditationes Sacrae and Human Philosophy.* Montanna: Kessinger Publishing (1996).

Bailey, M. and Redden, G., 2011. *Mediating Faiths: Religion and Socio-Cultural Change in the 20th Century.* Farnham: Ashgate.

Bakewell, J., 1996. *The Heart of the Matter: A Memoir.* London: BBC Books.

Bakker, J., 1980. *Eight Keys to Success.* Manchester: New Leaf Press.

Bakker, J., 1986. *Showers of Blessing.* Charlotte: PTL.

Bakker, J., 1996. *I Was Wrong.* Nashville: Thomas Nelson.

Bakker, J. and Abraham. K., 1998. *Prosperity and the Coming Apocalypse.* Nashville: Thomas Nelson Publishers.

Bakker, J., 2013. *The Time Has Come: How to Prepare Now for Epic Events.* Nashville: Worthy Publishing.

Barfoot, C. H., 2014. *Aimee Semple McPherson and the Making of Modern Pentecostalism.* London: Routledge.

Barnes, R. D., 2010. *Outrageous Invasions: Celebrities' Private Lives, Media, and the Law.* Oxford: Oxford University Press.

Barnes, T., 2011. *Celebrating Songs of Praise: 50 Years*. Oxford: Lion.

Barnhart, J. E. and Winzenburg, S., 1988. *Jim and Tammy: Charismatic Intrigue inside PTL*. Buffalo: Prometheus Books.

Barnouw, E., 1968. *History of Broadcasting in the United States*: Vol.1: *A Tower of Babel*: To *1933*. New York: Oxford University Press.

Barnouw, E., 1968. *The Golden Web: A History of Broadcasting in the United States*. Vol.2: *1933-1953*. New York: Oxford University Press.

Barnouw, E., 1970. *History of Broadcasting in the United States*. Vol. 3: The *Image Empire – from 1953*. New York: Oxford University Press.

Barnouw, E., 1990. *Tube of Plenty: The Evolution of American Television*. 2nd edition. New York: Oxford University Press.

Baron, M., 1975. *Independent Radio: The Story of Commercial Radio in the UK*. Lavenham: Terence Dalton.

Barr, A., 2001. *Songs of Praise: The Nation's Favourite*. Oxford: Lion.

Barron, L., 2015. *Celebrity Cultures*. London. Sage

Bass, B. M., 1985. *Leadership and Performance beyond Expectations*. New York: Free Press.

BBC., 1928. *BBC Handbook*. London: BBC.

BBC., 1932. *BBC Handbook*. London: BBC.

BBC., 1933. *BBC Handbook*. London: BBC.

BBC., 1934. *BBC Handbook*. London: BBC.

BBC., 1947. *BBC Handbook*. London: BBC.

BBC., 1955. *BBC Handbook*. London: BBC.

BBC., 1958. *The Story of the BBC*. London: BBC.

BBC, 1970. *BBC Audience Research in the United Kingdom: Methods and Service*. London: BBC.

BBC., 1975. *BBC: Religious Broadcasting*. London: BBC Publishing.

BBC., 1977. *What Do You Think of it So Far?* London: BBC.

Beachcroft, T. O., 1948. *British Broadcasting*. London: Longman Green & Co.

Beal, T., 2008. *Religion in America: A Very Short Introduction*. Oxford: Oxford University Press.

Beale, C., 1956. *Television and Religion*. Wallington: Religious Education Press.

Bedell, K. B., 1994. *Yearbook of American and Canadian Churches*. Nashville: Abingdon Press.

Beeson,T., 2006. *The Canons*. London: SCM Press

Beeson, T. R., 1972. *An Eye for an Ear*. London: SCM Press.

Bell, G. K. A., 1957. *Randall Davidson: Archbishop of Canterbury*. 3rd edition. London: Oxford University Press.

Benjamin,L.M., 1998. *Freedom of the Air and the Public Interest: First Amendment Rights in Broadcasting to 1935*. Carbondale: Southern Illinois University Press.

Bennis,W. and Nanus C. 1997. *Leaders. Handbook of Leadership: Theory and Practice*. New York: The Free Press.

Benson, D. C., 1973. *Electric Evangelism*. Nashville: Abingdon Press.

Berger, P., Davie, G. and Fokas, E., 2008. *Religious America, Secular Europe? : A Theme and Variations.* Oxford: Routledge.

Berger. P., 1982. From the Crisis of Religion to the Crisis of Secularity. *In:* Douglas, M. and Tipton, S., *Religion and America: Spirituality in a Secular Age.* Boston: Beacon Press.

Bertaux, D., 1981. *Biography and Society: The Life History Approach to the Social Sciences.* Beverley Hills: Sage.

Blackmore, G., 1956. *Shall the NCC Control Religious Broadcasting?* Wheaton: United Evangelical Action.

Bloch, M., 1963. *The Historian's Craft.* Manchester: Manchester University Press.

Bluem, A. W., 1969. *Religious Television Programming: A Study of Relevance.* New York: Hastings House.

Blumhofer, E., 1993. *Aimee Semple McPherson: Everybody's Sister.* Grand Rapids: Eerdman's.

Blumhofer, E. W., 1993. *Restoring the Faith: The Assemblies of God, Pentecostalism and American Culture.* Urbana: University of Illinois Press.

Bodroghkozy, A., 2018. *A Companion to the History of American Broadcasting.* New Jersey: John Wiley & Sons.

Bond, H. K. and Adam, E., 2020. *The Bible on Television.* London: T & T Clark.

Boorstin, D., 1961. From Hero to Celebrity: The Human Pseudo-Event. *In:* Marshall, P. D., *The Celebrity Culture Reader.* London: Routledge.

Boston, R., 1996. *The Most Dangerous Man in America? Pat Robertson and the Rise of the Christian Coalition.* New York: Prometheus.

Bowker, J., 1983. *Religious Beliefs and Practices in Britain Today*. London: BBC.

Bowler, K., 2013. *A History of the American Prosperity Gospel*. Oxford: Oxford University Press.

Bowman, E. G., 1991. *Eyes Beyond the Horizon*. Nashville: Thomas Nelson.

Boyle, A., 1972. *Only the Wind will Listen*: Reith of the BBC. London: Hutchinson.

Brierley. P., 2006. *Pulling Out of the Nose-Dive: A Contemporary Picture of Churchgoing. What the 2005 English Church Census Reveals*. London: Christian Research.

Briggs, A., 1961. *The History of Broadcasting in the United Kingdom*. Vol. 1: *The Birth of Broadcasting*. London: Oxford University Press.

Briggs, A., 1965. *The History of Broadcasting in the United Kingdom*. Vol. 11: *The Golden Age of Wireless*. Oxford: Oxford University Press.

Briggs, A., 1970. *The History of Broadcasting in the United Kingdom* Vol. 111: *The War of Words*. London: Oxford University Press.

Briggs, A., 1979. *The History of Broadcasting in the United Kingdom*. Vol. 1V: *Sound and Vision*. Oxford: Oxford University Press.

Briggs, A., 1985. *The BBC: The First Fifty Years*. Oxford: Oxford University Press.

Briggs, A., 1995. *The History of Broadcasting in the United Kingdom*. Vol. V: *Competition*. Oxford: Oxford University Press.

Briggs, A. and Burke, P., 2009. *A Social History of the Media: From Gutenberg to the* Internet. 3rd edition. Cambridge: Polity Press.

Brinkley, A., 1983. *Voices of Protest: Huey long, Father Coughlin and the Great Depression*. New York: Alfred A. Knopf Publishing.

Bronowski, J., 1973. *The Ascent of Man*. London: BBC Books.

Brown, C. G., 2001. *The Death of Christian Britain*. London: Routledge.

Brown, C. G., 2006. *Religion and Society in 20th Century Britain*. Harlow: Pearson Education.

Brown, C.G., 2019. *The Battle for Christian Britain*. Cambridge: Cambridge University Press.

Brown, S., 2008. The Canadian Comeback Kid. *In: Fail Better in Stumbling to Success in Sales & Marketing, 25 Remarkable Renegades Show How*. London: Marshall Cavendish/Cyan.

Bruce, S., 1988. *The Rise and Fall of the New Christian Right: Conservative Protestant Politics in America 1978-1988*. Oxford: Clarendon Press.

Bruce, S., 1990. *Pray TV: Televangelism in America*. London: Routledge.

Bruce, S., 1995. *Religion in Modern Britain*. Oxford: Oxford University Press.

Bunyan, J., 1849. *The Pilgrim's Progress from This World to That Which is to Come*. London: William Pickering.

Butler, J., 1997. Studies of Religion in American Society: State of the Art. *In*: Stout, H. S. and Hart, D. G., *New Directions in American Religious History*. New York: Oxford University Press.

Butsch. R., 2000. *The Making of American Audiences: From Stage to Television 1750-1990*. Cambridge: Cambridge University Press.

Caine, B., 2010. *Biography and History*. Basingstoke: Palgrave Macmillan.

Calvet, L. J., 1990. *Roland Barthes 1915-1980*. Paris: Flammarion.

Camporesi, V., 2000. *Mass Culture and National Traditions: The BBC and American Broadcasting 1922-1954*. Fucecchio: European Press Academic Publishing.

Cantril, A.H and Allport, G. W., 1941. *The Psychology of Radio*. New York: Peter Smith.

Carlyle, T., 1841. *On Heroes, Hero Worship and the Heroic in History*. New York: Appleton & Co.

Carnell, E. J., 1950. *Television: Servant or Master?* Grand Rapids: W.B. Eerdmans.

Carpenter, J. A., 1985. *Tuning the Gospel Fundamentalist Radio Broadcast and the Revival of Mass Religion 1939-1945*. Urbana: University of Illinois.

Carpenter, J. A., 1997. *Revive Us Again: The Re-Awakening of American Fundamentalism*. New York: Oxford University Press.

Carpenter, R. H., 1998. *Father Charles E. Coughlin: Surrogate Spokesman for the Disaffected*. Westport: Greenwood Press.

Carter, M. D., 1971. *An Introduction to Mass Communications: Problems in Press and Broadcasting*. London: McMillan.

Casanova, J., 1994. *Public Religions in the Modern World*. Chicago: Chicago University Press.

Chase Jr. F., 1942. *Sound and Fury: An Informal History of Broadcasting*. New York: Harper Brothers.

Chignell, H., 2009. *Key Concepts in Radio Studies*. London: Sage.

Clark, D. L. and Virts, P.H., 1985. *Religious Television Audience: A New Development in Measuring Audience Size*. Savannah: The Society for the Scientific Study of Religion.

Clericus, 1942. *BBC Religion*. London: Watts & Co.

Conger, J. A. and Kanungo, R. N., 1998. *Charismatic Leadership in Organisations*. London: Sage.

Cook, F.S., 1982. *Seeds in the Wind: The Story of the Voice of the Andes, Radio Station HCJB*. Colorado: The World Radio Missionary Fellowship.

Coppens, T., Downey, J. and Pusateri, C.J., 2001. Great Britain and USA. *In*: Haenens, L. and Saeys, F., Western *Broadcasting at the Dawn of the 21st Century*. Berlin: Meuton de Gruyter.

Crisell, A., 2002. *An Introductory History of British Broadcasting*. 2nd edition. London: Routledge.

Curran, J., 1982. Communications, Power and Social Order. *In*: Gurevitch, M., *Culture, Society and Media*. London: Methuen.

Curran, J. and Seaton. J., 1991. *Power without Responsibility*. London: Routledge.

Curran, J., 2002. *Media and Power*. London: Routledge.

Curran, J., 2009. Narratives of Media History Revisited. *In*: Bailey, M., *Narrating Media History*. London: Routledge.

Currie, R., Gilbert, A. and Horsley, L., 1977. *Churches and Churchgoers: Patterns of Church Growth in the British Isles since 1700*. Oxford: Clarendon Press.

Czitrom, D. J., 1982. *Media and the American Mind: From Morse to McLuhan*. Chapel Hill: University of North Carolina Press.

D'Haenens, L. and Saeys, F., 2001. *Western Broadcasting at the Dawn of the 21st Century*. Berlin: Mouton de Gruter.

D'Souza, D., 1984. *Falwell before the Millennium: A Critical Biography*. Chicago: Regency Gateway.

Davie, G., 1994. *Religion in Britain since 1945: Believing Without Belonging*. Oxford: Blackwell.

Davie, G., 2015. *Religion in Britain: A Persistent Paradox*. 2nd edition. London: Blackwell.

Dinwiddie, M., 1968. *Religion by Radio: Its Place in British Broadcasting*. London: George Allen & Unwin Ltd.

Dirlik, A., 2012. Charismatic Leadership and the Contradiction of Socialist Revolution. *In:* ed. Stutje, J. W., *Charismatic Leadership and Social Movements*. New York: Berghahn Books.

Donavan, J. B., 1988. *Pat Robertson: The Authorized Biography*. New York: McMillan.

Donne, J., 1624. *Devotion upon Emergent Occasions. Meditation XV11*, Montana: Kessinger Publishing 2010.

Downton, J., 1973. *Rebel Leadership: Commitment and Charisma in the Revolutionary Process*. New York: Free Press.

Doyle, M., 1991. *The Future of Television: An Overview of Programming, Technology and Growth*. Los Angeles: NATPE International.

Drinker, F. E. and Lewis, J. J., 1922. *Radio: Miracle of the 20th Century*. Philadelphia: National Publishing Company.

Durkheim, E., 1912. *The Elementary Forms of Religious Life* (Trans. Cosman, C., 2001). Oxford: Oxford University Press.

Durkheim, E., 1950. *The Rules of Sociological Method: and Selected Texts on Sociology and its Methods*. Glencoe: Free Press.

Dyer, R., 1982. *Stars*. London: British Film Institute.

Dyer. R., 1987. *Heavenly Bodies: Film Stars and Society*. Basingstoke: MacMillan.

Eckersley, P. P., 1941. *The Power behind the Microphone*. London: Jonathan Cape.

Eckersley, R., 1946. *The BBC and All That*. London: Samson Law Marston & Co.

Eliot, M., 1981. *American Television: The Official Art of the Artificial*. New York: Anchor.

Ellens, J. H., 1974. *Models of Religious Broadcasting*. Grand Rapids: W. B. Eerdmans.

Elliott, W. H., 1951. *Undiscovered Ends*. London: Peter Davis.

Ellul, J., 1973. *Propaganda: The Formation of Men's Attitude*. New York: Vintage Books.

Elvy, P., 1986. *Buying Time: The Foundations of the Electronic Church*. Great Wakering: McCrimmons.

Elvy, P., 1990. *The Future of Christian Broadcasting in Europe*. Essex: McCrimmon.

Elvy, P., 1991. *Opportunities and Limitations in Religious Broadcasting*. Edinburgh: CTPI.

Emmanuel, D., 1999. *Challenges of Christian Communication and Broadcasting: Monologue or Dialogue?* Basingstoke: Macmillan.

Emerson, R. W., 1983. *Uses of Great Men in Essays & Lectures 1841*. New York: Literary Classics of the United States.

Engel, J. F., 1979. *A Pilot Research Study of Channel 38, WCFC, Chicago*. Wheaton: Wheaton College Graduate School.

Engleman, R., 1996. *Public Radio and Television in America*. London: Sage.

Erickson, H., 1992. *Religious Radio and Television in the United States 1921 – 1991: The Programs and Personalities*. Jefferson: McFarland & Co.

Everitt, A., 2003. *New Voices: An Update*. London: Radio Authority

Falconer, R., 1977. *Message, Media & Mission: The Baird Lectures*. Edinburgh: St Andrews Press.

Falwell, J., 1987. *Strength for the Journey: An Autobiography*. New York: Simon & Schuster.

Falwell, J., 1997. *Jerry Falwell: An Autobiography*. Lynchburg: Liberty House Publishers.

Falwell, M., 2008. *Jerry Falwell: His Life and Legacy*. New York: Howard Books

Ferre, J. P., 1990. *Channels of Belief: Religion and American Commercial Television*. Ames: Iowa State University Press.

Field, C., 2017. *Secularization in the Long 1960s*. Oxford: Oxford University Press.

Finstuen, A., Wacker, G. and Wills, A. B., 2017. *Billy Graham: American Pilgrim*. New York: Oxford University Press.

Fishwick, M. and Brown, R. B., 1987. *The God Pumpers: Religion in the Electronic Age*. Ohio: Bowling Green Press.

Fore, W. F., 1987. *Television and Religion: the shaping of faith, values, and culture*. Minneapolis: Augsburg Publishing.

Fortner, R. S., 2005. *Radio, Morality and Culture*. Illinois: Southern Illinois University Press.

Fotherby, V., 2000. *The Awakening Giant: The Miraculous Story of the Full Gospel Business Men's Fellowship International*. London: Marshall Pickering.

Foulkes, W. H., 1937. *Radio Evangelism in The Message and Method of the New Evangelism*, edit Bader, J. M., New York: Round Table Press.

Frankl, R., 1987. *Televangelism*. Carbondale: Southern Illinois University Press.

Freed, P., 1968. *Towers to Eternity*. Waco: Word.

Gabor, G. and De Vriese, H., 2009. *Rethinking Secularisation and the Prophecy of a Secular Age*. Newcastle Upon Tyne: Cambridge Scholars Publishing

Gallup, G. Jr., 1982. *Religion in America*. Princeton: Princeton University.

Geertz, C., 1973. *The Interpretation of Culture*. New York: Basic Books.

Gentili,B. and Cerri,G., 1988. *History and Biography in Ancient Thought*. Amsterdam: J.C.Gieben.

Georgianna, S. L., 1989. *The Moral Majority and Fundamentalism: Plausibility and Dissonance*. New York: Mellen Press.

Gilbert, A. D., 1980. *The Making of a Post-Christian Britain*. London: Longman.

Ginsburg, C. and Poni.C., 1991. *Microhistory and the Lost Peoples of Europe*. Baltimore: John Hopkins University Press.

Goodman Jr., W. R. and Price, J. J. H., 1981. *Jerry Falwell: An Unauthorized Profile*. Lynchburg: Paris & Associates.

Gorham, M. A. C., 1948. *Sound and Fury: 21 Years in the BBC*. London: Percival Marshall.

Graham, B., 1997. *Just as I am: The Autobiography of Billy Graham*. London: Harper Collins.

Green, S. J. D., 2011. *The Passing of Protestant England: Secularization and Social Change 1920-1960*. Cambridge: Cambridge University Press.

Grisewood, H., 1956. *Christian Communication – Word and Image*. Geneva: World Council of Churches.

Gunter, B. and Viney, R., 1994. *Seeing is Believing: Religion and Television in the 1990s*. London: John Libbey.

Hadden, J.K. and Shupe, A., 1988 *Televangelism: Power and Politics on God's Frontier*. New York: Henry Holt.

Hadden, J. K. and Swann, C. E., 1981. *Prime Time Preachers: The Rising Power of Televangelism*. Reading: Addison Wesley Publishing.

Haley, W., 1948. *Moral Values in Broadcasting*. London: British Council of Churches.

Haldane, I., 1978. *Who and what is Religious Broadcasting for?* London: Independent Broadcasting Authority.

Halloran, J.D., 1975. *Communication and Community*, Strasbourg: Council of Europe

Hangen, T. J., 2002. *Redeeming the Dial: Radio Religion and Popular Culture in America*. Chapel Hill: University of North Carolina Press.

Harding, S. F., 2000. *The Book of Jerry Falwell: Fundamentalist Language and Politics*. Princeton: Princeton University Press.

Harmes, B., Harmes, M.K. and Harmes, M., 2020. *The Church on British Television: From* the *Coronation to Coronation Street*. London: Palgrave Macmillan.

Harrell Jr. D. E., 1985. *Oral Roberts: An American Life*. Bloomington: Indiana University Press.

Harrell Jr. D. E., 2010. *Pat Robertson: A Life and Legacy*. Grand Rapids: Eerdmans.

Harrison, H. and Dudley, C., 1979. *Second Fiddle*. Green Forest: New Leaf Press.

Hatch, N. O., 1989. *The Democratisation of American Christianity*. New Haven: Yale University Press.

Hendy, D., 2000. *Radio in a Global Age*. Cambridge: Polity Press.

Hendy, D., 2007. *Life on Air: A History of Radio Four*. Oxford: Oxford University Press.

Hendy, D., 2013. *Public Service Broadcasting*. Basingstoke: Palgrave Macmillan.

Henry, S. and Joel, M. V., 1984. *Pirate Radio: Then and Now*. Poole: Blandford Press.

Herberg, W., 1955. *Protestant, Catholic and Jew*. New Jersey: Doubleday.

Higgins, C., 2015. *This New Noise*. London: Guardian Books.

Hill, D. G. H., 1983. *Airways to the Soul: The Influence and Growth of Religious Broadcasting in America*. Saratoga: R & E Publishers.

Hill, D. G. H. and Davis, L., 1984. *Religious Broadcasting: A Selected Annotated Bibliography*. New York: Garland Publishers.

Hilmes, M., 2012. *Network Nations: A Transnational History of British and American Broadcasting*. New York: Routledge.

Hoover, S. M., 1982. *The Electronic Giant: A Critique of the Telecommunications Revolution from a Christian Perspective*. Elgin: The Brethren Press.

Hoover, S. M., 1988. *Mass Media Religion: The Social Sources of the Electronic Church*. Newbury Park: Sage.

Hoover, S. M., 2003. Religion Media and Identity: Theory and Method in Audience Research on Religion and Media. *In*: Mitchell J. and Marriage, S., *Mediating Religion: Conversations in Media Religion and Culture*. London: T & T Clark.

Hoover, S. M., 2006. Media. *In*: Ebaugh H.R., *Handbook of Religion and Social Institutions*. London: Springer.

Horkheimer, M. and Adorno, T. W., 1944. *The Culture Industry: Enlightenment as Mass Deception*. New York: Social Studies Association.

Horsfield, P. G., 1984. *Religious Television: the American Experience*. New York: Longmans.

Horsfield, P.G., 2015. *From Jesus to the Internet: A History of Christianity and Media*. London: Blackwell.

House, F., 1949. *The Church on the Air: The Work of the Religious Broadcasting Department*. London: BBC.

House, F., 1950. *Religious Programmes on Television*. London: BBC.

House, R. J., 1977. A 1976 Theory of Charismatic Leadership. In: Hunt, J. G. and Larson, L. L., *Leadership: The Cutting Edge*. Carbondale: Southern Illinois University Press.

Hovland, C. I., Lumsdaine, A. and Sheffield, F.D., 1949. *Experiments in Mass Communication*. New Jersey: Princeton University Press.

Howe, D. W., 2007. *What God Hath Wrought: The Transformation of America 1815-1848*. New York: Oxford University Press.

Howell, J. M., 1988. Two Faces of Charisma: Socialized and Personalized Leadership in Organisations. *In*: J. A, Conger and R. N. Kanungo., *Charismatic Leadership: The Elusive Factor in Organisational Effectiveness*. San Franscisco: Jossey-Bass.

Humbard, R., 1975. *To Tell the World*. Englewood Cliffs: Prentice Hall.

Hunt, S., 2011. Transformations in British Religious Broadcasting. *In*: Bailey, M. and Redden, G., *Mediating Faiths and Religion and Socio-Cultural Change in Twenty-First Century*. Burlington: Ashgate.

Hutch, R. A., 1990. *Religious Leadership: Personality History and Sacred Authority*. New York: Peter Lang.

Hutchinson, J. A., 1941. *We Are Not Divided: A Critical Historical Study of the Federal Council of the Churches of Christ in America*. New York: Round Table Press.

Independent Broadcasting Authority, 1976. *Television and Radio Handbook*. London: IBA.

Independent Broadcasting Authority, 1977. *Television and Radio Handbook*. London: IBA.

Independent Broadcasting Authority, 1984. *Religious Broadcasting Policy on Independent Television and Independent Local Radio*. London: IBA.

Independent Television Authority, 1962. *Religious Programmes on Independent Television*. London: ITA.

Independent Television Authority, 1964. *Religion in Television*. London: ITA.

Independent Television Authority, 1970. *Religion in Britain and Northern Ireland*. London: ITA.

Independent Television Authority, 1970/71. *Annual Report & Accounts*. London. HMSO

Inglis, F., 2010. *A Short History of Celebrity*. Princeton: Princeton University Press.

Jacobsen, D. G., 2011. *The World Christians: Who They Are, Where They Are and How They Got There*. Malden: Wiley Blackwell.

Jacobs,E. and Worcester,R., 1990. *We British: Britain Under the MORIscope*. London: Weidenfeld and Nicholson.

James, H., 1993. *Smile Pretty and Say Jesus: The Last Great Days of PTL*. Athens: University of Georgia Press.

Jorstad, E., 1993. *Popular Religion in America: The Evangelical Voice*. Westport: Greenwood Press.

Kaam, V., 1968. *Religion and Personality*. New York: Mage Books.

Kamms, A. and Baird,M., 2002. *John Logie Baird – A Life*. Edinburgh: National Museum of Scotland Publishing.

Kets De Vries, M., 1995. *Life and Death in the Executive Fast Lane*. San Francisco: Jossey-Buss.

Klapper, J. T., 1966. *The Effects of Mass Communication*. New York: The Free Press.

Knight, M., 1955. *Morals without Religion*. London: Dennis Dobson Ltd.

Knott, K., 1982. *Media Portrayals of Religion and their Reception*. Leeds: Leeds University.

Knott, K., Poole, E. and Taira, T., 2013. *Media Portrayals of Religion and the Secular Sacred: Representation and Chance*. Farnham: Ashgate Publishing.

Lacey, D. M., 1961. *Freedom and Communication 1914-2001*. Urbana: University of Illinois.

Lasswell, H. D., 1948. The Structure and Function of Communication in Society. *In*: ed. Bryson. L., *The Communication of Ideas*. New York: Harper & Brothers.

Lazarsfeld, P. F., 1940. *Radio and the Printed Page*. New York: Duell Sloan & Pearce.

Leishman, M., 2006. *My Father: Reith of the BBC*. London: BBC.

Leonard, M., 2004. *The Story behind the 60's 'Pirate Radio Stations'*. Heswall: Forest Press.

Lewin, K. and Lewin, G. W., 1948. *Resolving Social Conflicts: Selected Papers on Group Dynamics*. New York. Harper & Brothers.

Lewis, C.A., 1924. *Broadcasting From Within*. London: George Newnes

Lichty, L. W. and Topping, M.C., 1975. *American Broadcasting*. New York: Hastings House.

Linder,E.W., 2007. *Yearbook of American and Canadian Churches*. Nasville. Abingdon Press.

Lipset,S.M. and Raab,E., 1978. *The Policies of Unreason: Right-wing Extremism in America, 1790-1977*. Chicago: University of Chicago Press.

Lischer,R., 1987. *Theories of Preaching*. Durham: Labyrinth Press

Llobera. J., 1998. Historical Comparative Research. *In*: Searle, C., *Researching Culture and Society*. London: Sage.

Lochte, B., 2005. *Christian Radio: The Growth of a Mainstream Broadcasting Force*. Jefferson: McFarland & Co.

Lorimer, R., 1994. *Mass Communications: A Comparative Introduction*. Manchester: Manchester University.

Loveless, W. P., 1946. *Manual of Gospel Broadcasting*. Illinois: Moody Press.

Lowery, S. and De Fleur, M.L., 1983. *Milestones in Mass Communication Research*. New York: Longman.

Luccock, H. E., 1951. *The Best of Dick Sheppard*. New York: Harper Brothers.

Luckman, T., 1967. *The Invisible Religion: The Problem of Religion in Modern Society*. New York: Macmillan.

MacMillan, M., 2015. *History's People: Personalities and the Past*. London: Profile Books.

Madge,T.S. and Pusateri, C. J., 1988. Great Britain and USA. *In*: Rosen, P.T., *International Handbook of Broadcasting Systems*. New York: Greenwood Press.

Magil, A. B., 1939. *The Real Father Coughlin*. New York: Workers Library Publishers.

Maier, P. L., 1963. *A Man Spoke, A World Listened*. New York: MaGraw-Hill.

Marcus, S., 1973. *Father Coughlin: The Tumultuous Life of the Priest of the Little Flower*. Boston: Little Brown.

Marley, D. J., 2007. *Pat Robertson: An American Life*. Lanham: Rowman & Littlefield.

Marsden, L. and Savigny, H., 2009. *Media Religion and Conflict*. Farnham: Ashgate.

Marshall, H., 1938. *Dick Sheppard by His Friends*. London: Hodder & Stoughton.

Marshall, P. D., 1997. *Celebrity and Power*. Minneapolis: University of Minnesota Press.

Marshall, P. D., 2006. *The Celebrity Culture Reader*. New York: Routledge.

Martin, W., 1987. *Perennial Problems of Prime-Time Preachers*. Waco. Baylor University.

Martin, W., 2018. *A Prophet with Honour: The Billy Graham Story*. Grand Rapids: Zondervan.

Marx, K. E. F., 1972. *The German Ideology*. New York: International Publishers.

Massingberd, H., 1997. *The Daily Telegraph: Third Book of Obituaries: The Entertainers*. London: Macmillan.

Matelski, M. J., 1995. *Vatican Radio: Propagation by the Airways*. Westport: Praegar.

Matheson, H., 1933. *Broadcasting*. London: Thorton Butterworth Ltd.

Max-Wilson, P., 1976. *Stars on Sunday*. Pinner: Pentagon.

McCavitt, W. E., 1981. *Broadcasting Around the World*. Blue Ridge Summit: Tab Books.

McDonnell, J., 1991. *Public Service Broadcasting*. London: Routledge.

McDonnell, J., 1993. Religious Education and the Communication of Values. *In:* Arthur, C., *Religion and Media: An Introductory Reader.* Cardiff: University of Wales Press.

McDonnell. J., 2009. From Certainty to Diversity: The Evolution of Religious Broadcasting Since 1990. *In:* Geybels, H., Mels, S. and Walrave, M., *Faith & Media: Analysis of Faith and Media.* Brussels: P. I. E. Peter Lang.

McKay, R. 1956. *Aims of Religious Broadcasting.* London. St. Paul's Lecture Society.

McIntyre, I., 1993. *The Expense of Glory: A Life of John Reith.* London: Harper Collins.

McKibbin, R., 1989. *Classes and Cultures.* Oxford: Oxford University Press.

McLeod, H., 2007. *The Religious Crisis in the 1960s.* Oxford: Oxford University Press.

McLoughlin, W. G., 1960. *Billy Graham: Revivalist in a Secular Age.* New York: Ronald Press.

McLuhan, M., 1962. *The Gutenberg Galaxy: The Making of Typographic Man.* Toronto: University of Toronto Press.

McLuhan, M., 1992. *Understanding Media.* New York: Mentor.

McPherson, A. S., 1923. *Spreading the Word.* Los Angeles: Foursquare Publications.

McPherson, A. S., 1996. *This is That.* Los Angeles: Foursquare Publications.

McQuail, D., 1992. *Media Performance.* London: Sage.

McQuail, D., 2010. *McQuail's Mass Communication Theory*. 6th edition. London: Sage Publications Ltd.

Melton, J. G., Lucas, P. C. and Stone, J. R., 1997. *Prime Time Religion: An Encyclopaedia of Religious Broadcasting*. Phoenix: Oryx Press.

Messner, T. F., 1996. *Telling it My Way*. New York: Villard.

Milner, R., 1963. *Reith: The BBC Years*. Edinburgh: Mainstream Publishing.

Morris, C., 1984. *God-in-a-Box: Christian strategy in the Television Age*. London: Hodder & Stoughton.

Morris, C., 1990. *Wrestling with an Angel*. London. Collins Fount

Morris, J., 1973. *The Preachers*. New York: St. Martin's Press.

Mosco, V., 1978. *Broadcasting in the United States*. New Jersey: Ablex Publications.

Muggeridge, M., 1977. *Christ and the Media*. London: Hodder and Stoughton.

Murch, J. D. F., 1956. *Co-operation without Compromise: A History of the National Association of Evangelicals*. Grand Rapids: Eerdmans.

Mytton, G., 1999. *Handbook on Radio and Television Research*. London: BBC.

National Broadcasting Company, 1939. *Broadcasting in the Public Interest*. New York: NBC.

Neuendorf, K. A., 1990. *The Public Trust versus the Almighty Dollar in Religious Television: Controversies and Conclusions*. Norwood: Ablex Publishing.

Nicholas, S., 2006. *BBC Listener Research Department 1937-1950*. East Ardesley: Microform Academic Publishers.

Northcott, R. J., 1937. *Dick Sheppard and St. Martin's*. London: Longmans Green & Co.

Novarr, D., 1986. *The Lines of Life: Theories of Biography 1880-1970*. West Lafayette: Purdue University Press.

Oberdorfer, D. N., 1982. *Electronic Christianity: Myth or Ministry*. Taylor Falls: John L. Brekk & Sons.

Parker, E. C., Barry, D. W. and Smythe, D.W., 1955. *The Television/Radio Audience and Religion*. New York: Harper Brothers Publishers.

Paulu, B., 1981. *Television and Radio in the United Kingdom*. London: MacMillan.

Paxton, W., 1938. *Dick Sheppard: An Apostle of Brotherhood*. London: Chapman & Hall.

Peck, J., 1993. *The Gods of Televangelism: The Crisis of Meaning and the Appeal of Religious Television*. New Jersey: Hampton Press.

Perman, D., 1977. *Change and the Churches: An Anatomy of Religion in Britain*. London: Bodley Head.

Pierard, R.V. and Lewis, D.M., 2014. *Global Evangelicalism: Theology, History and Culture in Regional Perspective*. London: IVP.

Pollock, J., 1985. *The Billy Graham Story*. Grand Rapids: Zondervan.

Poloma, M., 1989. *The Assemblies of God at the Crossroads*. Knoxville: University of Tennessee Press.

Postman, N., 1985. *Amusing Ourselves to Death*. London: Methuen.

Pugh, P., 2017. *Headline Britons*. London: Icon Books.

Pusateri, C.J. 1988. *A History of American Business*. Illinois. Harlan Davidson

Quicke, A., 1976. *Tomorrow's Television*. Berkhamstead: Lion Publishing.

Quicke, A. and Quicke, J., 1992. *Hidden Agendas: The Politics of Religious Broadcasting in Britain 1987 – 1991*. Virginia Beach: Dominion Kings Grant Publications.

Rees, C. H. M. and Colbert, M., 1980. *Audience Reaction to Communion Programme*. London: Independent Broadcasting Authority.

Reith, J. C. W., 1924. *Broadcast over Britain*. London: Hodder and Stoughton.

Reith, J. C. W., 1949. *Into the Wind*. London: Hodder & Stoughton.

Renders, H. and Haan, B., 2014. *Theoretical Discussions of Biography: Approaches from History, Micro history and Life Writing*. Leiden: Brill.

Reville, N., 1991. *Broadcasting – The New Law*. London: Butterworths.

Roberts, O., 1972. *The Call: An Autobiography*. New York: Doubleday.

Roberts, P. I., 1924. *Radio Preaching: Far-Flung Sermons by Pioneers of Broadcasting*. New York: Fleming H. Revell Company.

Roberts, R., 1985. *He's the God of the Second Chance*. Tulsa: Oral Roberts Evangelistic Association.

Roberts, R. E., 1942. *H. R. L. Sheppard*. London: John Murray.

Robertson, E. H., 1956. *The Church on the Air: Some Thoughts on Religious Broadcasting*. London: Carey Kingsgate Press.

Robertson, P., 1972. *Shout It From the Housetops*. New Jersey: Logos International.

Robertson, P., 1991. *The New World Order*. Dallas: Word Publishing.

Rojek, C., 2001. *Celebrity*. London: Reaktion Books.

Rollyson, C., 1992. *Biography: An Annotated Bibliography*. Chicago: Pasadena & Englewood Cliffs.

Rosen, P. T., 1988. *International Handbook of Broadcasting Systems*. Westport: Greenwood Press.

Rosenthal, M., 2007. *Protestants and TV in the 1950s: Responses to a New Medium*. New York: Macmillan.

Scannell, P. and Cardiff, D., 1991. *A Social History of Broadcasting Vol.1. 1922-1939*. Oxford: Basil Blackwell.

Schneider, H. W., 1952. *Religion in 20th Century America*. Cambridge: Harvard University Press.

Schramm, W., 1975. *Mass Communications*. 2nd edition. Illinois: University of Illinois.

Schubert, P., 1928. *The Electric Word: The Rise of Radio*. New York: Macmillan.

Schuller, R., 2001. *My Journey: From an Iowa Farm to a Cathedral of Dreams*. New York: Harper.

Schultze, Q. J., 1990. *American Evangelicals and the Mass Media*. Grand Rapids: Academic Books.

Schultze, Q. J., 1990. Defining the Electronic Church. *In:* Abelman, R. and Hoover, S. M., *Religious Television: Controversies and Conclusions*. Norwood: Ablex Publishing.

Schultze, Q. J., 1991. *Televangelism and American Culture: The Business of Popular Religion*. Grand Rapids: Baker Book House.

Scott, C., 1977. *Dick Sheppard*. London: Hodder & Stoughton.

Seaman, A. R., 1999. *Swaggart: The Unauthorized Biography of an American Evangelist*. New York: Continuum.

Seaton, J., 2004. Writing the History of Broadcasting. *In:* ed. D.Cannadine., *History and the Media*. London: Palgrave Macmillan.

Seaton, J., 2015. *'Pinkoes and Traitors': the BBC and the Nation, 1974-1987*. Revised edition. London: Profile.

Secombe, H., 1985. *Harry Secombe's Highway*. London: Robson Books.

Sendall, B. C., 1982. *Independent Television in Britain*. Vol.1. London: Macmillan.

Seymour-Ure, C., 1996. *The British Press and Broadcasting since 1945*. Oxford: Blackwell.

Shepard, C. E., 1989. *Forgiven: The Rise and Fall of Jim Bakker and the PTL Ministry*. New York: Atlantic Monthly Press.

Sheppard, H. R. L., 1927. *The Impatience of a Parson*. London: Hodder and Stoughton.

Sheppard, H. R. L., 1932. *Sermon. St. Martin-in-the-Fields Calling*. London: Athenaeum Press.

Shurick, E. P. J., 1946. *The First Quarter of American Broadcasting*. Kansas City: Midland Publishing.

Siepmann, C. A., 1950. *Radio, Television and Society*. New York: Oxford University Press.

Smith, A., 1974. *British Broadcasting*. Newton Abbott: David & Charles Ltd.

Smith, J., 1995. *Understanding the Media: A Sociology of Mass Communications*. New York: Hampton Press.

Smyth, C., 1959. *Cyril Forster Garbett*. London: Hodder and Stoughton.

Sorenson, S., 2014. *The Collar: Reading Christian Ministry in Fiction, Television and Film*. Eugene: Cascade Books.

Southern Baptists, 1947. *Annual of the Southern Baptist Convention*. Nashville: Southern Baptist Convention.

Spencer, H., 1898. *The Principles of Sociology*. New York: D. Appleton.

Standford, M., 1998. *An Introduction to the Philosophy of History*. Oxford: Blackwell.

Stark, W., 1970. *The Sociology of Religion*. New York: Fordham University Press.

Sterling, C. H. and Kittross, J. M., 2002. *Stay Tuned: A Concise history of American Broadcasting*. 3rd edition. New Jersey: Edward Arnold.

Stoller, T., 2010. *Sounds of Your Life: The History of Independent Radio in the UK*. New Barnet: John Libbey Publishing Ltd.

Straub, G. T., 1986. *Salvation for Sale: An Insiders View of Pat Robertson*. Buffulo: Prometheus Books.

Street, S., 2002. *A Concise History of British Radio 1922-2002*. Tiveton: Kelly Publications.

Street, S., 2006. *Crossing the Ether: Public Service Radio and Commercial Competition*. Eastleigh: John Libbey.

Street, S., 2015. *Historical Dictionary of British Radio*. Plymouth: Rowman & Littlefield.

Stringfellow, W., 1982. *A Simplicity of Faith*. Nashville: Abingdon.

Stutje, J. W., 2012. *Charismatic Leadership and Social Movements: The Revolutionary Power of Ordinary Men and Women*. New York: Berghahn Books.

Suman, M., 1997. *Religion and Prime Time Television*. Westport: Praeger Publishers.

Sutton, M. A., 2007. *Aimee Semple McPherson and the Resurrection of Christian America*. Cambridge Mass.: Harvard University Press.

Svennevig, M., Haldane. I., Spreis, S. and Gunter, B., 1988. *Godwatching: Viewers, Religion and Television*. London: John Libbey.

Swatos, W. H. Jr., 1998. *Encyclopaedia of Religion and Society*. Walnut Creek: Altamira Press.

Tayer, L., 1988. Mass Media and Mass Communication: Notes Towards a Theory. *In*: Budd, R. W. and Rubens, B. D., *Beyond Media: New Approaches to Mass Communication*. New Brunswick: Transaction Books.

Temple, W. E., 1941. *Citizen and Churchman*. London: Eyre and Spottiswood.

Tidewell, G. L., 1993. *Anatomy of a Fraud: Inside the Finances of the PTL Ministries*. New York: John Wiley & Sons.

Tribe, D., 1967. *The Scandal of Religious Broadcasting*. National Secular Society. London.

Tulga, C. E., 1951. *The Case Against the National Council of Churches*. Chicago: Conservative Baptist Association of America.

Tunstall, J., 1983. *The Media in Britain*. London: Constable.

Turow, J., 1992. *Media Systems in Society*. London. Longmans

Tyson, J. N., 1990. *Paradigms of Religious Expression: An Analysis of Religious Broadcasting*. Austin: University of Texas.

Van Der Geest, H., 1981. *Presence in the Pulpit: The Impact of Personality in the Preaching*. Atlanta: John Knox Press.

Van Doren, C., 1915. *Biography as a Literary Form*. New York: Columbia University Press.

Vanderlaan, E. C., 1925. *Fundamentalism versus Modernism*. New York: H.W.Wilson and Co.

Voskuil, D. N., 1990. The Power of the Air: Evangelicals and the Rise of Religious Broadcasting. *In*: Schultze, Q. J., *American Evangelicals and the Mass Media*. Grand Rapids: Academic Books.

Voskull, D., 1983. *Mountains into Goldmines*. Grand Rapids: Eerdmans.

Wacker, G., 2014. *America's Pastor: Billy Graham the Shaping of a Nation*. Cambridge: Belknap Press.

Wallis, R., 2020. Genesis of the Bible Documentary: the Development of Religious Broadcasting in the UK. *In*: Bond, H. K. and Adams, E., *The Bible on Television*. London: T & T Clark 2020.

Ward, K., 1989. *Mass Communications in the Modern World*. London: Macmillan.

Ward, L. B., 1933. *Father Charles E. Coughlin*. Detroit: Tower Publications.

Ward, S. M., 1994. *Air of Salvation: The Story of Christian Broadcasting*. Grand Rapids: Baker Books.

Warren, D., 1996. *Radio Priest: Charles Coughlin the Father of Hate Radio*. New York The Free Press.

Weber, M. K. E., 1915. *The Theory of Social & Economic Organisations.* Trans. Parsons, T., 1947. New York: Free Press.

Welman, B., 1971. *Stars on Sunday.* London: Independent Television Authority.

White, R., 1988. *Falwell Gives Evangelicals a Pep Talk.* Orlando Sentinel.

Wigger, J. H., 2017. *PTL: The Rise and Fall of Jim and Tammy Faye Bakker's Evangelical Empire.* New York: Oxford University Press.

Williams, R., 1974. *Television: Technology and Cultural Form.* New York: Schocken Books.

Williamson, M., 2016. *Celebrity: Capitalism and the Making of Fame.* Cambridge: Polity.

Willner, A. R., 1984. *The Spellbinders: Charismatic Political Leadership.* New Haven: Yale University Press.

Winter, D., 2001. *A Winters Tale: Living Through an Age of Change in Church and Media.* Oxford: Lion Books.

Winters, M. S., 2012. *God Right Hand: How Jerry Falwell made God a Republican and Baptized the American Right.* New York: Harper One.

Wolfe, J., 1994. *God and Great Britain: Religion and National Life in Britain and Ireland 1843-1945.* London: Routledge.

Wolfe, K. M., 1984. *The Churches and the British Broadcasting Corporation 1922-1956. The Politics of Broadcast Religion.* London: SCM.

Wolfe. K. M., 1983. *Religious Broadcasting Now: British Religious Broadcasting in Perspective.* London. IBA.

Wolff, R., 2010. *The Church on TV: Portrayals of Priests, Pastors and Nuns on American Television Series.* New York: Continuum.

Woodhead, L. and Catto,R., 2012. *Religion and Change in Modern Britain*. London: Routledge.

Yin, R. K., 2014. *Case Study Research Design and Methods*. 5th edition. Thousand Oaks: Sage.

Young, P. D., 1982. *God's Bullies: Native Reflections on Preachers and Politics*. New York: Holt, Rineheart and Winston.

JOURNAL ARTICLES

Abelman, R. I., 1987. Why Do People Watch Religious TV? A Uses and Gratification Approach. *Review of Religious Research*, 29 (I2), 199-210.

Athans, M. C., 1987. A New Perspective on Father Charles E. Coughlin. *Church History*, 56 (2), 224-235.

Athans,M.C., 1998. Radio Priest Charles Coughlin. The Father of Hate Radio. *Catholic Historical Review*, 84 (3), 589-590.

Bailey, M., 2007. He Who Has Ears to Hear: Christian Pedagogy and Religious Broadcasting during the Inter-War Period. *Westminster Papers in Communication and Culture*, 4 (1), 4-25.

Balbi, G., 2011. Doing Media History. *Westminster Papers in Communication and Culture*, 8 (2), p.154-177.

Barnes, D. F., 1978. Charisma and Religious Leadership: An Historical Analysis. *Journal for the Scientific Study of Religion*, 17 (1), 1-18.

Berelson, B., 1958. The Present State of Communication Research. *Public Opinion Quarterly*, 22 (2), 178.

Bering-Jenson,H., 1993. Sister Aimee: The Life of Aimee Semple McPherson. *Insight on the News*, 9 (14), p.22

Bookbinder, A., 2003. Religious Broadcasting: Challenge to the Churches. *Epworth Review*, 30 (4), 7-13.

Boston, R., 2006. The End of the Line for Pat Robertson. *Humanist*, 66 (3), 37-38.

Bourgault, L. M., 1985. The Electric Church: The PTL Club. *Journal of Religious Studies*, 12, 76-95.

Bourgault, L. M., 1985. The PTL Club and Protestant Viewers: An Ethnographic Study. *Journal of Communication*, 35 (1), 132-148.

Brooke, C., 1985. What is Religious History? *History Today*, 36 (8), 43.

Brown, C. G., 2010. What was the Religious Crisis of the 1960s? *Journal of Religious History*, 34 (4), 468-479.

Brown, G., 1990. Jerry Falwell and the PTL: The Rhetoric of Apologia. *The Journal of Communications and Religion*, 14 (1), 9-19.

Bruce, S., 1994. The Inevitable Failure of the Christian Right. *Sociology of Religion*, 55 (3) 229-242.

Bruce, S. and Glendinning,T., 2010. When was Secularization? *British Journal of Sociology*, 61 (1), 107-126.

Burns, T. 2005. The Rationalism of Father Brown. *Perspectives on Political Science* 34(1), 42.

Caldwell, L.G., 1927. The Standard of Public Interest: Convenience or Necessity as Used in the Radio Act of 1927. *Air Law Review*, 10-11.

Campbell, D., 2008. The Legacy of Billy Graham. *Theology in Scotland*, 15 (2), p.75-79.

Camporesi, V., 1994. The BBC and American Broadcasting 1922-1955. *Media Culture & Society*, 16 (4), 625-639.

Cawthon, D.L., 1996. Leadership: The Great Man Theory Revisited. *Business Horizons*, 39 (2), 1-4.

Chester. G., 1949. How good is British Radio? *Quarterly Journal of Speech*, 35 (3), 320.

Clark, S.H., 2005. Created in Whose Image? Religious Characters on Network Television. *Journal of Media and Religion*, 4, 137-153.

Coleman, L. E. J., 1970. Christian Communication in the 1970s. *Review and Expositor: An International Baptist Journal*, 67 (1), 65-75.

Compuresi, V., 1994. The BBC and American Broadcasting 1922-55. *Media Culture and Society*, 16 (4), 625.

Conger, J. A., Kanungo, R.N., Menon, S.T. and Mathur, P., 1997. Measuring Charisma: Dimensionality and validity of the Conger-Kanungo scale of charismatic leadership. *Canadian Journal of Administrative Sciences*, 14 (3), 290-302.

Cooper, M., and Macaulay, M., 2015. Contemporary Christian Radio in Britain: A New Genre on the National Dial. *The Radio Journal – International Studies in Broadcast and Audio Media*, 13 (1/2), 75-87.

Crome, A., 2020. "Wonderful", "Hot", "Good" Priests. Clergy on Contemporary British TV and the New Visibility of Religion Thesis. *Religions*, 11(1), 1-15.

D'Antonio, M., 1998. Aimee Semple McPherson. *Biography*, 2 (9), 5-87.

Dickenson, S. H., 1983. Characterising the Message of the Electric Church. *Florida Communication Journal*, 11 (1), 16-26.

Dickson, G., 2012. Charisma: Medieval and Modern. *Religions*, 3 (3), 763-789.

Editor, 1977. Religious Affiliation. *Social Trends*, 8, 26-27.

Editor, 1975. Religious Broadcasting a Protected Area. Commission of the Roman Catholic Episcopal Conference: *The Furrow*, 26 (9), 572.

Edwards, N., 1974. Secularisation and Modernisation. *Journal of Popular Culture*, 8 (2),37

Field, C., 2013. Gradualism or Revolutionary Secularization: A Case Study of Religious Belonging in Inter-War Britain 1918-1939. *Church History and Religious Culture*, 93 (1), 92-93.

Fisher, H. A. L., 1908. A Sociological View of History. *The Sociological Review*, 1 (1), 61-77.

Fisher, R. and Tamarkin, S., 2011. Right Wing Organisations Do This Too: The Case of the Christian Coalition. *Journal of Community Practice*, 19 (4), 407.

Flake, C., 1982. The Electric Kingdom. *New Republic*, 186 (20), p.20-21.

Fore, W. F., 1988. Media, Religion and the Church's Task. *A Journal of Scholarly Reflection for Ministry*, 9 (4), 7-8.

Fore, W. F., 2007. The Unknown History of Televangelism. *Journal of the World Association of Christian Communication*, 54 (1), 45-48.

Frankl, R., and Hadden, J.K., 1987. A Critical Review of the Religion and Television Research Report. *Review of Religious Research*, 29 (2), 111-124.

Fritz, D. A., and Ibrahim, N. A., 2010. The Impact of Leadership Longevity in Innovation in a Religious Organisation. *Journal of Business Ethics*, 96 (2), 223-231.

Fuchs, O., 1993. How the Church deals with the Media. *Concilium*, 6, 80-90.

Gaddy, G. D., 1984. The Power of the Religious Media: Religious Broadcast Use and the Role of Religious Organisations in Public Affairs. *Review of Religious Research*, 25 (4), 289-302.

Gaddy, G.D. and Pritchard, D., 1985. When Watching Religious TV is Like Attending Church. *Journal of Communications*, 35, 123-131.

Garner, K., 2003. On Defining the Field. *The Radio Journal: International Studies in Broadcast and Audio Media*, 1 (1), 26-28.

Gentry, R. H., 1984. Broadcast Religion: When Does its Raise Fairness Doctrine Issues? *Journal of Broadcasting*, 28 (3), 259-270.

Gilgoff, D., 2007. The Preacher Who Put God into Politics. *US News and World Report*, 142 (19), 16-17.

Green, J. C., 1993. Pat Robertson and the Latest Crusade: Religious Resources and the 1988 Presidential Campaign. *Social Science Quarterly*, 74 (1), 157-168.

Hadaway, C. K., and Marler, P. L., 2005. How Many Americans Attend Worship Each Week: An Alternative Approach to Measurement. *Journal for the Scientific Study of Religion*, 44 (3), 307-322.

Hadden, J. K., 1987. Religious Broadcasting and the Mobilization of the New Christian Right. *Journal for the Scientific Study of Religion*, 26 (1), 1-24.

Harris, A., and Spence, M., 2007. Disturbing the Complacency of Religion. The Evangelical Crusades of Dr.Billy Graham and Father Patrick Peyton in Britain 1951-54. *Twentieth Century British History*, 8 (4), 481-513.

Harrison, H., Birks, M., Franklin, R., and Mills. J., 2017. Case Study Research: Foundations and Methodological Orientations. *Forum: Qualitative Social Research*, 18 (1), 1-17.

Harrison, J., 2000. A Review of Religious Broadcasting on British Television. *Modern Believing*, 41 (4) 3-15.

Haley, W., 1976. John Reith: A Man for One Season. *American Scholar*, 45 (4), 560-564

Hendy, D., 2012. Biography and the Emotions as the Missing 'Narrative' in Media History. *Media History*, 18 (3-4), 361-378.

Heyck, T. W., 1996. The Decline of Christianity in the Twentieth Century Britain. *A Quarterly Journal Concerned with British Studies*, 28 (3), 437-453.

Hoover, S. M., 1987. The Religious Television Audience: A Matter of Size of Significance. *Review of Religious Research*, 29 (2), 135-151.

Hoover, S. M., 1988. Audience Size: Some Questions. *Critical Studies in Mass Communications*, 5 (3), 265-270.

Hoover, S.M. and Wagner, D.K., 1997. History and Policy in American broadcast treatment of religion. *Media Culture & Society*, 19 (1), 7-28.

Hosseini, S. H., 2008. Religion and Media. *Journal of Media and Religion*, 7 (1-2), 56-69.

House, R. J., Spangler, W. D., and Woycke. J., 1991. Personality and Charisma in the US Presidency: A Psychological Theory of Leader Effectiveness. *Administrative Science Quarterly*, 36 (36), 364-396.

Howley, K., 2001. Prey TV: Televangelism and Interpellation. *Journal of Film and Video*, 53 (2/3), 23-37.

House, R. J. and Howell, J.M., 1992. Personality and Charismatic Leadership. *Leadership Quarterly*, 3 (2), 81-98.

Independent Broadcasting Authority, 1977. Reponses by the Authority to the Annan Report. *Independent Broadcasting*, 12, 36.

Jeansonne, G., 2012. The Priest and the President: Father Coughlin, FDR, and the 1930s America. *Midwest Quarterly*, 53 (4), 359-373.

Jenson,R.J., 1999. Father Charles E. Coughlin: Surrogate Spokesman for the Disaffected. *Rhetoric and Public Affairs* 2 (3), 520-522.

Johnstone, R. L., 1971. Who Listens to Religious Broadcasts Anymore? *Journal of Broadcasting*, 16 (1), 120.

Jolyon, M., 2000. Christianity & Television. *Studies in World Christianity*, 11 (1), 1-8.

Kay, W. K., 2009. Pentecostalism and Religious Broadcasting. *Journal of Beliefs and Values*, 30 (3), 245-254.

Kirkpatrick, S.A. and Locke, E.A., 1991. Leadership Do Traits Matter? *The Executive*, 5 (2) 48-60.

Krabbendam, H., 2014. Review of a Short History of Global Evangelicalism. Hutchinson,M. and Wolffe, J., 2012. *Church History and Religious Culture*, 94 (1), 163-165.

Kridel, T., 2007. Rethinking Religious Radio. *Broadcasting & Cable*, 137 (38),18.

Leigh, I., 1992. Regulating Religious Broadcasting. *Ecclesiastical Law Journal*, 2 (10), 287-304.

Lindsay, D. M., 2008. Mind the Gap: Religion and the Crucible of Marginality in the United States and Great Britain. *The Sociological Quarterly*, 49 (4), 653-658.

Litman, B.R. and Bain, E., 1989. The Viewership of Religious Programmes: A Multidisciplinary Analysis of Televangelism. *Review of Religious Research*, 30 (4), 329-343.

Lobsenz, N. M., 1969. Everett Parker's Broadcasting Crusade. *Columbia Journalism Review*, 8 (3), 30-36.

Lofton.K., 2011. Religion and the American Celebrity. *Social Compass*, 58 (3), 346-352.

Maddux, K., 2011. The Foursquare Gospel of Aimee Semple McPherson. *Rhetoric and Public Affairs*, 14 (2), 291-326.

Maddux, K., 2012. The Feminized Gospel: Aimee Semple McPherson and the Gendered Performance of Christianity. *Women's Studies in Communication*, 35 (1), 42-67.

Marsden, G., 1977. Fundamentalism as an American Phenomenon: A Comparison with English Evangelicalism. *Church History* 46 (2), 215-232.

Marszolek, I. and Robel, Y., 2016. The Communicative Construction of Collectivities: An Interdisciplinary Approach to Media History. *Historical Social Research*, 41 (1) 328-357.

Martin, D., 1986. The Church and the British Broadcasting Corporation 1922-1956. The Politics of Broadcast Religion. *Religious Studies*, 22 (2), 283-284.

Marus, R., 2007. Falwell Leaves a Complex Legacy. *Christian Century*, 124 (12), 10-11.

McGarry, J. G., 1952. Religious Broadcasting. *The Furrow*, 3 (5), 10-11.

Miles, A. P., 1943. Social Work and the Science of Society. *Society and Social Research*, 27 (6), 433-440.

Morrison, A.J., 1979. Mass Media Use by Adults. *American Behavioural Scientist*, 23 (1), 71.

Noonan, C., 2013. Piety and Professionalism. *Media History*, 19 (2), 196-212.

O'Day, R., 1985. What is Religious History? *History Today*, 35, 48-49.

Pradip, T., 2009. Selling God/Saving Souls. *Global Media and Communication*, 5 (1), 57-59.

Pritchard, G. G. D., 1985. When Watching Religious TV is Like Attending Church. *Journal of Communication*, 35 (1), 123-131

Razelle, F., 1993. Hidden Agendas: The Politics of Religious Broadcasting in Britain 1987-1991. *Journal for Scientific Study of Religion*, 32 (3), 307-308.

Rosenthal, M., 2001. This Nation under God: The Broadcasting and Film Commission of the National Council of Churches and the New Medium of Television. *The Communication Review*, 4 (3), 347-371.

Sandon, R., 1981. Religious Piety and Political Reaction. *Public Policy*. 6 (2), 609

Sayer, J. E., 1983. Father Charles Coughlin: Ideologue and Demagogue of the Depression. *Northwest Communication Association*, 15 (1), 17-30.

Soukup, P. A., 1993. Church Documents and the Media. *Concilium*, 6, 71-79.

Spector, B.A. 2016. Carlyle, Freud and the Great Man Theory More Fully Considered. *Leadership*, 12 (2) 250-260.

Stacey, W. and Shupe, A., 1982. Correlates of Support for the Electronic Church. *Journal for the Scientific Study of Religion*, 21 (4), 291-303.

Starkey, G., 2002. Radio Audience Research: Challenging the "Gold Standard". *Cultural Trends*. 12 (45), 45-90.

Starkey, G., 2004. Estimating Audiences: Sampling in Television and Radio Audience Research. *Cultural Trends*, 13 (1), 3-25.

Stoecker, R., 1991. Evaluating and Re-thinking the Case Study. *The Sociological Review*, 39 (1), 88-112.

Stoneman, T., 2017. Global Radio Broadcasting and the Dynamics of American Evangelicalism. *Journal of American Studies*, 51 (4), 1139-1170.

Stoneman, T. H. B., 2007. Preparing the Soil for Global Revival Station HCJBs Radio Circle 1949-59. *Church History: Studies in Christianity and Culture*, 76 (1), 115-166.

Sutton, M. A., 2005. Clutching to 'Christian' America. *The Journal of Policy History*, 17 (3), 308-338.

Swindler, A., 1989. Culture in Action: Symbols and Strategies. *American Sociological Review*, 51 (2), 273-276.

Tamney, J. B., and Johnson, S., 1984. Religious Television in Midldletown. *Review of Religious Research*, 25 (4) 303-313.

Tavokin, E. P., 2011. Mass Communication in the Modern World. *Herald of the Russian Academy of Sciences*, 81 (6), 608-613.

Teachout, T., 1996. Founding Father. *National Review*, 48 (15), 53-54.

Thomas, S., 1985. The Route to Redemption: Religion and Social Class. *Journal of Communication*, 35 (1), 111-122.

Underation, C., 2012. Sending the Vision: Symbolic Convergence Theory and Aimee Semple McPherson. *Atlantic Journal of Communications*, 20 (5), 274-289.

Virts, P., 1981. The Context of the Electric Church Controversy. *Religious Communication Today*, 4, 5-8.

Wall, J., 1988. Religious Newsmaker. *Christian Century*, January 6-13, 3.

Wallis, R., 2016. Channel 4 and the Declining Influence of Organised Religion on UK Television. The Case of Jesus: The Evidence. *Historical Journal of Film, Radio and Television*, 36 (4), 668-688.

Wigger, J.H., 2015. Blessed: A History of the American Prosperity Gospel. *Fides et Historia*, 47 (2), 47-48.

Williams, D. K., 2010. Jerry Falwell's Sunbelt Politics: The Regional Origins of the Moral Majority. *The Journal of Political History*, 22 (2), 125-147.

Willner, A., and Willner, D., 1967. The Rise and Role of Charismatic Leaders. *Annals of the American Academy of Political and Social Science*, 358, 77-88.

Wober, J. M., and Gunter, B., 1986. Television Audience Research at Britain's Independent Broadcasting Authority. *Journal of Broadcasting and Electronic Media*, 30 (1), 15-31.

Woodward, K. L., 2018. Dr. Christian. *Commonweal*, 145 (6), 20-23.

Yukl, G. A. and Van Fleet, D.D., 1982. Cross-Situational Multi Method Research on Military Leadership Effectiveness. *Organisational Behavior and Human Performance*, 30, 87-108.

Zaleznik, A., 1992. Managers and Leaders: Are They Different? *Harvard Business Review*, 70 (2) 126-135.

LEGISLATION, REPORTS, COMMITTEES & COMMISSIONS

BBC, 1939. *Audiences for Religious Broadcasting*. London. BBC Listener Research Department. BBC Written Archives Centre. File Ref: R9/9/3.

BBC, 1941. *Listener Research Report: Religious Broadcasting*: London. Listener Research Department. BBC WAC. File Ref: R9/66/1.

BBC, 1942. *Inquiry into Studio or OB Broadcasts*. London. Listener Research Department. BBC WAC. File Ref: R9/9/6.

BBC, 1943. *Religious Broadcasting: History and Current Practice.The First 10 Years 1922-1932*. London. BBC WAC. File Ref: R34/815/2.

BBC, 1947. *Controversy in Religious Broadcasting*. London. Church of England Archive Centre. File Ref: BCC/7/1/9/5/2.

BBC, 1954. *Audience Research Special Report*. Audience Research Department. London. BBC WAC. File Ref: R9/9/18.

BBC, 1955. *Audience Research Special Report*. Audience Research Department. London. BBC WAC. File Ref: R9/9/19.

BBC, 1955. *Religious Broadcasting and the Public*. London. Audience Research Department. London: BBC WAC. File Ref: R9/9/19.

BBC, 1958. *Consultation on Religious Broadcasting and Television*. London. BBC WAC. File Ref: R12/893/1.

BBC, 1959. *Religion on BBC Radio & Television*. London. BBC WAC. File Ref: R34/815/6.

BBC, 1977. *The BBC Response to the Annan Report*. London. BBC.

BBC, 1978/79. *BBC Audience Research Findings*. London. BBC Audience Research Department.

BBC, 1984. *Religious & Spiritual Programmes*. London. BBC Audience Research Department. BBC WAC. Ref. File: R9/164/1.

BBC Research Department, 1984. *Songs of Praise*. London. BBC WAC. Ref: File: R9/222/1.

BBC Research Department, 1995/1996. *Songs of Praise*. London. BBC WAC. File Ref: R9/1920/1.

Beale, C., 1952. *Scope and Character of Religious Television*. London. BBC.

British Council of Churches, 1950. *Christianity and Broadcasting*. London. Church of England Archive Centre. File Ref: BCC/10/5/29.

Broadcasting Act 1990, 38 & 39 Eliz. 11, c.42.

Cable and Broadcasting Act 1984, Eliz. 11, c.46

Central Office of Information, 1973. *Broadcasting in Britain*. London. HMSO.

Central Religious Advisory Committee, 1940. *Minutes*. London. BBC WAC. File Ref: R34/814/1.

Central Religious Advisory Committee, 1941. *Minutes*. London. WAC. File Ref: R32/67/1.

Central Religious Advisory Committee, 1946-1947. *Freedom of Religious Discussion*. WAC.File Ref: R6/21/5.

Central Religious Advisory Committee, 1946-1947. *Religion and the Post-War Reconstruction*. London. WAC. File Ref: R6/21/5.

Central Religious Advisory Committee, 1947-1948. *Progress Report*. London. CRAC.

Central Religious Advisory Committee, 1948. *Review of the Aims and Achievement of Religious Broadcasting 1923-1948*. London. Church of England Archive Centre. File Ref: BCC/7/1/9/5/1.

Central Religious Advisory Committee, 1977. *Religious Programmes Policy*. London. BBC WAC File Ref: R78/810/1.

Central Religious Advisory Committee, 1984, *Minutes*. London. BBC WAC File Ref: R78/811/1.

Church Assembly Board, 1945. *Towards the Conversion of England*. London. Church of England Commission on Evangelism.

Church of England, 1931. *The Religious Value of Broadcast Services and their Bearing on Public Worship*. London. Church of England.

Controversy Committee, 1928. *Minutes of a Meeting*. London. BBC WAC. File Ref: R6/19/1.

Convocation of Canterbury. *The Eighth Georgia v Regnante: Joint Committee*. Committees of the Lower House. London. SPCK.

Evangelical Alliance, 1983. *Evidence to the Home Office on Cable and Satellite*. London. Evangelical Alliance.

Evangelical Alliance, 1989. *Tele-Evangelists Cloud Broadcast Debate*. London. Evangelical Alliance.

Federal Communications Commission, 1960. *Report and Statement of Policy Research* Washington. FCC.

Federal Council of Churches of Christ 1908. *Report of the First Meeting of the FCC*. New York. Revell Press.

Federal Council of Churches of Christ. 1924. *Report on Evangelism*. New York. FCCC.

Federal Council of Churches of Christ 1938. *Broadcasting and the Public*. New York. Abingdon.

Federal Council of Churches of Christ 1946. *Biennial Report*. New York. FCCC.

Federal Radio Commission, 1927. *First Annual Report*. Washington. FRC.

Gallup Poll, 1978. *Evangelical Christianity*. Washington. Gallup.

General Synod, 1983. *Cable Television*. London. Church Information Office.

General Synod Commission, 1973. *Broadcasting Society and the Church.* London. Church Information Office.

Green Paper: *Radio Choices and Opportunities: a consultative document* 1987, Cmnd.92. London. HMSO.

Grisewood,H., 1987. *Religious Broadcasting.* IBA Collection. File Ref: A/X/0001/1. Bournemouth: Bournemouth University.

Gunter, B., 1984. *The Audience & Religious TV.* London: IBA Research Report.

Gunter, B., 1984. *Attitudes to Sunday Evening Religious Broadcasts on Television: Highway and Songs of Praise Compared.* London. IBA Collection: File Ref: IBA/00418.

Haldane, I., 1978. *Who and what is Religious Broadcasting for?* IBA Collection: File Ref: A/R/1700/17.

House, F., 1948. *Confidential Paper Prepared for CRAC.* London. BBC WAC. File Ref: R6/17/1

House, F., 1955. *Religious Broadcasting: 1945 – 1955.* Annual Conference of Religious Broadcasting Department. BBC WAC. File Ref: T16/183/3.

Hurwitz, D., 1983. *Audience Research in American Broadcasting.* Mass Communication Annual Convention, Oregon.

Independent Broadcasting Authority, 1980. *Audience Reaction to the Communion Programme.* IBA Collection File Ref: A/X/003/5.

Independent Television Authority, 1974/75. *Annual Report & Accounts.* London: ITA.

Independent Television Authority, 1978. *Stars on Sunday.* IBA Collection File Ref: A/X/0016/1.

Independent Television Authority, 1984. *Proposed International Conference on Religious Broadcasting*: IBA Collection File Ref: A/X/004/6.

Independent Television Authority, 1987. *The Future of Religious Broadcasting*. IBA Collection File Ref: A/X/0008/6.

Independent Television Authority, 1988. *Religious Broadcasting in the 1990s*: IBA. Collection File Ref: A/X/005/3.

Lang, R. J., 1965. *Is Religious Broadcasting Necessary*? Great Saint Mary's Conference, Cambridge. Great Saint Mary's.

Mass Media Commission, 1975. *Submission to the Annan Committee on the Future of Broadcasting.* London: Roman Catholic Church.

Moral Majority, 1985. *National Issues Survey.* New York. Aldine Publishing Company.

National Council of Churches, 1951. *Christian Faith in Action*. New York. NCC.

National Council of Churches, 1960. *The Role of Radio, Television and Films in Religion*. New York. NCC.

National Religious Broadcasters, 1950. *Annual Report*. Wheaton. United Evangelical Action.

National Religious Broadcasters, 1956. *NCC Advisory Council Policy Statement*. Washington. NRB.

National Religious Broadcasters, 1966. *Ten Reasons Why You Should Join and Support the National Religious Broadcasters*. Washington. NRB.

Nielson, 1981. *Report on Syndicated Programme Audience*. New York. Nielson Media Research.

Pius X1, 1936. *Vigilanti Cura*. Rome. Roman Catholic Church.

Pius X11, 1957. *Miranda Prorsus*. Rome. Roman Catholic Church.

Reith, J. C. W., 1925. *Report to the Crawford Committee*. London. BBC WAC. File Ref: R4/27/1.

Religious Broadcasting Department, 1995/96. *Songs of Praise*. London. BBC.

Report of the Broadcasting Committee 1926, (*Crawford Report*) Cmnd. 2599. London. HMSO.

Report of the Broadcasting Committee 1951, (*Beveridge Report*) Cmnd. 8116. London. HMSO

Report of the Broadcasting Committee 1962, (*Pilkington Report*) Cmnd. 1753. London. HMSO.

Roman Catholic Report to the Annan Committee, 1975. Catholic Archives Society.

Report of the Broadcasting Committee 1977, (*Annan Report*) Cmnd. 6753. London. HMSO.

Report of the Broadcasting Committee 1982, (*Hunt Report*) Cmnd. 8866. London. HMSO.

Sendall, B.C., 1955. *Religious Advisory Committee Meeting*. IBA Collection File Ref: A/X/001/2.

Sendall, B. C., 1971. *Stars on Sunday*. IBA Collection File Ref: A/X/0009/1.

Sendall, B. C., 1972. *Stars on Sunday*. IBA Collection File Ref: A/X/0009/5.

Silvey, R. J. E., 1956. *Religion of the Air: Audiences for Religious Broadcasting*, London. St Pauls Lecture Society.

Silvey, R.J.E., 1974. *Religious Broadcasting and the Public*. BBC.

Second Vatican Council, 1971. *Communio et Progressio*. Rome. Roman Catholic Church.

Sound Broadcasting Act 1972, 19 & 20 Eliz.11, c.31.

Television Act 1954, 2 & 3 Eliz.11, c.55.

Television Staff, 1978. *Stars on Sunday*. IBA Collection. File Ref: A/X/0016/6.

Green Paper: *Radio Choices and Opportunities: a consultative document* 1987, Cmnd.92. London. HMSO.

White Paper: *Broadcasting in the 90s, Competition, Choice and Quality* 1988, Cmnd. 517. London. HMSO.

THESES

Bell, A., 2008. *Radical Religious Rebels: The Rise and Fall of Jerry Falwell and the Moral Majority*. (Masters). East Tennessee State University.

Buddenbaum, J. M., 1979. *The Audience for Religious Television Programmes*. (Masters). Indiana University.

Coon, R. W., 1970. *The Public Speaking of Dr. William A. Fagal of Faith for Today*. (PhD). Michigan State University.

Cooper, B. G., 1962. *Religious Broadcasting in Britain 1922-1939*. Unpublished. (PhD). Oxford University.

Coyer, K., 2009. *Its Not Just Radio: Models of Community Broadcasting in Britain and the United States*. (PhD). Goldsmith's College, London.

Deller, R., 2012. *Faith in View: Religion and Spirituality in Factual British Television 2000-2009*. (PhD). Sheffield Hallam University.

Dennis, J. L., *1962. An Analysis of the Audience of Religious Radio and Television Programmes in the Detroit Metropolitan Area.* (PhD). University of Michigan.

Devlin, J. P., 2016. *The Relationship between the BBC and the Commercial Radio Sector in Promoting DAB in the United Kingdom.* (PhD). Bournemouth University.

Dubourdieu, W. J., 1933. *Religious Broadcasting in the United States.* Unpublished. (PhD). Northwestern University.

Halper, D. L., 2011. *A Media Ecology: Analysis of Early Radio 1920-1935.* (PhD). University of Massachusetts.

Hart, A., 2015. *Gods and Gurus in the City of Angels: Aimee Semple McPherson, Swami Paramananda and Los Angeles in the 1920s.* (Masters). California Polytechnic State University.

Hiadky, K., 2011. *Chasing the American Dream: Trinity Broadcasting Network and the Faith Movement.* (PhD). Florida State University.

Hilton, C. T., 1980. *The Influence of Television Worship Services on the Irvington Presbyterian Church.* (PhD). Drew University.

Hinch, T. A., 1989. *Viewing Religious Programmes: A Comparative Study of Two Audiences.* (PhD) University of Maryland.

Hoar, T. F. X., 2011. *Religious Broadcasting 1920-1980: Four Religious Pioneers and the Process of Evangelisation.* (PhD). Salve Regina University.

Jackson, T. G., 1991. *The Electric Church: An Analysis of the Phenomenon.* (PhD). California State University.

Jennings, R. M., 1967. *Policies and Practices of Selected National Religious Bodies as Related to Broadcasting in the Public Interest 1920-1950.* (PhD). New York University.

Kandiero, T., 1979. *The Management of Public Broadcasting: A Comparative Study of Great Britain, USA, Canada and Malawi.* (PhD), Brunel University.

Knock Jr., S. F., 1959. *The Development of Network Religious Broadcasting in the United States 1923-1948.* (Masters). American University.

Kornberg, J., 1964. *History & Personality: The Theories of Wilhelm Dilthey.* (PhD). Harvard University.

Ma, R., 2011. *The Status and Influence of the Contemporary American Christian TV Broadcasting.* (PhD). Shanghai University.

Mistenda, K., 1995. *An Evaluation of Protestant Religious Film and Television Broadcasting in the UK and the USA.* (PhD). University of Wales.

Osborn, H. B., 1940. *A Study of the American System of Broadcasting and its Control.* (PhD). University of Southern California.

Noonan, C., 2009. The Production of Religious Broadcasting: the Case of the BBC. (PhD). Glasgow University.

Pegg, M., 1980. *British Radio Broadcasting and its Audience 1918-1939.* (PhD). Oxford University.

Pohlman, M. E., 2011. *Broadcasting the Faith: Protestant Religious Radio a Theology in America 1920-1950.* (PhD). Southern Baptist Theological Seminary.

Robertson, I., 1993. *Beyond our Control: Regulation and De-Regulation in British Broadcasting.* (Masters). Manchester.

Robinson, H. W., 1964. *A Study of the Audience for Religious Radio and Television Broadcast in Seven Cities throughout the US.* (PhD). Illinois University.

Rosen, N., 1988. *The Electric Church*. (PhD). University of Southern California.

Rosenthal, M., 1999. *TV : Satan or Saviour: Protestant Responses to Television in the 1950's*. (PhD). University of Chicago.

Saunders, L. S., 1968. *The National Religious Broadcasters and the Availability of Commercial Radio Time*. (PhD). University of Illinois.

Simpson, N. A., 1989. *A Study of Religious Television Programmes in the UK*. (PhD), Edinburgh University.

Solt, D. C., 1971. *A Study of the Audience Profile for Religious Broadcasts in Onondaga County*. (PhD). Syracuse University.

Wallis, R., 1987. *Looking on Glass*. Unpublished. (Masters). Exeter University.

Wanner, C. N., 2016. *Transmitting the Word: A Cultural Analysis of Religious Broadcasting*. (PhD). University of Georgia.

Webb, G. T., 1987. *Religious Broadcasting and 'Another Life': A Study of a Christian Broadcasting Network's Soap Opera*. (PhD). University of Texas.

Weinberg, E. G., 2012. *Creating Heaven on Earth: Jim Bakker and the Birth of Sunbelt Pentecostalism*. (PhD). University of Kentucky.

Windsor, C. D., 1981. *Religious Radio in the 1970's: A Uses and Gratifications Analysis*. (PhD). Ohio State University.

PERIODICALS, NEWSPAPER/MAGAZINE ARTICLES & TV

Aikman, D., 2018. Killing Communism with Kindness. *Christianity Today*. 12th April, p.72-75.

Applebome, P., 1989. Scandals Aside TV Preachers Thrive. *New York Times*. 8th October, p.24.

Applebome, P., 1989. Bakker is convicted on All Counts: First Felon among TV Evangelists. *New York Times*. 6th October, p.1.

Applebome, P., 2007. Jerry Falwell: Moral Majority Founder Dies at 73. *New York Times*. 16th May, p.11.

Barfield, N., 1963. Obituary: Jess Yates. *The Guardian*. 16th April, p. 7.

Barnes, D., 2018. The Most Influential Evangelist of our Time. *Christianity*. 21st February, p.34-45.

Bisset, T., 1981. Religious Broadcasting Comes of Age. *Christianity Today*. 4th September, p.33.

Botham, N., 1993. My Love for Jess. *News of the World*. 5th July, p.5.

Brace, R., 1972. Wandering Innocent Among the Stars. *Yorkshire Post*. 11th January, p.4.

Brand, D., 1987. God and Money. *Time Magazine*. 3rd August, p.48-49.

Brinley, R., Rev., 1956. The Church Speaks. *Nelson Leader*. 6th July, p.4.

British Comedy Guide, The Rev. www.comedy.co.uk/rev.

British Secular Society, 1975. Scrap Religious Broadcasting. *The Stage*. 6th February, p.13.

Butt R., 2007. The Vicar of Dibley Effect: More Women Than Man Ordained. *The Guardian*, 14th November, p.13.

Carter, H. W., 2017. The Cautionary Tale of Jim and Tammy Faye Bakker. *Christianity Today*. 19th September, p.12-13.

Correspondent, 1925. Church Broadcasting: A Failure. *Radio Broadcast Magazine*. November, p.33-34.

Correspondent, 1934. Largest Pulpit in the World. *Radio Magazine*. 14th November, p.49.

Correspondent, 1944. Attended by Throngs. *Los Angeles Times*.10th October, p.13

Correspondent, 1952. The Church and Television. *Coventry Evening Telegraph*. 6th November, p.7.

Correspondent, 1955. Morals without Religion. *The Times*. 20th January, p.5.

Correspondent, 1959. Bishops Take Up Television Course. *The Times*. 17th April, p.6.

Correspondent, 1971. How Much Light Do these Stars Give Us? *Daily Express*. 27th November, p.21.

Correspondent, 1979. The Cost of Televangelism. *New York Times*. 2nd December, p.13.

Correspondent, 1987. Falwell Quits Warning PTL Ministry May End. *New York Times*. 9th October, p.14.

Correspondent, 2015. Father Brown. *Independent Catholic News*, 5th January, p.6.

Corry, J., 1987. Preachers Mastery of the Medium. *New York Times*. 2nd April, p.26.

Curran, C., 1974. Shooting Arrows into the Air: The Function of Religious Broadcasting? *The Listener*. 29th August, p.262.

Daroubakhsh, S., 2005. A Life and Times in Pictures. *Yorkshire Post*. 10th August, p.3.

Davidson, R., 1926. Broadcasting as a National Service. *Radio Times*. 17th December, p. 669.

Davies, C., 1974. Yates Loses His Job. *Daily Mirror*. 9th July, p.14.

Davison, P., 2016. Mother Mary Angelica. *The Herald*. 5th April, p.12.

Editorial, 1924. Radio Preaching and Its Problems. *Christian Century*. October, p.1654

Editorial, 1925. Religion that is Broadcast. *Radio Times*. 6th February, p.1.

Editorial, 1925. Religious Broadcasting. *Radio Broadcast*, November p.34

Editorial, 1931. Religion and the BBC. *The Times*. June 24th, p.13

Editorial, 1931. Religious Broadcasting. *Literary Digest*. June, p.22-23.

Editorial, 1932. The World We Listen In. *Radio Times*. 20th May, p.466.

Editorial, 1933. Why is Religion so for some of us? *The Listener*. 1st February, p.165.

Editorial, 1934. Broadcast Religion. *Radio Magazine*. June, p.49.

Editorial, 1934. John Charles Walsham Reith. *Radio Magazine*. May, p.7.

Editorial, 1935. The Archbishop's Plea. *Radio Times*. 13th September, p. 2.

Editorial, 1953. America's Television Bishop. *Yorkshire Post and Leeds Mercury*. 4th April, p.5

Editorial, 1954. Evangelist Billy Graham. *Time Magazine*. 25th October, p.54-55.

Editorial, 1965. Our Man at St Mark's. *Stage and Television Today*. 22nd July 1965, p. 10

Editorial, 1956. Time and Tolerance. *Broadcasting Magazine*. 3rd September, p.102.

Editorial, 1975. Bakker Religious Show. *Florence Morning News*. 7th September, p.5.

Editorial, 1981. Mass Media Evangelism: Bennett's Gift to Graham. *Christianity Today*. 13th January, p.13.

Editorial, 1986. Gospel TV: Religion Politics and Money. *Time Magazine*. 17th February, p.67

Editorial, 1987. Survey of Top TV Preachers. *Christianity Magazine*. 16th October, p. 46-49.

Editorial, 1988. Preacher Scandals Strengthen TV Evangelism: Falwell. *Orlando Sentinel*, 19th March, p.198.

Editorial, 1988. The State of Christian Broadcasting. *Christianity Today*. 20th March, p.48-50.

Editorial, 1988. White Paper on Broadcasting. *Broadcast*. 7th December, p.7-8.

Editorial, 1988. 1990 Broadcasting Bill. *Broadcast*. 14th October, p13-14.

Eesinoun,B., 1963. Reflections of a Radio Priest. *Focus Midwest*. February p.8-10.

Effron, L., Paparetta, A. and Taudte, J., 2019. The scandals that brought down the Bakkers, once among US's most famous televangelists. *ABC News*. 20th December.

Elliott, W. H., 1930. Vicars Letter. *St. Michael's Parish Magazine*. November, p.2.

Elliott, W. H., 1930. Religion on Air. *Daily Mail.* 6th December, p.5

Elliott, W. H., 1931. Christmas Address. *St. Michael's Parish Record.* 10th December, p. 233.

Elson, J., 1995. Mother Knows Best. *Time Magazine.* 7th August, p.58.

Engel, J. F., 1984. Great Commission or Great Commotion. *Christianity Today.* 20th April, p.33.

EWTN, 2016. The Quotable Mother Angelica. *National Catholic Register.* www.ncregister.com

Fea, J., 2008. *Born Again History.* usreligion.blogspot.com

Finnigan, J., 1972. The Spiritual Soft Sell of Father Emery Tang. *TV Guide.* 18th March, p.45.

Fineman, H., 2007. The Face of the Moral Majority. *Newsweek.* 29th April, p.14.

Fiske, E. B., 1973. The Oral Roberts Empire. *New York Times.* 22nd April, p.216.

Fitzgerald, F., 1981. A Disciplined Charging Army. *New Yorker Magazine.* 18th May, p.53-141.

Flynt, L., 2007. My Friend, Jerry Falwell. *Los Angeles Times.* 20th May, p.16.

Fore, W. F., 1975. Religion on the airwaves: In the public interest? *Christian Century.* September 17th, p 26-27.

Fox, M., 2016. Mother Mary Angelica. *International New York Times.* 29th March, p.10.

Freedman, S. G., 1987. Ideas & Trends: How Bakker Widened the Eye of the Needle. *Washington Post.* 14th June, p.26.

Funk, T., 2018. Fallen PTL Preacher Jim Bakker is Back with a New Message about the Apocalypse. *Charlotte Observer*. 17th February, p. 2.

Garbett, C. F., 1925. Broadcasting. *Southwark Diocesan Gazette*. March p.22.

Gilchrist, R., 1974. Jess Yates Plans a 'Stars on Sunday' Comeback on American TV. *Daily Mail*, 24th September, p.3.

Goddard, S., 1984. Jesus the Evidence. *Buzz*. April, p.20-25.

Goldsmith.B., 1983. The Meaning of Celebrity. *New York Times*. 4th December, p. 75-76.

Graham, B., 1983. The Future of TV Evangelism. *TV Guide*. 4th October, p. 4-11.

Grayston,K., 1951. Religious Broadcasting in Great Britain. *World Dominion*, January/February p.47-51.

Hailes, S., 2018. America's Pastor Now in the Arms of Jesus. *Christianity Magazine*, 21st February, p.7.

Harris, A., 1991. Jim Bakker Sentence Overturned. *Washington Post*. 13th February, p.5.

Harris, A. and Isikoff. M., 1986. The Bakker's Tumultuous Return. *Washington Post*. 12th June, p.3.

Hayward, A., 1993. Obituary: Jess *Yates*. *The Independent*. 12th April, p.17

Hickling, M., 2005. A Life in Times and Pictures. *Yorkshire Post*. 10th August. p.3.

Holsendolp, E., 1979. Religious Broadcasting Brings Rising Revenues and Creates Rivalries. *New York Times*. 2nd December, p.1.

House, F., 1952. Evangelise or Perish. *The Times*. 10th September, p.7.

Hull, J. D., 1987. The Rise and Fall of 'Holy Joe'. *Time*. 3rd August, p. 54-55.

James, C., 1974. O Lord Preserve Us. *The Sunday Observer*. 19th May, p.35.

John, K.E., 1987. Television Evangelists Have Been Tarnished by Scandal. *Washington Post* June 1st, p.37

Johnson, E., 2014. A Theme Park, a Scandal and the Faded Ruins of a Television Empire. *Religion & Politics*. 28th October, https://religionandpolitics.org

Juozapavicius, J., 2009. Oral Roberts, 91. A Trailblazer Televangelist. *The Star* 16th December 2009.

Knight, P., 1977. Giving More Scope to Religion. *Daily Telegraph*. 29th August, p.5.

Knight, G.R., 1991. Democratization of the American Church. www.digitalcommons.andrews.edu.

Knox, C., 1933. A Man Who Preaches. *Daily Mail*. 4th December, p.3.

Krebs, A., 1979. Charles Coughlin 30s Radio Priest. *New York Times*. 28th October, p.44.

Lang, J., 1977. BBC Religious Programmes. *Daily Telegraph*. 29th August, p.5

Longley. C., 1987. Broadcasting as Challenge. *The Times*. 6th July, p. 12.

Longley, C., 1988. The True Art of Teaching Religion. *The Times*. 24th September, p.12.

McPherson, A.S., 1923. Radio Opportunities. *Four Square*. December, p.24.

MacPherson, H., 1974. Shooting Arrows into the Air: The Function of Religious Broadcasting. *The Listener*. 29th August, p. 261.

Mann, J., 1982. The Mainline Churches Strike Back. *US News & World Report*. 6th August, p.60.

Martin, W., 1981. The Birth of a Media Myth. *New Yorker*. June, p.7-16.

McIntire, R. C., 1980. Oral Roberts. *Boston Globe*. 30th November, p.13.

Matzko, P., 2018. What Jim Bakker Can Teach American Evangelicals Today. 13th April, www.thegospelcoalition.org.

McCormick, R. P., 1937. On the Death of Canon Sheppard. *The Listener*. 3rd November, p.956.

McLendon, M.A., 1981. Jim Bakker Seen By Millions Known By Few. *The Saturday Evening Post*, April, p. 50-53.

Minnery, T., 1981. The Man behind the Mask. *Christianity Today*. 4th September, p.28-29.

Norman, R. C., 1938. Sir John Reith: An Appreciation. *The Listener*. 7th July, p.5.

Oastling. R.N.L., Russell, B. and Gregory, H., 1985. Legions Seek to Remake Church and Society. *Time Magazine*. 2nd September, p.48.

Obituary, 1957. Canon W.H. Elliott. *The Times*. 7th March, p.12.

Obituary, 1993. Jess Yates. *The Times*. 12th April, p.17.

Obituary, 2016. Mother Angelica: Television Nun. *The Telegraph*. 29th March , p.16.

Outlook, 1972. Never Set Out To Be Controversial. *Sheffield Morning Telegraph*. 25th April, p.3.

Page, C., 1989. Jim Bakker's Sentence is Too Harsh. *Chicago Tribune*, 29th October p.10.

Paley, W. S., 1931. Broadcasting Both Sides of the Atlantic. *The Listener*. 24th June, p.1052-1053.

Parker,E.C., 1949. The Potential of Radio. *Religion News Service* January 3rd.

PTL Club, 1985. 21st April.

PTL Club, 1985. 4th-7th November.

PTL Club, 1986. 7th January.

PTL Club, 1986. 3rd March.

PTL Club, 1986. 25th April

Ranalagh, J., 1983. Broadcasting for Breadth. *The Times*. 5th November, p.10.

Rankin, S., 2014. Confessor-in-Chief. *Christian History*, www.christianhistoryinstitute.org Issue # 111.

Reindorp, G. E., 1958. Unseen congregation. *Daily Mirror*, 19th June, p.7.

Richard, K, 2011. Frank Capra's Miracle Woman. *Christianity Today*, 13th December, p.18

Richards, B. Rev., 1956. The Church Speaks. *Nelson Leader*. July 6th, p.4.

Roberts, O., 1948. Holiness. *Pentecostal Holiness Advocate*. 27th May, p.3.

Robertson, P., 2006. 700 Club, March 13th Edition.

Robertson, P., 2020. Origins of Nickname. www.patrobertson.com

Rodgers, W. W., 1922. Broadcasting Church Services. *Radio Broadcast*. August. p.321.

Saxon, E., 1964. On Television. *Church Times*. 24th April, p.7.

Schneider, D., 2009. Oral Roberts: Fiery Preacher Dies at 91. *New York Times*. 15th December, p.1.

Schultze, Q. J., 1987. Fund-Raising: Did Oral Roberts Go Too Far? *Christianity Today*, 15th February, p.215.

Schultze,Q.J., 1988. The Wireless Gospel. *Christianity Today*. 18th January p.19-23.

Schultze Q.J., 2001. Evangelicalism, *Christianity Today*, 18th February, p.20

Shegog, E., 1989. Godwatching. *Sunday Telegraph*. 26th November, p.15.

Shegog,E., 1990. Religious Broadcasting. *Church Times*. 16th February, p.6.

Shepard, C.E., The Bakkers Lavish Lifestyle. *Charlotte Observer* 26th January 1986, p.10

Shepard, C. E., 1987. Jim Bakker Resigns from PTL. *Charlotte Observer*. 20th March, p.1.

Shepard, C. E., 1989. Jim Bakkers' Middle Name was Show Business. *Seattle Post Intelligencer*. 9th October, p.1.

Sheppard, H. R. L., 1925. Responses to Broadcasts. *St.Martin's Review*. p.303.

Sheppard, H. R. L., 1928. A Wider Scope than Wesley's. *The Radio Times*. 2nd March, p.430.

Sheppard, H.R.L., 1932. Sermon. *St. Martin-in-the-Fields Calling*, p. 32

Short, R., Songs of Praise. *The Radio Times*. 15th April 1976, p.1

Smillie, D., 2006. Prophets of Boom. *Forbes*. 18th September, p. 118-121.

Spence, H., 1948. The Man of the Lutheran Hour. *Saturday Evening Post*. 19th June, p.17-20.

Stearly, B., 1923. The Effects of Broadcasting on the Churches. *Radio Broadcast Magazine*. August, p.273-274.

Stolberg, S.G., and Shear M.G., Billy Graham Lies in Honour at US. *New York Times*, 28th February 2018, p.14

Taylor, C., 1947. The Church and Radio. *St.Martin's Review*, Issue No.1947, p.146-150.

Temple, A., 1954. Billy Graham at Harringay. *Daily Mail*. 21st May, p.4.

Temple, W. E., 1935. The Christian and the World Situation. *The Listener*. 4th September, p.375-376.

Trammel, M., 2007. Making Airwaves. *Christianity Today*. 26th January, p.87.

Turner, D. M. R., 1952. The Church and Broadcasting. *Montrose and Arbroath Review*. September 18th, p.4.

Vitello, P., 2016. Mary Mother Angelica, Popular TV Host, Dies at 92. *New York Times*. 27th March, p.10.

Ward, T., 1988. The Churches and Local Radio. *Church Times*. 26th February, p.12.

Welby, J., 2018. The Most Influential Evangelist of Our Time. *Christianity Magazine*, 21st February, p.37.

Welch, J. W., 1944. Religious Broadcasting. *St Martin's Review*. p.25.

Whale, J., 1979. The Gospel of the Losers. *The Sunday Times*. 2nd December, p.17.

Williams, W. E., 1957. Dick Sheppard. *The Times*. 28th August, p.17.

Wineke, W.R., 1971. The Problems and Prospects of Evangelical Radio. *Christianity Today*. 1st January, p.2-5.

Wood, H., 1934. Broadcasting – Here and in the USA. *Radio Magazine*. April p.17-18.

Woodward, K. L., Fineman, H., Mayer, A.J. and Lindsay, J., 1980. A Tide of Born Again Politics. *Newsweek*. 15th September, p.28-36.

Wyland, D., 2013. Reverend Billy Graham: Ordinary Man, Extraordinary Call. *inspirationalChristians.org*.

Williams, W.E., 1957. Seven Decisive Years for Sound and Vision. *The Times*. 28th August, p.17

Yancy, P., 1979. The Ironies and Impact of PTL. *Christianity Today*. 21st September, p.28-33.

PERSONAL COMMUNICATION

Bourn, I. K., 1940. *Letter from Bourn, General Secretary of the Women's Protestant Union*, 19th July. BBC Written Archives Centre. File Ref: R41/169/2.

Gielgud, V., 1930. *Letter to R.H. Eckersley.* 12th May. BBC WAC. File Ref: R20/176/2.

Gorham, M.A.C., 1946. *Memo: To J. Welch.* 17th January. BBC WAC. File Ref: R17/174/2.

Hind. K., 1990. *Commons Standing Committee F.* 25th January. Hansard Col.322, 323.

Iremonger, F.A., 1936. *Report to Sir Cecil Graves.* 7th May 1936. BBC WAC.File Ref: R4/72/1.

McDonnell, J., 2020. *Concluding Statement.* 14th March.

Newton, I., 1676. *Letter to Robert Hooke.* www.physicsforums.com

Powell, A., 1940. *Letter to William Paton at the World Council of Churches*: 3rd December. BBC WAC. File Ref: R4/72/1.

Reith, J. C. W., 1952. *Speech to the House of Lords.* 22nd May. Hansard Col.1297.

Sarnoff, D., 1947. *The Past and the Future of Radio.* New York Speech. IEEE Vol.99 Issue 10 2011.

Schultze, Q.J., 2020. *Concluding Statement.* 10th March.

Silvey, R. J. E., 1956. Lecture. *Religion of the Air: Audiences for Religious Broadcasting.* St. Pauls Lecture Society, London.

Trump, D., 2018. *The Great Billy Graham is Dead.* in @realDonaldTrump, February 21st.

Whates, A. E., 1935. *Letter to Sir John Reith*, 8th January. BBC WAC. File Ref: R41/179/1

APPENDIX 1

KEY U.K. MEDIA INSTITUTIONS
(Fast Facts)

BRITISH BROADCASTING CORPORATION (BBC)

Formerly the British Broadcasting Company formed in 1922, it became a Corporation licensed under Royal Charter in 1927.

The BBC is considered the oldest and probably the largest broadcaster in the world. It is funded by an annual licence fee, broadcasts in over 28 languages and is under the supervision of the UK Government Department of Culture, Media and Sport.

It is managed now by the BBC Board and Governed by a Chairman and a Director-General. Its first Director-General was John Reith and to this day the BBC aims to follow the Reithian directive to 'inform, educate and entertain".

Its headquarters are housed in Broadcasting House in central London, but nationwide and internationally has probably around 35,000 staff with an operating cost of approx. 5 billion pounds.

BROADCASTERS AUDIENCE RESEARCH BOARD (BARB)

BARB was founded in 1981 and replaces ITV's JICTAR (Joint Industry Committee for Television Audience Research) and the BBC's own research arm.

It is owned by the BBC, ITV, Channel 4, Channel 5, B Sky B, and the IPA (Institute of Practitioners in Advertising). BARB carries out continuous surveys with approx. 50,000 homes using electronically monitored meters in each of their sample homes across the UK.

This level of research and on-going reporting is key to television broadcasters in general, but especially to those in the commercial sector where results can seriously affect income as well as programme production.

CENTRAL RELIGIOUS ADVISORY COMMITTEE (CRAC)

Formerly called the 'Sunday Committee' in 1923, CRAC (as it was later to be named) was formed at the suggestion of John Reith, the first Director-General of the BBC. The members of the initial committee were appointed by the BBC, but broadly represented main–stream Christianity in Britain.

The committee was to be the BBC's link with churches and the primary source of advice about religious programmes. It also became a filter for criticism of the BBC's approach to religion which came from many sources including from those within the church.

CRAC was to be the model of advisory committees for the BBC in a number of subject areas and extended its influence still further with the establishment of ITV and in its interaction with various broadcasting committees. Its role ceased in 2009 and was replaced with the BBC Standing Conference on Religion and Belief.

INDEPENDENT LOCAL RADIO (ILR)

Better known as Commercial Radio, it began in 1973 made possible by the 1972 Sound Broadcasting Act. The London Broadcasting Company (LBC) was the first station on air followed shortly after by Capital Radio.

There are over 200 commercial stations in the UK, but as a result of deregulation provisions in the 2003 Communications Act most commercial stations now are neither independent nor local.

As of 2003 regulation for Commercial Radio fell into the hands of OFCOM after the disbanding of the Radio Authority.

INDEPENDENT RADIO NEWS (IRN)

IRN began broadcasting with the creation of Commercial Radio. Its role then, as now, is to provide a 24 hour national and international news. It is funded by stations receiving the service and it claims to have over 27 millions listeners in the UK with news content provided by Sky News Radio.

INDEPENDENT TELEVISION (ITV)

ITV was made possible by the Television Act of 1954 and set up in 1955 to break the monopoly of BBC television. ITV is a network of 12 regional television services covering England, Southern Scotland, Wales, the Isle of Man and the Channel Islands. Since the Broadcasting Act of 1990 it has been more commonly known as Channel 3. Programmes made in each region are shared and broadcast on the entire network. It remains the biggest and most popular commercial television channel in the UK even though its viewing figures have declined because of the era of multi-channel TV.

MEDIANET

Medianet is a network that supports, encourages and inspires Christians who work in and with the UK media. It was created in 2009 and took over its role from the former Churches Advisory Council for Local Broadcasting (CACB) and the Churches Media Council (CMC).

It holds a Church and Media Annual Conference with the aim to affirm media's vital role in society and to give positive practical support to its members to achieve the highest standards in media on both a national and international stage.

APPENDIX 1

OFFICE OF COMMUNICATIONS (OFCOM)

This Government Agency was created in 2003 and superseded the former regulators – the Broadcasting Standards Commission, the Independent Television Commission, the Office of Telecommunications, the Radio Authority and the Radio Communications Agency.

Ofcom is the "regulator for the UK communications industries with responsibilities across television, radio, telecommunications and wireless communication services".

Its remit is to balance choice and competition in the media industries with a duty to 'foster plurality, inform citizenship, protect viewers, listeners and customers and promote cultural diversity'.

OFCOM was established by the Office of Communications Act 2002 and empowered by the Communications Act 2003.

PREMIER CHRISTIAN RADIO

Premier Christian Radio which launched in London in 1995, was the first Christian Radio Station to be licenced under the new rules and regulations provided by the 1990 Broadcasting Act. It is wholly owned by the charity the Christian Media Trust.

It began broadcasting to London and Greater London on 3 Medium Wave wavelengths, eventually broadcasting to the rest of the UK on Sky and then in 2009 digitally on DAB Radio. Premier Christian Radio is now part of the Premier Media Group which publishes magazines and runs 2 other stations – Premier Gospel and Premier Praise.

RADIO JOINT AUDIENCE RESEARCH (RAJAR)

RAJAR was established in 1992 to operate a single-audience measurement system for the UK radio industry. The company was owned by the BBC and the Commercial Radio Companies Association (CRCA) subsequently the Radio Centre.

The method of audience measurement is through personalised diaries to be completed according to the individuals listening habits. There is current pressure to introduce a more electronic monitoring system.

Each quarter RAJAR'S figures are released to show how each station is performing.

SKY UK

Sky UK (formed from British Sky Broadcasting and B Sky B) is a telecommunications company which serves the UK and was launched in 1990 by media tycoon Rupert Murdoch.

Sky provides television, news, broadband internet and telephone services to consumers and businesses in the UK.

UNITED CHRISTIAN BROADCASTERS (UCB)

UCB is an international Christian broadcasting and media group which in the UK started broadcasting in 1986 with programming on various radio platforms until 2009 when it gained a national DAB Licence.

UCB UK is based in Stoke on Trent and aims to broadcast quality Christian radio programming, provide practical and insightful Christian television on satellite and acts as a support ministry for Christians

Apart from broadcasting UCB publishes Christian materials and runs a telephone helpline.

APPENDIX 2

KEY U.S. MEDIA INSTITUTIONS
(Fast Facts)

AMERICAN BROADCASTING COMPANY (ABC)

The Company was formed in 1943 as a radio network. It extended its operations into television in 1948, following in the steps of CBS and NBC. In 1953 the merger of ABC and United Paramount Theatres brought in a new era and the later connection with the Walt Disney Company and others, made it an equal force with CBS and NBC and probably one of the largest entertainment groups in the U.S.

COLUMBIA BROADCASTING SYSTEM (CBS)

The CBS News Network was formed by William S Paley in 1929 as part of the Columbia Broadcasting System. In the 1920s and 30s network news consisted primarily of 'events' coverage, including presidential speeches and election results, but eventually branched out with more foreign affairs topics. In later years they used the new television platforms and a substantial amount of intensive research on their programmes. But by the 1980s and 90s the CBS organisation had lost its supremacy to NBC and ABC.

CABLE NEWS NETWORK (CNN)

CNN was founded in 1980 by American media proprietor Ted Turner as a 24 hour cable news channel. CNN was the first all-news television channel in the US and provided global satellite connections, fast breaking national and international news, in-depth financial, political and sports coverage and has become a 'news junkies' paradise.

CNN grew in importance and in 1982 provided a second channel CNN Headline News, with half hour updates and effective tie-ins to other international networks.

CHRISTIAN BROADCASTING NETWORK (CBN)

CBN was founded by televangelist Pat Robertson in 1961. Its flagship variety programme *The 700 Club* became the blueprint for many other religious broadcasters.

The 700 Club features a daily news segment with commentary on certain stories, as well as interviews and is distributed to an average daily audience of one million viewers on cable and through syndication.

Pat Robertson, CBN's founder, once campaigned unsuccessfully for the Republican candidacy for the 1988 Presidential Election and also founded the interdenominational evangelical Christian Broadcasting Network University in 1977 which was renamed Regent University in 1990.

FEDERAL COMMUNICATIONS COMMISSION (FCC)

The FCC is an independent federal agency formed by the Communications Act of 1934. It replaced the Federal Radio Commission (FRC) and was established to regulate interstate and international electronic communications, wired and wireless and is accountable to Congress and funded by regulatory fees.

Its brief now works in six main areas relating to broadband, competition, spectrum, homeland security, media and public safety as well as modernising itself. It is reported to cost 388 million dollars to run and has about 1,700 employees.

THE FEDERAL COUNCIL OF CHURCHES OF CHRIST (FCCC)

The Federal Council of Churches, officially the Federal Council of Churches of Christ in America was formed in 1908 and was an ecumenical association of Christian denominations in the United States in the early 20th Century. It represented the Anglican, Baptist, Eastern Orthodox, Lutheran, Methodist, Moravian, Oriental Orthodox, Polish National Catholic, Presbyterian, and Reformed traditions of Christianity. It merged with other ecumenical bodies in 1950 to form the present day National Council of Churches.

FOX NEWS CHANNEL

Fox News is an American cable and satellite television news channel, established in 1996 and owned by the Fox Entertainment Group; a subsidiary of 21st Century Fox. The Channel has had much criticism because of its perceived bias reporting and its news interpretation, which is ironic in the light of its co-founder's (Roger Ailes) slogan of being *"fair and balanced"*.

It was estimated in 2015 that approximately 95 million households receive the Fox News Channel.

MUSIC TELEVISION (MTV)

MTV which launched in 1981 is an American cable and satellite television channel owned by the Viacom Media Network. The original mission of MTV was to be music television playing music videos 24/7, guided by video jockeys.

In the early years its target audience were young adults, then it moved primarily towards teenagers, but suffered in its ratings because of the growth of digital media.

The network's influence extended beyond the music industry with many of its international featured artists starting fashion trends based on their MTV videos. In addition television programmes, movies and commercials incorporated the MTV style – quick cut editing, slick, flashy imagery and loud rock music.

The brand MTV has expanded beyond the original MTV channel, including a variety of sister channels in the US, dozens of affiliated channels around the world and an internet presence through MTV.com and related websites

NATIONAL BROADCASTING COMPANY (NBC)

It was formed in 1926 by the Radio Corporation of America (RCA) after a number of earlier disputes between radio corporations and is therefore one of the oldest radio networks in America. By 1941 25% of radio stations were affiliated with NBC networks. But like many other groups there were mergers and take overs with a decline in radio and a move to television.

Throughout the 1950s and 60s NBC generally finished in second place in ratings behind CBS and then declined more in the 70s to third place. But with the help of General Electric by the late 90s NBC was once again the undisputed leader of network television with 5 top rated shows most weeks. Now NBC has developed even more with the help of international cable and satellite channels.

NATIONAL PUBLIC RADIO (NPR)

The creation of NPR was a result of the Public Broadcasting Act of 1967 which called for a new Corporation for Public Broadcasting to help foster a system of public radio stations.

The network based in Washington DC produces and distributes programming, manages the public radio systems, provides training and other services to its affiliated stations.

The funding for NPR comes from dues paid by its 600 member stations, sponsorships and foundation grants. Its flagship programmes *Morning Edition* and *All Things Considered* were two of the most popular radio programmes in the country.

NATIONAL RELIGIOUS BROADCASTERS (NRB)

NRB was established in 1944 and is the world's pre-eminent association of committed broadcasters and Christian communicators.

It states its mission is to 'advance biblical truth, to promote media excellence and to defend free speech'.

NRB supported the Cable Act of 1992 which benefited religious television stations. It is now an international association with over 1000 member organisations representing millions of viewers, listeners and readers. All Members subscribe to the NRB Statement of Faith and Code of Ethics.

NRB holds an Annual Convention attended by US Presidents, members of Congress, FCC Commissioners and international speakers.

SALEM MEDIA GROUP

Formerly Salem Communications Corporation, founded by Stuart Epperson in the early 1980s, it changed its name in 2015. It is an American radio broadcaster, internet content provider and a magazine and book publisher, focussed on family-themed content and conservative values.

Unlike many Christian broadcasters it is a for-profit corporation. Salem owns 115 radio stations, with 73 in the top 25 markets and 25 in the top 10. Tied with CBS Radio, it is the fifth largest radio broadcaster in the US.

TRANS WORLD RADIO (TWR)

TWR started in 1952, when the American Paul Freed set up the organization to reach Spain by broadcasting from Morocco. Later, TWR moved to Monaco. Other major transmitting sites include Guam, Bonaire, Sri Lanka, Cyprus, and Swaziland. Trans World Radio remains a multinational evangelical Christian media distributor. One of the largest Christian media organization in the world, it uses mediumwave or high-powered AM and shortwave transmitters, local FM radio stations, cable, satellite, internet, and mobile device technologies. Their programs can be heard in 190 countries in more than 230 languages and dialects.

TRINITY BROADCASTING NETWORK (TBN)

TBN was co-founded in 1973 by Paul Crouch, an Assemblies of God (AOG) minister and his wife Jan.

It is an international Christian based broadcast television network and probably the largest religious television network in the world with a flagship programme called *'Praise'*.

The organisation has a presence on almost every continent with networks in 13 languages serving 22 countries and claiming over one billion potential viewers.

APPENDIX 3

U.K. BROADCASTING REPORTS/COMMITTEES

Sykes Committee

Reported: 1923

Discussed: British Broadcasting Company funding by licence and its monopoly on broadcasting.

Recommended: Licence fee funding

No advertising

Broadcasting transfer from private to public

Outcome: The Company continued its monopoly and funding by licence

Crawford Committee

Reported: 1926

Discussed: Broadcasting organisation and its effect on viewers

Recommended: Broadcasting run by a public service corporation

No direct Parliamentary control

Licence fee funding for 10 years

Educational programmes

Outcome: The establishment of the British Corporation by Royal Charter

Selsdon Television Committee

Reported: 1935

Discussed: Television broadcasting and the Baird or Marconi systems

Recommended: Television broadcasting should be held within the public sector

A London station should be set up using both systems until one proved better

Outcome: The BBC's first television broadcasts from Alexandra Palace (eventually broadcasting with the Marconi system)

Ullswater Committee

Reported: 1935

Discussed: Broadcasting, including overseas, funding and the nature of programming

Recommended: Regional broadcasting decentralisation and expansion

Government control during national emergencies

Freedom to report anti-Government views

No funding by advertising

APPENDIX 3

                Increase in Licence fee

                News programmes' impartiality

                More schools broadcasting

                2 more BBC Governors

Outcome: Further expansion of the BBC and programmes

Hankey Television Committee

Reported: 1944

Discussed: Television services after the war

Recommended: BBC monopoly of television services

                Television in the regions

                High definition television on 405 lines

                Television receiver standards

                More co-ordinated research and development

                Television's financial independence

Outcome: A post war BBC television service, a monopoly until 1955 and expansion of BBC research and development.

Beveridge Committee

Reported: 1951

Discussed: BBC monopoly and funding

Recommended:	BBC continuing as sole broadcaster
	Charter renewal and Licence fee funding but under review
	Regional devolution
	Broadcasting of minority views
	More political broadcasting
	Trade Union recognition
Minority Report:	Selwyn Lloyd recommended the end of broadcasting monopoly
Outcome:	Selwyn Lloyd's recommendations were consolidated into a White Paper and ITV was set up

Pilkington Committee

Reported:	1962
Discussed:	Organising of whole broadcasting industry and programmes
Recommended:	Renewal of BBC Charter and Licence Fee funding
	Extending radio hours
	Adult education broadcasting
	Second television channel
	Colour television on 625 lines
	Local broadcasting

APPENDIX 3

Better television regulation

Outcome: Open University, BBC local radio, BBC2 and colour television licence

Annan Committee

Reported: 1977

Discussed: The whole broadcasting industry, new technologies and their funding, the role and funding of the BBC and IBA programme standards

Recommended: BBC funding by Licence fee

A fourth independent television channel

Long-term restructure and diversification of broadcasting

Establishment of Broadcasting Complaints Commission

Privatisation of local radio

Independence from direct political control

Outcome: Increased Licence fee and towards the development of Channel 4

Hunt Committee

Reported: 1982

Discussed: The organisation and future of cable broadcasting

Recommended: A cable regulatory authority

	Cable providers able to make programmes
	BBC and ITV programmes carried free
Outcome:	Expansion of cable broadcasting, eventually overtaken by satellite broadcasting

Peacock Committee

Reported:	1986
Discussed:	BBC funding and efficiency, cable and satellite broadcasting
Recommended:	Licence fee continues indexed to the RPI
	Radio 1 and 2 privatisation
	More broadcasting hours
	Independent production quotas
	ITV companies franchise auctions
	Removal of cable and satellite broadcasting restrictions
Outcome:	Charter renewal and licence fee (less than the BBC hoped for), BBC staff cuts and efficiency drive, night time broadcasting, independent production sector growth, deregulation of ITV and removal of cable and satellite broadcasting restrictions.

APPENDIX 4

HIGHLIGHTS OF U.K. & U.S. BROADCASTING LEGISLATION

UK	US
1904 THE WIRELESS TELEGRAPHY ACT Extended the Postmaster-General's powers to control wireless telegraph and made the establishment of the British Broadcasting Company (BBC) possible.	
	1912 RADIO ACT Places Secretary of Commerce in charge of radio regulation, station licences now required the Secretary to assign wavelengths
	1927 RADIO ACT First comprehensive radio legislation, established basic regulatory standards, declared public ownership of airways and government right to regulate. FRC (Federal Radio Commission) created to regulate radio.

UK	US
	1934 COMMUNICATIONS ACT has 'public interest, convenience and necessity' as a recurring theme and replaced FRC with the Federal Communications Commission whose powers extended beyond radio to include wire and wireless communication, both interstate and foreign.
1954 TELEVISION ACT The Act enabled the start of a commercial television service in the UK. It created the Independent Television Authority (ITA). The ITA was responsible to regulate the new service, making sure that commercials were clearly distinguishable from programmes.	
1964 TELEVISION ACT Consolidated the Television Acts of 1954 and 1963 defining the constitution, function and powers of ITV. It excluded sound-only broadcasts, but made reference to a possible second commercial channel.	

UK	US
1967 MARINE BROADCASTING (OFFENCES) ACT Legislation taking action against offshore Pirate broadcasters	**1967 BROADCASTING ACT** it amended the Communication Act of 1934 and established public radio and television based on the Carnegie Commission recommendations.
1972 SOUND BROADCASTING ACT Revised the Independent Television Authority (ITA) into the Independent Broadcasting Authority (IBA), which took responsibility for commercial television and commercial radio.	
1973 INDEPENDENT BROADCASTING AUTHORITY ACT Consolidated the Television and Sound Broadcasting Acts of 1964 & 1972.	
1979 INDEPENDENT BROADCASTING ACT Conferred power on the IBA to transmit a television service additional to the BBC and that already provided by the Authority (namely Channel 4).	

UK	US

1981 BROADCASTING ACT
It consolidated the previous broadcasting Acts of 1973, 1974, 1978 and 1980 including the removal of certain specified people broadcasting opinions. It extended the IBA's provision of programmes for Channel 4 and established the Broadcasting Complaints Commission.

1984 CABLE AND BROADCASTING ACT
Set up a Cable Authority to grant Licences and regulate the newly liberalised cable television industry.

UK	US

1990 BROADCASTING ACT
It repealed the 1949, 1967, 1981, 1984, and 1988 Acts. It aimed to reform the entire structure of British Broadcasting. The IBA was abolished and replaced by the Independent Television Commission (ITC) and the Radio Authority and a 'lighter touch' regulatory approach. It also directed that 25% of programming should be 'independent productions' and allowed religious groups to own and run radio stations. It also provided for a Channel 5 to be established, but retained all the elements of public service broadcasting.

1992 CABLE TELEVISION CONSUMER PROTECTION AND COMPETITION ACT.
the act purports 'to provide increased consumer protection and to promote increased competition in the cable television and related markets'. It built on the Cable Communications Policy Act of 1984 which brought in elements of regulation.

APPENDIX 5

I am radio
I am a university in your room
I am an opera sung by your fireside
I am an orchestra to set your feet a dancing
I am a band to enthuse your musical soul
I am an orator whose eloquence holds you still
I am a violin recital rendered by a master at your side
I am a statesman conferring with you on the nations needs
I am a diplomat voicing a foreign friendliness
I am a doctor coming to your home without charge
I am a banker watching your laid away pounds
I am a leader of industry analysing the economic trend
I am a newspaper describing events as they happen
I am a drama played in your parlour
I am a debate where you hear both sides of the day's problems
I am a football game with thrills by the score
I am a boxing championship with a seat at the ringside
I am a governess teaching your children each day
I am a scientist revealing wonders that you know not of
All these I am and more
I am a patriot kindling a new love of country
I am a preacher re-awakening your faith in human nature
Yes, poor, foolish men, just call me radio

Eric H. Palmer : *Daily Telegraph* (Sydney) 30th September 1927, p.13.

APPENDIX 6

VATICAN DOCUMENTS RE: MEDIA

Vigilanti Cura	(1936)	Encyclical Letter of Pope Pius X1 on the Motion Picture.
Miranda Prorsus	(1957)	Encyclical Letter of Pope Pius X11 on Motion Pictures, Radio and television.
Inter Mirifica	(1963)	Decree on the Means of Social Communication.
Communio et Progressio	(1971)	Pastoral Instruction on the Means of Social Communication by order of the Second Vatican Council.
Aetatis Novae	(1992)	Pastoral Instruction on Social Communications on the Anniversary of Communio et Progessio

APPENDIX 7

ARCHIVES CONSULTED

BBC Written Archives Centre
Peppard Road
Caversham Park
Reading
RG4 8TZ
UK

BBC Listener Magazine Archive
Bournemouth University
Fern Barrow
Poole
Dorset
BH12 5BB
UK

St Martin-in-the-Fields Archive Centre
Trafalgar Square
Charing Cross
London
WC2N 4JJ

Lambeth Palace Archives
Lambeth Palace
Lambeth Palace Road
Lambeth
London SE1 7JU
UK

Church of England Records Centre
15 Galleywall Road
South Bermondsey
London
SE16 3PB
UK

City of Westminster Archive Centre
10 St.Ann's Street
Westminster
London
SW1P 2DE
UK

IBA Archive
Centre for Media History
Bournemouth University
Fern Barrow
Poole
Dorset
BH12 5BB
UK

Churches Advisory Council for Local Broadcasting Archive
Central Hall Westminster
Storeys Gate
Westminster
London
SW1H 9NH
UK

British Library
Special Collections
96 Euston Road
London
NW1 2DB
UK

The Newsroom
The British Library
96 Euston Road
London
NW1 2DB
UK

Protestant Radio & Television Centre Collection
The Walter J. Brown Media Archives & Peabody Awards Collection
The University of Georgia
Athens
GA 30602
USA

The National Council of Churches Collected Records 1908-Current
Swarthmore College Peace Collection
500 College Avenue
Swarthmore
PA 19081 – 1399
USA

Records of the National Religious Broadcasters
Billy Graham Center Archives
501 College Avenue
Wheaton
IL 60187
USA

British Film Institute
Reuben Library
Belvedere Road
Lambeth
London
SE1 8XT
UK

Parliamentary Archives,
House of Lords,
Westminster,
London
SW1A 0PW
UK

New York Times Article Archive
www.archive.nytimes.com/ref/membercenter/nytarchive

Time Magazine Archive
www.content.time.com/time/archives

The British Newspaper Archive
www.britishnewspaperarchive.co.uk

Church Times Digital Archive
UK Press Online
www.ukpressonline.co.uk

The Times Digital Archive 1785-2013
www.gale.com/intl/c/the-times-digital-archive

BBC Radio Times Archive
www.genome.ch.bbc.co.uk

BBC Listener Historical Archive 1929-1991
www.gale.com/intl/the-listener-historial-archive

APPENDIX 8

INTERVIEWEES

Dana	18th October 2017	Winner for Ireland of Eurovision Song Contest in 1970. Worked with Mother Angelica on EWTN in 1990s for 8 years.
Blair Crawford	1st June 2018	Religious Producer Sheffield's Radio Hallam from 1981-1988.
David Heron	21st June 2018	Chairman of Premier Christian Radio 1996 – 2007.
Steve Goddard	3rd July 2018	Editor of *Buzz Magazine* 1982 – 1987.
Pam Rhodes	5th July 2018	*Songs of Praise* Presenter 1987 to Present Day.
Peter Meadows	16th August 2018	Communications Secretary Evangelical Alliance 1984-1982.

APPENDIX 8

Canon David Winter	5th September 2018	Head of BBC Religious Radio 1982-1985. Head of BBC Religious Broadcasting 1986-1989.
Rev. Cindy Kent	12th October 2018	Broadcaster and former member of Central Religious Advisory Committee (CRAC).
David L'Herroux	10th March 2019	CEO of United Christian Broadcasters (UCB)
Professor John Wigger	9th July 2019	Professor of Social & Cultural History University of Missouri. USA.
Jeff Bonser	16th July 2019	Former Director of Churches Advisory Council for Local Broadcasting (CACLB).
Rev. Brandon Jackson	16th July 2019	Former Religious Advisor to Yorkshire Television's *Stars on Sunday*.
Dr. Jim McDonnnell	3rd October 2019	Head of UK Catholic Communications Centre 1990-2002.

APPENDIX 9

ILLUSTRATIONS

John C.W.Reith
(Reproduced by kind permission of BBC Written Archives)
p.180

Rev. Dick Sheppard
(Reproduced by kind permission of St. Martin-in-the Fields Archive Centre)
p.184

Rev. W.H. Elliott
(Reproduced by kind permission of Westminster City Archives)
p.188

Aimee Semple McPherson
(Reproduced by kind permission of the Revival Library)
p.192

Father Charles Coughlin
(Reproduced by kind permission of Alamy Images)
p.198

Mother Mary Angelica
(Reproduced by kind permission of EWTN)
p.201

Dr.Billy Graham
(Reproduced by kind permission of the Billy Graham Evangelistic Association)
p.204

APPENDIX 9

Oral Roberts
(Reproduced by kind permission of the Oral Roberts Evangelistic Association)
p.208

Pat Robertson
(Reproduced by kind permission of Mark Foley)
p.212

Jerry Falwell
(Reproduced by kind permission of Liberty University)
p.216

Jim & Tammy Bakker
(Public Domain)
p.332

Jess Yates
(Reproduced by kind permission of Alamy Images)
p.346

Index

A

American Broadcasting Company (ABC), 22, 48, 82-83, 120, 133, 205, 218, 250, 359, 379, 440, 455.

Angelica, Mother Mary 4, 6, 54, 123, 128, 201-203, 235-236, 382, 366, 386, 439, 441, 444, 447-478.

About Religion, 133, 268, 312.

Adorno, Theodor W.17, 400.

All Gas and Gaiters, 276

American Religious Identification Survey (ARIS), 30.

Andrew, Agnellus 103, 262.

Annan Report, 5, 140-141, 143, 170-171, 266, 362, 421, 427, 432.

Anno Domini, 138

Arbitron, 318

Ariel, 8, 215

Armstrong, Ben 6, 11, 50, 111-113, 121, 138, 164, 214, 252, 255, 283, 293, 318, 358, 385.

Audience Research Department, 303-304, 307, 313, 325, 427.

Ayer, William Ward 82, 253, 255.

B

Bacon, Francis 293.

Baird, John Logie 23.

Bakker, Jim 9, 32, 48, 55, 126, 201, 213, 222-223, 293-294, 332-345, 354-356, 358-362, 366, 370, 383, 385-386, 411, 415, 436-437, 440-442, 444-446.

Bakker, Tammy Faye 126, 330-334, 339-340, 360, 362, 415, 437.

BARB, 314, 316, 450.

Barnhouse, Donald Grey 83.

Baverstock, Donald 134.

BBC Religion, 56, 91.

Beale, Colin 105-107, 118, 168, 388, 427.

Bertermann, Eugene R. 254-255.

Blackburn, Tony 144.

Bonser, Jeff 269, 479.

British Council of Churches (BCC), 6, 96, 104, 116-117, 243, 262, 264, 267, 269, 286, 380, 398, 428.

Beveridge Committee, 25, 102-103, 131, 379, 463.

Beveridge Report, 117, 262, 286, 432.

Beyond Belief, 137.

Bookbinder, Alan 256.

Boorstin, Daniel J. 5, 46, 73, 176, 178, 228, 389.

Briggs, Asa 11, 16, 21, 26, 55, 64-65, 114-118, 170-172, 174, 230-231, 286-287, 368, 374, 390.

Brighter Sunday Campaign, 92.

Broadcasting Act 1981, 151, 173.

Broadcasting Act 1990, 5, 28, 57-58, 146, 157, 159, 160-161, 174, 268, 271, 384, 428, 452, 471.

Broadcasting Magazine, 254, 284, 440.

Brown, Rev.Robert R. 76.

Buddenbaum, J.M. 7, 52, 296-297, 301, 322, 323-324, 433.

Bunyan, John 2

Buzz Magazine, 153.

INDEX

C

Cable and Broadcasting Act 1984, 151, 173, 428.

Carlyle, Thomas 5, 41, 71, 175-176, 178, 228, 367, 372, 392.

Carnegie Commission, 26, 381, 469.

Carnell, Edward 124.

Cathedral of Tomorrow, 125.

Catholic Hour, 84, 378.

Cawston, Richard 137, 154.

Christian Broadcasting Network (CBN), 48, 50, 79, 126, 128, 152, 202, 213-216, 300, 332, 339-341, 343, 381, 436, 456.

Central Religious Advisory Committee (CRAC), 4, 6, 61, 88, 147-148, 181, 243, 259, 266-267, 346, 367, 369.

Charismatic Movement, 37.

Charlotte Observer, 334, 356, 359-360, 442, 446.

Chesterton, Gilbert K. 278.

Chignell, Hugh i, 392.

Choirs on Sunday, 135, 346, 348-349.

Christian Broadcasting Council, 158.

Christian Century, 214, 238, 241, 245, 281, 321, 423, 425, 439, 441.

Christian Coalition, 215, 223, 239, 389, 419.

Christian Faith in Action, 250, 283, 431.

Christian Forum, 107.

Christian Living, 95.

Christian Outlook, 90.

Christianity and Broadcasting Report (1950), 262.

Christianity and Social Order, 98.

Christianity Today, 10, 127, 164, 205, 233, 236, 238, 240, 284, 343, 361-362, 373-374, 436-437, 440-441, 444-448.

Church of England's Convocation Report, 92, 115.

Churches Advisory Council for Local Broadcasting (CACLB), 8, 269, 381, 452, 475.

Closed Period, 133.

Columbia Broadcasting System (CBS), 3, 22, 48, 78-80, 84, 120, 198, 247, 365, 378, 380, 455, 458-459.

Coggan, Archbishop Donald 350.

Concordat, 99.

Coughlin, Father Charles 4, 6, 54, 79, 198–201, 234-235, 391-392, 404, 414, 416, 422, 424, 443.

Crawford, Blair 145, 478.

Crawford Committee, 19, 377, 432, 461.

Credo, 138.

Cross Rhythms, 146.

Curran, Charles 139, 170, 174, 438.

Curran, James 7, 11, 17, 64, 393.

D

Daily Service, 4, 90, 134, 306, 309, 31.

Daroubakhsh, Serena 348.

Davidson, Archbishop Randall 258, 285, 388.

Dilthey, Whilhelm 41, 72, 435.

Donne, John 225.

Dunham, Dr. Franklin 108.

De Hann, Dr. Richard 128.

Durkheim, Emile 17, 29, 46, 67, 394-395.

Dyer, Richard, 46, 74, 178, 229, 395.

E

Eckersley, Peter 19.

Electric Church, 4, 123, 125-126, 128, 331.

Elliott, Wallace H. 4, 6, 55, 60, 90-91, 98, 188-192, 231-232, 367, 371, 395, 440-441, 444.

Elsner, Theodore 83.

Emerson, Ralph Waldo 41, 72, 176, 178, 396.

Eternal Word Television Network (EWTN), 202-203, 236, 441, 478.

Evangelical Alliance, 151, 157-158, 173-174, 269, 429.

Evangelicals, 10, 51, 63, 81, 165, 244, 252-253, 255, 264, 283, 360, 410, 414-415, 444.

Everyman, 39, 138-139.

Explaining the Christian Way, 95.

F

Faith for Today, 249, 282, 433.

Fagal, William A. 249, 251, 282, 433.

Fahey, Father Denis 200.

Falwell, Jerry 4, 6, 32, 54, 127, 201, 216-224, 239-241, 293-294, 335, 344, 366, 371, 380, 382, 396, 398, 415, 417, 426, 433, 437, 441.

Falwell, Macel 219, 222.

Family Holvak, 274.

Father Brown, 278, 289, 417, 438.

Father Dowling Mysteries, 274.

Father Ted, 277.

Federal Communications Commission (FCC), 23, 48, 80, 82, 126, 166, 202, 334, 378, 429, 456, 459.

FEBC, 3, 85, 86, 379.

Federal Council of Churches of Christ (FCCC), 3, 6, 8, 48, 79-80, 83-84, 120, 243, 244-247, 249-251, 253, 281,365, 369, 376, 378, 380, 429, 456.

Federal Radio Commission (FRC), 23, 78, 80, 193, 365, 377, 429, 456.

Ferrers, Earl 157.

Fisher, Archbishop Geoffrey 275.

Flynt, Larry 219, 223.

Forces Service, 100.

Forrest, John 134-135.

Freed, Paul 86, 113, 380, 397,459.

Frontiers of Faith, 84, 120.

Full Gospel Business Men's Fellowship International (FGBMFI), 331.

Fuller, Charles E. 80.

Fundamentalists, 31,129.

G

Gallup, 30, 50, 144, 299, 307, 323, 331, 358, 397, 429.

Garbett, Cyril Foster 6, 61, 88, 132, 181, 258-260, 275, 285, 412, 442.

Gielgud, Val 292.

God and the World through Christian Eyes, 95, 97.

Goddard, Steve 154, 173, 442, 478.

Godwatching, 58, 70, 174, 314, 326, 413, 446.

Going My Way, 274.

Gorham, Maurice A.C. 105, 118, 302, 324, 398, 449.

Graham, Billy 4, 6, 32, 54, 83, 107, 125, 128, 137, 154, 192, 204-208, 218, 236-237, 366, 370, 379-380, 396, 398, 405-406, 408, 414, 417, 420, 439, 447-449, 476.

Great Man Theory, 40-41.

INDEX

Grisewood, Harman 150, 164, 172, 398, 430.

Gunter, Barry & Viney Rachel 7, 58, 398.

H

Hadden Jeffrey & Swann, Charles 6, 53, 296.

Haley, William 66, 96, 103-104, 116, 230, 398, 421.

Hankey Television Committee, 21.

Harrison, Henry 331, 340.

HCJB, 3, 85, 366, 378, 393.

Hell Town, 274

Hearst, William Randolf 83.

Heritage Village, 333

Heron, David 160, 478.

Highway, 5, 61, 135-137, 169, 315-316, 326, 367, 371, 383, 411, 430.

Hind, Kenneth 158.

Hints for Sunday Speakers, 92.

Hoover, Stewart M. 38, 49-50, 54, 63, 71, 78, 113, 131, 164, 166, 168, 194, 199, 213, 238, 322-323, 327, 361, 400, 410, 421.

Hope FM, 146, 159.

Horsfield, Peter G. 7, 53, 68, 164, 174, 322- 323, 324, 400.

Hour of Power, 125, 382.

House, Francis 43-45, 72-73, 102-103, 105-107, 112, 117-118, 164-165, 221, 258, 262, 284-285, 309, 325, 358, 389, 396, 400, 403, 410, 421, 429-430, 443, 449-450, 477.

Humbard, Rex 84, 125, 298, 340, 380.

I

I'm Going to Ask You to Get Up Out of Your Seat, 137.

Independent Broadcasting Authority (IBA), 26, 62, 311.

Independent Television (ITV), 25, 132, 148, 156, 159, 168, 172, 265, 267-268, 286-287, 311-312, 315, 326, 345, 350-352, 354-355, 362, 367, 401-402, 411, 415, 430-431, 453, 468, 469, 471.

Inglis, Fred 5, 46,176,178, 228-229, 402.

Iremonger, Frederick A. 4, 95-96, 181, 191, 232, 449.

ITA's Programme Schedule Committee, 352.

Independent Television Commission (ITC), 7, 58, 152, 156, 159, 268, 471.

J

Jackson, Rev.Brandon 351, 353, 479.

James, Clive 350.

Jerusalem Trust, 57.

Jesus the Evidence, 5, 154, 173, 367, 383, 442.

Jesus of Nazareth, 5, 133.

Jesus Then and Now, 153.

JICTAR, 311, 314, 450.

Joan and Betty's Bible Story programmes, 95.

Johnstone, R.L. 7, 52, 112, 299, 323, 422.

Joint Religious Radio Committee (JRRC), 6, 83, 246.

K

KDKA, 21, 75, 376.

Kent, Cindy 143, 479.

KFSG (Kalling Four Square Gospel), 193.

L

Lasswell, Harold D. 15, 403.

Lazarsfeld, Paul F. 15, 403.

L'Herroux, David 146.

Littler, Gareth 158.

Lift up Your Hearts, 90, 305, 309.

Listen America, 127, 220.

Listener Research Department, 7, 58, 104, 232, 302, 305-306, 311, 324-325, 408, 426

Living Your life, 133.

Longley, Clifford 271.

Look up and Live, 84, 120.

Los Angeles Times, 195, 233, 240, 438, 441.

M

Macleod, George 98.

MacFarland, Charles S. 6, 245, 251.

Maconachie, Sir Richard 99.

Maier, Walter 4, 78-79, 83, 247, 249, 251, 378, 404.

Marconi, Guglielmo 19, 85, 376, 462.

Marine & Broadcasting (Offences) Act, 144.

Marshall, P.David 5, 18, 73, 177-179, 211, 228- 229, 231, 233, 324, 358, 389, 391, 397- 398, 405.

Marx, Karl E.F. 17, 405.

Mayo, Rev. John 90, 181.

McDonnell, Jim 28, 67, 147, 172, 174, 248, 261, 288, 371, 374-375, 405-406, 449.

McLuhan, Marshall 18, 64, 164, 393, 406.

McIntyre, Carl 255.

McKay, Rev. Roy 107.

McPherson, Aimee Semple 4, 6, 31, 54, 76, 192-197, 232-234, 336, 366, 376, 386, 389, 413, 416, 418, 423, 425, 434.

McQuail, Denis 16, 64, 406-407.

Meadows, Peter 158, 478.

Meeting Point, 137.

Melodies of Christendom, 95, 306.

Meyer, Sir Christopher 207.

Moody Bible Institute, 76, 377.

Moral Majority, 4, 127, 220-223, 239-241, 335, 382, 397, 426, 431, 433, 437, 441.

Morris, Colin 56, 106, 138.

Morse, Samuel 18, 75, 164, 278, 393.

Muggeridge, Malcolm 57, 107.

Murder in the Cathedral, 4, 95.

Mutual Broadcasting System, 81, 366, 378-379.

N

National Association of Evangelicals, 81, 120, 253, 255, 283, 366, 407.

National Broadcasting Company (NBC), 3, 22-23, 48, 79-80, 82-84, 112, 120, 245-247, 365, 377-378, 380, 407, 455, 458.

National Council for Christian Standards, 158.

National Council of Churches (NCC), 4, 6, 11, 84, 120, 243, 250-251, 253-254, 283, 293, 366, 413, 424, 431, 457, 476.

National Radio Pulpit, 77, 245, 378.

National Religious Broadcasters, 3, 6, 8, 50, 81-82, 120, 205, 243, 252-253, 255, 281, 284, 293, 366, 431, 436, 476.

New York Times, 45, 73, 121, 123, 164-165, 203, 216, 229, 234-238, 241, 295, 322, 359, 437- 438, 441-443, 446-447, 477.

News of the World, 348, 363, 437.

Newton, Sir Isaac 14.

Nicolls, Basil 99.

Nielson & Arbitron, 294-295.

O

Old Time Gospel Hour, 127, 298.

Our Man at St.Mark's, 276.

P

Parker, Everett, C. 6, 246, 249, 251, 282, 422.

Peace Pledge Union, 60, 186.

Peacock Committee, 156, 383, 466.

People's Service, 90, 309.

Pilkington Committee, 5, 26, 134, 144, 381, 464.

Pope Paul V1 124,165.

Postman, N. 122,164, 408.

Potter, Judge Robert 335.

Powell, Sir Alan 98.

Praise the Lord (PTL), 7, 8, 9, 126, 222-223, 241, 293, 301, 324, 330-340, 343-345, 354-355, 358-362, 382-383, 386-87, 402, 411, 413, 415, 417, 438, 442, 445-446, 448.

Premier Christian Radio, 5, 147, 159-160, 367, 453.

Prosperity Gospel, 210, 336, 344, 355.

Protestant Film Commission, 83.

Protestant Radio Commission, 83, 249-250.

Public Broadcasting Act, 26, 458.

R

Rader, Paul 76.

Radio Act 1912, 77.

Radio Act 1927, 3, 111, 417.

Radio and Television Commission (RTC), 247.

Radio Authority, 155, 158-159, 168, 268, 396, 452-453.

Radio Broadcast Magazine 245, 281, 284, 289, 392, 438-439, 446-447.

Radio Caroline, 25-26, 144-145, 381.

Radio Chapel Service, 77, 376.

Radio Choices and Opportunities, 155, 173, 430, 433.

Radio Cracker, 159.

Radio Greenbelt, 146.

Radio Magazine, 89,114, 438-439, 448.

Radio Times, 8, 89-90, 93, 98, 105, 114-116, 169, 302, 377, 439, 447, 477.

RAJAR, 311, 384, 453, 454.

Ranelagh, John 152.

Reith, John C.W, 4, 6, 20, 55, 59-60, 65, 87-88, 91, 95-98, 102, 105, 117, 180-184, 191, 229-230, 257-258, 264, 366-368, 371, 374, 379, 390, 403, 407, 409, 432, 439, 449.

Reithian Sunday, 182, 264.

Religious Broadcasting and the Public Report (1955), 308.

Religious Broadcasting Challenges the Churches Report, 256

Religious Broadcasting Department, 4, 95-98, 101,103-104, 106, 117, 133, 263, 307, 378, 400, 432.

Renton, Timothy 157.

Restricted Service Licences, 146, 159.

Rev. 289.

Review of the Aims and Achievements of Religious Broadcasting 1923-1948, 257.

Rhodes, Pam 134-135, 478.

Roberts, Rev. William H. 244, 251.

Roberts, Oral 4, 6, 32, 54, 84, 125, 166, 192, 208-212, 214, 218, 237-238, 294, 296, 332, 340, 344, 366, 380, 399, 409, 441, 443-444, 446.

Robertson, Pat 4, 6, 32, 50, 54, 126, 192, 201-202, 212-216, 223, 238-239, 294, 332, 344, 366, 370, 381, 383, 389, 394, 399, 404, 412, 417, 420, 456.

Rojek, Chris 5, 46, 74, 176, 178, 228, 410.

Round, Henry J. 19.

S

Salem Media Group, 128.

Sarge, 274.

Sarnoff, David 368.

Schramm, Wilbur L. 15, 63, 129, 410.

Schuller, Robert 123, 125, 294, 298, 340, 382.

Schultze, Quentin J. 10, 51, 54, 63, 112, 165, 168, 211, 238, 256, 283-284, 358, 369, 371, 374-375, 410, 414, 446, 449.

Secombe, Harry 61, 136, 169, 349, 383, 411.

Seeing is Believing, 10, 58, 316, 326, 375, 398.

Selsdon Committee 21, 378, 462.

Selywn Committee 260.

Sendall, Bernard 352.

700 Club, 126, 213-214, 239, 298, 332, 381.

7th Heaven, 275.

Sheen, Bishop Fulton J.84, 366.

Shepard, Charles E. 55, 334, 358-360, 411, 446.

Sheppard, Rev.Dick 4, 6, 55, 60, 90, 98, 114, 181, 184-188, 230-231, 258, 367, 377, 404-405, 408-409, 411, 444, 447-448.

Sherrill, Henry Knox 6, 250-251.

Silvey, Robert J.E. 7, 58, 302-303, 307, 324, 432-433, 449.

Sister Kate, 274.

Something Beautiful for God, 137.

Songs of Praise, 5, 62, 134-135, 137, 169, 315- 316, 326, 346, 367, 371, 381, 387, 427, 430, 432, 447-478.

Sound Broadcasting Act 1972, 144-145.

Southern Baptist Convention, 81, 282, 412.

Southern Baptist Hour, 246.

Southern Religious Radio Conference (SRRC), 246-247.

St. Martin-in-the-Fields, 8, 186, 231, 411, 447.

St. Martin's Review, 95, 185-186, 306.

St. Michael's Chester Square, 189.

St. Paul's Cathedral, 61, 187-188.

Stars on Sunday, 5, 7, 9, 62, 134-135, 137, 169, 330, 345-346, 348-355, 363-364, 367, 371, 381, 405, 415, 430, 432-433, 442, 479.

Stevens, Paul. M. 247.

Stobart, John C. 94.

Stoller, Tony i, 26, 171, 287.

Sunday Break, 133.

Sunday Committee, 4, 6, 88, 181, 451.

Sunday Half Hour, 4, 100, 307.

Sunday Policy, 4, 91.

Sustaining Time, 3, 79-80, 82, 124, 126, 246, 253, 366, 378.

Swaggart, Jimmy 4, 32, 126, 201, 222-223, 294, 366, 383.

Sykes Committee, 19, 376, 461.

T

Taylor, Cyril 260, 306.

Tang, Father Emery 249, 282, 441.

Televangelists, 4, 32, 51, 58, 121-122, 125-129, 132, 201, 207, 212, 296, 298, 338, 355, 359, 366, 440.

Television Act 1954, 148.

Television Act 1964, 311.

Temple, William E. 54, 98, 100, 116-117, 193-194, 195-196, 205, 236, 413, 447.

The Anvil, 99.

The Bible Study Hour, 83.

The Bridal Call, 194.

The Call, 210, 234, 237, 409.

INDEX

The Cathedral, 276.

The Christian and the World Situation, 98, 116, 447.

The Family Channel, 215.

The Hour of Decision, 48, 83, 125, 205, 379.

The Impatience of a Parson, 186, 231, 411.

The Listener, 7-8, 10, 58, 66, 104, 116, 170, 232, 302, 305-306, 311, 324-325, 377, 408, 426, 438, 444-445, 447, 474, 477.

The Lutheran Hour, 52, 79-80, 247, 379.

The Man Born to Be King, 4, 55, 95.

The Miracle of Seed Faith, 210.

The Old Fashioned Revival Hour, 80, 379.

The Pilgrims Hour, 80.

The Protestant Hour, 246.

The Scope and Character of Religious TV Report 105.

The Sunday Debate, 137.

The Times, 25, 66, 93, 115, 118, 168, 172-173, 232, 288, 309, 325, 363, 438-439, 443-445, 448, 477.

The Way to God, 95.

Think on These Things, 90.

Thomas Road Baptist Church, 216, 218-219, 223.

Time Magazine, 127, 167, 222, 235, 241, 288, 322, 344, 362, 437, 439-441, 444, 477.

Towards the Conversion of England Report 262, 286, 428.

Traditionalists, 244, 264.

Trans World Radio, 3, 86, 145, 366, 380, 459.

Trinity Broadcasting Network, 333, 382, 434.

U

Ullswater Commitee 21, 378, 462.

Undiscovered Ends, 60, 192, 231, 395.

United Christian Broadcasters, 146, 383.

V

Vatican Radio, 85.

Vicar of Dibley, 277.

Viewpoint, 137.

Vision Broadcasting, 152, 159, 383.

W

Wallis, Richard i-iii, 114, 173, 273, 362, 414, 425, 436.

Weber, Max K.E. 17, 43, 44, 46, 72, 176, 178, 228, 367, 372, 415.

Welch, James 4, 55, 95-99, 101-102, 105, 115, 118, 191, 448-449.

Whale, John 153.

Whittemore, Rev. Lewis B. 76.

Wigger, John H. 333, 344, 360, 415, 426.

Wildish, Fran 152.

Williams, Sir William Emrys 25.

Winter, David 139, 479.

White-Thomson, Leonard J. Bishop of Ely, 261.

Y

Yates, Jess 7, 62, 135, 346-357, 362-363, 437, 442, 444.

Yorkshire Post, 113, 351, 362-363, 437-439, 442.

Yorkshire Television, 62, 134-135, 345-346, 348-349, 354, 479.

Lightning Source UK Ltd.
Milton Keynes UK
UKHW020214240922
409349UK00003B/205